THE
TRAVELS
OF THE
JESUITS
IN
ETHIOPIA:

CONTAINING

I. The Geographical Description of all the King-doms, and Provinces of that Empire; the Natural and Political History; the Manners, Customs, and Religion of those People, &c.

II. Travels in *Arabia Fælix*, wherein many Things of that Country, not mention'd in other Books of this Nature, are Treated of, as a particular Description of *Aden, Moca*, and several other Places.

III. An Account of the Kingdoms of *Cambate, Gingiro, Alaba*, and *Dancali* beyond *Ethiopia* in *Africk*, never Travelled into by any but the *Jesuits*, and consequently wholly unknown to us.

Illustrated with an exact MAP of the Country, delineated by those Fathers, as is the Draught of the true Springs and Course of the *Nile*, within *Ethiopia*, besides other useful Cuts.

The whole Collected, and Historically Digested by *F. Balthazar Tellez*, of the Society of *JESUS*; and now first Translated into *English*.

London, Printed for *J. Knapton*, in St. *Paul's Church-yard*; *A. Bell*, in *Corn-bill*; *D. Midwinter*, in St. *Paul's Church-yard*; *W. Taylor*, in *Pater-Noster-Row*; and Sold by *J. Round*, in *Exchange-Alley* in *Cornbill*; *N. Cliffe*, in *Cheapside*; *E. Sanger*, at the *Posthouse*, and *A. Collins*, at the *Black-boy*, in *Fleet-street*; and *J. Baker*, in *Pater-Noster-Row*, 1710.

FZA 2

D1522229

THE

PREFACE.

THE *Defign of this Collection being to entertain the Publick,*
with fuch valuable Travels as have not yet appear'd abroad
in Englifh, it is thought none can be more acceptable than
this Hiftorical Account of Ethiopia, *for as much as lefs*
has been hitherto writ of it, than of many others, and
what we have, for the moft part very uncertain and fabulous. The
beft Piece extant among us is in Purchas's Collection, *and that only an*
Abridgment of Francis Alvarez *his Hiftory of this Empire : He was*
the firft European *that treated of it on his own knowledge, having*
been there fome years with a Portuguefe Embaffador, *and to do him*
Juftice, appears to have been a Man of Judgment and Integrity, which
Qualities have gain'd him Reputation, and render'd his Book, tho' fmall,
very Valuable. But as has been faid, Purchas *only abridg'd him,*
and he could not in a few years give a perfect Account of that large
Monarchy; befides that Purchas *is grown fcarce, and too bulky for*
every Reader. Of later years Ludolphus *has writ the Hiftory of*
Ethiopia, *wherein he labours much to fhow the World his Skill in the*
Ethiopick *Language, and relies more than is convenient on the Rela-*
tions of one Gregory *an* Ethiopian, *not fo well qualify'd in many*
Refpects, as the Jefuits, *who were all Learned and Able Men, whom*
he makes it his bufinefs to contradict, as much as in him lies, notwith-
ftanding he is beholding to them for the beft part of his Hiftory. The
frefheft Account of this Nation we fpeak of is Poncet's *Voyage thither*
in the year 1698. *fo very concife, that little can be expected from it.*

The work here prefented to the Publick is methodically digefted by a
Learned Jefuit *employ'd in it by his Society, and confequently had the*
Advantage of confulting all that had been writ on the Subject by fuch
of them as had been there, whom he always fairly quotes. The firft
of them is F. Peter Paiz, *of whom a Manufcript Treatife of* Ethiopia
is preferv'd at Rome, *reaching from the year* 1555. *till* 1622, *when he*
dy'd in that Empire. The next is F. Emanuel d'Almeyda, *who was*
feveral years Superior there, Travell'd over thofe Countries, and
monftrous Mountains, and Read all their Books, the better to enable
himfelf to give a fatisfactory Account. Thirdly, The Patriarch Don
Alfonfo Mendez, *who liv'd there Ten years, and writ the Hiftory of*

Ethiopia

Ethiopia *in* Latin. *Besides these, he had the Annual Letters written by the Fathers of the Society, from the year* 1556, *till* 1656. *as also the Commentaries of* F. Jerome Lobo, *resident there Nine years, and examin'd all other Books, whither ancient or modern treating of this Subject, and compar'd them together. This may suffice, as to the Work in General, leaving the Reader to make his own Judgment of the performance.*

It is to be observ'd that this upper Ethiopia, *lying between the Tropick of* Cancer *and the* Equinoctial, *is sometimes call'd* Oriental, *or* Eastern, *as lying Eastward of all the other* African Ethiopia, *which stretches along the* Ethiopick Ocean, *that is* Angola, Guinea, Cabo Verde, &c. *However, according to ancient Authors, it is often call'd* Occidental, *or* Western, *to distinguish it from the former more* Eastern Ethiopia, *beginning on the Eastern Shore of the* Red Sea, *and containing the Countries of* Arabia, Madian, *and others as far as* Palestine, *all of them in* Asia, *whereas this* Ethiopia *we speak of is in* Africk. *So that the upper* Ethiopia, *or* Abissinia, *or* Prester John's *Country, lies between two* Ethiopias, *the one in* Africk, *and the other in* Asia, *and is call'd* Eastern *in Regard of that which is to the* Westward *of it, and* Western, *on Account of the other that is to the* Eastward.

The Gallas *often mention'd in this History, enter'd the Kingdom of* Ethiopia, *by the way of* Ballii, *about the year* 1537. *and by degrees made themselves Masters of* Ballii, Fategár, Doaró, Ogé, Bizamó, Oifate, Angota, Cambate, *and several other Provinces lying between them. There are at present above Sixty Herds, or Tribes of those People, tho' only Four came in at first, and were it not for the Wars among themselves, they would have long since conquer'd all this Empire.*

THE

THE ABISSINE EMPIRE,

as it now is; and the true Source of the Nile.

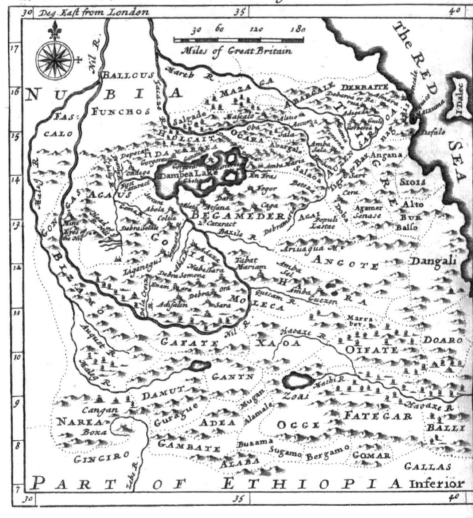

THE
TRAVELS
OF THE
JESUITS
IN
ETHIOPIA.

BOOK. I.

CHAP. I.

Of the Name of Prester John, *vulgarly given to the Emperor of* ETHIOPIA; *the occasion of that Mistake, and the proper Name of this Empire.*

THE *Portuguese* Nation having extended their Discoveries and Conquests along the Coasts of *Africk*, and proceeded thence to the, before unknown, remotest Eastern Shores; *Europe* was not only enrich'd with the precious Spices and other valuable Commodities of those Parts; but improv'd with the Knowledge of new Monarchies and Empires, Spacious Provinces, Wealthy and Large Islands, Warlike Nations, and variety of Countries, to which the ablest Cosmographers.

Improvement of Cosmography.

graphers were before utter Strangers ; so that we may say, the World is beholding to the *Portuguefes* for this increase of Wealth, and addition of Extent.

Difcovery of Ethiopia. Among the other Regions we came acquainted with, by means of this wonderful difcovery of *India*, one was the Upper *Ethiopia,* which lies next to *Egypt*, vulgarly call'd *Prefter John*'s Country, of which tho' many Authors have writ much, yet was it fo varioufly, and with fuch unintelligible Confufion, that fome difcours'd, and others deliver'd Fables of it, that he would do no fmall Service to the Publick, who fhould untye or cut afunder thefe *Gordian* Knots, and lead the way out of this dark and intricate Labyrinth. At this Time we have fuch true and certain Information of the Affairs of that Empire, by fuch means as are mention'd in the Preface, and will appear to thofe who read thefe Travels, that I could not but think I fhould much oblige all curious Perfons, and perform a work moft acceptable to Men of Erudition, in giving a full Account, in this Volume, of all we now know concerning thofe Parts of *Ethiopia*, not only as to Temporals, but alfo in Relation to Religion, the whole Truth, as to both Points being now certainly found out ; fo that I may be bold to fay, I can offer this as a Hiftory altogether new, notwithftanding fome may think it very old and much handled by others; becaufe Truth it felf, which always prevails, will afford it fuch a Grace, as is an Ornament to all Novelty.

Ancient falfe Accounts. I concluded this work would be the more acceptable, in regard I am fully fatisfy'd that the Accounts of thofe Parts are either corrupted by the Fictions of fabulous Authors, or elfe very imperfect, for want of fufficient and credible Information, which has given occafion to forge the moft Chimerical and ufelefs Stories of it in the World, and even more pernicious than the fam'd Romances, which being full of Witty Inventions, and deliver'd in a lofty Stile, ferve to divert the Readers, as Learned and Ingenious Fables ; whereas thefe other Writers, have endeavour'd to impofe upon the unwary, by reprefenting their vile Forgeries for valuable Truths.

Name of Ethiopia whence. To come to the point, before we launch out into the Affairs of this Upper *Ethiopia*, it will be convenient to fhow its proper Name, for as much as Hiftorians have fpoken very varioufly of it, and having err'd in the very Beginning, no wonder they fhould afterwards utter fo much Impertinence, like thofe of whom the Prophet fays, *They are eftrang'd from the Womb, they go aftray as foon as they be born, fpeaking lies*, Pfal. 58. 3. The name given in *Portugal* to that Empire, or its Emperor, was that of *Prefter John,* or *Presbyter John*, as may be feen at large in *Joam de Barros*

Dec.

Dec. 3. Lib. 4. *Diogo de Couto* Dec. 4. Lib. 10. *Nicolas Godinho,* *Hist. Ethiop. Lib.* 1. and *Damiam de Goes,* 3 par. *Chron. Reg. Eman.* *cap.* 6. where he calls that Emperor *Precious John.*

But with their good leave, who gave thefe Names, I muft de- *Miftake a-* clare all thefe were meer Fables concerning this *Precious John* ; for *bout Pre-* it is now plainly and evidently made out by the *Portuguefes* who *fter John.* have been there fince, and by the Religious of the Society, who travers'd over almoft every ftep of this *Ethiopia,* and view'd it from End to End, that they found not there the leaft Footfteps of fuch Holy Names and Celebrated Titles ; and no Man in this *Ethiopia* makes the leaft queftion of this Truth, being wholly ig- norant of any fuch Name there Emperor has, and they are fur- priz'd when we ftile him fo, as not finding any thing in all their Language that bears the leaft Refemblance with this Title of *Prefter John,* or may fo much as allude to it ; whatfoever the *A-* *byffinian Zagabazo,* mention'd by *Damiam de Goes,* as alfo in this Hiftory, as being fent into *Portugal* with a fort of Embaffy, did endeavour to invent, to find out fome means of adapting this Name to his Tongue ; which is no better grounded, than what *F. Lewis de Urreta,* in the Hiftory of *Ethiopia* Dreamt, when he faid, this Emperor was call'd *Baldigian.*

It is therefore moft certain, and beyond all controverfy, that *Advantage* neither this Emperor, nor the Empire from him, has any claim *of clear-* to the Title of *Prefter John;* and tho' Philofophers may be of Opi- *ing Names.* nion, that this controverfy about the Name is not Material, for as much as it is what they call, an Argument about a Word, however we fee that among Learned Men, he often underftands Things beft, who is moft acquainted with the Names, and we fhall next fhow what was the occafion of giving this Name to the King of *Ethiopia.*

To this Purpofe it muft be obferv'd, that, as is plainly prov'd *Prefter* by *F. Nicholas Godinho, Hift. Ethiop. lib.* 1. *Pet. Iarric. in Thezaur* John *rer. Indic. tom.* 2. *cap.* 14. and *Patriarch. Alfonf. Mendez in Hift.* *where.* *Ethiop. lib.* 1. *cap.* 1, *and* 2. the Name of *Prefter John,* or *Pref.* *byter John,* did belong to a Chriftian Emperor, tho' a *Neftorian,* and fubject in Spirituals to the Patriarch of *Babylon,* as were thofe Chriftians, they call in *India,* of the Mountains, or of St. *Tho-* *mas,* which may be feen in *F. Antony de Gouvea,* in his Learned Book he compos'd, of the Journey undertaken to vifit thefe Chri- ftians by that great Prelate *Don F. Alexius de Menefes.*

This Emperor liv'd in the Mountains of *Afia,* his Sirname be- ing *Jehanan,* deriv'd from the Prophet *Jonas,* which the *Europe-* *ans* chang'd into *John,* and it was common to all the Kings of that Monarchy, as that of *Pharoah* was to the Kings of *Egypt* ;
that.

that of *Ptolomey* afterwards to the fame; and that of *Cæfar* to the *Roman* Emperors. The Addition of *Prefter* is an Abbreviation of *Presbyter*, and this Title is faid to have been given him, on account of a Crofs that was always carry'd before him, as is among us before Archbifhops.

How mifplac'd in Ethiopia. — Now the aforefaid Authors agree, that the giving this Name of that Chriftian Emperor in *Afia*, to the King of *Ethiopia* in *Africa*, proceeded from the miftake of the *Portuguefe Peter de Covillam*, fent with *Alfonfo de Payva* by King *John* II. of *Portugal*, in the year 1467, by Land, to difcover both *India*, and that fo much talk'd of Chriftian Emperor call'd *Prefter John*, of whom there was fome very dark Knowledge in *Portugal*, and an earneft Defire of better Information. This *Portuguefe*, in his Return from *India* to *Gran Cairo*, hearing much Talk at *Adem* and *Suaquem*, through which he pafs'd, of the *Abyffine* Emperor, who was there nearer to him, as that he was a Chriftian, carry'd a Crofs in his Hand, and that in his Country there were Monafteries of Religious Men; and having heard no News, in all thofe parts of *India* he Travell'd through, of any Chriftian Prince Inhabiting *Afia*, he concluded there was no occafion for him to proceed any further in fearch of what he did not know to have any Being there, being then fo near what they told him was to be found in *Ethiopia*. Thus he perfwaded himfelf he had met with that his King fent him in fearch of, and that without doubt this fame was the very *Prefter John*, fo much fought after, and fo little known in *Portugal*.

Error spread through Europe. — Upon this Notion, *Peter de Covilham* went away immediately himfelf to *Ethiopia*, firft fending an Account from *Cairo* to King *John* II. of what he imagin'd he had found, directing feveral Letters to him by fundry ways. And as it often happens, that pleafing News is rather believ'd than examin'd; fo this found fuch a general Acceptance and Approbation, that the *Abyffine* Emperor of *Ethiopia* was immediately declar'd to be the *Prefter John* of *Afia*, firft in *Portugal*, and afterwards throughout all *Europe*; the true one being thus bury'd in Oblivion, and the fuppofititious cry'd up and applauded.

Prefter John extinct. — This Miftake was back'd and confirm'd, by the total Extinction of *Johannan*, or *Prefter John* in *Afia*, with all his Monarchy; fo that not fo much as the Name of any Chriftian Emperor reigning in *Afia* being now brought into *Europe*, and the Fame of this Chriftian Monarch, fo near to *Egypt* increafing with the difcovery of *India*, the *Europeans* had fome Colour for their general miftake, abfolutely concluding, efpecially the *Portuguefes*,

ses, trading to the Red Sea, that this King of *Ethiopia* was the
so much sought after and celebrated *Prefter John.*

Marcus Paulus Venetus, in his *Itinerary* very much strengthned Cathay
this vulgar Error, writing, That the great King call'd *Prefter not found.*
John us'd to reside at *Archico,* which is the first Town belonging
to *Ethiopia,* within the *Red Sea* ; but that this is absolutely false
we shall see hereafter : Now this *Ethiopia* we speak of, is as remote from *Cathay,* where the true *Johanan* seems to have resided,
as *Spain* is from *Peru* ; for I am of opinion that this Emperor of
Asia was that same Christian King that dwelt in *Cathay,* of whom
S. *Antoninus,* Archbishop of *Florence* makes mention, and who
has been so long, and with so many Toils, and Hazards, in vain,
sought after, by the Religious Men of the Society, who have
in *India* indefatigably traversed immens'd Lands, and unknown
Seas, in search of this hidden Monarchy, till at last they came
to this conclusion ; That there remains nothing at present in all
the *East,* but the bare Names of the Fields, in which this Celebrated *Cathay* Stood, and its Emperor *Prefter John* reignd.
And yet this Notion is so strongly rooted in some Mens Opinions,
that they still expect this hidden *Cathay* will be found out, and
that more particularly among the *Portuguese,* some of whom are
so Credulous as to believe, there is still a great Island in our Seas,
not only Undiscovour'd, but Inchanted ; and so they to this Day
expect the discovery of the hidden King of *Cathay.*

Having clear'd these Points above, I must now add, that the *Names of*
proper name of the *Higher Ethiopia,* or next to *Egypt,* whereof Ethiopia
we are here to Treat, is *Abassia,* and consequently that of its *and its*
Inhabitants is *Abassines.* They themselves call it *Abex,* laying the *Kings.*
Emphasis on the last Syllable, which, according to our way of
Writing, must be pronounc'd *Abesh,* or rather *Habesh,* the *Por-*
tuguese pronouncing the *x* here, as we do *sh* ; as we see the
Latins change the *x* into *ss,* calling the Country *Abassia,* and the
People *Abyssines.* These People call a King *Nugue,* and the Em-
peror *Nuguea Nagasta,* which is as much as King of Kings.

The Name of *Abassia,* according to *Strabo,* was given it on Account of its being surrounded with great Deferts and Wil-
dernesses, which the *Egyptians* call *Abasses.* The Learned Patriarch of *Ethiopia, Don Alfonso Mendes,* in Hist. *Ethiop.* l. 1. c. 1.
says, It might perhaps be so call'd from *Abaxa,* the Capital
City of the Kingdom of *Adel,* adjoyning to *Ethiopia,* whose Emperors were once Masters of it, even as the same Kingdom of
Adel was call'd *Zeylonian* from the Port of *Zeyla.* But *F. Ma-*
nuel de Almeyda, says, The Names of *Abassia,* and *Abissinia,*
have no certain Signification, no more than those of many

        B   other

other Kingdoms and Empires, better known to us by our Acquaintance with their People, than by the Origin of their Denominations. This is certainly its proper Name, but it has other Appellatives, as thofe of the Higher *Ethiopia,* the Inner *Ethiopia,* and *Ethiopia* above *Egypt,* of which we fhall fpeak hereafter.

C H A P. II.

Of the Countries Comprehended under this Empire of Abiffinia, *or the* Upper Ethiopia, *what Kingdoms now belong to it, and which are taken from it ; and the extent and limits of fome of them.*

Several Ethiopia's.

THE firft thing to be taken Notice of, is, That this Name of *Ethiopia* is very Comprehenfive, as including all thofe Regions, whofe Inhabitants are Black, who are all call'd *Ethiopians.* This fame name alfo denotes thofe Countries lying along the *Red-Sea,* on the fide of *Arabia,* as far as *Palaftine,* which in Holy Writ are call'd *Ethiopia* ; and the fame Name is given to all the Lands beyond *Egypt* down the *Red Sea,* not only as far as Cape *Guardafu,* which is in Twelve Degrees Latitude, but to all thofe extending to the Cape of *Good Hope,* and then turning that Cape all along as far as *Angola* and *Cabo Verde,* the Inhabitants whereof are all call'd *Ethiopians.* To diftinguifh that which lies on the fide of *Arabia,* it is call'd the *Oriental* or *Eaftern,* as lying to the Eaftward ; whereas the other, on the Oppofite fide of the *Red Sea,* lying more to the *South* and *Weft,* is therefore call'd *Southern* and *Occidental,* or *Weftern.*

Divifion of Africk.

However, Modern Geographers, as may be feen in *Johnfon's Atlas,* reduce *Ethiopia* into a narrower Compafs, dividing *Africk* into Six Regions, which are *Egypt, Barbary, Biledulgerid, Zahara,* or *Lybia,* or the Defert, the Country of the Blacks, and *Ethiopia,* each of which has its peculiar Limits affign'd it, as may be feen in the aforefaid *Atlas* ; where, fpeaking of *Ethiopia,* it is divided into Two Parts, the one call'd the Upper or Inward, the other the Lower or Outward ; which laft, according to the Moderns, comprehends the Southern part of *Africk,*

ftretching

ftretching beyond the Tropick of *Capricorn* to 35 Degrees of *South* Latitude, and is call'd the Lower *Ethiopia*, in regard to its Pofition from the Upper, of which I fhall prefently fpeak, being divided into Five feveral Regions, viz. *Congo, Monomotapa, Cafraria, Zanguebar*, and *Aiana*.

We do not here treat of this Lower *Ethiopia*, but of the Upper; which is fo call'd for Two Reafons. The *Firft*, becaufe the *Nile* comes down from it to Water the Plains of *Egypt*, and for the fame Reafon it is call'd *High Ethiopia*, and *Ethiopia above Egypt*. The *Second* Reafon is, becaufe it is nearer than the other to the *Arctick* Pole, which is always above in Regard to us, as the Prince of Poets obferves, *Illic Vertex femper nobis fublimis. Georg.* 1. and this *Ethiopia* being neareft to the Pole, is therefore call'd the Upper, or the Higher. *This Ethiopia, why call'd the Upper.*

In this Upper *Ethiopia*, under the *Torrid Zone*, which fome would have made not Habitable, is the *Abiffinian* Empire, commonly call'd *Prefter John*'s Country, of which we are here to treat. And in regard that there are moft notorious Errors in the Defcription, and laying down of thefe Countries, not only in *Ptolomey*'s Maps, but in thofe of *Ortelius, Mercator*, and the New *Atlas*, publifh'd in 1653. I thought it convenient to infert here a Map of this *Ethiopia*, drawn by fome of the ableft Men of the Society, and particularly by the moft Reverend Patriarch of *Ethiopia, Don Alfonzo Mendez*, and by *F. Manuel Almeyda*, a Perfon of great Learning and Sincerity, both whom we here principally follow. *Abiffinia.*

As for the length of this Empire, thefe grave Fathers fay, that meafuring it from *North* to *South*, in a ftrait Line, upon the Antient Limits, which were on the *North* a Country call'd *Focay*, lying above *Suaquem*, and on the *South* another call'd *Bergamo*, it extends Nine Degrees, *Bergamo* being in Eight Degrees of *North* Latitude, and *Focay* in Seventeen. But at prefent, the Country poffefs'd by this Emperor, is ftill fmaller, becaufe we muft not reckon from *Focay*, but only one Degree above *Mazua*, beginning in Sixteen Degrees of *North* Latitude, and thence to *Bergamo*, which as has been faid is in Sixteen, and in it is contain'd the number of Leagues ufually allow'd to Eight Degrees, according to the Variety of *German, Italian, Spanifh*, or other Leagues. *Its Length.*

The Breadth of this Empire is to be taken from the Coaft of the *Red Sea*, to the Banks of *Nile*, including the turn the faid River makes towards *Egypt*, after compaffing the Kingdom of *Gojam*, and making it a Peninfula, which may be about 140 *Por-* *Breadth.*

tuguese Leagues, and *F. Manuel de Almeyda* says, he knows this to be true, as having Travell'd it over some Times.

Extent North and South. The North side is not to begin at *Suaquem*, as *John de Barros* would have it, but a Degree above *Mazua*, and is to bend a little towards the *South-West*, till it ends in the Country of the *Agaus*, in Fourteen Degrees Latitude, and so it will be 140 Leagues in Length. That diligent Author must give us leave to tell him he is in the wrong in saying, That this *North* side reaches to the Island of *Meroe*, which he pretends is call'd *Noba*, whereas *Nuba*, or *Nubia*, is a Kingdom to the Northward of it, along the River *Nile*. And in the Ninth Chapter, I shall show there is no other Island *Meroe*, but the Kingdom of *Gojam*, of which I shall soon speak.

Mistakes of Geographers. Having settled the Bounds of this Empire, it plainly appears, how much the antient Maps Err, and not only they, but the Modern of *Mercator*, and *Johnson's Atlas*, in the Charts of *Abyssinia*, which they stretch from 22 Degrees *North*, to 16 or 17 of *South* Latitude, where they place the Lake *Zayre* or *Zambre*, out of which they say the *Nile* flows. Along this side *Mercator*, places the Kingdom of *Gojam*, because he had heard that the *Nile* rises in it; so that they allow this Empire 39 or 40 Degrees from *North* to *South*, whereas, as I have said, it extends but Eight or Nine. They also assign the Breadth from *East* to *West*, from the *Red Sea* to the River *Niger*, and the Borders of *Congo*, or *Monicongo*, which is above 400 Leagues. Thus these Geographers bestow all those vast Countries on the *Abissinians*, because they are none of their own, nor they bound to make good their Gift.

Of John de Barros. The Famous Historian *John de Barros*, in the 3d. Decad. of his *Asia*, l. 4. c. 1. is not so bountiful as the aforesaid Authors, for he cuts off no less then 27 Degrees of their Allowance, leaving only 14, from the Kingdom of *Adea*, which he says is the Southermost, and places in Six Degrees of *North* Latitude to *Suaquem*, which he places in 19 and 20 Minutes; but he may cut off Four Degrees more, for the Dominions of the *Abissinians* never extended to *Suaquem*, and in our Days they reach but little beyond *Mazua*, which is in 15 Degrees; and there must be One or Two Degrees retrench'd on the *South*, because *Adea* is not in Six, but betwixt Seven and Eight Degrees of Latitude. Tho' *John de Barros* was a diligent Historian, yet what he delivers as to this particular is from the Relations of the *Portuguese*, who went into *Ethiopia* with *Don Christopher de Gama*, some of whom return'd to *Portugal* and gave him that Information; but they had not Travell'd over all *Ethiopia*, nor resided there many years;

nor

nor do we know that they had any Inftruments to take the Height
of the Sun, and obferve the true Latitudes of thofe Countries, as
thofe Fathers did. whom I here quote ; all which will appear
more plainly by our Map.

This *Abiffine* Empire being fo little known in *Europe*, there *Kingdoms*,
could not be any certain Accounts of it, and hence fprung all *wrong*
thofe miftakes, not only as to its Limits, but alfo the mifplacing *nam'd and*
and mifnaming of Kingdoms, and the making feveral Kingdoms *plac'd.*
of one. To inftance in that of *Tigre*, which is but one Kingdom
in *Ethiopia*, and the firft beginning on the *Eaft*, as fhall be foon
fhown ; yet of this One Kingdom the Maps make Three, for
they call one *Tigray* near the Line, another they place in
Ten degrees of *North* Latitude, calling it *Tygre*, and betwixt
thefe another by the name of *Tygre Mahon*, and befides thefe,
another farther on, with the Title of *Barnagaes*, which is all
but fo many feveral Names, the Kingdom being but One,
call'd *Tygre:* Which is much fuch a Miftake, as if a Man,
defcribing of *Spain*, fhould there lay down one Kingdom
call'd *Portugal*, another by the name of *Lufitania*, and a
Third by that of *Lisbon*. Nor is *Barnagas*, or *Baharnaga-
es*, for fo it fhould be Writ, a Kingdom ; but a proper
Name, fignifying the Governor of the Countries near the
Sea, confifting of Three fmall Territories, belonging to the
fame Kingdom of *Tygre;* whereof *Debaroa*, a fmall Town
Eighteen Leagues from *Mazua*, is the Capital.

Johnfon's new *Atlas*, in his Map of *Abiffinia*, after fet- *Errors in*
ting down Three Kingdoms of *Tigray*, *Tigre-mahon*, and *Ti-* Johnfon's
gre, fays the Kingdom of *Tigray* is fubjeft to that of *Ti- Maps.*
gre-mahon, which is all Chimerical, there being but one
Kingdom of *Tigre* in *Ethiopia*, as has been faid. So F.
Francis Alvares, of whom I fhall have occafion to fpeak
hereafter, in his Hiftory of *Ethiopia*, calls *Tigre*, by the
Name of *Tigre-mahon*, giving the Kingdom the Name of a
Town, which is otherwife call'd *Auzen*. He alfo makes
Barnagaes a diftinft Kingdom, contrary to what I have
faid, and will appear by our Map ; in which the whole
Abiffine Empire, is delineated, with all the Kingdoms within its Limits, tho' at prefent, moft of them are not fubjeft
to that Emperor ; even as in making a Map of *Italy*, all
the Countries and Dominions comprehended under that Name
are fet down, though they belong to feveral Princes. The
Kingdoms which ftill own'd the faid Emperor at the Time
when the Patriarch *Don Alfonfo Mendez* was there, are *Kingdoms*
thefe, *Tigre*, *Dambea*, *Begameder*, *Gojam*, *Amahara*, *Narea*, in Ethio-
and pia.

and Part of *Xaoa*. The leſſer Provinces, below the Dignity of Kingdoms, ſubject to him are, *Maxaga, Salent, Ogara, Abargale, Holcait, Salgade, Cemen, Salaoa, Ozeca,* and *Doba.*

The Kingdoms formerly belonging to him, but now taken from him, are *Angot, Domo, Ogge, Balli, Adea, Alamale, Oxelo, Ganz, Betezamora, Guraque, Buzana, Sufgamo, Bahargamo, Cambat, Boxa, Gumar, Conch, Damot, Doba, Mota, Avra, Holtea, Oyfat, Guedem, Ganh, Marrabet, Manz* and *Bizamo.* By which it plainly appears, that this Emperor has not at preſent half the Kingdoms his Predeceſſors were poſſeſs'd of; the other better half has been wreſted from them by the *Galas,* of whom I ſhall hereafter ſpeak at large; and now, ſince their new revolt from the Catholick Church, they have loſt others, according to the freſheſt News come from thence, as we ſhall ſee in its place.

Tigre Kingdom.

I will now give a ſhort Deſcription of the Principal Kingdoms, that ſtill belong to the *Abiſſinian* Emperor, beginning with that of *Tigre,* the firſt of this Empire in all reſpects. This Kingdom begins at *Mazua,* which is a ſmall Iſland near *Arquico,* the firſt Port of the Continent of this *Ethiopia,* of which we ſhall often make mention, and it ſtands in Fifteen Degrees of *North* Latitude, being ſubject not long ſince to this Emperor, but the *Turks* depriv'd him of this his beſt Sea Port. From *Mazua* or *Arquico,* this Kingdom runs Ten or Twelve Leagues along the Coaſt of the *Red Sea,* towards the Mouth of it, as far as *Dafalo;* which was alſo a ſort of Port of this Kingdom, tho' not much frequented, becauſe the Sea is there very Shoal: But even this Port the *Turks* of *Mazua* took from them, and all the People betwixt *Mazua* and *Dafalo* are Subject to them, being moſt of them *Mahometans.* Thus the *Abiſſine* Empire was wholly depriv'd of Sea Ports, which was an unſpeakable loſs.

Fremona Town.

South Weſt of *Mazua,* almoſt in the midſt of this Kingdom of *Tigre,* ſtands a Town call'd *Maegoga,* but more commonly *Fremona,* famous, and much ſpoken of in the Annual Letters of the Fathers of the Society, becauſe there the Patriarch *Don Andrew de Oviedo* reſided and dy'd, and there the Fathers, his Companions, continu'd till they chang'd this Life for a better, and afterwards others always remain'd there, that came into *Ethiopia,* till the Total change I ſhall ſpeak of hereafter. This Town is in Fourteen Degrees and a Half of *North* Latitude, by Obſervations frequently taken there with the Aſtrolabe. The Length of this Kingdom is about Ninety Leagues, and the Breadth Fifty, being the largeſt and beſt in *Abiſſinia.*

The

The Kingdom of *Begameder* Borders on *Tigre* to the *North* Begame-
Eaft, on the due *Eaft* it has the Kingdom of *Angot*, and thence der *King-*
runs along the Kingdom of *Amahara*, which is its Southern *dom.*
Boundary, till it comes to the *Nile*, which is its Limit on the
Weft. Between thefe Two Kingdoms of *Begameder* and *Amaha-*
ra, runs the River *Baxilo*, which is very large, and after parting the faid Kingdom, lofes it felf in the *Nile*. The Length
of it is from *Larta* to the *Nile*, being about Sixty Leagues; the
Breadth from *North* to *South*, Twenty, and no more; for as
much as fome Provinces are at prefent difmember'd from it,
including the which, it would be as Broad as Long.

I fhall fay fomething of the Two Kingdoms of *Gojam* and Gojam
Dambea, in regard they are both belonging to the Celebrated *Kingdom.*
Nile, which rifes in the one, and receives its increafe from the
other. *Gojam* lies *North Weft*, and *South Eaft*, and is about Fifty
Leagues in Length; the Breadth from *Eaft* to *Weft* being about
Thirty, reckned from one Bank of the *Nile* to the other; for
this River rifing, as will be faid hereafter, almoft in the midft
of the Kingdom, takes a compafs, and enclofes it quite round,
becoming as it were a Ditch or Intrenchment to fecure it every
way in Return for having given it Birth.

North of *Gojam* lies the Kingdom of *Dambea*, well known for Dambea
the great Lake in it, which the *Abiffinians* call the Sea of *Dam-* *Kingdom.*
bea, and the *Nile* runs into it, as fhall be fcon defcrib'd. This
Kingdom is only Twenty Four Leagues in Length, and Ten or
Twelve in Breadth; but if we add to it this Lake, which lies
along the *South* and *South Eaft* fide, it will be near as many
Leagues more.

The Length of the Kingdom of *Amahara* from *Eaft* to *Weft*, Amahara
is about 40 Leagues. *Narea* is the laft Kingdom, now fubject to *Kingdom.*
the Emperor, we fhall fpeak of it hereafter, and the Map will
fhow the reft of them.

CHAP.

C H A P. III.

Of the River Nile, *whose Source is in this* Ethiopia, *of the Great Lake of* Dambea, *and how the said River runs through it, and continues its Course towards* Egypt.

Search after the Source of Nile.

THE most remarkable thing discover'd in this *Ethiopia*, was the Head, or Spring of the *Nile*, formerly so eagerly sought after by all Antiquity, for the finding whereof, the Greatest Men us'd their utmost endeavours. It is said of *Alexander the Great*, that the first Question he ask'd, when he came to *Jubiter Ammon*, was, Where the *Nile* had its Rise ? And we know he sent discoveries throughout *Ethiopia*, without being able to find out this Source. The same is recorded of *Philadelphus* and *Sesostris*. Historians also tell us of *Cambises*, that he travers'd much Land, with a Mighty Army, as if this Discovery were to be made by Force of Arms, and yet all prov'd in vain ; for at last he return'd with the loss of abundance of Men and without finding the Spring, as *Lucan* observes, l. 10.

Et pastus cade suorum, innoto te Nile *redit.*

Julius Cæsar was so desirous of knowing this Spring, that discoursing in *Egypt* with that Grave Old Man *Acboreus*, and enquiring, Where the *Nile* had its Origin ? He went so far as to tell him, It was the thing he most coveted to know in the World ; *nihil est quod noscere malim, Quam Fluvii causas, per sæcula tanta latentis :* Adding, That he would quit his Country *Rome*, for the satisfaction of discovering that Source, *Spes si mihi certa videndi Niliacos Fontes, Bellum civile relinquam.* This Spring lying still conceal'd after so much search, Men at last concluded, that Nature had decreed this Secret should not be reveal'd, as *Claudian* observes, *Secreto de Fonte cadit, nec contigit ulli, hoc vidisse Caput ; fertur sine Teste creatus.* *Pliny* Nat. Hist. lib. 5. cap. 9. says, This Spring was not known in his Days ; yet adds, that by means of *Juba*,

Mistakes about the River Niger.

King of *Mauritania*, it was said to come from a Lake call'd *Nilis*. Some have made it to proceed from the River *Niger*, but there is no such River in this *Ethiopia*, notwithstanding all the Fables F. *Urreta* Writes of it.

And

And tho' *Mercator* and others in their Maps make this *Niger* the Weſtern Boundary of *Ethiopia*, yet they place it higher up in *Africk*, above 400 Leagues Weſt from the *Red Sea*, and conſequently very remote from our *Ethiopia*, which, as has been ſaid, ſcarce reaches 150 Leagues Weſt from the *Red Sea*, and this will appear by our Map: So that the ſaid River *Niger* muſt lye 250 Leagues wide of *Abyſſinia*. The new *Atlas*, in both the Maps of *Africk* and *Ethiopea*, places a Lake he calls the Black Lake, near the Kingdom he names *Tigray*, in betwixt 3 and 4 Degrees of North Latitude, whence he ſays, proceeds a River call'd *Niger*; but as I have before declared, there is no ſuch Kingdom as *Tigray* in *Ethiopia*, and that of *Tigre* is not in the Latitude he mentions, nor has it any ſuch Lake; ſo that it is plain there is no River *Niger* among the *Ethiopians*.

Several Sacred Writers were of Opinion, that the *Nile* was the River in *Paradiſe*, call'd *Gihon* by *Moſes*, and that it ran thence under the Earth and the Sea itſelf, till it guſh'd out in *Ægypt*: Thus we ſee how great Strangers the Ancients were to the Source of the *Nile*; and the Reaſon they could never find it, was its lying ſo far up in *Africk*, and the way to it all barr'd with thoſe monſtrous high and impaſſable Mountains of *Abyſſinia*, from which the River caſts itſelf down moſt dreadful Precipices; beſides that, the Nations lying in the way are the fierceſt and moſt barbarous in the World. Now the Diſcoverers ſent upon this Errand, meeting with thoſe impregnable Mountains and vaſt Deſarts, we ſhall ſpeak of hereafter, choſe rather to return, and give out, that the Spring was Enchanted and never to be found out, than to hazard their Lives with ſo little probability of Succeſs. *About the* Nile.

It is now time to come to ſpeak of what is certainly known at this Time, after being ſo long conceal'd, which we have from the Annual Letters and other Accounts, of ſeveral Fathers of the Society, who were Eye-Witneſſes of what they Write, and more particularly among them the Patriarch of *Ethiopia*, Don *Alfonſo Mendez*, F. *Emanuel de Almeyda*, and F. *Jerome Lobo*, who all curiouſly view'd thoſe Springs, and writ the Truth of what they ſaw, and eſpecially the laſt, who is moſt particular in theſe Affairs, in the Commentaries of his long Peregrination, which he communicated to me at his Return to *Portugal*, in the Year 1673.

Here in *Abyſſinia*, almoſt in the midſt of the Kingdom of *Gojam*, ſpoken of in the laſt Chapter, and in 12 Degrees Latitude, inclining to the Weſtward, is a Country they call *Sacahala*, inhabited by a Nation they name *Agaus*, moſt of them Heathens, and ſome, who at preſent only retain the Name of Chriſtians. This *True Source of* Nile.

C　　　　　　　　Country

Country is Mountainous, as are most Parts of *Ethiopia,* tho' there are others higher about it. Among these Mountains, is a spot of Plain, not very Level, about a Mile in Extent, and in the midst of it a little Lake, about a Stones throw over. This Lake is full of a sort of little Trees, whose Roots are so interwoven, that walking on them in the Summer, Men come to two Springs, almost a Stones throw asunder, where the Water is clear and very deep, and from these two the Water gushes two several ways into the Lake, from which it runs under Ground, yet so as its Course may be discern'd by the Green Grass, gliding first to the Eastward for about a Musket-shot, and then turns towards the North.

Its Course and Increase
About half a League from the Source, little over or under, the Water begins to appear upon the Land, in such quantity as makes a considerable Stream, and then presently is joined by others; and after having run with all its Windings about 15 Leagues, it receives another considerable River, bigger than the *Nile* itself, and call'd *Gema,* which there loses its Name. A little farther, when its Course begins to be to the Eastward, it receives two other Rivers, call'd *Kelty* and *Branzy,* and close by is the first Fall or Cataract, of which we shall speak anon. Thence the River runs almost East, and flows into the great Lake, which in that Country they call'd the Sea of *Dambea* for its greatness, as being in that Kingdom, of which we shall treat in the next Chapter. It is distant from the Source of the *Nile* about 20 Leagues in a strait Line.

Crosses a Lake.
The *Nile* crosses this Lake over a Point of it, which stretches to the Westward, and flows out of it again in Summer, with much the same quantity of Water it goes in : Nor does it only seem to be the same in quantity alone, but even in quality ; for when the Lake is very smooth, the Current of the *Nile* is perfectly discern'd crossing it, and carrying some small Sticks and Straws, which usually drive with the Stream ; the Water of the Lake standing still, as if that haughty River disdain'd to mix its Waters with any others, and only took its Passage over the Lake, which is there between 6 and 7 Leagues across.

Encompasses the Kingdom of Gojam.
We have now discover'd the Source of the *Nile,* which before was thought to be enchanted, and was only concentred in the midst of a Kingdom, which is a part of the *Upper Ethiopia.* This River, as has been said before, encloses almost all the Kingdom of *Gojam,* and the compass it takes is not amiss represented by a Snake not quite turn'd round ; but with those Windings here set down in the Map, represented for the better understanding of it. The Extent of it from the Turning at the Entrance into it, to the South East Point, next the Kingdom of *Xaoa,* may be

[margin note:] Passage alluded to by Ludolf, History of 1682 p 46

be about 50 Leagues, and the Breadth from betwixt the two oppofite Parts, of the River which encompafs it, about 30 ; but when
the River turns again, it comes within 10 or 12 Leagues of its
Source, as plainly appears in the Map annex'd.

The *Abyffinians* call the Lake above men.ion'd *Bar Dombea*, fig- Dambea
nifying the Sea of the Kingdom of *Dambea*, which is in 13 De- *Lake.*
grees and a half of North Latitude, and on the South Side the faid
Lake is about 20 Leagues in length; on the North Side 35; but if
were we to reckon the Windings of all the Bays it makes into the
Land, it would be much more. The Compaffings on the South
Side are not fo many, but will make 30 Leagues. The Breadth
meafur'd over the middle and deepeft Part, will reach to 10 or
12 Leagues. The Water of it is very clear, light and wholefome,
and has in it abundance of Fifh of feveral forts; as alfo great numbers of Sea-Horfes, which come out to Graize on the Land, in the
plaineft Parts, where they deftroy much Provifion. There are
fome Men who live by killing them; they Eat their Flefh, and of
their Skins make *Alengas*, fo they call a fort of Lafhes they ufe for
their Horfes; for in *Ethiopia* they have no Spurs, the want whereof is fupply'd by thefe *Alengas*, which gird and cut. There are
no *Crocodiles* or *Alligators*, generally fpeaking, in this Lake, as
there are in other Parts of the *Nile*, fo that the Cattel Graize fe-
curely on its Banks, and all the People dwelling about them,
enjoy the Sweetnefs of its Waters, without thofe Frights others
are fubject to along the *Nile*, after it enters *Ægypt*. However,
it is moft certain there are no *Tritons* nor *Sirens* in this Lake, as
Johnfon was inform'd, and he tells us in his Map of *Ethiopia*, in
his *Atlas*, publifh'd *An.* 1653.

Ptolemy call'd this Lake *Coloe*; *John de Barros* gives it the Name *Wrong Names*
of *Barcena*, it is likely, from an Ifland which is near the Place, *given it.*
where the River flows out. *Mercator* and *Johnfon* in their Tables of *Abyffinia*, call this Lake by two Names, the South Part
Zambre, and the North Part *Zaire*; but its true Name, as has
been faid, is *Bar Dambea*. There are many Iflands in it, faid in
all to be 21, fome of them large, as is that they call *Dek*, in which *Iflands in it.*
there are plow'd Lands, which employ 40 Yoke of Oxen. In 7
or 8 of thefe Iflands there are Monafteries of Religious Men, which
were formerly very great; being hot they produce good Oranges
and Limons, and all forts of Fruit that has Thorney Trees.

The *Abyffinians* Navigate this great Lake in a fort of Veffels they
call *Tancoas*, which are like *Almadies*, or little Boats, not made of *Boats made*
Wood, but of a fort of Rufhes they call *Tabua*, whereof there is *of Rufhes.*
great Plenty in this Lake, each of which is as thick as a Mans
Arm, and a Fathom in length; and they are fatisfy'd with thefe

Veffels

Veffels, which are as handfome as thofe who make them. This *Tabua* grows alfo in the other Lakes, and all along the *Nile*, where it is fmaller and longer than that of this Lake, and *Pliny* defcribes his Rufh *Nat. Hift. lib.* 13. *cap.* 11. and it is the fame they call *Papyrus*, of which was made the Paper the Antients us'd to write on, whence to this Day that we now have is call'd Paper. The Antient *Ægyptians* made Boats of the fame to Sail on their *Nile*.

Errors of Mercator and Johnson. Many were of Opinion, that the *Nile* had its Source in this Lake, which, as has been faid, only affords it a Paffage; yet, tho' feveral others fall into it, none has any other Paffage out of this Lake but that of the *Nile*; which fhows, that *Mercator* and *Johnfon* were both mifinform'd, when they fay, that from this Lake flows the River *Zaire*, which after watering the Kingdom of *Congo* falls into the Weftern Ocean, and two other Rivers, which they pretend, meet in another Lake on the Borders of *Angola*, whence *Mercator* fays, the River *Coanza* flows. However, moft certain it is, that only the *Nile* runs out of this Lake, and the *Coanza* has a far different Source.

Gathering of Waters. Neverthelefs, many feveral Rivers fall into this Lake of *Dambeà*, and all the great Mountains of that Kingdom difcharge all their Waters into it, as do the other Hills and Plains about it; which vaft Bulk of Water much Swells the Lake, and therefore in Winter the *Nile* is very confiderably increafed by it, becaufe all thofe Waters have no other Mouth to run out at, but only that the *Nile* has made; fo that all the prodigious quantity of Waters gather'd by the Lake in Winter, ferves to aggrandize the Name of the River.

Rivers falling into the Nile. Befides this, the *Nile*, after coming out of this Lake, and before it leaves *Ethiopia*, receives many very confiderable Rivers, as the *Gamarà*, *Abeà*, *Bayxò*, *Anquer*, and others, that may be feen in the Map; and laftly, the *Tacazè* is loft in it farther towards *Ægypt*. Thus we fee the Learned *Mayolus* was mifinform'd, when he fays, the *Nile* has this peculiar Privilege, *That it Swells with only its own Waters, and fcarce admits the Society of any other River*; *whereas the Sea receives very many. Mayol. Dieb. Canicul. Colloq.* 11. *verbo Fluvius.*

Its winding Courfe into Egypt. As foon as the *Nile* is out of this Lake, its Stream runs almoft directly South Eaft, and fo paffes by the Kingdoms of *Begamedèr*, *Amaharà* and *Oleca*, leaving them on the Eaft; then turning towards the South, it leaves the Kingdoms of *Xaoa* on the South Eaft; and again winding to the Weft, North Weft and North, leaves *Ganz*, *Gafates* and *Bizamò* on the South Weft and Weft, and pierces into the Countries of the *Gongas* and *Cafres*, and further

ther on, paſſing by thoſe of *Faſcalò*, enters thoſe of the *Ballous*,
or *Funchos*, being, according to *F. Emanuel de Almeyla's* well
grounded Opinion, the ſame as *Nubia*; and thence it glides on
towards *Ægypt*, which lying North from the Source of *Nile*,
Claudian had good Reaſon to ſay, the *Nile* came from the South.
Epig. de Nilo. This River draws all that infinite quantity of
Water after it, as has been ſaid, which, tho' very Clear and Chry-
ſtalline at its firſt coming out of the Lake, yet afterwards runs
through Flats of Black Earth, where it is muddy'd, and having
loſt its Native Purity, well deſerves the Epithets the Prophet
Jeremy gives it of thick and troubled. To this alſo the Poets allude, who call it ſlimy and blackiſh. For this Reaſon, ſays *Pie-
rius*, the *Nile* was call'd *Melon*, that is, Black, from the black-
neſs of its Waters. It is this muddineſs that cauſes the *Nile* to
fertilize *Ægypt* ſo wonderfully, that being ſatisfy'd with the Bleſ-
ſings it receives this way, it neither wants the Commodities of
the Land, nor the Rains from Heaven.

C H A P. IV.

Of the Cataracts, and the over-flowing of the Nile, *and
the Opinions of the Antients concerning them ; as alſo
of the other Rivers of* Ethiopia, *and particularly
the* Tacazé, Zebec, Haoax *and* Mareb.

THE *Nile* by reaſon of the prodigious Height of the Rocks, *Cataracts or*
　among which it has its Courſe, even within *Ethiopia*, has *Falls of* Nile.
ſome dreadful Falls, which the Antients call'd Cataracts. The
firſt of theſe is near a Town of the *Agaus*, call'd *Depeqhan*, 9 or
10 Leagues before it enters the Lake of *Dembea:* The ſecond is 5
or 6 Leagues after its coming out of the ſaid Lake, near a Territory of the Kingdom of *Begameder*, call'd *Alata*. At the firſt Cataract the River falls plum down a very craggy ſteep Rock, along
which the Water ſcatters very much, and a great deal of it diſ-
perſes into a thick Miſt, or mizling Rain, which being carry'd
away with any Wind, is ſeen at a great diſtance like a large beautiful Cloud that is diſſolving into continual Rain.

The

The Noise of the rebounding Water and the Whirlpool it makes, falling into a deep Cavity surrounded with Rocks, is so violent, that it resembles a continual and dreadful Clap of Thunder, which for a great compass round about deafens the Ears and torments the Head. For this reason I do not question, but that nearer to *Egypt* there are those Cataracts, so famous among the Antients, which, tho' little greater than these, says *F. Emanuel de Almeyda*, will cause the Country for a League about to be uninhabited, or at least the Inhabitants will in a short time become Deaf ; because that violent Noise must of necessity offend the Drum of the Ear. The Fall of the first Cataract is about 50 Spans, that is, 12 Yards and a half high ; that of the second is twice or thrice as much, and accordingly the Noise of the Water is double.

I will now say something in relation to the other Secret of this renowned River, which was as much talk'd of as unintelligible, being the Cause of its Swelling in the Months of *August* and *September*, so as to overflow and fertilize the spacious Plains of *Egypt* ; for it being then Summer there, and the Antients not knowing where the *Nile* had its Source, they could not conceive whence that Inundation should proceed, which was equal to a Sea.

F. Urreta says, the mighty Storms which prevail at that Time about the Cape of *Good Hope*, are by Subterraneous Passages communicated to the Lake whence this River proceeds, and expelling the Water with their Violence, cause it to drown the large Plains of *Egypt*. This is as extravagant a Notion as many more of that Author who could find no difficulty in conveying the Storms of the Cape of *Good Hope* about 900 Leagues under Ground ; for so far that Cape is from the Source of the River, to disturb the Lake of *Dambea*, which is so still and peaceable, that *F. Emanuel de Almeyda*, who liv'd several Years on a Peninsula it makes, affirms, that after observing all its Qualities with the greatest exactness, he could never find the least Ground for laying such an Imputation to its Charge.

Some Authors believ'd, that the Swelling Surges of the Sea being drove through the Pores of the Earth, caus'd this Lake to Swell to such a degree, as to vomit out so vast an Inundation of Waters. Others fancy'd, that these Floods proceeded from the Snows melting on the Mountains of *Ethiopia :* However, tho' the Snows may in some measure help, they are not the Prime Cause of that Inundation. I will not trouble the Reader with many other Notions of Authors on this Account, who knowing nothing of it, invented whatsoever their Imaginations could dictate ; for
the

the reafon of the fwelling of the *Nile*, in *July*, *August* and *September*, is as well known in this *Ethiopia*, as in *Portugal* the caufe of the rifing of the *Tagus*, *Mondego*, or other Rivers in *December* and *January*; which is becaufe it is then Winter with us, and fo in *Abyffinia*, the depth of Winter is in *July*, *August* and *Sep-* *The true Reatember*, and it is a plain cafe, that a River muft needs fwell, *fon.* which before it leaves *Ethiopia*, for the fpace of above 150 Leagues, receives into it almoft all the Rivers and Brooks of thofe Parts, all which at that time are full fraught; befide the vaft quantity of Water added to it by the mighty Lake of *Dambea*, the common Receptacle of all the Waters falling from all the Mountains round about it. And the fame *Nile* after leaving *Ethiopia*, in its many windings before it comes to *Egypt*, for above 300 Leagues, fwallows up all the Rivers and Brooks it meets in the way.

The *Nile* carries all this immenfe quantity of Waters during thofe Months, and coming into the fpacious Plains of *Egypt*, when it is Summer there, fpreads over, and fills them with fuch abundance of Water, Slime and Mud, it brings along with it, that thofe, who are not acquainted with the Caufe, can only admire the Effect. Thus, by what is here faid, thefe two fo long hidden *Secrets of* Secrets of the fource of the *Nile*, and the caufe of its Inundation, *Nile's Source,* are made manifeft to the World; and it plainly appears what an *and over-* infinite multitude of Waters run out of the Lake from fo many *flowing dif-* Rivers along with the *Nile*; as alfo with what fury that pro- *covered.* digious weight of Water muft needs caft it felf down the Mountains of *Ethiopia*, and rufh on towards *Egypt*, till it refts in the *Mediterranean*.

This demonftrates the impoffibility of what fome Authors affirm, faying, That the *Grand Seignior* pays a certain Tribute to *Impoffibility* the *Abyffine* Emperor, left he fhould divert the Courfe of the *of diverting* *Nile*, but may fuffer it to go Water the Plains of *Egypt*, and to *the Courfe of* the end that when the Floods are too great, he may turn away *Nile.* the Water, near the Ifland *Meroe*, to the Red-Sea, for fear the Lands be drown'd and the Crop fpoilt. All which is fabulous and impoffible, as will appear to any fenfible Man, who will but confider how impracticable it is to divert any of our common Rivers, when they overflow and beat down Houfes and all that ftands in their way; much more the *Nile*, which has a Courfe of fo many hundred Leagues, and gathering all the Waters of fo many Kingdoms and Provinces, comes into *Egypt* with fuch an Immenfity of Water, that it forces it felf into the *Mediteranean* at feveral Mouths, about *Alexandria*, oppofite to the Ifland of *Cyprus*, after it has it felf appear'd all over that Country like a large Sea.

　　　　　　　　　　　　　　　　　　　　　　　　One.

Confirmation   One Argument may be brought againſt the Impoſſibility of
of it.   diverting the Courſe of the *Nile*, which is that the Hiſtory of
India informs us, the great *Alfonſo d' Albuquerque* had a deſign of
meeting the Emperor of *Ethiopia*, in order to turn away the *Nile*
to the Red Sea, cutting a new Channel and ſtopping up that
which flow'd towards *Egypt*, to render thoſe Fields barren;
which are the Great *Turks* Granaries; which Work the Author
of that great Commanders Commentaries declares to be very eaſie,
and to be done with very little Trouble, as he expreſſes it.   But
with their leave who entertained that Conceit, I muſt be free to
ſay, that Work was not only difficult, but altogether impoſſible,
becauſe that River never had, nor can ever have any other Courſe,
but what the Author of Nature gave it at firſt, nor is it in the
Power of Man to turn it away and find it a new Paſſage to the Red-
Sea.   The reaſon is, becauſe there are above 100 Leagues from the
neareſt Part of the River to the Red-Sea, and all that Country
the moſt horrid Rocks and Mountains it is poſſible to imagine, as
we ſhall ſee hereafter; and what Force would ſuffice to hew
down ſuch Mountains and break through the Boundaries God
himſelf has plac'd, which as the Scripture tells us, is no better
than ſtriving againſt the Stream.

Having ſpoken as much as is neceſſary of the *Nile*, let us now
ſay ſomething of the other noble and mighty Rivers, which riſe
Tacazè River. in and Water this *Ethiopia*, among which the *Tacaze* is well
known and famous. *Mercator* ſays this is the River *Ptolemy* calls
Aſtaboras, and he ſeems to be in the right, as I ſuppoſe the *Aſta-*
pus mention'd by the ſaid *Ptolemy* to be the *Nile*. The *Tacaze*
has it ſource on a Ridge of Mountains, call'd *Arynagna*, on the
Frontiers of the Kingdom of *Angot*, next that of *Begameder*,
where at the Foot of the higher Mountain, which lies to the
Eaſtward, three ſeveral Springs guſh out violently within a Stones
Throw of one another, and joyning their Waters make a great
Stream, which runs to the Eaſtward for ſome Days Journey,
betwixt the Territories of *Daphaná*, and *Hoage*, lying North of it.
Then it croſſes the Kingdom of *Tigre*, cutting through the midſt
of *Sirè*, a Province of the ſaid Kingdom, leaving the beſt Lands
of that Province on the Eaſt, and its famous Deſart *Aldobá* on the
Weſt, where formerly there were many Anchorites, as in *Thebaida*
of *Egypt*.

This River *Tacaze* is not quite ſo large, yet not much inferior
to the *Nile*, and has ſome very deep Places, in which there are
Water-Horſes. Crocodiles of an extraordinary magnitude, as alſo Water-Horſes,
which *F. Emanuel d' Almeyda* teſtifies he ſaw there, and ſaid,
they are properly call'd Horſes, as being like them in the Head,
and

and particularly the Ears, tho' their Legs are short and their Tails shorter, and they have no Hair, but a bare Skin, and very smooth. It has also much Fish of other sorts, and the same *F. Emanuel d'Almeyda*, assures us they here show'd him in a Bowl, that Fish, which in *Latin*, from the Effect it produces, they call *Torpedo*, and we the Cramp-Fish; for that laying hold of it with his Hand, it immediately caused such a Numbness, that he presently let it go, not thinking fit to continue that dangerous Experiment. This same River passes on by another Province they call *Holcait*, whence it runs into very low Lands of *Cafres*, and leaving them, visits the Kingdom of *Deqhin*, inhabited by a sort of *Moors*, whom we call *Baullous*, and on the Coast of *Suaquem*, they are nam'd *Funchos*, as may be seen in our Map. Then meeting with the *Nile*, loses it self in that River, which receives a considerable increase from its Waters.

There is another celebrated River call'd *Zebee*, said to be greater than the *Nile* it self, rising in a Territory call'd *Boxa* in the Kingdom of *Narea*, which is the most Southerly, and whereof we shall speak hereafter. It begins its Course Westward, and a few Leagues farther turns to the Northward, and runs about the Kingdom of *Gingiro*, of which we shall also give an Account, making it a sort of Peninsula, as the *Nile* does the Kingdom of *Gojam*. After leaving this Kingdom it takes its course to the Southward, and some say it is the same that falls into the Sea at *Mombaza*. *Zebee River.*

There is another very large and notable River, call'd *Haoax*, almost equal to the *Nile*, rising betwixt the Kingdoms of *Xaoa*, which is to the North of it, *Ogge* to the South, and *Futegar* to the East. It takes its course to the North-East, and receives the Waters of another great River call'd *Machy*, which comes out of the Lake *Zoay*, in the Kingdom of *Ogge*, and being increas'd by this Addition, the *Haoax* runs into the Kingdom of *Adel*, by us call'd *Zeyla*, entering it at a Province call'd *Auca Garrele*, being the Place where the Fathers *Bernard Pereyra* and *Francis Machado*, of whom I shall speak hereafter, continued some time, till the Perfidious *Mahometan* King put them to Death, in Hatred, to Christianity. It Rains very little in that Country, but Providence has made amends for that want, with the Water of this River, which being drawn out into several Channels by the Inhabitants, waters their Fields and fertilizes the Valleys, so that it is one of the most plentiful Countries of those Parts in Grain and Cattle. And so generous is this River, that tho' it is master of so much Water, it leaves it all in those Fields it runs through, *Haoax River.*

D

as if it thought it more Honour to be bury'd in the Earth, than lose it self in the Sea.

Mareb River.
 There is another great River of the same nature, call'd *Mareb,* which rises in the Kingdom of *Tigre,* Two Leagues from *Barea* or *Fremona,* to the Westward, whence it runs to the South, and entring some Lands of *Cafres,* which are naturally Sandy, hides it self in them for a considerable space; but if they dig Two Yards they not only find Water to drink, but good Fish, as *F. Emanuel d' Almeyda* says, he was assur'd by *John Gabriel,* who was then Commander of the *Portugueses,* of whom we shall speak hereafter, being a Man of Sincerity and Conscience. A little farther on, this River rises again and coming into the better Country of the Kingdom of *Deqhin,* bestows all the Treasure of its Waters on those Fields, as if it forgot to go any farther and meet the Sea.

P. Urreta's Fabulous History.
 It is not amiss here to observe that *F. Urreta,* in his Fabulous History of *Ethiopia,* says this is call'd the Black-River, because it runs through a Country of Blacks, as if any River in *Ethiopia* did run through a Country of Whites. This is the same he says, forms Three Lakes, from one of which he tells us a River flows, which always runs over Stones of great Value, and falling into the Sea at *Melinde,* has a great Fishery of Pearls, and Amber-Greece at its Mouth. So full of precious thoughts is that Chimerical Author.

Chap. V.

Shewing that the Island Meroe, *which Authors place in* Ethiopia, *is the Kingdom of* Gojam, *where the* Nile *rises.*

Falshood in Barros's History, and others.
 THE famous *Portugueze* Historian, *John de Barros,* following the Opinion of several Geographers, in his 3 *Decad. lib.* 4. *cap:* 1. places the celebrated and fabulous Island of *Meroe* within the Bounds of *Ethiopia,* and makes the North side of this Empire to run from *Suaquem* to the end of this Island, which he says is now call'd *Noba.* Of the same mind was formerly *Pomponius Mela,* saying the Island *Meroe,* was the Head of the Empire

pire of *Ethiopia*. *Diodorus Siculus, lib.* 1 and 17. places this Island in *Egypt*, where he says, it is the largest and most renowned, and had its Name from the chief of its Cities, which took it from a Sister of *Cambyses* its first Founder, who dy'd there, for it is a Thing very ancient for Places to become famous by the Death or Misfortunes of great Persons.

Pliny, lib. 2. *cap.* 15. also places this Island in *Ethiopia*, and *More Fables.* makes it the chief of many he says there are in it and the Head of that Country. Some raise the number of these Islands to 700. This Author and many others tell wonders of this Island and of the abundance of Gold, Silver, Brass, Iron, Ebony, and other precious Commodities they pretend Nature has bountifully bestow'd on it, which were it not all fabulous must render it the chief of those they call Fortunate.

Having duly examined the Maps and view'd *Ptolemy*'s Tables, *Meroe Island.* I find they place this Island in *Ethiopia*, in 13 Degrees of North Latitude, telling us, that in 11 Degrees Latitude, a River, which *Ptolemy* and most other Authors say is the *Nile*, and the *Aftaboras*, supposed to be the *Tacaze*, meet and then part again in 12 Degrees Latitude, and afterwards join again between 16 and 17 Degrees, and within this distance remaining between the two Branches, he says is the Island *Meroe*, of which same Opinion is *John de Barros*, adding that it is now call'd *Noba*. The new *Atlas* of *Johnson*, says the *Nile* and *Tacaze* meet and form that Lake, which he also calls *Gueguere*. But *Pliny* and *Solinus*, quoted by the same *Ptolemy*, as also *Ortelius* and *Mercator* say, those are only two Branches of the *Nile*, and not part of the *Nile* and part of the *Tacaze*, and that they form that Island, which they call *Gueguere*.

All these are mere Fancies, for want of true Information; *Errors disco-*
ver'd. for the Patriarch *Don Alfonso Mendez*, F. *Emanuel d' Almeyda*, and the other Fathers, who liv'd several Years in *Ethiopia*, in 12, 13 and 14 Degrees Latitude, cross'd over the *Nile* and the *Tacaze* many times, and most diligently observ'd all Things, do declare, it is most certain, that these two Rivers do not meet, within the Dominions of the *Abyssinians*; but have their Springs and run on 70 Leagues distant from one another, little more or less, as long as they continue in *Ethiopia*, as may be seen in our Map; and they farther add, that the *Nile* never divides it self into two Branches within that Empire.

Now what shall we say to those Authors and ancient Histories, *Meroe Island,*
is the King-
dom of Go-
jam. who so confidently inform us, that the Island *Meroe*, form'd by the *Nile* alone, or by the *Nile* and *Tacaze*, is in *Ethiopia*, and place it between 12 and 13 Degrees of Latitude? This Point being

being duly weigh'd and confider'd, among the moft learned Perfons of the Society, that went over into *Ethiopia*, they all concluded, that the Kingdom of *Gojam*, where the *Nile* rifes, and which the fame *Nile* encompaffes about, and makes a Peninfula, is the famous Ifland *Meroe* of that River, in *Ethiopia*, of which fuch Wonders are told. A proof whereof is, that thofe Authors place the faid Ifland, between 12 and 13 Degrees, which is the Latitude that Kingdom is in ; befides the faid Kingdom is known to be almoft furrounded with the Waters of the *Nile*, fo that it is a Peninfula. It is alfo certain that there is no other Ifland in the faid Latitude, whence it follows of neceffity, that if there be any fort of Ifland in that Part, it is the Kingdom of *Gojam*, that is the fo renowned *Meroe*. Now thofe Authors knowing very little of it, or where to place it, they had the more encouragement to enrich it at Pleafure, fince it coft them nothing but letting their Pen run ; for fince they could not tell where it was, they refted fatisfy'd that no body would call them to Account for what they faid.

Confirmation of it. A farther Confirmation of this Opinion is, the Breadth of 30 Leagues, which thefe Authors affign the Ifland *Meroe*, little more or lefs, which is the fame of the Kingdom of *Gojam*; but they are out in the Length, making the Ifland 100 Leagues long, whereas the Kingdom of *Gojam* is little above 50. The Cataracts of *Nile*, which thefe Authors place on the North Point of the Ifland *Meroe* next to *Egypt*, are in two Places, the firft near a Village of the *Agaus*, call'd *Depeqban*, 9, or 10 Leagues before the River falls into the Lake of *Dambea*, as was faid before; and the fecond after its coming out of the fame Lake, near a Town call'd *Alata*.

Proof out of Ptolemy. Nor can it be faid that the *Nile* forms this Ifland *Meroe* out of *Ethiopia*, becaufe we do not find that River makes any fuch Ifland in all its Courfe from *Ethiopia* to the *Mediterranean*. Befides that *Ptolemy* and the beft of other Authors place this Ifland within *Ethiopia*, and *Ptolemy* being himfelf an *Egyptian* could not be ignorant of it, if the *Nile* had form'd fuch an Ifland in *Egypt*. Befides that the Inhabitants of this Ifland were Black, as *Lucan* tells us, which agrees with the *Ethiopians* and not with the *Egyptians* : thus fays that Poet, *Pharf. lib.* 10.

———*Gurgite vafto*
Ambitur nigris Meroe *fecunda colonis.*

Nor can it be said that any of the Islands I mention'd above to be in the great Lake of *Dambea* is that of *Meroe*, because they are very small and inconsiderable in Comparison of that vast Island which Authors make 100 Leagues in length, and I say is 50 at least, if it is the Kingdom of *Gojam*, as it seems to be.

By what we have said, it appears, that *Ethiopia* contains those two hidden Treasures of the World, so much spoken of, which are the Source of the *Nile* and the Island *Meroe*; both of them more valuable by Fame, than in Reality; for the Source of the *Nile*, is like that of any other ordinary River, and perhaps more inconsiderable; and the Kingdom of *Gojam* differs little from any other of the Kingdoms of *Ethiopia*, in which there are none of those Mines of pure Gold, nor those Mountains of Precious Stones, wherewith Historians enrich'd this Island, which in this particular resembles the Fortunate Islands, on whom greater Encomiums were bestow'd, than there are Blessings found in them.

C H A P. VI.

Of the Red-Sea, which leads into this Ethiopia, *and the Reasons, why it is so call'd.*

IT was said before, that this Empire towards the East, commences on the Banks of the Red-Sea; and in regard that all the Religious Men of the Society, who enter'd *Ethiopia* went that way, and that we shall have frequently occasion to speak of it and of its Mouths, which are two Channels, the one next *Arabia* and the other on the side of *Abyssinia* which lead into this Sea, and give it a Communication with the *Indian* Sea; and for as much as there has been great debates among the Curious, how it came to be call'd the Red-Sea, I therefore thought, that after treating of the *Nile*, it would be convenient to say something, briefly to this Particular.

The *Red Sea* is in length about 380 Leagues; on the Right Hand entering lies *Arabia Felix*, on the Left *Ethiopia* above Egypt, otherwise call'd *Abyssinia*, or *Abassia*, on whose Coast are the Ports of *Dalee*, *Maxua* and *Suaghem*, besides others of less Note, but none of them at present belong to the *Abyssine* Emperor.

Description of the Red-Sea.

ror. Betwixt the two Coasts, almost in the midst lies the Island call'd *Jabel Mandel*, or *Nahum*, [all other Geographers call it *Babel-Mandel*] and a little beyond it begins a Chain of Islands, so close to one another, that very often 6 or 7 appear together in a Row, and this Ridge of Islands is as it were a Line that cuts it all in length, as the *Apennine* Mountain does *Italy*, and may be seen in our Map. The Children of *Israel* crossed this Sea near *Egypt* when they fled, and in that Place it is said to be but 3 Leagues over to *Arabia*, which was enough to stop them and to drown the *Egyptians*.

Its several Names. This Sea has several Names given it, some call it the *Arabian* Gulph, because it stretches along so far on the Coast of *Arabia*: Others name it the *Streight* or Sea of *Mecca*, because it leads to that City, where *Mahomet*'s Tomb is. The *Greeks* call it *Erythrean*, and from them all others the *Red Sea*; whereas its Waters are as clear as those of the other *Indian* Seas, and hence came the Question, why it should be call'd the *Red Sea*.

Reasons assign'd for them. The first Reason alledg'd is from the Red Clay or Earth, some pretend there is on the Shores, which with the Reflection of the Sun causes theWater to look Red: To make good which Affertion, they ought first to have prov'd, that there were such Red Shores; for tho' there may be some Reddish Earth, yet it cannot cast so great a Reflection, as to affect such a large Sea, which like all others, would rather take its Colour from the Air above, or from the Earth under it, than from the Banks. *Pliny Nat. Hist. lib. 6. cap. 23.* seems to strengthen the aforesaid Opinion, by saying it receives the Colour from the Reflection of the Sun Beams; but in the same Place he says it might be so call'd from the powerful King *Erythrus*, who reign'd in those Parts, and was bury'd on the Shore, whence the Sea had the name of *Erythrean*, which in *Greek* signifies Red, and thence all other Nations took it; of which Opinion are *Philostratus, Solinus, Pomponius Mela, Curtius, Ortelius, F. La Cerda*, and *F. Benedict Fernandez* upon *Exodus*. This Etymology has many followers besides those above nam'd, who seem more complaisant in submitting their Judgments to such Authors, than nice in examining into the certainty of the Truth.

From the Slaughter of the Ægyptians. I should not much blame those, who might urge this Sea was call'd Red, from the great quantity of *Ægyptian* Blood shed in it, when *Pharoah* and all his Army of Horse and Foot perish'd there; where the Slaughter being so great, the Sea could not but be dy'd with the Gore. It is very remarkable, in order to make good this Opinion, that *Moses* in the 14th Chapter of *Exodus*, so often mentioning this Sea, as he does, in speaking of the Passage of the Children of *Israel*, never in the said Chapter once calls it the Red

Sea,

Sea, till after the Slaughter of the *Egyptians*. And it was ufual among the *Jews* to give Names to Places on account of extraordinary Deaths, as the Place where *Uzzah* was Slain by God was call'd *Perez-Uzzah*, or the Smiting of *Uzzah*; and fo the Field bought with the Money for which *Judas* fold our Saviour, had the name of the *Field of Blood*. Nor is there any Author to be found, that ever call'd this the Red Sea, before God deftroyed the *Egyptians* in it; for *Mofes* was the firft and ancienteft of all the Authors in the World, as is fully prov'd by the Learned *P. Francis de Mendoza, Tom. 1. in Reg. Hift. Annal.* 2. *Prooem Annot.* 12.

There may be two Objections againft this Opinion: The firft, that *Mofes* calls this the Red Sea, in the 10*th* and 13*th* Chapters before the Slaughter of the *Egyptians*; to which we anfwer, that he writ his Hiftory long after the paffing of the Red Sea, and therefore might give it the Name it had then receiv'd, tho' not proper to it before the Thing happen'd. The other Objection may be, that the *Egyptians* were not Slain with the Sword, but drowned, and that caufes no Effufion of Blood, to make the Sea Red. To this we anfwer, that here were two forts of Deaths, for the *Vulgate* fays, that the Lord looking upon the Hoft of the *Egyptians, flew them, and overthrew the Wheels of their Chariots*, and the *Egyptians* feeing this Slaughter would have fled, and then the Sea came upon them. Befides, in the Confufion of flying they might kill one another, and many be hurt and over-run by the Horfes and Chariots, and fo much Blood-fhed.

Objections Anfwered.

The *Portuguezes* us'd many Endeavous to difcover the Reafon of calling this the Red Sea, and particularly the Great *Alfonfo d' Albuquerque*, the firft of the Nation who enter'd the Mouth of it, as did alfo the famous *Don John de Caftro*, who went into the *Red Sea* with the Governor *Don Stephen de Gama*, and by what both of them found, the Opinion of thofe who fay that Water is Red becaufe of the Red Bottom, was much confirm'd and prevail'd. This the aforefaid *Alfonfo d' Albuquerque* teftifies in his Commentaries; for he being with his Fleet at the Mouth of that Sea, faw from his Ships a Stream of very Red Sea Water gufh out at the Mouth of the Streight, and it reach'd up it as far as a Man could fee; and afking the Moorifh Pilots *the Caufe of that Rednefs*, thefe are the Words of the Hiftorian, *they anfwer'd, That the Commotion the Tide caufed in the Water, becaufe the Sea was there Shoal and had little Depth, occafion'd the Colour upon the Flood and Ebb*: And he adds, that the faid *Alfonfo d' Albuquerque* concluded it was fo, and that the Bottom of the Sea was the Caufe of it.

Rednefs from the Shores.

Don

Don John de Castro examined this Matter more nicely, as appears by his Journal, and by what the Historian *John de Barros* relates of him. He observing the Redness of the Water, as he sailed along that Sea, *order'd some of the Water to be taken up in Buckets,* says the above named Author, *which being brought up he found to be much more clear and Crystalline, than that without the Mouth or Streight; not so satisfy'd, he caused some Seamen to dive, who brought him a Red Matter from the Bottom, in the Nature of Coral in Branches, and some covered with an Orange Colour Down,* &c. Thus we find that the Redness proceeds from the Ground, appearing thro' the clear Water, which deceives the Eyes, so as that they take that Colour to be in the said Water, which is only in the Bottom of it.

From the Bottom.

Notwithstanding these Observations, there is more Reason to believe, the Redness of this Sea proceeds from abundance of Red Weeds there are in it, as appears by the Account given by the Reverend and Learned Patriarch *Don Alfonso Mendez,* who speaks as an Eye-witness in his Treatise, concerning the Time when the Faith of *CHRIST* enter'd into *Ethiopia,* Chap. 2. His Words are these:

From Weeds

In our way from Mazua *to* Suaquem, *which is commonly gone in* 5 *or* 6 *Days, we spent* 45, *whereof we were* 15 *ashore, and observed three several Colours in that Sea: The first Blue, which is in the deepest Part; the second Green, where there are many Flats, because it is generally very Shoal, and this Greenness it has from the Green Slime that lies on the Rocks; the third Colour is not Red, but Violet Colour, which in some Parts spreads all over the Superficies, and in others lies in Spots, some thicker than others, according to the Cause they proceed from; being certain Holes full of Red Weeds, not very tough, which the Sea, when boisterous, casts upon the Shore, and we had them often in our Hands. Besides, we made another Experiment, which remov'd all Cause of doubting, and was, that being on a Calm Day when the Water was still, in the midst of many Red Spots, we order'd some Youths to Swim, and they pull'd up those Tufts of Weeds; and as they threw them away, the Red Spots ceased, the others about them still remaining.* Thus far this Judicious Person.

Three Colours.

In my Opinion, this doubt is not only clear'd, but we now perceive, why the *Portuguezes* have not only call'd this Sea Red, but Violet Colour, which Distinction we do not find in Authors, who only speak of the Redness and not of the other Violet, tho' that Sea has of late had both Names, and the Colours are different. So where this Sea is so deep, that the Weeds do not reach near the Superficies, it looks Blue, and somewhat Blackish, which is usual in any deep Water. And again, where the Weeds are Red,

or

or of a Violet Colour, they cause that variety already spoken
of.

This Truth is confirm'd by what the great Doctor of the Church *The Redness*
of *S. Jerome* says, which is, that the Cause of calling this Sea Red *from Weeds.*
comes from the word *Suph*, which is *Hebrew*, us'd in Holy Writ,
in speaking of this Sea, and that *Suph* signifies Red; and as it is
well observ'd by our Learned *F. Barradas* upon *Exodus*, the *Septu-*
agint always translate *Suph* Red, and some *Hebrews* tell us, that
Suph is the Name of a Red Weed growing in this Sea, and the
Sun glancing on these Waters, through which the Colour of those
Weeds is seen, makes them look Red tho' they are not so. This
Point is learnedly handled by our *F. Pineda*, in his 4*th* Book upon *Solomon*, and that which clenches all we have said to this
Point, is, what our above quoted Patriarch says, *viz.* That the
Arabs call that Weed we have spoken of *Suph*, and in *Ethiopia*
they give the same Name to an Herb like this in all Respects,
which they bring up in their Gardens, and use the Flower of it
for Dying their Cloth Red, and Eat the Seed: And thus it is
plain, that Sea is call'd Red from those Weeds growing on its
Bottom.

This is what has occurr'd concerning the *Red Sea*, which we
shall often speak of in this Work; and having made so long a
Stay upon it, we will now cast Anchor on its Coast and enter
Ethiopia, to give an Account of that Empire.

CHAP. VII.

Of the Climate, the prodigious high Mountains, the Fer-
tility, Trees, and other Product of Ethiopia*; and*
of the several sorts of Animals, both Wild and
Tame.

TIME has always been the ablest and best Master in all falli- *Time the*
ble Points, such as are the Notions and Opinions of Men. *best Master.*
This is most evident in relation to the Judgment Ancient Astro-
nomers made of the Number and Qualities of the Heavenly
Spheres, which they declared to be Ten, and of an incorruptible
Matter, which Opinion they concluded was not only venerable,
E   but

but would be ever unchangeable in the Schools, and yet in Time abler Mathematicians by infallible Obfervations found out that which is now generally receiv'd, *viz.* That there is no need of, nor are there fo many Heavens as the Ancients pretended, and that even thofe Three, which are generally allow'd of, are not incorruptible, as they would have perfwaded us. So that Time, tho' fo old a Mafter, ftill teaches fome Things that are new.

Miftakes of the Ancients. But what wonder that Men fhould err in Things that relate to Heaven, whither they cannot fly, with the weight of their corruptible Bodies, when we fee how much they have been miftaken in Earthly Matters, which are near and obvious? What could be more receiv'd in Antiquity, than the Opinion which taught that all thofe Countries were not Habitable, which lie under the Torrid, and under the two Polar, Arctick and Antarctick, Zones; the firft as too hot, and the others as too cold? Yet Time, notwithftanding that fo receiv'd Opinion, has demonftrated, that there are People living near both the Poles; and that in the Center of the Torrid Zone, where they imagin'd the People muft be burnt up, there are infinite Nations, and fome of them enjoy as Temperate a Climate as there is in *Europe*, in the belt Parts of *Spain*, or the cooler *Lombardy*.

Temperate Regions in the Torrid Zone. There has been no occafion to make the leaft doubt hereof, fince the Conquefts and Difcoveries of the *Portuguefes*, and we have an evident Proof of it in this our *Abyffinian Ethiopia*, which lying betwixt 8 and 17 Degrees of North Latitude, all under the Torrid Zone, is yet fo far from being inhabitable for too much Heat, that it is generally as Cold and Temperate as *Portugal*, infomuch, that in many Parts they have none of our Summer Heats, nor are ever fenfible of the furious fcorching of the Dog-Days among us; but on the contrary they are more afraid of the Cold.

Different Winters in Ethiopia. But as there is a great diftance betwixt thofe Countries, fo do the Climates vary. Hence it is, that the Maritime Parts of this Empire, as from *Mazua* to *Danghali*, along the Red Sea, have their Winter in *December* and *January*, as it is in *Portugal*, and reaches 10 or 12 Leagues up the Inland, being very mild, without any fharp Cold or exceffive Rain, as if Nature gave it the Rain Water to moiften or fertilize the Land, and not to moleft or trouble the Inhabitants. Farther up the Country there is no want of troublefome Rains, till you come to fome high Mountains, call'd *Bizan*, two Days Journey fhort of *Debaroa*, where the Winter is from the 10th of *June* till the end of *September*; and thus F. *Emanuel d' Almeyda* fays, he found it in all the Countries of this Empire he travell'd through: So that the Winter throughout all the Inland of *Ethiopia*, is in the fame Months as it is on the Coaft of

India

India from *Diu* to Cape *Comori* ; and on the Coast of *Ethiopia* it is at the same time as in *Portugal*, whereas it is contrary on the Coasts of *Arabia*, lying from the Mouth of the Red-Sea, to the Islands of *Curia-Muria*, where the Winter is in *June, July, August* and *September*, as on the Coast of *India*; and up the Inland of *Arabia* it is in the Months of *November, December, January* and *February*, as in *Portugal.*

All the Emperor of *Ethiopia*'s Dominions he now possesses are Mountainous, except the Kingdom of *Dambea*, the greatest Part whereof is Plain along the great Lake, and has rich Fields of Fat fertile Land for about 20 Leagues in length, little more or less, and 4 or 5 in breadth. The other Kingdoms, *viz. Tigre, Begameder, Gojam, Amara*, and the Provinces of *Cemen, Ogarà, Sagado, Holcait, Xaoa* and *Holecà*, are almost continual Mountains of a prodigious Height, and it is rare to travel a Days Journey without meeting such steep, lofty and craggy Hills, that they are dreadful to behold, much more to pass over. All the Mountains in *Portugal* compar'd to those of *Ethiopia*, are meer Mole-Hills. Those who have crofs'd the *Alps* and *Pyrenean* Mountains, and the *Apennine*, which cuts *Italy* in two, all of them so famous in *Europe*, and have seen those of *Ethiopia*, declare, the others are but easy and low Eminences to these last. *Vast Mountains.*

Thus Nature, which in several Places seems to sport, producing wonders, so here it works the same marvellous Effects in Mountains, far exceeding the highest Clouds, and in Valleys so deep, that they look as if they were going to hide themselves in the very Center of the Earth and lowest Abyss, and accordingly the first partake of the excessive Cold of the second and third Regions of the Air, and the latter of the Fire of Hell. Some of these Mountains, which the Natives call *Ambas*, stand by themselves apart from all others, are prodigious high, all upright, as if they had been hew'd with a Chisel, with only one or two ways to get up to them, with much difficulty, and on the top they have Water and a Plain, where the Inhabitants live, as it were in an impregnable Fortress, erected by Providence for the Defence of the *Ethiopians*, who hitherto have not the Skill to make any Martial Works. There are many of these throughout all this Empire, but most of all in the Kingdom of *Amara*, which is now next to the *Gallas*, who would before now have made themselves Masters of it, were it not for the Retreat of these *Ambas*, or Fortresses made by Nature, without the help of Man. *They serve for Fortresses.*

It is wonderful to see these vast high Rocks, some of them like Pyramids, others round, as if they were turn'd at the Top and Bottom; others like square Towers, as handsomly wrought as if *Their several Shapes.*

E 2 they

they had been hew'd out, and were Natural Columns, boldly rising above the Clouds, as it were to support the Sky, as the Poets feign'd of *Atlas*.

The worst is, that very often in passing from one Kingdom to another, some of these Mountains must of necessity be cross'd, as happens in going from *Fremona*, which is almost in the middle of the Kingdom of *Tigre*, 45 Leagues from *Mazua*, to *Dancaz* and *Dambea*, where among many other Mountains Travellers must cross one call'd *Lamalmon*, and before they come to the first ascent of that they are at the Foot of a vast high Mountain call'd *Guca*, which is as it were the Foundation or Pedastal of *Lamalmon*. It

Lamalmon and Guca Mountains.

is half a Days Journey to ascend this Mountain, always rounding it, for it goes continually winding by very narrow Paths, cut along the side of the Hill, with such dreadful Depths and Precipices, either looking up or down, that if the Caravan ascending happens to meet with the other descending, unless they take special care where they set their Feet, they are absolutely lost, and

of the names of the Lam by Bruce

tumble down those frightful Depths, beating the Travellers to pieces, and losing the Goods they carry. The Commodities they generally load are *India* Stuffs and Salt.

Dreadful deep Valleys.

On the top of this Mountain *Guca*, is a large Plain above a League in compass, where the tir'd Travellers and Caravans rest themselves, the better to prosecute the rest of their Journey ; for the next Day they enter upon a most tiresome Ridge, so sharp and narrow, that it is frightful to behold, much more to pass along it, being Perpendicular on both Sides, and the Valleys on either of them so wonderful deep, that the sight cannot reach the bottom of them. As soon as pass'd this Ridge, they are at the Foot of a Mountain, almost all of it made of one entire upright Rock, which rising out of the Ground, represents an excessive high and strong Bulwork. This is the most difficult Part of all the way, and yet Nature has provided a sort of Steps like Stairs, with windings both ways, but all extraordinary uneoth, and the Steps or Rocks sometimes two or three Cubits high ; so that it is wonderful, that

Frightful Ascent.

the Beasts of Burden can climb, and keep their Feet, tho' they are there unloaded ; for in this Place there are abundance of People who live by taking the Burdens off the Beasts, till they pass those Difficulties.

Plain on the Mount.

This Mount is about 300 Fathom high, and on it Nature has made a very plain Flat, being about half a League in Compass, and a Musket-shot Diameter ; and this Eminence they call by the Name of *Lamalmon*, representing in some measure a Chair without Arms, for the Rock on the highest Part of the Plain resembles the Back of the Chair, being as Perpendicular as if hew'd out

with

with a Chizzel; under which is that which answers to the Seat of this wonderful Chair, where there is a Town, safe enough against all Attacks of any Enemy, were it but as well provided with Necessaries for human Life; yet they have good Water, with which they make what amends they can for the want of Provisions, whereof there is no Plenty.

From this height is discover'd, almost all the Kingdom of *Tigre,* and towards the East appears a vast Chain of excessive high Mountains, running from this of *Lamalmon,* with another like it towards the North and North East, and all together making a great Bow, in the midst of which the Hills and Mountains of *Tigre,* tho' very high, look like inconsiderable Hillocks. Tho' the famous *Carthaginian Hannibal,* from the Top of the *Alps* encourag'd and comforted his Soldiers with the pleasing sight of the spacious and delightful Plains of *Italy ;* here, on the contrary, the most covetous and ambitious Person, at the sight of these dismal Mountains, might well lay aside all Thoughts of subduing such uncooth, such craggy and such dreadful Places, which as bad as they are to behold, are much more hideous to climb. And surely, only those, who, as the Prophet did, *Lift up their Eyes to the Hills from whence cometh their Help,* can with the sweet Thoughts of Heaven make those almost impassable Mountains of *Ethiopia* tolerable, as the Religious Men did. And I must confess I am so much out of Humour with the bare Relation, and so far distant view of one of these Mountains, that I forbear speaking of the others, which *F. Emanuel d' Almeyda* took the pains to describe, as having undergone the trouble of passing over them. [*Chains of Mountains.*]

It follows next to say something of the Fertility of the Country, and Gold being esteem'd the most precious Product of the Earth, there are said to be very rich Mines of it in *Ethiopia ;* it is most certain, at least, that many grave Authors are very free in bestowing abundance of such Mines on it ; and many believe there are really such Mines in *Ethiopia,* but that they will not have them discover'd, for fear lest their Fame should move the *Turk* to invade them, as he has already done more than once, and together with their Treasure, deprive them of their Liberty, which is more precious than Gold. Such is the vile nature of this Metal, that if you want it you are miserable, and if you have too much you are in Danger. The Gold they have at present is taken out of some Rivers in small Grains, like Seed-Pearl, and there is no other Money in the Country, especially for Strangers, but this Gold, which they dispose of by weight. [*Gold in Ethiopia.*]

But.

Iron, Lead, and Salt. But what they want in Gold, they have to fpare in Iron, which has alfo its value; nor do they want Lead. Salt is their moft general Commodity, and they have almoft brought it to ferve inftead of Money, all other Goods being commonly fold for it at Fairs. This Salt is not like that we have in *Europe,* made of Sea-Water; but Providence has furnifhed them with in-exhauftible Mines of it, being as it were Rocks of Salt on the Borders of the Kingdoms of *Tigre* and *Angot,* from which they hew out Pieces like Bricks.

Fertility. The Land, for the moft Part, where it can be till'd, is very fruitfull, for in many Places, tho' the *Abyffinians* are not over in-duftrious, it yeilds three Crops in a Year of Wheat, Barley and Millet, and many other forts of Grain that grow in *Portugal.* There is great Plenty of a fmall Grain they call *Tef,* which is the proper Food of the Country, as natural to the Ground, and of fufficient Nourifhment, and is fo very fmall that one fingle Grain *Tef, a fmall Grain.* of Muftard-Seed will make ten of this *Tef,* tho' it is longifh, but very thin and flender. Yet tho' the Soil be fo Fertile, there is often Eamine in *Ethiopia,* either caus'd by the Locufts, a frequent Plague there, or by the marching of Soldiers, from one Country to another, which is a worfe Plague than the Locufts, becaufe they only de-vour what they find in the Fields, whereas the others fpare not what is laid up in the Houfes.

Amadmagdo and Affazoe, Plants of great Virtue. All the Odoriferous and Medicinal Herbs that *Europe* produces are found here, and among them one they call *Amadmagdo,* which draws out the Splinters of broken Bones that remain loofe in the Flefh. There is another Herb they call *Affazoe,* which has fuch Virtue againft Poifon, that the moft Venomous Snakes touching it, are quite ftupify'd and fenfelefs; and what is yet more won-derful, the very fhadow of it does not only fcare away but be-numbs any Snake; fo that as S. *Peter's* fhadow miraculoufly wrought Cures, this Plant naturally deftroys Poifon. Befides whofoever eats the Root of this Plant retains its Virtue for many Years, and may go among all forts of Poifonous Snakes without fearing any Hurt from them; nay he has fo much Power over them, that his very fhadow ftuns them.

Cotton, Sugar Canes and Fruit. The Fathers of the Society write, that they often faw feveral *Abyffinians,* who had eaten thefe Roots, handle the moft venomous Vipers, as if they had been Eels, and put them about their Necks, like Collars; and kill them when they pleas'd. The Country alfo produces much Cotton, growing on Shrubs, like thofe of *India;* abundance of *Senna, Lemmons, Citrons, Oranges,* and *Figs* like ours. In fome Parts there are good Pearls, efpecially in the King-dom of *Dambea,* and to fweeten the want of other Fruits, which do not grow here, Providence has given it very large and well

tafted

tasted Sugar Canes, particularly in the Islands of the Lake of *Dambea*. There are but few Grapes, which is no small dissatis-faction to those who have tasted the Juice they afford; however the Fathers always made some Wine there for Consecrating at Mass, and to drink some Months in the Year; but 'tis likely it was not much since *F. Emanuel Fernandez*, on the 10th of *June* 1568, writ to the Reverend Father General of the *Jesuits S. Francis de Borja*, that for want of it, he sent for Grapes and squeez'd them to say Mass with the Juice. Yet he adds, he had found by Experience it would keep, and in 20 Days was excellent Wine, which lasted almost a Year.

F. Peter Phys writes, that being at the Court of *Abyssinia*, in the Year 1604, and desired by the Emperor himself, to say Mass, he forbore, for want of Wine of Grapes, not one drop of it being found in all the Court. *F. Belchior da Sylva*, residing in *Ethiopia* as Vicar to the *Portuguese*, sent to consult the Divines at *Goa*, whether Mass might be said with Wine squeez'd out of Raisins? Whereas were there such Cisterns full of Wine as *F. Urreta* speaks of, there would be no occasion for putting that Question, or saying Mass with such Wine as he propos'd. *Want of Wine.*

The *Ensete* is a Tree peculiar to *Ethiopia*, not unlike the *Indian* Fig-Tree, and growing so thick in the Body, that two Men can scarce Fathom it; when cut down close to the Ground, 5, or 700 and sometimes 1000 sprout out from it, I say when it is cut down, for it bears no other Fruit to Eat, being itself the Tree that grows, and the Fruit that is eaten, either cut out in Slices and boil'd, or the Leaves made into Meal for Pap, or Hasty-Pudding, which 'tis likely is not very well relish'd, tho' in some Parts it is the common Food of the Ordinary sort of People. *Ensete-Tree.*

Ethiopia has all sorts of Tame Beasts that are common in *Europe*, as Horses, Mules, Cows, Oxen, and other Cattel in vast numbers, this being the Principal wealth of the Country, as it us'd to be in former Times, when the World, tho' it abounded not so much in Gold, was in the Golden Age; and it is very fine to see the mighty Herds of large Cows, and stately Oxen, grazing in the Fields, especially in the Kingdom of *Tigre* and Country of the *Agaus*. *Tame Cattel.*

They have abundance of noble Horses, and of the true Breed, Black, Roan, Bay, Grey, Dappled, Cream-colour'd, Pyebald, and others as Mettlesome and Sprightly, as the *Spanish Andaluzians*, and when well manag'd they Gallop, Trot, Pace, Curvet and Wheel, as well as the best of ours. They make their Saddles very light and sure, all like our Manage-Saddles, but rising higher, both before and behind; their Stirrups very small, and the Stirrup-Leathers long; but they put only their Great Toe into the *Horses.*

Stirrup,

Mules.

Stirrup, so that it is likely they cannot sit so fast. For the most part, even when they go to the War, their Horses are led, and they Ride on Mules, which are very gentle, large and beautiful; which Custom they retain, as an Inheritance from the *Jews*, of whom they are descended, as we shall see hereafter; for it is plain in Holy Writ, that the Kings did not Ride on Horses, but pamper'd Mules.

Elephants and Wild Beasts.

There are abundance of Wild Elephants, and no tame one was ever seen in the Country. There are also Ounces, Wolves, Foxes, Monkeys, Cattamountains, Civet-Cats, Hares, Rabbits, Tigers, and many very large Lions, some of which they breed up Tame, when very small, but can never trust them much. In the Year 1630, a Countryman kill'd a Lyon, near *Maegoga*, in the Kingdom of *Tigre*, which was Eight Cubits long from the Tail to the Neck, and he kill'd him all alone, fighting him in open Field, without any other Weapon, but only two Horsemans Darts, in this manner. This Fierce Creature was so blooded with the many Men it had devour'd, beside the Oxen, and other Creatures it had torn in Pieces, that it was thought necessary to use Art to deliver Travellers from such a mischievous and dreadful Creature. To this purpose they dug a great Pit in the way this bloody Beast us'd to come down from the Mountains. On a sudden it came upon two Shepherds, who had just dug the Pit; the Eldest of them, bid the other, who was his Brother, to secure himself, by flying in Time, for he was resolv'd to try what he could do with his Darts, and when he could do no more, he would trust to his Heels, for he was very nimble. Having so said, and being left alone, he put himself into a Posture to receive his formidable Enemy, which being come within the cast of his Dart, he let it fly so dexteroufly and with such Force, that he struck the Lyon through one Shoulder, which made the Monster Roar, shake its Mane, and leap furiously from side to side, till it fell into the Pit, that had been provided for that purpose; where the Victorious Country-Man pierc'd it several Times with the other Dart, many Wounds being necessary to destroy so potent an Adversary, till he made an end of the bloody Creature.

Wild Ass.

There are many sorts of Wild Beasts, which I do not mention, because they are not very strange in their shape, and will speak of two, which are more remarkable for their Rarity. The first is that they call, the wild Ass, being as big as a good Mule, Fat, Sleek and well Shap'd, only the Ears disgracing it, and from them had the Name, tho' in all other Respects it deserves not so mean a Denomination. It is wild, but easily tam'd, and what there are of them, are brought into *Ethiopia*, from certain Woods beyond the Countries the *Gallas* are at present possess'd of. The most

moſt remarkable thing in them, is the Curioſity wherewith they are by Nature diverſify'd, ſtrip'd and painted, for acroſs the Loins they have a black Circle, which is, as it were, the beginning and foundation of the reſt, for both ways from it there run other Circles or Stripes intermix'd, the one Jet Black, the other Aſh-colour'd, all of them ſo proportionable, ſo orderly, and uniform, ſo equal in breadth and ſo exact in length, that nothing can exceed it in the fineſt Painting. And as this Creature's Body either ſpreads on the Back, or contracts on the Neck, Head and Legs, ſo theſe Circles or Stripes go on proportionably, as if Nature, when moſt at leiſure had undertaken to beautifie and ſet it off, to humble others which bear nobler Names, but are much inferior to it in Perfection. The Emperor *Sultan Segued*, ſent one of theſe as a Preſent to a *Baſſa* of *Suaqhen*, of whom an *Indian Moor* bought it for 2000 *Chequins*, to carry it to the Great *Mogol*. P. *Emanuel d'Almeyda* ſays, he prevail'd with the ſame Emperor to ſend another to the *Baſſa* of *Suaqhen*, for his Civility to the *Jeſuits*, in their Paſſage; and he carry'd it to *Conſtantinople*, to the Great *Turk*, which gain'd him a favourable Reception and diſpatch of his Buſineſs, by reaſon of the Rarity of the Preſent; for very often valuable Gifts go farther in diſpatch of Affairs than good Service.

Here is another Creature they call *Giratacachem*, ſignifying *Slender End*, which ſeems to be the largeſt Creature on the Earth, yet known, for it is much bigger than the Elephants, tho' not ſo groſs of Body. Men mounted on good Horſes eaſily paſs under it; the Fore-legs being 12 Spans, or four Yards high, the Hind-legs ſomewhat ſhorter; the Neck Proportionable and long to reach the Ground and Graze, for that is its Food. I am of Opinion this is the *Struthio-Camelus*, the Ancients ſpeak of, for as they Write, it is more like the Camel, than any other Creature. Thus much of the Beaſts of the Earth, the Fiſhes and Birds in *Ethiopia* are almoſt the ſame as in *Europe*.

(right margin) Giratacachem, *or* Struthio-Camelus.

F   CHAP.

CHAP. VIII.

Of the several sorts of People in this Empire, of their
Features, Inclinations, and Habit, and of some of
their Customs, as to Eating, their Marriages and
Behaviour towards the Dead.

Several Na-
tions.
HAving spoken briefly of the Climate, Product, and Animals
of *Ethiopia*, we will now be more particular concerning the
main point, which is the Men. These Countries are inhabited
by great variety of People, *Christians*, *Mahometans*, *Jews* and
Gentiles. These last for the most part live in the Kingdom of
Gojam, and are some of them *Agaus*, others *Gafates*, and many
Gallas, to whom the Emperor himself has there given considerable
Lands, as also in *Dambea*, to make use of them in his Wars,
against other Races of *Gallas*, who are more Barbarous and his
Enemies.

Jews.
There were always *Jews* in *Ethiopia*, from the Beginning, without including those who came with *Melileec*, and some of them
have been converted to Christianity, and they formerly had large
Possessions of Lands, almost all the Kingdom of *Dambea*, and the
Provinces of *Ogara* and *Cemen*; but the Empire being now drawn
into a narrower compass by the *Gallas*, the *Ethiopians* have streight-
ned the *Jews*, and drove them out by Degrees. However in
Cemen they defended themselves most couragiously, being much
assisted by the great Height and Cragginess of their Mountains,
yet the Emperor *Sultan Segued* subdu'd them of late Years, so
that the most and best of them being kill'd in sundry Encounters,
such as remain'd submitted to the Will of the Conqueror, or
dispers'd themselves into several Parts. Of these there are many
in *Dambea*, some were baptiz'd and live by Weaving, or else by
making of Darts, Plows, and other such like Necessaries, being
great Smiths.

Another sort
of them.
Besides, betwixt the Emperor's Dominions and the *Cafres* dwelling near the River *Nile*, and now free from any Subjection to
the Empire, there are still many of these *Jews*, whom they there
call *Falaxas*, which signifies, Strangers, and it may be suppos'd,
they also came into *Ethiopia* out of the Captivity of *Salmanasar*,
or afterwards, when they were expell'd, at the Destruction of
Jerusalem by *Titus* and *Vespasian*, and therefore the *Abyssinians*, tho'
many

many of them were also *Jews*, descended from those who came with *Melilecc*, the Son of the Queen of *Sheba*, by *Salomon*, always treated them as Strangers, God so ordering, that they should have no settled Dwelling on the Earth, who would not receive the King of Heaven. These have still *Hebrew* Bibles, and sing the Psalms very scurvily in their Synagogues.

The next sort of People are *Mahometans*, who live throughout all the Empire, intermixt with the Christians, and are almost the third Part of the Inhabitants of *Ethiopia*. Some of them live by Tillage, others are Factors, for no Christians being permitted to resort to the Sea-Ports, they are sole Masters of all the great Trade, and carry Gold to the Sea, whence in return, they bring Silks and Stuffs, and not being over Conscientious, they make their Advantage of this Factorship, getting Estates out of other Men's Goods. *Mahometans.*

As there are divers sorts of Nations, so is there also variety of Languages, for the *Moors* speak their own *Arabick*, the *Jews*, *Hebrew*, but with as much corruption in the Words, as there is in their Lives and Manners. They are moderate Eaters, but exceed in drinking, whether it be Wine, if they can come at it, or their Ale, call'd by them *Sava*, with quantity whereof they make amends for the want of better Liquor. *Languages.*

Almost all these People are understanding and of good Dispositions, not cruel or bloody, easie in forgiving of Wrongs, nor have they many fallings out among them; and what they have are seldom decided by the Sword; but for the most part by Cuffs and Cudgels. They are naturally very submissive to Reason and Justice, and consequently upon any Quarrel, as soon as ever they have done Cudgelling, they put the matter to a Reference, or lay it before the Lord of the Place; both sides pleading by word of Mouth, without our Tedious Bills and Answers, which are so many Volumes of Cheat and Fraud, and when Judgment is given, they stand to it without any Muttering, Reply, Discontent, or Appeal, and so save all the Noise and Babbling of Lawyers and Costs of Sute. *Good disposition of the People.* *No Lawyers.*

In the Kingdom of *Tigre*, they are not so apt to forgive, if there be any Blood-shed; but if a Man chance to be kill'd, the Enmity continues betwixt the Kindred of the Dead Man, and the Party who kill'd him for many Years; which they call having Blood betwixt them, and therefore that of the Slain, is not wash'd away, but by all that of the Slayer, or much of his Friends and Relations. They are not free from Malice; and are generally light and unsteady, which is of very ill Consequence, and appear'd in their changing to and from the Catholick Faith, as we *Revenge and unsteadiness.*

F 2 shall

shall see hereafter. They are apt to Swear, and as ready to break their Oaths; and this Inconstancy, is the occasion of their frequent Rebellions, where the Mutinous have the Remedy at hand, for if they miscarry, they beg the Emperors Pardon, who readily grants it, and they are as good Friends as before, tho' the offence be never so heinous.

Habit, and Beds.
A word now of their Habit. Within less than 60 Years last past, none but the Emperor, and some of his Kindred and Favourites, were allow'd to wear any thing but Breeches, and a Piece of Cloth they cover themselves with, and serves for many uses; for in the Day Time it is a Cloak, and at Night a Blanket and Sheet, their Bed generally being only a Hide, they call *Nete*, which is instead of a Quilt. There is something more of Curiosity in the Boulster or Pillow, which is a sort of Wooden Fork call'd *Bercuma*, whereon they rest not their Head, which lies hollow, but the Neck, and this they do to avoid lying upon their Hair, it being curiously dress'd, as we shall see. This is hitherto the usual Bed of all the greater number, and even considerable People; tho' of late some of the Prime Men have got their corded Couches, on which they lay the aforesaid Hides; and some of the Princes and greatest Lords have *India* Quilts, brought them from the Ports of the Red Sea, with Silk Borders to them, and those who have two or three of these, keep their Beds in their outward Rooms, for the Couches serve them instead of Chairs, and on them they lay the two Quilts, that both may be seen plainly, the Border of the one hanging down below the other, so exposing both to view, for the Grandeur of that Couch, like the Man *Martial* speaks of, who endur'd the Distemper of his Body, to show the Richness of his Bed.

Habit of the better sort.
The Breeches and Piece of Cloth I mention'd above, are at present the Habit of the common sort; those who are better to pass wear a sort of *Indian Banyan's* Vest, not quite open, but only to the Waste, and closed with small Buttons. They have little Collars, and the Sleeves very streight and long, so that they lie in gathers on the Arms, and these they call Shirts, tho' in reality they are not so. They are generally made of a sort of *Cambaya* Callicoes, or of a blue Stuff brought from thence, like a Fustian; and over them they wear fine *Ethiopian* Cloth, or Silk, sew'd together in the middle, without any other Fashion. Some of the richer great Men, make those Shirts of Tafteta, or Sattin, or Damask, and have *Turkish* Vests of Velvet, or Brocard of *Mecca*, and these wear no Cloth over them, that they may show their Silk.

The

,,The Breeches worn by the prime Men of Quality, are after *Breeches.* the *Moorish* Fashion, reaching down to their Feet and wrinkled, and these from the Knee downward are made of Damask or Velvet; but all above that being hid under the Vest, they all, and even the Emperor himself, agree it is so much Silk lost, and therefore they make them of course Cloth, which is often seen as they sit down; but they never trouble themselves about such Niceties; so free are they from that Vanity, which reigns among us, of wearing Silks upon Silks, some outwardly for Ostentation, and others underneath meerly for Superfluity. But as these Breeches of the better sort are close, so those of the other People are after the old Fashion, as wide at bottom as at the top, which is very cumbersome, and thus they are generally very ill dress'd and awkward.

We must speak one word of their Hair, which is the covering for the Head, both of Men and Women, and which they *Dressing of* much value themselves upon. They let it grow, tho' it will not *Hair.* be of any great length, but being frizly and thin, they have many ways of ordering it, especially the Men, for the Women leave all loose but the fore part, whereas the Men braid and make it up after several Fashions; and to this purpose they keep it well daub'd with Butter, which is all the sweet Essence and Perfume they have, never regarding, as we do, that strong Scent of greasie Hair, full of Dust. And those People having much idle Time, they spend the greatest part of the Day in that Employment; but we have little occasion now to reflect upon the *Ethiopians* on this account, when so many Hours are among us sacrific'd to such Follies.

Ill Company was ever reckon'd a contagious Distemper, which *Errors of E-* easily infects those who are near it, and if this be of long stand- *thiopians.* ing, it is not easily to be cur'd. The *Abyssinians* live among *Mahometans* and *Gentiles* and their Errors are of that sort the Prophet speaks of, when he says, *They are estranged from the Womb,* Psalm 58, and 3. for as we shall see hereafter, before they became Christians, they observ'd the Law of *Moses,* and since they embrac'd the Faith of *Christ,* they never sincerely renounc'd the *Jewish* Perverseness; whence it comes, that they Circumcise themselves to this Day, as the *Mahometans* do, who live among them, and even the *Gentiles* of *Ethiopia,* that they may not be affronted with the Name of Uncircumcised.

And even in the manner of Baptizing their Children they con- *Baptism.* form'd to what the Old Law prescrib'd to Women, touching their coming to the Temple to be purify'd; for they Christen'd the Males on the 40th Day, and the Females on the 80th, nor would they

they admit them to Baptism before those Days, even in case of Necessity; nay, at the Time when they receiv'd the Faith of *Rome* by the preaching of the Fathers of the Society, they very unwillingly forbore Circumcision, so prevalent are ill Customs when they have once taken Root.

Sitting and Eating. They generally sit on the Ground; the Great Men on Carpets, and the rest on Mats, and therefore their Tables are low, and all round, on which they have no Table-Cloths, much less any Napkins; but they wipe their Fingers on *Apas*, which is a sort of Bread they make of several sorts of Meal, as Wheat, Millet and Peas. The Table is cover'd with these *Apas*, and on them, without any other Plates or Dishes, the Meat is laid, whether it be Roast or Raw, as they Eat it; but if they happen to have any Hen or Mutton Broth, or their usual Pap, wherein they dip their *Apas*, these Things are serv'd up in Black Earthen Porringers, cover'd with those they call *Escambias*, being like Caps made of fine Straw; and this is the usual Service at all, and even the Emperor's Table: So that what was look'd upon as a Rarity in *Sicily*, at the Table of King *Agathocles*, who valu'd himself upon Eating out of Earthen Ware, is here usual at the Table of these Emperors, with only this difference, that *Agathocles*, tho' he had much Gold was serv'd in Earthen Ware, in Memory of his Father, who had been a Potter; whereas these who think themselves to exceed the Sun in Nobility, delight in Gold, but Eat out of Earthen Ware.

Raw Beef Eaten. They always Eat Beef raw, and call it *Berindt*, this being the Meat they most delight in, which they Salt and Pepper very well, if they have it; and the better sort, if they can get the Gaul of the Beast that is kill'd, think they have a great Dainty. To make the most of that delicious Sauce, they beat the Piece of Beef they have before them very well, and squeeze out that Savoury Juice on it, and when well soak'd in, they Eat it, and their Palate is so Enur'd to that Gaul, that nothing relishes better with them. But they find yet another stranger Dainty in the Beast, which is taken from the finest Part of the Filth in the Guts, season'd with Salt and Pepper, which serves them instead of the best Mustard, and is reckon'd a most curious Sauce, call'd by them *Manta*; but only Princes and very great Persons can attain this Royal Dish, because it requires much Pepper, which all Men have not.

Women grind the Corn. As plain and as ordinary as these their Dishes are, it costs them no small Pains to Dress them; for having no Mills, they are fain to grind all Things by Hand, which Work is so peculiar to the Women, that even the meanest MaleSlaves will not do it upon any Account. A Woman Grinds as much daily as will make 40 or 50 *Apas*, which

which must be made every Day, for they are good for nothing the Day after, and confequently it is a great Toil, and requires many Slaves and much Wood, to make the *Apas* they Eat and the Ale they Drink. Thefe are the Mills one boafted of, faying, that the Emperor had 500 of them in his Camp, and he might well have faid 3000, for it plainly appears this proceeds from want of Induftry, rather than Grandeur.

Their Wine is none of the celebrated *Chios* or *Falernum*, but *Liquors.* made of 5 or 6 Parts Water put into a Jar, with one part of Honey, and a handful of parch'd Barley, which makes it ferment; then they add fome Bits of a fort of Wood they call *Sardo*, which fo qualifies it, that in 5 or 6 Days it lofes the fulfomenefs of the Honey, and tho' it be not fo well tafted as our Wine, is more wholefome. They never Drink whilft they are Eating, but after all is taken away, as many of the Antients us'd to do, who brought in the Goblets when the Difhes were remov'd, and this the *Ethiopians* do to fuch excefs, that it is wonderful to think how they can hold fo much; fo that, tho' this Wine is very weak, yet the quantity makes it have the fame Effect as the beft in *Europe*, for turning the Brain, making the Tongue run, and weakning the Legs.

As for their Marriages, they contracted them till our Days, in *Marriages.* fuch manner, that they were not really valid, becaufe they did it with a *tacit*, or exprefs Confent, that they might part whenfoever the Man and Wife happen'd to difagree, and they there gave Security for Performance. The Principal Motives for parting were the Breach of Matrimonial Vows on either fide, want of Children, or Strife among themfelves, and this laft being very frequent among Married People, Divorces are as common. But as to the Point of Breach of Faith they eafily reconcil'd it, the Offender giving fome of his Goods to the Party wrong'd, and hence it is, that Married People have each of them their own Chattels and their Lands apart, and if they Eat together, each brings what they have drefs'd, fuch are their Marriages.

The Reconciliation is not fo eafy, if the Quarrel be on account *Divorce.* of Diflike, or Contention at Home: In this Cafe they repair to the Judge, to whom thefe Caufes belong, and there being only a Verbal Procefs it is foon decided, and as foon as Judgment given, they are both Free and may Marry where they pleafe, fo that the *Ethiopians* are fooner reconcil'd to a Wife defam'd by Adultery, than to a peevifh one. The *Jefuits* took no fmall Pains to reduce thefe People to contract Marriages after the true Catholick manner, by reafon this Error had prevail'd for fo many Ages, and this was one of the Caufes why they afterwards fell off.

They

Duties to the Dead. They bewail their Dead for many Days together, beginning their Lamentations very early in the Morning, and holding on till the Day is far advanc'd. There the Parents, Kindred, and Friends of the Party deceas'd meet, with many Women Mourners, like the ancient *Praefica,* among the *Greeks* and *Romans* who were hir'd for the Solemnity of that Lamentation, which among the *Abyssinians* is done to the Beat of Drums, clapping their Hands, striking their Breasts and Faces, and uttering such dismal Expressions, in a doleful Tone, that they torment the Head, and grieve the Heart. They bring to the Place of Mourning the Dead Person's Horse, if he had any, his Launce, his Shield, his Cloaths and other Weapons. They bury the Dead in the Churches, and make their Offerings to the Clergy, who say their Psalms and other Prayers for them. They also make Offerings to the Churches, and bestow Alms on the Poor, killing Cows to divide among them, with abundance of *Apas* and Wine, which they do the 3d, the 7th, the 30th and the 40th Days, and at the Years End; and yet they deny'd Purgatory, but were easily convinc'd, by their own Prayers and Alms offer'd for the Dead.

Lamentations When they receive the News of the Death of any near Relation, or of their Lord, or their Lord's Son, or Daughter, they immediately cast themselves on the Ground, with such heavy falls that some die of them, others are maim'd, and others come off with broken Heads, Arms, or Legs. Those who do not thus cast themselves on the Ground, are look'd upon as disaffected to the Deceas'd: The *Gafates* instead of falling down, beat themselves and wound their Heads and Arms, of which Follies, I know not which is the most tolerable.

CHAP.

C H A P. IX.

Of the Custom observ'd by the Abyssine *Emperors, of keeping their Sons in the Fortress of* Amba-Guexen; *the Description of that Place, and of the Ceremonies us'd in taking them out from thence to be promoted to the Throne.*

AMong the other most remarkable Customs in *Ethiopia*, there *Occasion im-* was one relating to the Emperor's Sons, which being very *prisoning of* singular, shall be here taken notice of. About the Year 1260, *Princes*. an Emperor call'd *Igbunu Amalac*, who then reign'd in *Ethiopia* had Five Sons, or Nine according to others, to whom the Father, before his Death, very earnestly recommended Unity among themselves, and being willing to leave them equal in their Inheritance, since they were equal in Parentage, order'd they should all Reign alternatively, every one his Year, beginning with the Eldest. and so descending, according to their Ages. So they did for some Years, but not many, for the World was always the same, and there is none that will admit of any Partner in Empire, because Majesty is not divisible, as has been found by Experience.

Accordingly it happed, that the Youngest of these Princes had not Patience enough to wait so long for his Year of Government. His Name was *Free-Hecan*, and he was the more provok'd to see that those who had govern'd did Eat together at the same Table, and he with the rest, whose turn of ruling was not yet come, were left to the second Table, and were to go out into another Room to wash their Hands, because it is look'd upon as ill manners in *Ethiopia* to wash their Hands before their Betters. These things put the Prince upon contriving, how he might once come by the Empire, without being subject to such Changes and alternating. These Thoughts possessing his Breast, he could not rest, but not knowing how to ascend the Throne sooner, he resolv'd that when his turn came, he would put an end to that Ceremony of Annual Government, like that the *Greeks* feign'd of the *Theban* Brothers.

It being very hard to conceal a mighty Design, without imparting it to somebody; this Prince at length communicated his Resolution to a Friend, acquainting him in Secret, That when it was his Year to Reign, he would seize all his Brothers, and put

G them

them into a very ftrong *Amba*, being one of thofe naturall Fortrefles we have before fpoken of, where he would fecure them for ever coming out, that fo he might perpetuate the Empire in himfelf. There is no Secret that deferves the Name, after it has once broke out of the Breaft where it lay conceal'd; nor is there any Caufe to complain of being betray'd by another, when a Man could not keep his own Secret. The unfortunate *Free-Hecan* was taken in his own Snare, like the improvident Perfon the Prophet fpeaks of, who fell into the Pit he had made, *Pfal.* 7. 16.

It happened that the Friend he entrufted, immediately acquainted the Brother then reigning with the Secret. He confidering the Danger he was in, and liking the Contrivance, concluded that the natural Fortrefs of *Amba-Guexen*, was very fit for that purpofe, and before he could be feized himfelf, clapt up not only the projecting Brother, but all the reft with him; and foon after put his own Sons into the fame Place, for Ambition is jealous even of them, as was feen formerly in *Herod*, and at this Day in the Barbarous Cuftom obferv'd by the *Ottoman* Family, and many other wicked Tyrants, who think not any Power fecure, unlefs it be cemented with Blood. *Mercator* in his Map of *Ethiopia*, and *Johnfon* in his, call this Mountain where the Princes were kept *Amara*, but they were mifinform'd, for the Name of it is *Amba-Guexen*, tho' the Kingdom it ftands in is *Amara*.

That Cuftom abrogated. This Cuftom was obferv'd in *Ethiopia* for 200 and odd Years, till the Emperor *Nahod*, Father to *Onac-Segued*, who was the laft Prince of that Country, that came out of the Penitential Life of *Amba-Guexen*, broke it off, upon the following occafion. He had a Son, he doated on betwixt Eight and Nine Years of Age. This innocent Child being one Day by his Father, a great Man of the Court, who was a Privy Councellor, and happen'd to be prefent, faid to the Emperor, Sir, *this Child is grown very big*; but he who was no Child in Capacity, underftanding what that Councellor's Obfervation tended to, and as it were ftruck to the Heart with the Expreffion, fixing his Eyes full of Tears on his Father, faid, What, *am I grown up for* Amba-Guexen? Thefe words fo fenfibly affected the Emperor, that affembling the great Men of his Court and Privy Councellors immediately, he took an Oath in their Prefence, and made them Swear, that no Son of his, or any other Emperor fhould ever be put into that Prifon; and this has been punctually obferv'd ever fince, as the Fathers, who have been in *Ethiopia* do teftifie, and that the Emperor *Sultan-Segued*, who died in the Year 1632, as we fhall fee hereafter, had feveral Sons, and never thought of fhutting them up in that
Prifon,

Prison, that Custom of confining the Princes being wholly a-bolish'd.

This is the Reason, the greatest Statesmen agree in this Point *Wicked Po-*of Politicks, that a King in many Cases, is to behave himself, *licy.* even towards his own Children, rather as a publick Person, than as a Father; and tho' innocent Princes suffer in that Place, yet when the Distemper is dangerous, it is allow'd to cut off a Limb, rather than hazard the whole Body, notwithstanding the Member must be taken off where it is found; for *Tacitus An. lib.* 14. well observes, great Evils can scarce be redress'd without some Injustice, but the publick Advantage makes amends for the wrong done to private Persons. So that considering the Inconstancy of the *Abyssinians,* and their Aptness to set up new Princes, spro-vided they be of the Blood Royal, it was a very prudent Practice to keep them so confin'd, tho' very uneasie to them.

We will now describe the Place, where those unfortunate Princes were shut up. On the Borders of the Kingdom of *Ama-* *Amba-Guex-*hara, next to that of *Xaoa,* stands that *Amba*; which they call *en described.* *Guexen,* being an impregnable Mountain, Perpendicular, like a natural Fortress of solid Rock. The breadth of it on the top, along the Slope of the Rock, may be about half a League, but at the Foot it is half a Days Journey about. The Height is so great, that a Stone cast out of sling by the strongest Arm, will not reach the top. The Ascent, tho' not so difficult at first afterwards grows so painful, that even the Cows, which in this Country skip like Goats, cannot get up, or down, unless hoist-ed with Ropes, or Thongs. At the top of this way stood a House built with Stone and Clay, and Thatch'd, like all others, being the Habitation of the Guards of those wretched Princes, who liv'd there as if they had been Enchanted. In the midst of the Plain, on the top, there are two Pools, being the Work of Na-ture, with Springs of their own, one of which serves to drink and the other for washing.

To render this Prison yet more intolerable, it is to be observ'd, *Its Barreness.* that the Country being all craggy, there is no Fruit-Tree to be found throughout it, nor any other, except some Wild Cedars, and a few Shrubs and Bushes, no other sort growing there to sweeten the Bitterness of that Confinement. Close by one of those Pools, a Hill rises, on which there are two Churches, the one Dedicated to God the Father, the other under the Invocation of the Blessed Virgin. Near to them live some of their Religious Men, and some *Depteras,* who are as it were Canons, or bene-fic'd Clergy-men and Chanters of the said Churches. Formerly there were about 14 of those Religious Men, there are still Six or

Seven, the *Depteras* having Families of Wives and Children, are always more numerous.

Poor dwellings for Princes.

By what has been said it sufficiently appears that the Retreat of *Amba Guexen* was not very comfortable; yet there the Poor Princes refided, dwelling in little Houfes of Stone and Clay, lin'd on the Infide with Straw. At the firft fhutting of them up there, they were promis'd the 3d part of the Revenues of all the Empire; but time convinc'd them, how eafie it is to promife that which is never defign'd to be perform'd; for they had only fome Lands about their Prifon affign'd them.

Their rigid Reftraint.

There alfo liv'd fome Perfons of Note on *Amba-Guexen*, and others near to it, who reliev'd one another, being as it were their Stewards, and at the fame time watch'd and obferv'd them fo ftrictly, that no Creature whatfoever was permitted to come near; nor was there any Meffage, or Letter deliver'd to them, but what was firft examin'd by thefe fever: Goalers, who, purfuant to the fevere Rules there obferv'd, kept thefe diftreffed Penitents fo much under, that they would not allow them to wear any better Cloaths than the ordinary, which were of Cotton, for fear left the mending of their Garb fhould infpire them with greater Thoughts.

An Inftance of it.

It was there reported, touching this Point, that one of thefe nice Guards feeing one of the Princes better clad than was allow'd by the Rigour of the Law, he not only reprov'd him and acquainted his Father, but it feems he lay'd violent Hands on him, that it might be a warning to him never to think of fuch Cloaths any more, unlefs he would have the Seams fo fettled again. It happened, that a few Years after, that fame Prince came to be Emperor, and the Keeper remembring what he had done, took care to fecure himfelf, for fear of falling into his Hands whom he had fo roughly handled. But the Emperor, who had not forgot how he had been treated, caus'd him to be fought out and brought before him; and he full of Dread and Apprehenfion, caft himfelf at his Prince's Feet, begging Pardon for his Offence. The Emperor bid him rife, and caus'd him to be Richly clad. in return for the good Cloaths he had forbid him. giving him a Gold Bracelet of great Value, and faying, *You did your Duty well, and ferv'd your Mafter faithfully, go back to your Employment and execute it with the fame Zeal.* This Emperor doubtlefs acted like a Difcreet and not a revengeful Man; yet this Paffage fhow'd, how natural it is for Men to alter their Minds, as they change their Conditions; for he thought it fit to have others treated in the fame manner as he had miflik'd himfelf.

What

What has been here faid, plainly fhews the Hardfhips were undergone in that Confinement, whereof neverthelefs *F. Urreta* writ fo many Fables, as if he would perfwade us there had been another Terreftrial Paradife conceal'd in that Place, but this is the real Truth we have here deliver'd, as many Religious Men of the Society teftifie, and may be feen in *F. Francis Alvarez's* Book, *chap.* 56. And *F. Emanuel d' Almeyda,* who actually faw what we here defcribe, adds, that if this *Amba* be compar'd to many others there are in *Ethiopia,* there will be above 100 found that exceed it in all Points, as being much higher and more difficult of Accefs, having more and better Water within them, and containing larger and more fruitful Fields, for thofe on this *Amba* produce nothing but Beans, Barley, and fome Wheat ; whereas others are much more fertile and better; all that made this more or lefs fortunate, was its being the appointed Prifon for thofe innocent Penitents, which caus'd it to be more talk'd of both in *Ethiopia* and without it.

We will next relate, in what manner they drew out of this Place of Captivity, the Prince that was to fucceed the Emperor *Manner of* Deceas'd, which was done after long Confultation, and much en- *taking out the* quiry made into the Behaviour of him that was to be Enthron'd. *Prince to be* As foon as it was refolv'd, which of them it was to be, the Go- *Enthron'd.* vernor or Vice-Roy of the Kingdom of *Tigre* march'd with fome Forces, and encamp'd at the Foot of the *Amba,* then he and the Principal Men prefent went up, and entring the Cell of the Prince they had pitch'd upon, put a fort of Gold Pendant into his Ear, which they call *Belul,* and was the Token of his E-lection. This done they fent word to the other Princes, who all met there to own the new Emperor and Congratulate him; which they could not but do with much Regret, fince all of them expecting fome happy Hour to be deliver'd from that Purgatory, they faw one go out to Reign, whilft they were continu'd in Mifery, without any hopes of finding the leaft Commiferation for Sighs and Tears.

The new Emperor being gone down, the Governors march'd out with all the Army to meet him, and as foon as they came *His Corona-* near, alighted all together, upon a Signal by him given, mount- *tion.* ed again, and taking him into the midft of them, conducted him with abundance of Mufical Inftruments, as Drums, Waites, and Kettle-Drums, and many other Tokens of Joy, after the manner of the Country, to his Royal Tent, which they call *Debana,* where he alighted within, and all the reft without it. Then a dignify'd Clergy-man, whom they call *Seraie Macare,* a-nointed him with Sweet-Oyl, whilft the others Sang Pfalms.

This

This done, they clad him in the Royal Robes, and plac'd on his Head the Crown, consisting of several Pieces of Gold and Silver, fix'd on a Thing like a Hat, on the top whereof was a Cross. Next they put a naked Sword into his Hand to denote Justice, and seated him on the Regal Throne. Then the *Ker Ace*, who is his first Chaplain got up on a high Place and made Proclamation, *We have caused such a one to Reign.* As soon as this was heard, the Standers by and all the Army and other People, made great Acclamations of Joy, and all came in order to kiss his Hand.

This is the Truth of what was practis'd touching the Confinement of the Princes of *Ethiopia* and the Election of their Emperors; and all the rest that was invented and Printed by *F. Urreta*, is to be look'd upon as the Product of a Head bent towards making of Fables, and fruitful in Fictions. Unless it be that the said Author intended to show the World how such an Election ought to be manag'd, assigning Rules and Ceremonies for the performing of it, as was done by *Xenophon*, who writ the Life of his renowned *Cyrus*, not as he really liv'd, but as he ought to have done; to give the World a Pattern of an accomplish'd Prince, as there had been many of Tyrannical Kings.

F. Urreta condemned.

CHAP. X.

The manner how these Emperors take and declare their Empresses, and of the Government of the Abyssine *Empire.*

Polygamy of the Emperors.

THE Common Enemy of Mankind has always endeavour'd to introduce Looseness of Life and Behaviour in all Parts, where Ignorance in Matters of Faith has prevail'd. In *Ethiopia*, as well as many other Parts of the World, the ill Custom has always been practiz'd from great Antiquity, of the Emperors having several Wives, all of them reputed Lawful, besides others unlawful; which evil Custom is so ancient in this *Ethiopia*, that it seems to have been brought by *Melilec* from *Jerusalem*, as learnt of his Father *Solomon*, when he went thither to visit him, as shall be said hereafter.

And

And notwithstanding *F. Francis Alvarez* writes of the Emperor *Fran. Alva-* *Onag Segued*, who was first call'd *David*, in whose Days the said *rez contra-* Father went into that Country, that he had not many Wives, *dicted.* either the Father was misinform'd, or this might be so when he arriv'd there; for it is evident by the Account the Fathers of the Society had several Times from the excellent Prince *Raz Sella Christos*, of whom we shall often have occasion to speak, that he had many, and some of them Gentiles, to please whom, like his Ancestor *Solomon*, he consented to have Idols for them in his Court: So that on one side was the Church of God, and on the other the Heathen *Pagod*, so vilely are they mislead, who having the Regal Power, suffer themselves to be blinded by Affection.

As for those Emperors marrying the Daughters of *Mahometan* *Those Empe-* or *Pagan* Kings, or other Great Men, causing them first to be Bap- *rors marry'd* tiz'd, it was so common, that even King *James*, brought one, *the Daughters* Daughter to the *Moorish* King of *Adea*, with a design to Marry *of* Mahome- her, and treated her as a Wife, but that he dy'd before they were *tans and* united by Matrimony, as is testify'd by *F. Peter Pays*, who was Pagans. then at the Court.

Those they generally marry'd were the Daughters of Subjects of Noble Families, whereof there are many in the Kingdom of *Tigre* and some other Provinces; yet sometimes they did not Regard their Quality, but rather their Natural Endowments, saying, that the Wives Birth adds nothing to the Emperor, and she is sufficiently ennobled by being preferr'd to his Bed. When any of these Ladies was pitch'd upon, she was brought to Court, and there *Their Nupti-* kept in the House of some of the Emperors Kindred, that they *als.* might be the better acquainted with her good Qualities. Being satisfy'd as to them, the Emperor and she went together to Church on a *Sunday*, to hear Mass and receive the Blessed Sacrament, all the Court being in their best Apparel upon that Occasion. From the Church they both return'd to the Palace, where the *Abuna*, who is as it were their chief Bishop, us'd to perform the Matrimonial Ceremonies. Then the Emperor din'd at his Table alone, as he always does, without being seen by any Body, as will be declared hereafter: The Queen din'd in another Room with many Ladies, and the Clergy-men and *Depteras* were nobly treated in others.

This is as to Eating, for in order to Drink they all constantly meet every Day, tho' at great Entertainments there is more plenty *The Enter-* of Wine and a greater number of Guests. The Custom as to this *tainment.* particular is, to place in the middle of the Imperial Chamber many Pots of Liquor, leaning against certain Wreaths of Straw, for the easier pouring of it out, and the Cups go round, begin-

ning

ning with the Emperor and Emprefs, both which have a Curtain
drawn before them when they Drink, that they may not be feen,
and fo down to the reft, according to their Quality. Whilft they
Drink, and fometimes with the Cup in their Hands, they Difcourfe and tell feveral Stories, as long as the Liquor lafts; for as
foon as that is out, there is an end of the Company; but it feldom
fails in the King's Lodgings till the Night is well advanc'd and
Sleep comes on, when every one drops where he is, and fo the
Feaft ends, but there is no Liquor left.

The Emprefs's Title. Thus the Nuptial Solemnity concludes ; but the Emprefs has
not yet the Title of *Itigue*, which is her Highnefs, or Majefty. In
order to receive this Title, fome Days or Months after, as the Emperor pleafes, the Queen comes from her Houfe to the Palace, for
her Houfe is always feparated from his, and within another Enclofure, tho' near at Hand, and fitting down near the Emperor's
Throne, which is his Couch, on a Step fomewhat high, fhe is
there clad in rich Apparel, and then one of the Principal dignify'd
Clergy-men in the Court goes out into the Court, and ftanding
upon a Chair as making Proclamation, utters thefe Words with a
loud Voice: *Anagafna Danguecera Chem;* which fignify, *We have
caus'd our Slave to Reign:* Which all the People prefent anfwer
with loud Acclamations, and from thence forwards they give her
the Title of *Etbié*, or Highnefs.

Emprefs Dowager honour'd. It is to be obferv'd, that as long as the Emperor's Mother lives,
if fhe was Emprefs and Wife to the Emperor deceas'd, the Wife
of the Emperor actually Reigning is not call'd *Etbié*, but that Honour is always given to the Old One; infomuch, that not only
the Wife of the new Emperor, but he himfelf, tho' he be not her
Son, calls her Mother, and Honours her as if fhe were really
fo.

Great Men all Deacons. They never Crown her, nor was it ever practifed with any
Queen of *Ethiopia.* As for a Scepter, the Emperors themfelves ufe
none ; and as for what fome have faid, that a Crofs was the Scepter of the Emperors of *Ethiopia*, it was a miftake ; for tho' they
carry'd a little Crofs in their Hands, they did it not as a Token of
Empire, but of their being Deacons, which Order they all of them
receiv'd, as did moft of the Great Men, that they might not in the
Churches be left without the Curtains, or Chappels, as Lay-Men
are always, and Communicate there, but that they might go in
and receive with the Clergy.

Ethiopians call'd the Emperors Slaves. That fort of Proclamation above mention'd, *viz. We have caus'd
our Slave to Reign*, may feem odd to any Stranger; but is fo ufual
in *Ethiopia*, that whenfoever the Emperor beftows on any Man,
tho' it be one of his own Brothers, any Employment, which they
call

call *Xumete*, the Honour is always attended with that great Expreſſion : *We have conſtituted ſuch a One our Slave, Viceroy, or Governour, of ſuch a Kingdom, or ſuch a Province.* Theſe are the Words of the Proclamation. They tell us of a *Portugueze* among the *Abyſſinians*, who having receiv'd ſome ſuch Honour from the Emperor, and not liking the Title of Slave to the Monarch of *Ethiopia*, being born in a Country where the Kings call their Subjects Children, he offer'd a great Sum to the Cryer, that he might not call him Slave, but barely ſuch a one, which the Officer durſt not do ; and the Reaſon of it is, becauſe the Emperor looks upon them all as Slaves, and they do not think it any undervaluing to them to be ſo.

There is but one only Sovereign who Rules and Governs in the Provinces and Kingdoms we have ſaid belong to this Empire, nor has he any other King under him ; for he of *Dancali*, who is a *Mahometan*, and he of *Gingiro*, who is a *Heathen*, are not properly Subjects, nor pay any Tribute to the Emperor, tho' as to a powerful Neighbour they reſpect and in ſome manner acknowledge him for their Superior. He takes and gives all the Lands at Pleaſure ; yet in the Kingdom of *Tigre* particularly, there are ſome, the Dominion whereof he never takes from certain Families, deſcended from the ancient Poſſeſſors. Such are thoſe of the *Barnagaes*, and the *Xumos*, or Governors of *Seraoé, Syré, Temben* and others. So in *Dambea*, the Power of the *Cantiba* never departs from the Race of the ancient Poſſeſſors ; but the Emperor once in two Years, or every Year, or half Year, takes theſe Commands from ſome Perſons, and beſtows them on others of the ſame Families, according to their Merits, or his Pleaſure. *All Lands at his diſpoſal.*

The worſt of it is, that not only theſe but all other Governments in his Kingdoms and Provinces, are rather ſold than given ; for no Man has them without paying down as much as he expects he can make by them and be a Gainer. Now the Candidates being many, they generally carry the Poſts who bid moſt, and thus they give more than they are honeſtly worth ; ſo that to ſave themſelves they devour the People, and ſell inferior Poſts and Commands to the higheſt Bidders, and thus all Things here are expos'd to Sale ; and theſe Great Men being Lords and Judges, and having abſolute Power over the Lives and Fortunes of the Subjects, they are generally more like Robbers than Governours. *All Commands ſold.*

It is true there lies an Appeal from them to the Supream Courts and the Emperor, but there are few that dare Appeal, which is declaring themſelves the Governor's or Viceroy's Enemies, and then they fear he may find ſome ſpecious pretence to undo them. When the Governor's Command is expir'd, which ſhould ſeem to be *No Redreſs againſt Oppreſſors.*

H

be a proper Time to bring in any Complaint againſt him, either by Favour or Corruption he prevails with the Emperor to put out a Proclamation againſt laying any ſuch Information againſt him, or any of his Family for any thing they have done: And thus by means of this Jubilee, and entire Remiſſion of theirs and the Sins of others, all the Outrages and Extortions committed are bury'd in Oblivion. This is all the Account thoſe Governors are call'd to for their Adminiſtration, and ſo eſtabliſh'd among them, that they look upon it as no Sin, or take any Care to Redreſs it; but if any one is ſcandaliz'd at it, they ſay, This ſame is and ever was the Form of Government in their Country, and it will cauſe great Troubles to alter it; ſo tenacious are Men of ancient Cuſtoms, that they will rather be in the wrong their own way, than ſtand corrected by others.

Beteudets, Prime Miniſters ſuppreſs'd. There was formerly under the Emperor a high Dignity they call'd *Beteudet*, which imports, the Beloved, or the Favourite, and there were two to honour'd, the one of the Left and the other of the Right Hand. Theſe two had all the Power of Government, for the Emperor ſpoke to no Man, nor would he ſuffer himſelf to be ſeen but by very few; and thoſe two *Beteudets* did all Things. But of late Years the Emperors are grown more familiar, and ſuffer themſelves to be ſeen and talk'd to by all Men; by which means they have found they had no uſe for that high Dignity, becauſe the two *Beteudets* were Kings, and the Emperor had only the Name, for which Reaſon they ſuppreſs'd the Charge; inſtead

Raz now Prime Miniſter. whereof they conſtituted another call'd *Raz*, which ſignifies Head; becauſe he who has that Employment is next the Emperor, Head of all the great Men in the Empire; he is firſt Councellor and Prime Miniſter, both in Civil and Military Affairs, and is Generaliſſimo, as Commanding for the moſt Part in all Wars of any Moment.

Lord Steward. Next under him is another they call *Bellatineche Goytâ*, which ſignifies Lord of the Servants, being like a Lord Steward, and he has Power over all Viceroys, Generals, *Xumos*, or Governors, and over the *Azages*, and *Umbares*, who are the Judges of the Empire. There is another at Court call'd *Tecâcaſe Bellatinoche Goyta*, ſignifying, Lord of the Leſſer Servants, or an under Steward, who only commands the Houſhold Servants, which are all mean; for the Emperor is far from being ſerv'd by the Sons of Kings, as *Urreta* feign'd. whereof there are none in the Empire, but even not by thoſe of good honeſt ſubſtantial People, for he has none but Slaves of ſeveral ſorts; ſome of them *Agaus*, others *Gonga's*, and others *Cafres*, or *Ballous*; yet theſe he often makes *Xumo's*, and raiſes them to the greateſt Employments at Court. Nor is this any way reflected.

flected on, and the Emperor fays, he does it becaufe he finds none
faithful but thofe People he breeds up and raifes from nothing,
tho' all of them are not fo, but it feems they are more trufty than
others.

Under the *Bellatinoche Goyta* are all the other Viceroys, and Go- *Great Officers.*
vernors of Kingdoms and Provinces, and the Commanders of the
Emperors Camp, being thofe of the Van, the Rear, the Right and
Left, as alfo the Courts and Minifters of Juftice ; the chief whereof
is that of the *Azages*, which looks like the Judges of the King's
Court in *Spain* and *Portugal*, but that they make no Diftinction
betwixt Judges of the Court and of thofe for Criminal and Civil
Affairs; only there are fome of the Right and fome of the Left
Hand, and under them the *Umbares*, which fignify the Chairs, fo
call'd, becaufe they Sit whilft the Plaintiff and Defendant ftand,
and to thefe, if they belong to the Court, all Appeals in Caufes
either Civil or Criminal, throughout the Empire, are firft brought ;
as alfo all Caufes belonging to the Court or Camp, which are the
fame Thing in this Country, are firft try'd before them. Thefe
are alfo of the Right and Left Hand, and from them the Appeal
goes up to the Court Judges.

There are no Proceedings in Writing, but all Caufes are com- *Judicial Pro-*
menc'd and concluded by word of Mouth, as has been faid ; nor *ceedings.*
are any Witneffes heard but the Plaintiffs, and therefore for the
moft part Judgment is given for him, becaufe he brings what E-
vidence he pleafes: But the Defendant may invalidate their Credit, and does it all the ways he can ; yet the Succefs of the Caufe
depending on that, the Plaintiff has ftill a great Advantage, efpecially when without any Remorfe of Confcience he bribes the Evi-
dence, which is to be done with eafe and cheap enough in *Ethiopia*, as well as in other Countries.

A Criminal convicted of Murder is by the Judges delivered up
to the Kindred, Children or Wife of the Party murder'd, which *Murder, how*
Cuftom, befides many others, they have retain'd from the *Jews.* *punifh'd.*
Thofe Relations either fell the Murderer's Life, or put him to Death
after what manner they pleafe. When the Murther cannot be
prov'd upon any one Man, all the Inhabitants of the Place where
the Fact was committed, are fin'd, and the dread of this Punifhment prevents much Bloodfhed.

C H A P. XI.

Of the Abyssinian *Soldiery, and the manner of their Camp ; of the City* Aczum, *and other Towns and Buildings ; and of the Revenues and Taxes of this Empire.*

Abyssines good Soldiers.

IT may be said in general, that the *Abyssinians* are good Soldiers; for they Ride well, are strong, well made, and enur'd to Hardship, enduring Hunger and Thirst to a Miracle, which is the Commendation *Agesilaus* gave his Soldiers, saying, *They could Fight with Hunger and Thirst.* So these continue in the Field most part of the Year, patiently suffering all Weather, as the scorching Heats, the sharp Cold, and violent Rains, and this with very little Food. They are bred up to War from their Infancy, and grow Old in it ; for those who are not Husbandmen are Soldiers, and to that purpose the Emperor gives them Lands to live on, which they enjoy as long as they serve ; but if they fail he gives them to others, and this is all their Pay; which is the Reason he can raise a great Army with little Charge.

Their Weapons.

The Weapons they use are a sort of short Spears, the Staves of them thin, and the Iron of one sort narrow, like burs, and of the other broad, but thin ; the one to be darted strongly, the other to fence with in close Fight, with one Hand ; for the other holds the Buckler, which is made of wild Buffalo's Hide, very strong. Each Soldier generally carries two of these Spears or Darts. The narrow ones they dart, as was said, with such Fury, that they pierce Coats of Mail and Bucklers ; the broader they keep to continue the Fight, as we do with Sword and Buckler. The better sort have Swords, but very rarely make use of them, only wearing them in time of Peace, by way of Ornament, and therefore they endeavour to have a Gilt or Silver Hilt, and the Scabbard of Velvet, or some other Silk ; when they talk with any body, they hold them in their Hands, and so walk; but when they go in the Streets the Servants carry them under their Arms. Some wear Daggers under their Breasts, with the Hilt towards the Right, and the Point to the Left. They also carry Clubs of hard Wood and heavy, which they call *Bolotas,* with Daggers in them, which they use

when

when they come to grapple together, and sometimes they dart them.

The Horse have no Weapons to fight with but short Lances, such of them as have Coats of Mail, which are but few, do not care for Bucklers, as being less encumber'd, but they carry some of the narrow pointed Spears above mention'd, to dart at a distance. *Horse.*

The Emperor, when he gathers all his Force, brings into the Field 30 or 40000 Men, 4 or 5000 of them Horse, the rest Foot. Of the Horse about 1500 are sizeable, and some of them very fine and strong. About 7 or 800 of these Horse wear Coats of Mail and Head-Pieces, all the rest both Horse and Foot, have no other Arms than have been said above, the Spears and Bucklers. They have above 1500 Fire Arms, but there are seldom above 3 or 400 Musquetiers in any Action, and those for the most part so ill train'd, that they never fire above once; nor can it be otherwise, because Powder and Ball are so scarce, that very few have any to Exercise at other Times, and those few Principal Men that do, use a Rest which they have not leisure to do in their Wars with the *Gallas* and others; so that they are little the better for their Learning. *Abyssine Army.*

There being no such Martial Discipline among them, as we have in *Europe*, and consequently their Armies, Batallions and Squadrons, not being so regularly drawn up, the first Shock begins and ends their Battels; either the one side or the other turning their Backs, and the other pursuing; nor do they think much of running away, because it is daily practis'd. *No Discipline.*

The aforesaid number of Troops, or a much less, makes an extraordinary great Camp, by reason the other People that follow the Army are far more numerous than the Soldiers, and the Baggage very much; and this is because they commonly go to the War with their whole Families, Wives and Children, and the Queen herself goes; and there is need of many Women to make their *Apas*, which are their daily Food, as has been said, as also their Wine; and all these Hangers on, with the Merchants and other Followers, amount to so great a number, that where there are 10000 Soldiers, there never are less than 30000 Souls, and if the Emperor be there 100 or 120000. *Multitudes following the Camp.*

Here the Emperor, Great Men, Ladies, Commanders, and many Soldiers, have abundance of Tents, which are set up in very good Order, and always the same: For the Emperor's Tents being 4 or 5 very beautiful ones, are plac'd in the Center, and then leaving a large space between on the Right, Left, Front and Rear of them, are those of two Churches he carries with him, and those of the *Manner of encamping.*

Queen

Queen and Great Men, who have all their fixt Places ; then thofe
of the Officers and Soldiers, according to their Pofts ; thofe of the
Vanguard before, thofe of the Rear behind, and the two Wings
on the Right and Left. The Camp thus pitch'd, takes up a very
great Space, and is certainly very graceful to behold, efpecially in
the Night, by reafon of the Multitude of Fires lighted.

Of marching.   When they are to march, the *Titaurari,* fo they call him that
performs the Duty of a Major, or Quarter-Mafter General, goes
before, and pitches upon the Ground for encamping, where he
fticks a Lance, which fhows that the Emperor's Tent is to be fet up
there, and by that every Man knows what Place belongs to him.
On their march they obferve no Order, but before the Emperor
go the Waites and Kettle Drums, and he always mounts and
alights within his Tent ; and if he happens to alight by the way,
thofe who are neareft make a Ring, hiding him with their Cloaks,
and they bring him a Couch, which is always carry'd near at
Hand, on which, cover'd with Carpets and Cufhions of rich Silk,
he ufes to reft him.

Diforders of   Moft of thefe People carry no Provifions, and they who have
the Army.   any, when it is fpent live as well as all the reft upon what is given them, or they take in the Country Towns they march through,
which they leave as much undone, as the *Gallas* their Enemies
could do, were they in their Places, efpecially when the Army
continues any time on the fame Ground, for there is no other way,
but for the Emperor, or General, to affign them certain Towns,
which they rob of all forts of Provifions, and under that colour
all the reft goes ; fo that the Inhabitants have no other Remedy
but Patience, and may fay with *Job, The Lord hath given and
the Lord hath taken away, bleffed be the name of the Lord.* This is alfo the
Reafon why the *Gallas* fo eafily make Inroads into the Empire, and on
the contrary the Emperor's Forces cannot go far into their Lands ;
becaufe they do not Sow, nor have they any Stores of Provifion
laid up, but live upon the Milk of their Cows, and when they
have occafion, eafily drive them away, retiring themfelves, and
leaving the *Ethiopians* the defert Fields, which obliges them to retire fpeedily, or Starve.

How the Em-   About the Emperor march his *Azages* and chief Men, attend-
peror moves.   ing him, and he always travels with his Crown on his Head,
made up of feveral Pieces of Gold and Silver, with fome Seed
Pearl; for precious Stones were never fo much as feen in *Ethiopia.*
He alfo wears his Silk Hat, brought from *India,* like thofe us'd
there ; none of thofe Curtains, which formerly were, being now
carry'd about him, that he might be feen by no Man. On the
contrary he fometimes quits his Mule and Prances on his Horfe.
                                                When

When the Enemy is near, the Army marches clofe and in better order ; all the Divifions in their Pofts, and neither the Van advances far, nor the Rear ftays much behind. The Wings are ftretch'd out, the Emperor being in the Center with fome of his Guards, great Men and Ladies, leaving a fufficient Interval for the Baggage to be enclos'd and in fafety. *Damian de Goes*, writ a Treatife, *de Moribus Abyffinorum*, from which *Illefcas* took what he relates in the 2d Part of his Pontifical Hiftory, *lib.* 6. *cap.* 22. but neither of them had fuch certain Information of what they deliver, as we have.

The Learned *Mercator*, in the 3d part of his *Atlas*, defcribing *Ethiopia*, fays, there are few Cities among the *Abyffinians*, and would have been more in the Right, had he faid, there were none, as he is where he writes, they live in Villages. The new *Atlas* publifh'd in *Spanifh ann.* 1653, follow'd *Mercator*. At this time there is no fettled City in all *Ethiopia* ; formerly the Town of *Aczum* was very famous among the *Abyffinians*, and ftill preferves fomewhat of its Renown ; and this place feems to have *Aczum Town.* been a City, at leaft they look upon it as moft certain, that the Queen of *Sheba* kept her Court there, and that it was the Refidence of the Emperors for many Ages after, and they are Crown'd there to this Day. This is the City *Aczum*, or *Auxum*, often mention'd by the learned Cardinal *Baronius* in his Ecclefiaftical Annals, as we fhall fee hereafter ; at prefent it is only a Village of about 100 Houfes. This place is Three Leagues from *Fremona*, and about 45 from *Mazua*, in 14 Degrees and a half Latitude. There are to be feen many ancient Ruins, particularly thofe of a fpacious Church, which appeas to have been of 5 Ifles, 165 Foot in Length, and 75 in Breadth.

The moft magnificent Thing that appears here, are certain very *Obelisks.* tall Stones, in the nature of Obelisks, or Pyramids; the biggeft of them 78 Foot in Length, the Breadth at the Foot Seven Foot Six Inches. It is cut as it were in fmall Cufhions, each of them about half a Yard Square; the fmalleft of them being between 25 and 30 Foot high are rude mifhapen Stones. Some of thofe which feem to have been talleft are thrown down, and they fay, the *Turks* entring *Ethiopia* overthrew them. The end of erecting thefe Pyramids may reafonably be fuppos'd to have been for Monuments, near their Graves; which was the Defign of the *Egyptians* in their fo famous Pyramids. Here is alfo a Stone fet up with a large Infcription, in *Greek* and *Latin* Characters, but they do not make any Senfe. The Ceremonies here us'd at the Coronation of Emperors were many, whereof enough ftill remains, we fhall
fpeak.

speak of them hereafter at the Coronation of the Emperor *Sultan Segued.*

The Imperial Camp the only City. There is no City at this time in *Ethiopia*, only the King's Camp resembles a Royal City and the Capital of the Empire. It may deserve the name of a City, not in regard of the Buildings, but for the Multitude of People, and the good order observ'd in taking up their Ground, especially the Place where they Winter, which is generally the same, but never for many Years. When the Fathers of the Society were there, the Emperor repair'd to a Place call'd *Dancaz,* which lasted near 10 Years; but the same Emperor in 13, or 14 Years before that had 5, or 6 other Places, in each of which he continu'd 2, 3, or 4 Years. This has been always the Custom of *Ethiopia,* and when he removes, for the most part there is nothing remains to be seen, but, *Fields where* Troy *Town stood.*

Frequent removes. These frequent removals, are occasion'd in the first place by the small expence in building their Houses, as shall be soon shown; and secondly with regard to the several Wars they have in Hand, sometimes with one Enemy, and sometimes with another; but above all, for want of Wood. First the Ground is chosen, where there may be Plenty of Wood; but no order being observ'd in falling the Trees, the Mountains and Valleys are soon left bare, and then they presently think of removing to another Place, where there is Wood; and they are amaz'd to hear, that in *Europe* and other Parts of the World great Cities can continue long in the same Place without being in great want of Wood.

None but Villages in Ethiopia. Excepting the Emperor's Camp, or that of some great Man, there is no Habitation throughout the whole Empire, that can deserve the Name of a City, nor so much as of a great Town. They are all Villages, some greater and some smaller; but such as can claim no other Title. Of these, in some Provinces and Territories there are many so close together, that all the Country seems to be inhabited; other Parts are less Populous, and many are quite Desart. Thus we may judge they are all open, without Walls, or other Enclosure; only in the Kingdom of *Amahara* and some others, such as are on the Frontiers, next the *Gallas,* who so infest them with continual Incursions, that they cannot so much as Till the Land, these, being seated on *Ambas* and high Mountains, have also some sort of Walls of dry Stone.

Buildings. The Houses are generally of Stone and Clay, I mean those of the better sort, for the rest make their Walls of Stakes drove close together and cover'd with Straw. Only on the Sea Coast of the Kingdom of *Tigre* the Roofs are terrass'd; but for the most

part

part fo low, that a Man may reach them with his Head. Moft of
the Houfes are round; yet fome they build long, as were commonly thofe of the Emperors, which they call *Sacala*, and thence
this fame Name fignifies the Palaces of the Emperor, or great Men.
The round ones, if they be any thing large, they call *Behet Nugu*,
importing a Royal Houfe; for *Behet* is a Houfe, and *Nugu* a King.
The great Lords and Rich Men adorn thefe Houfes with Quarters
of Cedar, fo clofe to one another that they ferve inftead of Wainfcot, and this Wainfcot they bind and fasten together with Lines
of feveral colours, fo that they look handfome enough, and are
pleafant and convenient for ground Rooms. Every Man of
Quality has 6, 8, or more of thefe Houfes, or Rooms within
large Enclofures, which are made of dry Stone, 6, or 7 Spans
high, and on the Top of them they raife clofe Hedges, full of
Thorns. At this time, as will be faid hereafter, they have fome
knowledge of Lime, and have built fome Churches and a few
Houfes with Lime and Stone.

The Revenues of this Empire are very fmall, and as *F. Emanuel* *Revenues.*
d' Almeyda teftifies, that he had it from the Emperor *Sultan Se-*
gued's own Mouth, thefe Princes never had any Treafurers; fo
that whatfoever *F. Uretta* writes concerning this Point is all Chimerical; I will therefore give *F. Emanuel d' Almeyda*'s Account.
' The Kingdom of *Narea*, fays he, yields more Gold than any
' other of this Empire. The Emperor now reigning affirms that
' from all Antiquity, never fo much was brought to any one, as to
' *Malac Segued*, who reign'd from the Year 1563, till 1596; and
' of all that came to the faid *Malac Segued* every Year, only one
' amounted to 5000 *Oqueas*, as fome report, which many do not
' look upon as certain. For the moft Years it did not exceed
' 1500 *Oqueas*, which are 15000 Pieces of Eight. This fame Sum
' our Emperor, (meaning *Sultan Segued*) receiv'd for fome Years;
' but now he has not ufually above 1000 *Oqueas*. Thefe came
' to him Five Years fince, when I was in the Country of the
' *Damotes*, and their Viceroy, who was then the Catholick and
' Brave *Buco* went to fetch them, through the midft of the *Gallas*
' and *Cafres*, but from that time to this, *Narea* being it fefted by the
' *Gallas* and the great Men of that Kingdom at variance, in all
' thefe 5 Years, the Emperor has receiv'd but 500 *Oqueas*; yet it
' is hop'd that for the future he will not fail of 1000, which is
' the ufual Tribute at this Time.

' Some Lands of *Gojam* Yearly yield 1100 *Oqueas* in Gold by
' way of Tribute, little more or lefs; tho' fometimes the Emperor
' has beftow'd all thefe Lands, or part of them on fome great
' Men, as his Sons, or Brothers, and they fpend that Revenue.

I

' The

'The same Kingdom yields 3000 Pieces of Cloth, worth a Piece
'of Eight each; besides 200 *Bezetes*, being very large and close
'Cloths made of Cotton, with a Pile, or Shag on the one side, like
'our Carpets, each of which is worth an *Oqnea*, little more or less.
'Formerly, they say, the same Kingdom paid 3000 Horses; but
'it is to be observ'd that most of that Kingdom were, and still
'are ordinary Nags and low priz'd Beasts. This Tribute has
'ceas'd, because, since the *Gallas* drew near and made continual
'War on that Kingdom, the Emperor *Malac Segued* thought
'good to remit this Duty, the better to enable those People with
'their Horses to defend themselves against the *Gallas*. All that
'*Francis Alvarez* adds, touching this Point, of what he saw
'brought to Court in the Days of *David* the Emperor; and the
'Ceremonies and Magnificence he there describes, of the manner
'of bringing this Tribute, was a Contrivance to show it, like
'many more perform'd before him and his Companions, that they
'might have something to talk of in strange Countries.

'The Emperor receives no Tribute in Gold from any other
'Kingdom of his Empire; but the Governors he places over them
'give it him for their Commands; so that he receives 25000
'Pieces of Eight from several Governments, which they call
'*Xumetes*, in the Kingdom of *Tigre*; from the *Xumates* of *Dambea*
'5000; from those of *Begameder*, *Amahara*, *Noleca* and *Xaoa*,
'something, but less, because those Countries are infested by the
'*Gallas*. Of this sort of Revenue, the former Emperors receiv'd
'much greater Sums than the present, because they had many
'more and much larger Kingdoms; part whereof are now
'possess'd by the *Gallas*, and others pay no more Subjection,
'because the *Gallas* are got betwixt them and the Emperor's Do-
'minions.

'They have some Passes on Mountains, where all Commo-
'dities pay a Duty. Sea Ports on the Ocean no *Abyssinian* Emperor
'ever had any; on the Red-Sea they had *Mazua*, but the *Turks*
'have long since been Masters of it. Most of the Duties pay-
'able on those Passes the Emperor has given to great Men, with
'the Lands, where they are; but that of *Lamalmon* he keeps for
'himself, which yields him the value of 100 *Oqueas* a Year.

'The Emperor has some Lands, which are like Royalties, from
'which he draws 10, or 12 Loads of Provisions. Besides this he
'has another Duty of Provisions, an Account whereof the Hus-
'bandmen of *Dambea*, *Gojam*, *Begameder* and some other Provinces
'pay each a Load, little more or less; but most of this he has
'given to several of his Commanders. What comes from *Dam-*
'*bea*, being about 10, or 12000 Loads, he divides among some
'   'Soldiers,

' Soldiers, on whom he has not beftow'd Lands, gives fome Alms
' to the Poor, and diftributes among fome Men and Women of
' Quality, who are in Want at Court.

' There is one confiderable Tax in *Ethiopia*, which was impos'd
' lefs than 80 Years fince, by which every Man that has Cows,
' every three Years pays him one out of Ten; and the Country
' being full of Cattel, moft of which is Kine, this Tribute a-
' mounts to a great Value, and the Kingdoms and Provinces are
' fo diftributed, that fome of them pay it every Year. This they
' call Burning, becaufe they burn a Mark upon that they chufe
' for the Emperor; but it may deferve the Name for other Rea-
' fons, in regard that the Officers, who are to gather this Cattel,
' commit fo many Infolencies on the poor Country People, that
' they ruin, and confume them. Befides this every Loom that
' Weaves Cotton-Cloth, if belonging to a Chriftian, pays one of
' thofe Cloths; if to a *Mahometan*, a Piece of Eight, and by this
' Duty he gathers every Year in *Dambea* and the Neighbouring
' Parts 1000 Cloths. He has the fame Revenue in other King-
' doms, but has beftow'd it on thofe Lords to whom he has
' given the Lands of thofe Countries.

' Thefe are the Revenues of the *Abyffine* Empire, which being
' fummon'd up, it plainly appears are inconfiderable enough;
' not only in regard of what Fame has fpread abroad, but of
' what might be expected from fo many Kingdoms and Provinces.
' However, befides all this we have here mention'd, which in a
' poor Country amounts to much more than can be imagin'd in
' others, that which makes this King great, is his being abfolute
' Lord of all the Lands within his Dominions; fo that he can
' take away and give them all as he thinks fit; for neither great
' nor fmall poffefs any thing but by the Emperor's Gift, and all
' they have is a Bounty during Pleafure. And it is fo ufual,
' for the Emperor to chop, change and take away, every Year, or
' two, or three, or in the midft of it, the Lands any Man has,
' and to beftow them on another, that it is never thought much
' of, and very often, one Plows, another Sows, and a third reaps.
' Hence it is that no Man improves what he has, or fo much as
' Plants a Tree, as knowing it is a mighty rarity for him that
' Plants to gather the Fruit. It is the Emperor's Advantage that
' they fhould all fo entirely depend on him; for thus they all
' ferve him in Peace and War, fome for fear of lofing the Lands
' he has given them, and others in hopes of getting thofe they
' have not; and for this reafon they make him their Prefents,
' according to their Ability, for generally he gets moft, who gives

' moft,

' molt, and he has least, who presents least.   These are the Words
' of *F. Emanuel d' Almeyda.*

C H A P. XII.

Wherein a short Account is given of the Gallas, *who*
are at present the greatest Enemies of the Abys-
sinians.

Gallas, *where*
they live.
WE shall have often occasion in this History to speak of the
Gallas, who are at present the Scourge God has made use
of against the *Abyssinians,* and therefore I have thought it necessary to give some Account of them in this place.   In order to
it, we must first observe that the most Southern parts of this Empire are, the Kingdom of *Cambate* due South, that of *Narea*
South West, and that of *Bali* South East.   From the Kingdoms of
Narea, and *Cambate* to the Sea there are several hundred Leagues ;
but from that of *Bali* to the Sea, going directly from North West
to South East, there are less than an hundred Leagues to the Coast
of the Ocean, which Sailers call the Desert Coast, and is the nearest to *Ethiopia,* as lying next the Kingdom of *Bali,* formerly belonging to *Abyssinia.*   These Lands that lie betwixt *Bali* and the
Ocean are the proper Country and Habitation of the *Gallas.*

Suppos'd to be
Jews.
The most received Opinion among learned Men is, that these
People are originally descended from those *Jews,* who on occasion
of the Transmigrations, or Dispersions of the said Nation under
Salmanasar, Nebuchadnezzar, Titus, Adrian, and *Severus* settled
on that Part of the Borders of *Ethiopia ;* and that from them came
those we now call *Gallas,* or *Callas,* which signifies, Milks, chang-
ing the C into G, as is frequently done in other Nations : so the
Abyssinians changing *Calla* into *Galla,* gave the Name to these
Jews and to other *Greeks* and *Assyrians,* who mix'd with them,
Gallas, or *Callas* signifying White Men, for *Calla* in the *Hebrew,*
signifies Milk, and they were call'd Milks, to denote they were
White ; and still these People are call'd *Gallas,* that is Whites,
tho' they are now Black.   So the Race of the *Portugueses,* who
enter'd *Ethiopia,* with *Don Christopher da Gama,* are still by the
Abyssinian

Abyffinians call'd *Portuguefes*, as being defcended from them, tho' they are now *Abyffinians* and of their Colour. In the fame man-ner thefe *Gallas* having no Education and converfing continually with Barbarous Nations, are become fome of the moft brutal of all the *Cafres.*

The firft time this Plague broke out of their own Country, *Their firft* where they dwelt and enter'd *Ethiopia*, was in the Days of the *coming into* Emperor *David*, otherwife call'd *Onag Segued*, of whom I fhall *Ethiopia.* fpeak hereafter; and their Irruption was at the fame time that the *Moor Granbe* of *Adel*, had made an Incurfion and conquer'd a confiderable part of the Empire, for Misfortunes never come alone, and their firft Inroad was by the Kingdom of *Bali*, on which they border'd.

The Irruption of thefe Barbarians into *Ethiopia*, was like an *Their Con-* Inundation from a mighty River, which fwelling over all the *quefts* Plain, fpares nothing that ftands in its way, but bears down all it meets, Men, Cattle, Corn, and Buildings; fo that when the Emperor *Sultan Segued* began his Reign, thefe Savages had fub-du'd moft of the largeft Kingdoms of *Ethiopia*, from that of *An-goa*, which now lies almoft Eaft of them, to the Southward through *Doaro, Oifat, Bali, Fategar, Oge*, part of *Xaoa, Bizamo*, and *Damut*, which lies Weft of *Gojam*, and they are now Mafters of thefe Kingdoms, and of many Provinces lying between them; and had not Providence fo order'd it, that they fhould be con-tinually at War among themfelves, one Hord, or Race againft another, there would not by this time be one Foot of Land in the whole Empire, but what they would be Mafters of. To this end alfo Providence farther feems to have order'd that the Kingdoms remaining under the *Abyffine* Emperor fhould be full of pro-digious high and craggy Mountains, where the Horfe of the *Gallas* cannot eafily make their Inroads, which is their way of Warring.

Tho' at firft thefe People were of a white Race, yet as in Procefs *Their Barba-* of time they loft their Colour and turn'd Black, fo for want of *rity.* Improvement, and through too much mixing with Barbarians, they became at length fo very brutal, that their way of living is more hideous than their Colour. They are Heathens, or rather neither Chriftians, *Mahometans*, nor Gentiles, for they worfhip no Idols, and have very little knowledge of God. However, fince they have Peopled the Lands of the Empire, being in the midft between the Chriftians, and the *Mahometans* of *Adel* and *Adea*, they have taken to Circumcifion, rather becaufe it is the Cuftom of the Country, than as an Act of Religion.

Not-

Manner of living.

Notwithstanding their being all Black, yet they show their Progenitors were not so, for they have not flat Noses, like the *Cafres*, nor thick Lips, like those of *Angola*; but have generally very good Features, and are well shap'd and many of them rather deep Tawny than Black. They neither Till, nor Sow, nor gather any thing the Land produces; all the spacious Vales and rich Plains they are Masters of, only serve to afford their Cattle such Sustenance as the Earth naturally produces. They look after their Flocks, drink their Milk and eat their Flesh, which is all their Food, without any Bread, so easily are these Barbarians fed. Yet when they enter the Lands of the *Abyssinians* and find any Bread they do not mislike, but eat it, with a very good Appetite, and yet will not Sow.

Policy to defend themselves.

The reason they alledge for it is, that so the *Ethiopians* or other Enemies may not be able to over-run their Lands; for as soon as the *Gallas* perceive an Enemy comes on with a powerful Army, they retire to the farther Parts of the Country, with all their Cattle, which is all their Wealth, and taking that they take all away; then have the *Abyssinians* several Days march to come at them, for which they cannot carry Provisions, according to their little forecast, and there being none on the Lands of the *Gallas*, as not being Till'd, they must of necessity either turn back, or perish. This is an odd way of making War, wherein by flying they overcome the Conquerors; and without drawing Sword, oblige them to encounter with Hunger, which is an invincible Enemy; tho' at the same time the *Gallas* fight against themselves, as always wanting Bread, to prevent their Enemies eating it sometimes; so that they are like the Dog in the Manger, that will neither eat Hay himself, nor suffer the Horse to eat it.

Cruelty to Children.

The *Gallas* for the most part are barbarous and cruel, using their own Children more inhumanly than even the Wild-Beasts; for they take no care of breeding them up or providing for them, during the first Six, or Seven Years after they are marry'd, but rather throw them about the Fields, a Savageness odious to Nature, which has given the fiercest Lyons and Tigers a Sense of Tenderness for their Young. However they are generally Men of their Words, and of no ill Disposition, as was seen in some that were bred up in the Emperor's, and other great Men's Houses,

Good Qualities.

who all prov'd so tractable, that the best of the *Abyssinians* did not exceed them; and some of them, who imbrac'd the Catholick Religion, were as constant in maintaining it under Torments, as they had been ready to profess it in Words.

They

They are generally valiant and brave. For defensive Armour, *Weapons.* they have only Targets of double Oxes Hides, and of late some are of Wild Buffalo, which is very strong; their offensive Weapons are such small Spears as has been said the *Abyssinians* use, and Wooden Clubs which they also cast, like those People. The first of the *Gallas* fought all a foot, but now they have Horses, tho' not so good, or nobly tempered, or of so choice a Breed as the *Ethiopians*; but very hardy, because they keep them in Breath, making them run half a Day together at half Speed.

The Saddles they use are very light, and easily made, their Stir- *Horsmanship.* rups very thin, and small, because they don't put their Feet into them, but only their Great-Toes, which they learnt of the *Abyssinians*, who all do so, and therefore they all and even the Emperor himself always ride barefoot. I do not approve of the Custom, much less of the *Roman*, who us'd no Stirrups at all, nor had so much as a Name to call them by, for in all the *Latin* Tongue there is no proper word to express them. Nor can we approve of the Practice of the *Numidians*, who had neither Stirrups, nor Bridles to their Horses, since it is certain that Bridles and Stirrups make Men sit faster and rule their Horses better.

That which always made the *Gallas* dreadful is their great Re- *Resolution.* solution in joyning Battle, where they absolutely conclude they will either Conquer, or Die; and this is the Reason they have obtain'd so many Victories over the *Abyssinians*, tho' these were still more numerous, and had better Arms and Horses. The *Gallas*, when they make an Incursion seldom exceed 7, or 8000, but these are chosen Youths, and sworn to stand by one another, and therefore the Emperor *Sultan Segued* was wont to say, *That the Ethiopians could not stand the first shock of the Gallas, and therefore he always suffer'd them to run deep into the Country, that they might Plunder, and cool, and at their return, when they were loaded with Booty, thinking only how to get home and enjoy their Prize, and their first Fury much abated, then he lay in wait for them on the way, and call'd them to account for what they had robb'd, not only recovering the Prey, but sacrificing their Lives to his Resentment.*

They have no King, or Sovereign among them, but every Eight *Government.* Years they chuse a sort of Consul or Governor, whom they call *Luva*, and obey him as their General. The first thing he does, as soon as enter'd upon the Government, is to gather all the best Men he can, and make an Inroad into the Empire, killing and plundering all in his way, to gain himself and his Soldiers Wealth and Fame, for the unfortunate *Ethiopia* is the *India* they resort to for what they want. This first Irruption they call

Dela

Dela Grito, which is as much as, a General Muster. It is an E-stablish'd Custom among them, never to cut the Hair of their Heads, till they have kill'd an Enemy in War, or some Wild-Beast, as a Lyon, or Tiger, and as soon as that is done they pole their Heads. On the top of it they leave a Lock, as is the Fashion of the *Japonefes,* which they much value themselves upon, as a Token of their Valour, not inherited from their Parents, but obtain'd by their own Merit.

This may suffice, as to the *Gallas,* and much less would have satisfy'd the *Abyffinians,* who are not only oppress'd but utterly undone by these Barbarians, Almighty God making use of them to chastise them for their Sins and Errors, as he made use of the *Philistines* to humble the Children of *Ifrael,* and both Nations did and do still deserve it, the *Jews* for their Rebellion, and the *Ethiopians* for their Schism.

C H A P. XIII.

How the Abyffinians *came to the knowledge of the true God, by means of the Queen of* Sheba, *who went to see* Solomon, *and of the Son she had by him; with an Account of what seems to be real and what fabulous, touching the coming of that Queen, and her Son by him.*

Ethiopian *Histories.*

THE *Abyffinians* have but a very imperfect Knowledge of their Histories and ancient Times, for want of the Curiosity of writing Books, which are the Treafury wherein we lay up the precious Wealth of Knowledge, valu'd by *Solomon* more than mighty Kingdoms; and those few Books they have, their Monks take great care to keep from the Catholicks, becaufe of the strong and irresistible Arguments they draw from them to confound the Errors of *Diofcorus* and *Eutyches.* However I will here deliver, what can be gather'd out of a very ancient Book of theirs, which is to them like another Gospel, and kept with extraordinary Veneration in the Church of *Auxum,* or *Aczum,* being the ancient Metropolis and prime Seat of all the *Abyffine* Empire, there

there being a moſt poſitive Tradition among them, that there was the Reſidence of the Queen of *Sheba,* and there is no queſtion but for many Ages it was the Court of the *Abyſſine* Emperors. I will here briefly relate, what is very largely contain'd in that Book and others of theirs, and what is unanimouſly receiv'd among all thoſe People, which is,

That a mighty Potent Queen, call'd *Azeb* or *Maqueda,* reign- ing in *Ethiopia,* ſhe was inform'd of the great Power and Wiſdom ***Queen of*** of *Solomon,* by one *Tamerin,* a Merchant of hers; and being de- ***Sheba.*** ſirous to ſee and hear *Solomon,* ſhe came to *Jeruſalem* with a migh- ty Retinue of the greateſt Princes and Lords in *Ethiopia,* and abun- dance of Treaſure. There *Solomon* gave her the Knowledge of the true God, and returning home at the end of Nine Months, ſhe was deliver'd of a Son begotten by *Solomon,* who was call'd *Meni- lehec,* and by another Name *David.* This Son afterwards went to *Jeruſalem* to ſee his Father *Solomon,* by whom he was magnificent- ***Menilehec*** ly entertain'd, and he caus'd him to be anointed and Sworn King ***ber Son.*** of *Ethiopia,* by *Sadoc* and *Joas* the Prieſts; and when well inſtru- cted in the Law of God, which he was to cauſe to be obſerv'd in his Country, he aſſign'd him ſeveral of the firſt begotten of *Iſrael* to attend and ſerve him in *Ethiopia,* and furniſh'd him with all Officers and Servants belonging to the Royal Houſe of *Juda,* as alſo a High Prieſt and Levites, and Men learned in the Law of *Moſes.*

Then the aforeſaid Book proceeds to give an Account how theſe firſt begotten, at the Inſtigation of *Azariah,* the Son of *Sadoc* the ***Fable about*** Prieſt, took an Oath to one another to carry away with them the ***the Ark.*** Ark of the Covenant, which they call'd the Heavenly *Sion;* and that going by Night to the *Temple,* Providence ſo ordering it, they found the Gates open, and put the Ark upon a Cart, and being attended by abundance of People, with much Wealth, and great Acclamations, they travell'd ſo ſwiftly, that *Solomon,* who went to recover the Ark, could not overtake them, and with the ſame Expedition they croſs'd the *Red Sea,* as joyfully as the Children of *Iſrael* had done, with only this Difference, that the *Iſraelites* paſs'd it on Foot, without being wet, and they flying in their Chariots; ſo that the Sea obey'd the former, and the Air was ſubſervient to the latter.

This Book farther tells us, that when Queen *Maqueda* under- ſtood that her Son already made King was coming, and brought along with him all thoſe firſt begotten, as alſo the Ark of the Hea- venly God of *Sion,* ſhe went out with great Solemnity to meet them, and plac'd the Ark in the Temple of the Land of *Maqueda,* all the People of *Ethiopia* receiving the Knowledge of the true God; there

being

being none at that time, throughout all the World, to compare to King *Solomon* in *Judea*, and to Queen *Maqueda* in *Ethiopia*. It further adds, that the Queen afterwards resign'd the Kingdom to her Son *David*, and oblig'd him and his Great Men to Swear by the Heavenly *Sion*, that they would never after admit any Woman to the Throne of *Ethiopia*, nor any but the Male Race descending from *David*.

All these Stories are told much at large in that Book of theirs, which they look upon as of undoubted Reputation. As to what they say, that the Queen of *Sheba* went out of *Ethiopia* to *Jerusalem*, the *Abyssinians* believe it to be beyond all Controversy. It is true, those precious Sweets the Scripture tells us, the Queen of *Sheba* carry'd with her, are rather to be found in *Arabia Felix* than in *Ethiopia*, and in the same *Arabia* we find the *Sabean* Region, which is the proper Land of Frankincense, as appears by all Authors who have treated of it, and so says the Prince of Poets, *Georg.* I.

Arabia the Country of Perfumes.

India *mittit Ebur, molles sua Thura* Sabæi.

Besides the Name of *Sheba*, or as the *Latin* has it *Saba*, denotes that the Queen was of this *Sabean* Country, which is in or near *Arabia Felix*. Many Holy Expositors have also declar'd that this Queen was of *Arabia* and not of *Ethiopia*; of this Opinion are *Justin, Cyprian, Epiphanius, Cyril* of *Alexandria*, Cardinal *Baronius, Suarez*, and others. But *Josephus* in the 2d Book of his Antiquities, says, the Queen of *Sheba* was of *Ethiopia*, and *Origen, St Augustin, S. Anselm* and others, quoted by F. *Toledo*, are of the same Opinion; but that Author adds, that *Arabia* is not far distant from *Ethiopia*, and so she might be Queen of *Ethiopia* and *Arabia*, and *Josephus* says, she was also Queen of *Ægypt*.

Opinions concerning this Queen.

F. *Peter Pays* of the Society, a Man of great Sincerity, whom we shall often speak of, being taken by the *Turks* in that Part of *Arabia*, was carry'd with his Companion F. *Antony* of *Montserat*, from *Dofar* to *Xaer*, and thence to *Senaan*, and they gave an Account, that in that Journey through *Arabia*, they found a Parcel of very large and wonderful ancient Ruins of Old Structures, and enquiring of the Natives concerning those Antiquities, they answer'd, That Place had been formerly the Pen for the Queen of *Sheba*'s Cattel; and it may be suppos'd, adds the said Father very discreetly. that the said Great Queen was Mistress of *Ethiopia*, and of that Part of *Arabia* lying opposite to it, beyond the *Red Sea*; and thus we may reconcile the Authors, who say she was Queen of *Arabia* with those who affirm she was Queen of *Ethiopia*, and hence

hence she might carry the Gold, since this is to be found in *A-byssinia*, as are Sweets and Frankincense in *Arabia*. A farther Confirmation of this Opinion is the Name the *Abyssines* give this Queen, saying, She was call'd *Maqueda* in *Arabick*, but the Name she goes by in their Book is *Neguesta Azeb*.

Near to *Auxum* or *Aczum*, in the Kingdom of *Tigre* in *Ethiopia*, there is still a small Village call'd *Saba* or *Sabaim*, where they say the Queen of *Sheba* or *Saba* was Born. There is also another Village call'd *Azebo*, which answers to the Name of *Azeb*, and another call'd *Beth David*, signifying the House of *David*, and in the *Ethiopian* Books this Queen is sometimes call'd *Saba*, sometimes *Azeb*, and sometimes *Maqueda*. *Her several Names.*

In the first Book of *Kings*, chap. 10. and in the second of *Chronicles*, chap. 9. She is call'd Queen of *Sheba*, or according to the Vulgate *Saba*; in S. *Matthew*, chap. 12. where our Bible has the Queen of the South, the *Ethiopick* Version has *Neguesta Azeb*, which is the same Thing; for *Neguesta* signifies Queen, and *Azeb* in *Arabiek* is the South Wind, and our Saviour call'd her so, because *Ethiopia* and *Arabia* lie to the Southward of *Jury*. *In Scripture.*

It is farther said of this Queen in that Book, that she built a City, which was Capital of *Ethiopia*, calling it *Debra Maqueda*, which they say is the same as *Auxum* or *Aczum*, and for many Ages was the Court and Capital of *Ethiopia*, and in it, they say, the Queen of *Sheba*, as soon as she came from *Jerusalem*, built a stately Temple, in Honour of the true God; which same they add, Queen *Candace*, whom they call *Andake*, afterwards consecrated to our Saviour *JESUS CHRIST*, and to the blessed Virgin his holy Mother. *Auxum City and Temple.*

I am sensible there are many Fabulous Notions among what has been said in this Chapter, and therefore as to the Point of the Queen of *Sheba*'s having a Son by *Solomon*, it seems no difficult matter to believe, and the Patriarch *Don Alfonso Mendez*, has endeavour'd to prove it; nor is it hard to credit that he who took to Wife the Daughter of *Pharoah*, and lov'd without measure the *Moabites, Edomites, Sidonians, Hittites*, and others, should contract Affinity with the Royal Family of *Ethiopia*; which is further confirm'd by the *Abyssinians* to this Day, calling all the Offspring of their Kings *Israelites*, and these must of necessity by their Laws be descended of the Male Line of the Sons of *Menilehec*, the Son of *Solomon* and the Queen of *Sheba*; and for this same Reason the Arms of *Ethiopia* are a *Lyon*, with this Inscription in an Orle, *The Lyon of Judah hath overcome*. *Arms of Ethiopia.*

*Queen of
Sheba brought
Judaism into
Ethiopia.*
I make no Question, as the Patriarch *Don Alfonso Mendez,* and the other Fathers of the Society who were there, do declare, that the Queen of *Sheba* was a Native of this *Ethiopia,* and introduc'd in it the Customs of the Court of *Jerusalem,* with Circumcision and the other Ceremonies of the *Jewish* Law, which continu'd even in the Days of our Saviour, and the preaching of the Gospel, as appears by the Pilgrimage the Eunuch of Queen *Candace* undertook to the Temple of *Jerusalem,* whom S. *Philip* the Deacon, as appears in the *Acts* of the Apostles, *chap.* 8. *ver.* 27. found reading the Prophet *Isaiah;* whence it may be inferr'd, that he observ'd the Law of *Moses* They were so tenacious of these Customs, that we shall hereafter see how obstinately they adher'd to Circumcision, the keeping of the *Sabbath,* or *Saturday,* and other *Jewish* Ceremonies.

*Resemblance
between Jews
and Ethiopi-
ans in Cu-
stoms.*
A further Confirmation of this Truth we find in the exact Resemblance there is betwixt the Customs of the *Jews* and those of the *Abyssines* in Peace and War, and in the Administration of Justice, for whatsoever we read in Holy Writ is there to be seen represented to the Life. The aforesaid Patriarch, who was one of the most learned Men in *Spain* as to Holy Writ, owns this of himself, that after his coming into *Ethiopia,* he understood many Passages of the Scripture he was before ignorant of, by comparing the Customs of those People with what the Bible relates, and that it is so undoubtedly an establish'd Opinion in *Ethiopia,* that this Queen was Born there, of her introducing the *Jewish* Rites, and of several Places retaining her Name, that it would be there look'd upon as no less Folly to deny their Emperors descending from *Solomon,* than it would be in *Rome* to say, that City was not built by *Romulus* and *Remus;* or in *Spain,* that their Kings did not descend from the *Gothi,* or theirs in *Portugal* from King *Alfonso Henriquez.*

*Fabulous
Stories.*
As for the Story of the Ark of the Covenant, stolen by *Azariah* and his Companions, all of them first begotten Sons, and the Miracles of their flying through the Air, and making their escape from *Solomon,* it is a Fable much like that of *Dedalus* his flying; when he escap'd out of *Crete* into *Italy;* and if the Inhabitants of that Island, were, as St *Paul* writes of them, in his Epistle to *Titus* C. 1. *v.* 12. *always Liars,* the *Abyssines* are nothing inferior to them in this particular, as the Fathers of the Society found by sufficient Experience; so that all the Relation was doubtless the Author's Invention, to gain Reputation to that Church and its *Tabot,* which is the Altar Stone, saying it stood on the Ark of the Covenant.

For the better understanding of what they pretended to urge, as to this particular, we must observe that in *Ethiopia* they call an
Altar

Altar Stone *Tabot*, which Name signifies the Ark of the Covenant, Tabot, *an* and the same they give to *Noah's* Ark. It is also well known, *Altar Stone,* that in the Infancy of Christianity, the Altars were of Wood, and &c. like little Chests, and there were no other Altar Stones, till the Time when St. *Silvester* Pope began to Consecrate Altar Stones; But leaving in St *Peters* Church the little Wooden Chest, which had for so many Years serv'd as an Altar to so many holy Popes, and on which none but his Holiness is now permitted to say Mass.

From this ancient Custom of the Church, seems to be deriv'd that which the *Abyssines* still observ'd, of saying Mass on little *Rather a Chest* Chests, and therefore they gave it the Name of *Tabot*, signifying *to say Mass* the Ark of the Covenant, and they thought they added much Re- *on.* putation to their Church of *Auxum* or *Aczum*, by saying their Chest or *Tabot*, was the very Ark of the Old Testament that was in *Solomon's* Temple, and that God brought it so miraculously in-to *Ethiopia*; the Inventor of this Fable never reflecting, that it is directly contrary to the holy Text, 2 *Machab.* Chap. 2. v. 4 and 5. where it is said, *That the Prophet being warn'd by God, commanded the Tabernacle and the Ark to go with him, as he went forth into the Mountain where* Moses *climb'd up, and saw the Heritage of GOD. And when* Jeremy *came thither, he found an hollow Cave, wherein he laid the Tabernacle and the Ark, and the Altar of Incense, and so stop'd the Door.*

This the Scripture delivers plain enough, but they will not hear of it, much less submit to what the Fathers of the Society urg'd *Ethiopians* upon this Point, so positive are Men in their Errors, that some *obstinate.* make their Appetite their God, and others have no Gospel but their Opinion. The *Abyssines* to gain more Respect to this little Chest of theirs, always kept it so close and conceal'd, that they would not show it even to their Emperors. They call it by way of excellency *Sion*, or *Seon*, as they pronounce it, and for the same Reason the Church, where they kept this to them so precious a Relick, being dedicated to the Virgin *Mary*, had the Name of S. *Mary* of Seon.

Not many Years since, perceiving that the Catholick Faith be- *Hide their* gan to spread abroad, and fearing lest this little Chest of theirs *honour'd* should be taken away, or disregarded, the most Zealous of their *Chest.* Monks remov'd it thence, and very privately convey d it to the Territory of *Bur* near the Red Sea, where they hid it among close Thickets and vast high Mountains, in order at a convenient Time to restore it to its ancient Place, in the Church of *Auxum* or *Ac-zum*, where in all likelyhood it now is, since their Revolt, of which we shall speak hereafter.

This

This is what is known in *Ethiopia*, concerning the Religion they followed from the Days of the Queen of *Sheba*, till the Conversion of Queen *Candace*'s Eunuch to the Faith of *CHRIST*, which is above 1000 Years; for according to the Computation of our most diligent Writer *F. Cornelius a Lapide, in Synopf. ad Tom. Gen. &c.* from the building of *Solomon*'s Temple till the Birth of *CHRIST*, there elaps'd 1017 Years. We will next come to the Emperors that Reign'd after the Queen of *Sheba*.

C H A P. XIV.

Of the Emperors that reign'd in Ethiopia *after* Solomon's *Son, and particularly of one call'd* Lalibela.

Number of Emperors.

THIS Empire is of great Antiquity, and had always a Succession of Emperors, tho' in their Books they only make mention of them since the Days of the Queen of *Sheba*; and from that Time to the Birth of our Saviour they reckon 24 Emperors, and from our Saviour to the present Emperor *Faciladas* there were 68. [*Observe this Emperor was at the Time the Author writ, which was in the Year 1659, and the same may be taken notice of in other Places, where he speaks of the present Time.*] I will here give a brief Account of these Kings, which *F. Emanuel d' Almeyda* faithfully translated at large from their Book of the Church of *Auxum* or *Aczum*, and another Book of the Emperor *Sultan Segued*, and I will adjoin the Years answerable to those of the *European* Emperors, that we may guess about what Time they reign'd.

Queen of Sheba.

The first Royal Person nam'd in those Books is the Queen of *Sheba*, who is there also call'd *Negueſta Azeb*, which is the same as Queen of the South, as our Saviour call'd her in the Gospel. This Queen, as was said in the last Chapter, went to *Jerusalem* in the fourth Year of *Solomon*'s Reign, and had by him a Son call'd *Menilehec*, by another Name *David*. It is said of her, that after her return Home, she reign'd 25 Years, and her Son *Menilehec*

Menilehec her Son.

rul'd 29 Years, and according to this she liv'd to the 29th Year of *Solomon*, and her Son was 11 Years contemporary with him, and the other 18 with *Rehoboam*.

Menilehec

Menilehec had a Son call'd *Sagdur*, and there was a Succeſſion 24 *Kings be-fore our Sa-viour.* of 24 Kings from Father to Son till King *Phacen*, who was contemporary with *Auguſtus Cæfar*, and in the 8th Year of this *Phacen* our Saviour was Born. From this Year of the Birth of our Saviour, till 527 there were 13 Emperors in *Ethiopia*, at which Time 13 *Others.* two Brothers call'd *Abra* and *Abza* rul'd jointly in a peaceable and friendly manner, a Thing rare between Brothers ſwaying the ſame Scepter, which allows of no Brotherly Affection, nor Fidelity to one another, according to that certain Rule of *Lucan*, lib. 10. *Nulla fides regni ſociis, &c.* In the Days of theſe two Brothers S. *Frumentius* came into *Ethiopia*, ſent by S. *Athanaſius*, as we ſhall relate, and it is likely his coming was in the beginning of their Reign.

After them Three other Brothers call'd *Azfa*, *Azfed* and *Amey* 3 *Brothers Reign at once.* reign'd jointly, of whom it is ſaid, that for their better Governing in Peace, and without interfering with one another; they divided the Days into 3 parts, which was doubtleſs an odd ſort of Government, and ſubject to more Confuſion; yet the *Abyſſinians* will perſuade us, that it proſper'd well with them. Their Succeſſors were *Arado*, *Aladoba* and *Amiamid*, and at this Time their Books ſay, many Religious Men came from *Rum*, who, as ſhall be ſhown, enter'd the Kingdom of *Tigre* about the Year 424 little over or under. After *Amiamid* reign'd *Tacena*, and then *Caleb*, who anſwers to the Time of the Emperor *Juſtinian* in *Europe*, which was about the Year of Grace 521; and this *Caleb* is the ſame that Cardinal *Baronius*, and the Acts of the Holy Martyr S. *Aretas*, call *Elesbaan*. The *Roman* Martyrology, and the ſaid *Baronius* call him a Saint, and as ſuch he is reckon'd, as ſhall be ſhown hereafter.

From the Year 521, till 960, when *Del Noad* reign'd, there *A Time of Uſurpation.* was a Succeſſion of 19 Kings, and at this time the Line of *Solomon's* Poſterity was interrupted, and a Family call'd *Zague* enter'd upon the Government, and held the Empire 340 Years, for ſo many there are from 960 to 1300, about which time, according to the Catalogues of theſe Emperors, and the general receiv'd Opinion of *Ethiopia*, *Iohunn Amalat* Reign'd, in whom the Poſterity of *Solomon* was reſtor'd to the Empire, and thoſe are the only Emperors there taken notice of, for I do not now ſpeak of thoſe, who intruded themſelves into the Empire, which did not belong to them.

From this *Iohunn*, who Reign'd about the Year 1300 till *Zara* *The right Line reſtor'd.* *Jacob*, who Govern'd about 1437, they reckon 16 Emperors. In the Days of this *Zara Jacob* the *Florentine* Council was held, as ſhall be hinted hereafter, and this was he that deſir'd to reduce his Empire to the Catholick Faith, and in order to it writ Letters
and

and sent some of his *Abyssinians* to Pope *Eugenius* the 4th, who then govern'd the Church, and answer'd him in a Letter mention'd by the Emperor *David*, or *Onad Segued* of *Ethiopia*, as will be seen hereafter, in a Letter he writ to Pope *Clement* the 7th. After *Zara Jacob* follow'd *Beda Mariam*, and after him *Escander*, or *Alexander*, in whose Days *Peter da Covilham* came into *Ethiopia*, about the Year 1491. The next was *Audeseon*, who Reign'd but 6 Months, and then *Naod* Rul'd 13 Years, answering to the Year of our Lord 1500. Next came *Onag Segued*, otherwise call'd *David*, in whose Days *Don Roderick de Lima* enter'd *Ethiopia*, with the Embassy from King *Emanuel* of *Portugal*, and with him went *F. Francis Alvarez*, often mention'd in this History. *David* began his Reign in 1507, and held it till 1540. In his Days the *Moor Granbe* enter'd *Ethiopia*, destroying and conquering the greatest part of it, as we shall see hereafter.

AsnafSegued or Claudius Emperor. *Asnaf Segued*, otherwise call'd *Claudius*, or as the *Ethiopians* name him *Glaudios*, succeeded his Father *David*, to succour whom *Don Christopher da Gama* came into *Ethiopia* with 400 *Portugueses*, who restor'd the Empire and slew *Granbe*. This Emperor ascended the Throne in 1540, and dy'd in 1548. Then follow'd *Adamas Segued*, by another Name *Minas*, and this was he who persecuted and banish'd the Patriarch *Don Andrew de Oviedo*. His Successor was *Malac Segued*, who began his Rule in 1573, and dy'd in 1597. In his Days dy'd the aforesaid Patriarch *Don Andrew*, and the other Fathers his Companions, as shall be shown, this Emperor neither persecuting, nor favouring them, but suffering them to live at *Fremona* and administer the Sacraments to the *Portugueses*. The next *Jacob* rul'd 7 Years; then *Za Danguil*, after whose Death *Jacob* reign'd again, whose Competitor was *Socinios*, otherwise *Sultan Segued*. The Controversie lasted 3 Years, *Socinios* prevailing in the end and governing 25 Years, without including the 3 the Civil War lasted, for there are so many from 1607, when *Jacob* dy'd, till 1632, when he ended his Reign with his Life.

All these make 99 Emperors descended from *Solomon*, and it is no small Reputation to the *Abyssines*, to show so great Antiquity, and produce a Line of Kings for so many Ages to this Time, when that Empire is much decay'd, by the Neighbourhood of the *Gallas*, and the Tyranny of the *Turks*, as this History will show. (*I know not how to reconcile the Author to himself here, saying the Emperors were 99, whereas before he says, there were but 24 before Christ, and from thence till his writing 68, which in all make but 92.*) I have not here taken notice of the Queen Women not taken notice of. of *Sheba*, or of Queen *Candace*, or the Empress *Helen*, because it

is

is not the Custom of the *Abyssines* to Name Women in these Catalogues of theirs, wherein they also follow the Custom of the *Jews*, from whom they descend, who, as *S. Jerome* observes, did not use to take notice of Females, in their *Genealogies*.

We have thus given a very brief account of the Emperors of *Ethiopia*, descended from *Solomon* in a direct Male Line, for a- *Lalibela, a great Emperor.* mong them they do not admit of those who descended by the Females. I took no notice of those, who usurp'd the Empire, during that Interval the Family of *Zague* Rul'd, for the reason before given; but among them there was one call'd *Lalibela*, who prov'd very potent, had great Dominions and was extraordinary fortunate, not only in regard of his long peaceable Possession of the Empire, which lasted 40 Years, and for leaving a Son to succeed him, who govern'd as long; but also for his greatness of Mind, in erecting sumptuous Structures, which perpetuated his Name in *Ethiopia*. He caus'd many notable Architects to be brought out of *Egypt*; where there were always some famous, since the raising of the celebrated Pyramids, and spent 24 Years in building 10 admirable Churches, after an unusual and won- *Churches* derful Method, for they were all hew'd out of solid Rocks, and *hew'd out* most curiously contriv'd. So that as in other stately Works we *of solid Rocks.* admire how much they increase by the addition of the Stones the Workmen lay on; in these prodigious Churches the Work increas'd as the Stone diminish'd, for all the advancing of the Structure depended on what was hew'd from it. The Names of the Churches were these, *S. Emanuel, S. Saviour, S. Mary, the Holy Cross, S. George, Golgotha, Bethlehem, Marcoreos, the Martyrs* and *Lalibela*. This last, which is the chiefest, and finest Structure retain'd the Name of the Founder of them all, well deserv'd by a Prince so magnanimous and of such singular Piety, who in a Country where there ever were such mean Structures, and so great a Scarcity of Builders, had Resolution and Treasure enough to bring those notable Artists from so far, which must be an extraordinary Expence, and to erect such singular Works, worthy to be reckon'd among the most sumptuous and wonderful in the World. The particular Description of these Churches I leave to *F. Francis Alvarez*, who saw them himself, as he writes in his History.

On Account of these Renowned and Pious Works, the com- *Lalibela* mon People look'd upon this Emperor as a Saint, and perhaps he *reckon'd a* might be so; I will here set down what we find written con- *Saint.* cerning him, in a Book of theirs. *On the 17th of June*, says the Book, *the blessed, unspotted Contemplator of the Heavenly Mysteries, Lalibela, Emperor of* Ethiopia, *went to rest: When this Saint was*

L born,

born, his Parents educated him in the Fear of God; and when he was grown up a Youth, the Emperor his Brother was told, that he should possess his Empire and sit upon his Throne; whereupon he grew envious, sent for him, and order'd him to be whipt, but the Stripes did not touch him, the Angel of the Lord delivering him, which Angel reveal'd to him, that he should build the Ten Churches, and when he had done building them, he rested in Peace.

Abraham
another.

Thus far their Book, which is no Gospel, but relates many Aprocryphal Stories, as *F. Emanuel de Almeyda* informs us, and as such I look upon what *F. Francis Alvarez* tells us, that he saw written in a Book they kept in that Church, wherein it is said, That a King, whose Name was *Abraham,* liv'd there a retir'd Life, for the space of 40 Years, and that he was a Priest, and said Mass every Day, for which an Angel daily supply'd him with Bread and Wine. I question not but he was a Holy Man, if the Angel came thus to attend him; but it does not appear that there was any such Emperor then in *Ethiopia.*

This short Account of the Emperors of *Ethiopia* will give us some Light, for the better understanding of this History; and as we have seen the Original of the Knowledge of the true God in *Ethiopia*; so shall we now see how the Faith of JESUS CHRIST came into this Empire. The famous *Portugueze* Historian *James de Conto* Decad. 7. lib. 1. cap. 8. brings a long Catalogue of the Emperors of *Ethiopia,* but not upon such certain Information.

C H A P. XV.

At what Time and in what manner the Knowledge of the Faith of CHRIST was brought into Ethiopia; a Proof of it out of the Ethiopian Books; a farther Confirmation of it.

AS to the Knowledge of the Faith of JESUS CHRIST, it is a most unquestion'd Tradition among the *Ethiopians*, that they receiv'd it by means of the Eunuch and great Favourite to *Candace*, Queen of *Ethiopia*, of whom mention is made in the Acts of the Apostles, *chap.* 8. I will here deliver this Story in the same Words it is written in the aforemention'd Book of *Auxum*, or *Acxum*, whence F. *Emanuel de Almeyda* took it, and it runs thus.

Before the Queen of Sheba *went to* Jerusalem *to hear the Wisdom of* Solomon, *all the People of* Ethiopia *were Heathens; but at her Return, she brought them the History of* Genesis, *and they continu'd in the* Jewish *Law, till the coming of* CHRIST. *After that, Queen* Candace's *Eunuch's going to* Jerusalem *to pay his Worship on the Feast of the* Passover, *was the cause of their becoming Christians, for the Gentiles, who embrac'd the Jewish Law, went to* Jerusalem *at the* Passover, *becaus it was not lawful for them to offer Sacrifice in their own Country, but in the Place where the Name of God was call'd upon. And as the said Eunuch was returning, the Angel of the Lord spoke to* Philip, *and said to him,* Arise and go towards the South to the way that goes down from *Jerusalem* to *Gaza* in the Desert. *He went thither and found an* Ethiopian, Eunuch *to Queen* Candace *of* Ethiopia, *who was Treasurer of all her Wealth and came to adore in* Jerusalem, *and was returning into his Country in his Chariot; and* Philip *coming up, heard he read a Prophecy of* Isaiah, *and ask'd him,* Whether he understood what he read? *He, answer'd,* How should he understand it, unless some body taught him? *And intreated* Philip *to come up into his Chariot, which he did, and taking occasion from what he ask'd, concerning that Prophecy, he preach'd to him* JESUS CHRIST, *converted, instructed him in the Faith and baptiz'd him. Then the Spirit took away* Philip, *and he saw the Eunuch no more, He continuing his Journey very joyfully, for what*

had

Story of Q. Candace.

had hapned to him, came into Ethiopia, *and to his Miftreffes Palace, and telling this Story, they believ'd in the Gofpel of the Grace of JESUS CHRIST.* Thus far the *Ethiopian* Book, which is almoft the fame we read in the above-quoted place of the Acts of the Apoftles.

Ethiopia the firft Country Converted,

The Hiftories of *Ethiopia* farther add, That, when our Saviour was born, *Bacepa* Reign'd, being the twentieth King from *Menilehec*, the Son of *Solomon.* (*Note here, that the Author before calls this King* Phacen, *and fays he was the 24th Emperor from* Menilehec, *which is a grofs miftake, as well as that before obferv'd.*) It is no fmall honour to the *Abyffinians* to have been the firft of all Forreign Nations that embrac'd the Faith of CHRIST, after the Apoftles began to fpread it through the World ; and fo it is many Fathers expound thofe Words of the 68 *Pfalm, ver.* 31. Ethiopia *fhall foon ftretch out her Hands unto God;* becaufe it fubmitted to CHRIST before any other Province in the World.

But imperfectly

But that Eunuch being no Bifhop, nor fo much as a Prieft in *Ethiopia,* and having but an imperfect Knowledge of the Myfteries of the Faith, as being inftructed and baptiz'd upon the Road, and that by *Philip,* who was a Deacon, and neither Apoftle, nor Bifhop, who are the Fathers of fpiritual Life, and by Impofition of their Hands can in Spirit beget Sons, that may alfo be Fathers, his Preaching was not in fuch perfect Knowledge as might be requifite, and they only receiv'd a confufe Idea of the Faith of CHRIST, and continu'd in the Obfervation of the Law of *Mofes,* till S. *Athanafius* was preferr'd to S. *Mark's* Chair at *Alexandria,* in the Year of our Lord 326; for in his Time God ordain'd the Faith fhould extend all over *Ethiopia,* and that there fhould be a Bifhop in it and Priefts.

S. Matthew not in Ethiopia.

As for S. *Matthew's* coming into this *Ethiopia* and preaching the Gofpel, it is a thing the *Abyffinians* know nothing of, and altogether groundlefs, and when the *Jefuits* told them, that our Hiftories gave an Account of it, they anfwer'd, It muft be underftood of the lower *Ethiopia,* which ftretches from *Suaghem* up the Inland, as far as *Egypt;* for they never knew any thing of S. *Matthew,* or any other Apoftle coming into their Country, as their Books teftifie, and all thofe affirm, who among them value themfelves upon having any Knowledge of Antiquity.

The occafion and manner of the Faith of CHRIST being more formally introduc'd into *Ethiopia,* in my Opinion, was that we find in *Ruffinus* his Ecclefiaftical Hiftory, *lib.* 1. *cap.* 9. The learned Cardinal *Baronius* gave fuch entire Credit to him, that he inferted all his Relation in the 3d Volume of his Annals, in the Year of Grace 327, when he thinks it happen'd, which had been

before

before done by *Socrates*, *Sozomen* and *Theodoret*. Yet none of the four knew certainly, which the Country was they spoke of; thinking it enough to say, that the great Conversion they treated of happen'd in the Lower, or Hither *India*, as it really was. But *Ruffinus* was mistaken, in placing it, beyond the Gulph of *Persia*, between the *Parthians* and the *Medes*, whereas he should have brought it into this *Ethiopia*, near the Red Sea. And whereas the Connexion there is between this Story of *Ruffinus*, and that the *Abyssinians* tell us of their Conversion, was before unknown; it has pleas'd God to discover this Truth to the Fathers of the Society, who were there, by reading our Books, and those of *Ethiopia*, comparing them both together. To come to the Relation *Ruffinus* in his Tripartite History speaks thus.

‘ A certain Philosopher born at *Tyre*, whose name was *Me-*   Ethiopia
‘ropius, being desirous to Travel through *India*, left his Coun-   *when converte*
‘ try, taking along with him two Children his Nephews, whom   *ed out of*
‘ he instructed in the liberal Arts. The Youngest of them was   Ruffinus.
‘ call'd *Edesius*, the Elder *Frumentius*. Having travell'd and seen
‘ all he desir'd, he return'd towards *Tyre*, but falling short of
‘ Water and Provisions, was oblig'd to put into a certain Port
‘ of Barbarians with his Ship. It is the Custom of that Nation
‘ when any Ship arrives there, to enquire of the Neighbouring
‘ People, whether the Peace they have made with the *Romans*
‘ holds good, and if they hear of any Breach, they immediately
‘ fall upon the Mariners, and kill all the *Romans* they find among
‘ them. On this pretence they seiz'd on the Philosopher, taking
‘ the Ship and killing all the Men in it. The two Children were,
‘ at this Time, ashore, resting themselves, and conning their Lessons.
‘ The Barbarians seeing them, and being mov'd to Compassion, spar'd
‘ their Lives, and carry'd them as a Present to their King, who
‘ was so fond of them, that he made *Edesius* his Cup-Bearer,
‘ and finding *Frumentius* more solid and understanding entrusted
‘ him with all his Writings, and Accounts. The King dying,
‘ appointed the Queen to Govern his Dominions, till his Eldest
‘ Son, then under Age, was capable of the Administration; and
‘ gave the two Youths their Liberty, and free leave to go where-
‘ soever they pleas'd.

‘ They being about to prepare to return into their own Coun-   Frumentius
‘ try, the Queen earnestly intreated them to stay, and assist her   Governs.
‘ in the Government, till such time as her Son was of Age to
‘ manage it himself, being destitute of Persons of such Experience,
‘ and whom she could so well trust as they. This she did chiefly
‘ on account of *Frumentius*, whose Wisdom was such, that he
‘ alone could have govern'd larger Kingdoms; for *Edesius* was a
‘ plainer

'plainer Man. They two having the ordering of all Things,
'God mov'd the Heart of *Frumentius*, who was a Christian, ob-
'serving that *Roman* Merchants resorted to that Country, to en-
'quire, whether there were any Christians among them, whom
'he sent for, show'd them extraordinary Kindness, and allow'd
'them great Privileges, to the end they might meet in some Towns,
'and there offer up their Prayers, after the *Roman* manner. He
'himself would be present, and invited the People of the Country
'with Gifts and Kindness, allowing them to Embrace the Faith
'of CHRIST, to which he drew many of them. When the
'Prince was of Age and Discretion to take the Government upon
'him; tho' both he and his Mother us'd all endeavours to retain
'the two Brothers, they could not prevail.

It made Bi-
shop.

'Returning homewards, *Edesius* made all Speed to *Tyre*, to
'see his Parents and Kindred; but *Frumentius* went to *Alexandria*,
'where S. *Athanasius* had not long been Patriarch, to whom he
'gave an account of all his Adventures, and the good Disposition
'there was in that Country for a plentiful Harvest of Souls,
'telling him it would be convenient to send some Bishop thither,
'to take Charge of those Churches and Christians there were al-
'ready. S. *Athanasius* assembling the Bishops, looking upon *Fru-*
'*mentius*, and considering his Actions, his Words, his Zeal, and
'Understanding, said to him in the midst of them all. *Whom
'can we find equal to your self, on whom the Divine Spirit may so
'much reside, and operate?* And Consecrating him Bishop, he
'order'd him to return, with his Blessing, and the Grace of the

Converts E-
thiopia.

'Lord. *Frumentius* returning for *India*, was so full and replenish'd
'with the virtue of the most high, that he wrought many Mi-
'racles, not inferiour to those of the Apostles, by which many
'became Christians in those Parts of *India*, many Churches were
'built, and many Priests ordain'd. This we do not deliver without
'good grounds, only upon Hearsay, but having had it from the
'Mouth of *Edesius* himself, who had been Companion to *Fru-*
'*mentius*, having met him at *Tyre*, where he was a Priest. These
'are the Words of *Ruffinus*, inserted by *Baronius* in his 3d Vo-
'lume, in the Year of CHRIST 327.

This Story we find almost in the same Words and Method,
in several *Ethiopian* Books, and particularly in that they so
highly value of the Church of *Auxum*, or *Atzum*, which delivers
it thus.

The same from
the Ethi-
opian Books.

'After many Years were past, a Merchant came from *Tyre*,
'with two Servants, the one call'd *Fremenatos* and the other *Sy-*
'*dracos*, and the Merchant falling sick, dy'd near the Sea, in the
'Dominions of *Ethiopia*; for which Reason the Youths were
brought

' brought to the King, who was well pleas'd with them, and or-
' der'd they should be with his own Sons. They wonder'd
' much at the People of *Ethiopia*, and ask'd them, How they
' came to believe in the Faith of CHRIST, because they saw
' them Pray and Adore the most Blessed Trinity, and that their
' Women wore the Sign of the Holy Cross on their Heads, and
' they prais'd God, who had been so merciful to those People, as
' that they should believe without preaching, and receive the Faith
' without an Apostle. They continu'd in that King's Court
' whilst he liv'd, and at his Death he discharg'd and gave them
' leave to go whither they pleas'd.

' *Sydracos* therefore return'd to his own Country *Tyre*; and *Fre-*
' *monatos* went to the Patriarch of *Alexandria*, desiring him to
' provide for the Salvation of the *Ethiopians*, and told him all he
' had seen, and how they believ'd, without having been taught
' by the Apostles. The Patriarch rejoyc'd very much, and gave
' great Praise to God, for his mercy in acquainting them with his
' Holy Faith. Then he said to *Fremonatos*, you shall be their
' Pastor, for God has chosen and rais'd You. Then after Ordaining
' him Priest, he made him Bishop of *Ethiopia*; and he returning
' baptiz'd the Natives, and ordain'd many Priests and Deacons,
' to assist him, and was much honour'd and respected by all Men.
' And because he brought Peace, they call'd him *Abba Salama*,
' which signifies Father of Peace, or Peaceable. His coming into
' *Ethiopia* was in the Reign of *Abra* and *Azba*, Brothers, who
' receiv'd the Doctrine of Holiness, as the dry Earth receives the
' Rain from Heaven. Thus far the Book of *Auxum*, or *Azxum*.
In another containing the Life of *Abba Tecla Haymanot*, of whom
we shall speak hereafter; it is expres'd, that the Patriarch of *Alex-*
andria who consecrated *Fremonatos* and sent him into *Ethiopia*
was S. *Athanasius* ; and this is the Tradition and Belief of all
those, who in this Country know any thing of History.

Both these Histories, as well the *Ethiopian*, as ours agree that *Consent be-*
S. *Athanasius* was the Patriarch, who Consecrated *Fremonatos*, or *tween the two*
Frumentius; and all the *Ethiopian* Books consent that this was *Relations.*
the beginning of the Conversion of the *Abyssines* to the Faith
of CHRIST, there being no material Difference; for they only
vary in not calling *Meropius* by his Name, and not saying he was
a Philosopher, but a Merchant of *Tyre*, and that he dy'd a natural Death, and that the younger of the Lads was call'd *Sydra-*
cbos, and in calling *Frumentius Fremonatos*, which does not at all
lessen the Credit, or the Connection of the Story.

For as to the first Point, the *Ethiopian* Writers might per- *Difficulties*
haps not know the Name of *Meropius*, who was a Stranger *reconcil'd.*
and

and as for saying he dy'd a natural and not a violent Death, either they might believe so, or be asham'd to own such a piece of Barbarity and Cruelty of their Country, as the murdering of a Stranger that came upon their Coast. Nor is it any Contradiction to call him a Merchant and not a Philosopher, for it is well known that many of the Ancient Philosophers were also Merchants, as *Solon, Thales, Crates, Zenon, Hippocrates,* and *Plato*; which Custom was also at *Tyre,* where the Merchants were not only Philosophers, but also Princes and Governours, as appears by those Words of *Isaiah* chap. 23. v. 6. *Who hath taken this Counsel against* Tyre, *the crowning City, whose Merchants are Princes, whose Traffickers are the honourable of the Earth?* And the Traders of *Tyre,* had settled their Trade towards *India,* on the Red-Sea, at the Port we now call *Tor,* or *Gibel-Tor,* as being at the Foot of Mount *Sinai,* and in sight of it and the *Arabs* calling a Mountain *Gibel,* they therefore call'd Mount *Sinai, Gibelter,* because it stands over the Town of *Tor.*

Tyrians trading to India. Here it is likely *Meropius* embark'd for *India,* being of *Tyre,* and this might be the Port he directed his Course to in his return, but was forc'd into *Maxua,* 45 Leagues from *Auxum,* or *Axxum,* the Metropolis of *Ethiopia.* By reason of this Trade, the *Tyrian* Mariners were as well acquainted with the Red-Sea, as the *Mediterranean,* on whose shore their City stood, and those who came from *India* for *Tyre* by Sea, must needs run up the Red-Sea to *Tor,* or some other nearer Harbour, whence they might Travel by Land to *Tyre*; but they putting into *Maxua* were carry'd to *Auxum,* or *Axxum.*

Ethiopia call'd India. Nor was *Etesius* mistaken, in calling *Ethiopia* by the Name of *India*; but *Ruffinus* was out in not knowing, and misplacing it. For the People of *Phœnicia, Syria,* and *Egypt* give the Name of *India* to all that Tract of Land, which stretches out to the Eastward from *Suez,* on both sides the Sea, and particularly to *Ethiopia* above *Egypt,* which is the *Abyssine* Empire we speak of. *Marcus Antonius Sabellicus Ænead.* 10. lib. 8. writes out of *Herodotus,* that a great number of People swarm'd out of *India* into *Arick,* and being settled and increasing there, gave it the name of the Country they came from, calling it *India*; as we see the *Vandals,* gave the name of *Vandalia* to that Province of *Spain,* we corruptly call *Andaluxia*; and *Virgil* speaking of the *Nile,* which has its Source in *Ethiopia,* as has been observ'd, says it rises among the *Indians.*

Usque coloratis Amnis devexus ab Indis. Georg. 4.

Eucherius

Eucherius on the 1st Book of Kings, calls the Queen of *Sheba*, *Indian*; and *Procopius* on *Isaiah*, *Ethiopian*. Which name was ever after continu'd to the *Abyssinians*, as appears by a Letter Pope *Alexander* the 3d sent the Emperor of *Ethiopia*, in the Year 1174, by *Philip*, a Physician, mention'd by Cardinal *Baronius* in his 12th Volume, the Superscription whereof runs thus, *Charissimo in Christo Filio, illustri & magnifico Indorum Regi, &c.* To our most dearly beloved Son in CHRIST, the Illustrious and Magnificent King of the *Indians*, &c. *Marcus Paulus Venetus*, who travell'd all over the East, about the Year 1300, calls *Abyssinia* the middle *India*; yet not properly, because to be call'd the middle, there ought to be another below it, however the name of *India* is allow'd.

Nor is the Connexion between these two Relations any way lessen'd by the *Ethiopian* Books calling *Frumentius*'s Companion *Sidracos* and not *Edesius*; for as much as it is an ancient Custom of Masters to give new Names to their Slaves, as we see in *Daniel* and his Companions, one of whom, *viz. Ananias*, was by the Prince of the Eunuchs call'd *Shadrac*, which is the same as *Sidrac*, or *Sidracos*. In the Name of *Frumentius* the Alteration was small at first; calling him *Fremonatos*, and many other Names are much more alter'd in *Ethiopia*, for they call S. *Sylvester*, *Solpetros*; S. *Damasus*, *Damaris*; S. *Dionysius*, *Dionaceos*; S. *Ildefonsus*, *Decios*, and so others. Four Leagues Eastward of *Auxum*, or *Aczum*, which was their Metropolis, as appears by a Place in S. *Athanasius*, which we shall soon quote, stands a Town, the most famous and frequented in all the Kingdom of *Tigre*. It is call'd *Fremona*, where the Fathers of the Society had their first and principal Residence, and it seems to have been so to S. *Fremonatos*, and he to have taken this first Name from it. **Names frequently chang'd.**

Afterwards, the People observing the Sanctity of their Prelate, and that he had made Peace betwixt God and them, they call'd him *Abba Salama*, which signifies, Peaceable Father. From him to *Simon*, who was the *Abuna*, that rebell'd with *Elos* against the Emperor *Sultan Segued*, and was kill'd at the Battel of *Sada*, in the Year 1618, as shall be said hereafter, they reckon 95 *Abuna's*; and this Holy *Abba-Salama*, or *Fremonatos*, was still living in the Year 356, which was the 20th of the Emperor *Constantius*, when that Emperor being an *Arian* Heretick, had put *George* an *Arian* Patriarch into *Alexandria*, in the Place of S. *Athanasius*, as is to be seen in the Life of that Saint and many other Books; and the Saint absconding, the wicked Emperor thought he was fled into *Ethiopia*, to his Son *Frumentius*, and therefore writ to the *Ethiopian* Monarch and Governors of *Auxum* or *Aczum*, that Letter S. *Athanasius* **Frumentius call'd Abba-Salama.**

nasius

nasius mentions in his first Apology, entitul'd thus : *Hæc adversus Frumentium Episcopum Auxumeos, Tyrannis ejus loci Scripta sunt :* That is, This was writ to the Governors of *Auxum*, against *Frumentius* the Bishop of that Place. And in the Letter, the heretical Emperor testifies, that *S. Frumentius* was confecrated Bishop by *S. Athanasius* in these Words : *Ye know and remember, unless ye pretend to be Ignorant of such Things as are notoriously manifest, that* Frumentius *was chosen to this Rank by* Athanasius, *a Man guilty of all sorts of Ills*. And to conclude, he orders them, in case *Athanasius* be among them to send him to *Alexandria*, to be punished, and with him *Frumentius* to be instructed, and confirm'd by George the *Arian* Bishop. Cardinal *Baronius* handles this Point, *Anno Christi* 356. *num*. 18.

Bellarmin his mistake. This makes out a mistake in the said Cardinal *Baronius*, who in his Notes on the *Roman* Martyrology on the 27th of *October*, where in the said Martyrology he makes mention of our *S. Frumentius* or *Fremonatos*, says, that in the Days of *S. Athanasius* there were two Bishops, who bore the Name of *Frumentius*, the one confecrated by that Saint, Bishop of the Lower *India*, whose Feast is kept on that Day, and of whom we here treat ; and the other Bishop of *Auxume*, a City in *Egypt*, of whom *S Athanasius* makes mention in his first Apology. But *S. Frumentius* and the Bishop of *Auxume* or *Auxum*, is the same with him of the lower *India* ; for *Auxum* was the Capital City of it, as has been shown. Nor does *Ptolemy*, tho' an *Egyptian* and of *Alexandria*, in his Tables or Geography, Name any City call'd *Auxume* in *Egypt*, but in *Ethiopia*, above *Egypt*, which is this we speak of, and in the same Place where the Ruins of it are now, and he calls it a Royal City, as may be seen in the 5th Book of his Geography, *cap* 8. and in the 4th Table of *Africk*.

Besides the same Letter from *Constantius* plainly proves, that *Auxum*, where *Frumentius* was Bishop, and which is there spoken of, was not a City in *Egypt* ; for there are these Words in it : *Therefore send the Bishop* Frumentius, *as soon as possible into* Egypt, *to the most Venerable* George, *and other Bishops in* Egypt, *who have the Supream Authority in treating and judging of Bishops*. So that had *Auxume*, where *Frumentius* was Bishop, been a City in *Egypt*, there was no need for the Emperor to order him to be brought into *Egypt*, and be presented before the Bishops of *Egypt*. But as *Ruffinus* Error of Ruffinus. was mistaken in placing the hither *India*, whereof *Edesius* spoke to him, near *Parthia*, so Cardinal *Baronius* err'd in not placing the City *Auxume* in this lower *India*, or *Ethiopia* above *Egypt*, but in *Egypt* itself ; which may sometimes happen to those who do not write what they saw, but what they receive from others.

A

A further Proof hereof is, that the Governors of *Auxum* are in that Letter call'd *Tyranni*; for this Name the *Romans* gave to all Kings and Great Men who were not their Subjects, as those of *Ethiopia* were not; whereas all *Egypt* was theirs, since the Days of *Augustus Cæsar* and *Cleopatra*, who was the last Queen of *Egypt*.

The King to whom the two Lads *Edesius* and *Frumentius* were presented as Slaves, was in all likelyhood *Agder*, between whom *Two Kings* and *Bacenà*, who reign'd in our Saviour's Days, the Catalogue of *reigning* Kings of *Ethiopia* places 13 others. The Child at his Death left *jointly.* under Age to govern, was perhaps *Abrà*, who seems to have associated to him in the Kingdom another younger Brother call'd *Azba*; for all the *Ethiopian* Books tell us, that when S. *Frumentius* return'd into *Ethiopia*, consecrated Bishop by S. *Athanasius*, two Brothers call'd *Abrà* and *Azba* reign'd jointly, and that in their Days there were great Numbers converted to the Law of *CHRIST*.

Genebrardus in his Chronicon makes mention of them, by the *At what* Name of Defenders and Spreaders of the Christian Religion, and *Time.* that in the 17th Year of their Reign, the Faith extended wonderfully; but he was mistaken, in making them an hundred Years more Modern than they really were; for he says they liv'd in the Year of *CHRIST* 460, whereas the utmost they could live to must be 360, because the said two Brothers were reigning when S. *Frumentius* return'd from *Alexandria*, consecrated Bishop by S. *Athanasius*, who was lately made Patriarch, and begun to be so in the Year 326: So that S. *Frumentius* might return about 330, and he being still alive in 356, as has been shown, the two Brother Emperors could not probably Survive 360.

I suppose all those who shall happen to read this History, will *Ethiopia the* not make a Question of *Ethiopia's* being the lower *India*, where *Lower* India. *Meropius* landed in his Return to *Tyre*, and where S. *Frumentius* was first a Captive or Slave, and afterwards Bishop of *Auxum* or *Aczum*, and Apostle of that Nation; since in it we find an Agreement of all Circumstances of Name, Place and Actions, and did not the Power of Truth so strongly unite the Relation of *Ruffinus* and the Histories of *Ethiopia*, there could not be such Consonance between them.

By all that has been said it appears, that the Faith of *CHRIST* was brought in Form into *Ethiopia* by means of S. *Frumentius*, sent *When fully* by S. *Athanasius*, Bishop of *Alexandria*, in the Year of our Lord *converted.* 330, little more or less; for S. *Athanasius* dy'd in the Year of Grace 372, according to the best Account of Cardinal *Baronius.* *Tom.* 4. *p.* 331, and that Saint governing his Church 46 Years, his beginning being under *Constantine* the Great, who commenc'd his Reign in 326, and this Passage of *Fremonatos*, being in the beginning of S. *Athanasius*'s Rule, it follows, as has been said, that the Faith of CHRIST came into *Ethiopia* about the Year 330, little ever or under. The *Roman* Martyrology makes mention of S. *Frumentius* sent by S. *Athanasius* to this Conversion, on the 27th of *October*.

C H A P. XVI.

At what Time the Monastical Life began in Ethiopia; *with an Account of the Holy King* Kaleb.

WE have fix'd the Time, when the Knowledge of the Faith of CHRIST began more regularly in *Ethiopia*; it remains now to clear another Point, very considerable in itself, and very acceptable to the Curious, which is, at what Time the Monastical Life first came into that Empire; and in regard this Affair is much controverted, there being variety of Opinions about it, and much Falshood intermix'd with some Truth : Therefore I will here deliver what the most Reverend Patriarch of *Ethiopia, Don Alfonso Mendez* writ concerning it, in the Information he gave upon Oath, after he had with indefatigable Labour fairly extracted all he found relating to this Point in the *Ethiopian* Books, and Authors that treat of such Affairs, being himself then in *Abyssinia*.

Monks when first in Ethiopia.

' It is likely, (says he) that S. *Athanasius* did not send S *Frumentius* into *Ethiopia* alone, but that he gave him some Councellors and Affistants, of those he always had about him, who were try'd Monks of Exemplary Lives, bred up under S. *Antony*, then living, for whom he had so great an Esteem, that he writ his Life, and boasts of his Friendship and Instructions; whereof he gave Testimony when going to *Rome*, in the Year 340, being call'd by S. *Julius*, then Pope, to answer to the Calumnies laid to his Charge by the *Arians*, who took along with him *Isidorus* and *Ammonius*, two chosen Monks; the sight of whom drew the Eyes and inflam'd the Hearts of the *Roman* Court and Nobility, to imitate the Monks of *Egypt*, as S. *Jerome* testifies, *Epist.*
16.

' 16. *ad Principiam, Palladius Hiftor. Laufiac. cap* 1. mentions
' *Ifidorus*'s bearing *S. Athanafius* Company; and that *Ammonius*
' did fo, *Socrates* teftifies 4 *Hift. Ecclef. cap* 18.
' I am perfwaded, that S. *Athanafius* gave S. *Frumentius* fuch
' Companions, by the Words of S. *Jerome Epift.* 7. *ad Latam,*
' where inviting her to fend her Daughter *Paula*, then a Child, to
' her Grand-mother S. *Paula*, the Elder, that fhe might there be
' fed among the Lillies of Purity, he fays, *From* India, Perfia *and*
' Ethiopia, *we daily receive Troops of Monks.* And that it may
' appear, he does not fpeak of that *Ethiopia* which bordeis on *A-*
' *rabia*, where *Mofes* took his *Ethiopian* Wife, but that it was
' this above *Egypt*, in the 17th Epiftle to *Marcellus*, he fays, *What*
' *need we mention the* Armenians, *the* Perfians, *the* Indians, *the* Ethio-
' pians, *or* Egypt, *clofe by abounding in Monks?* From which Places
' we may collect, that the Religious Life enter'd *Ethiopia* toge-
' ther with the Faith of *CHRIST*; for according to the Compu-
' tation of Cardinal *Baronius, Tom.* 4. *anno* 372. S. *Jerome* was
' Born in the Year 342, which was the Time, a Year over or
' under, when S. *Frumentius* converted all *Ethiopia*; for about that
' Time muft fall the 17th Year of *Abra* and *Azba*, and he dy'd
' in 420: And in that Interval of Time, when he writes, the
' Monaftical Life did fo flourifh in *Ethiopia*, that Swarms of Monks
' went thence to vifit the Holy Places.
' Tho' there were already Monks in *Ethiopia* in the Days of S.
' *Jerome*, yet 50 or 60 Years after his Death, there was a great
' Increafe of them by many Monks that came in, who the *Ethio-*
' *pian* Hiftories of the Monaftery of *Auxum*, and of all the other
' Churches, fay, came from *Rum* and from *Egypt*. Thefe, it may
' be gather'd, enter'd that Country betwixt the Years 470 and
' 480. The moft renown'd of them are Nine, who fettled and
' erected Monafteries in the Kingdom of *Tigre*; which we find
' exprefly declar'd in the Life of *Tecla Haymanot*, in the Chroni-
' cles of *Auxum*, and in many other Books.
' Thefe Chronicles tell us, that after the Days of *Abra* and *Azba*,
' in whofe Time S. *Frumentius* was confecrated Bifhop, till the
' coming of thefe Religious Men, there were Six Emperors, *Azfa*,
' *Arded* and *Amey*, Brothers, who they fay divided the Days in-
' to 3 Parts, and took their Turns round in the Government, *A-*
' *rado, Aladoba*, or *Saladoba* and *Amiamid*, whom others call *Ala-*
' *mid*, and others *Alamida*; and whom F. *James Gualterius* in his
' Chronicle, rightly places in the 5th Century, under this laft
' Name. It will not be impertinent here to tranflate the very
' Words of the Chronicle of *Auxum*, which are thefe. *In the*
' *Days of* Amiamid *many Monks came from* Rum, *who fill'd all the*
Empire,

' Empire ; *Nine of them ftay'd in* Tigre, *and each of them erected a*
' *Church of his own Name.*

' To Eight of them the People of the Country gave Names af-
' ter their manner, from fomething that befel them, and only one

Nine famous ' call'd *Pantaleo* preferv'd his own. The Names are thefe, *Abba*
Monks. ' *Arogavy*, fignifying the Old Man, becaufe he was the Eldeft and
' Superior of them all ; *Abba Pantaleon, Abba Guarima, Abba A-*
' *lef. Abba Sahami, Abba Afe, Abba Licanos, Abba Adimata* ; *Ab-*
' *baos*, whom they call'd *Guba*, fignifying Swollen, becaufe he
' building his Church on a very high Mountain, where he liv'd
' alone, thofe that pafs'd by the Foot of it faid, *What high Swollen*
' *Monk is this ?* Whence this Nickname ftuck by him. Thefe
' Monks wrought extraordinary Miracles, by which they convert-
' ed a great Part of *Ethiopia*. Among the reft, they tell one of a
' great Serpent that was about *Auxum*, which devour'd many
' Men and much Cattel, and burft afunder by their Prayers. Thus
' far the Books of *Auxum*. In the Life of *Tecla Haymanos* there is
' writ as follows. *He came to the Monaftery* Damo, *built by* Abba
' Agaravi, *one of the Nine Saints that came from* Rum *and* Egypt,
' *in the Days of* Alamida, *the Son of* Saladoba, *and Predeceffor to*
' Tacena. *Thefe Nine are fo many Stars that gave Light to all the*
' *World, &c.* And fo they run on in their Praifes.

' *Rum* mention'd in thefe two Places, is not *Rome*, which the

Greece call'd ' *Abyffines* always call *Romea*, as well in their Vulgar Tongue as
Rum. ' in the learned of their Books, but *Greece*, *Thrace* and *Conftanti-*
' *nople* ; becaufe *Conftantin* removing the Seat of his Empire thither,
' and defigning in all Refpects to make it equal to *Rome*, would
' have it fo in Name alfo, calling it *New Rome*, as we read in fe-
' veral Imperial Laws, Councils, and *Greek* Hiftorians ; and with
' the Emperor and his Court all the Prime Nobility of *Rome* came
' thither, and the *Turks* afterwards making themfelves Mafters of
' *Conftantinople*, it may well be fuppos'd, from *Romans* they came
' to be call'd *Rumes*. That Emperor dividing the adjacent Lands
' of *Thrace* among his Pretorian Bands, that fo they might forget
' their Poffeffions in *Italy*, they all fettled there : whence *Thrace*
' came to change its firft Name, being from the New *Roman* In-
' habitants call'd *Romania*, which Name it ftill retains throughout
' all the *Eaft* : And as all the *Weftern* People are call'd *Frangues*,
' from the *Francs* or *French*, who went to Conquer the Holy Land,
' fo all the *Greeks*, and any other *Europeans* thereabout Subject to
: the *Turks*, are call'd *Rumes*, becaufe many of their Anceftors were
' *Romans* ; and fo *Conftantinople* and *Greece*, *Rum* for the fame Rea-
' fon. Hence came that which we find in our Hiftories of *India*,
' as *John de Barros, Couto, Maphaus, &c.* that the *Portuguezes* always

' ways forbid any *Rumes* coming thither, and they often fought
' with and overthrew them, they being *Turks*, *Greeks* and *Euro-*
' *peans*, for none then came from *Rome*.

' Thus, when thofe Hiltories tell us, that thofe Nine Monks
' came from *Rum*, we mult underftand from *Greece* and *Conftan-*
' *tinople* ; and from the Name of one of them, in which all agree
' there was no Alteration, that is *Pantaleon*, being doubtlefs a
' *Greek* Name, we may conclude that the reft were alfo *Greeks* and
' *Egyptians*, and not *Latins*.

' We farther fuppofe, that they were all of the Order of St.
' *Antony*, which at that Time flourifh'd not only in *Egypt*, that
' Saint's Native Country, but was then fpread through all *Greece*.
' For not to fpeak of the reft, they fpeak thefe very Words of *Abba*
' *Aragavi*, the Eldeft of them, in the Life of *Abba Tecla Hayma-*
' *not*, viz. That *Abba Aragavi* took the Habit of a Monk of S. *Pa-*
' *chomius*, S. *Pachomius* of S. *Macarius*, S. *Macarius* of S. *Antony*,
' *(which Words we fhall relate more at large in the* 16*th Chapter, when*
' *we fpeak of* Abba Tecla Haymanot, *who was defcended from* Abba
' Aragavi. Now if he being the Eldeft and their Superior, was
' of the Order of S. *Antony*, how could the reft chufe but be of the.
' fame ? Let us now take particular Notice of the two Names of
' *Abba Pantaleon* and *Abba Aragavi* ; for by them we fhall difco-
' ver the true Year thofe Nine Monks came into *Ethiopia*, and the
' Time that *Tecla Haymanot* liv'd in.

' In order to prove that thofe 9 Monks enter'd *Ethiopia* be-
' tween the Years 470, and 480, it mult be allow'd, as an un- *King* Elef-
' doubted Truth, that in the Year 522 *Elesbaan*, whom they call baan, *or*
' *Kaleb*, the Son of *Tacena*, and Grandfon to *Alamida*, of both Kaleb.
' whom we have fpoken, was Emperor of *Ethiopia*. This King
' *Elesbaan*, or *Kaleb*, was a Saint of great Renown, and as fuch,
' honour'd by the Church, and inferted in its Martyrology, on the
' 27th of *October*. *Simeon Metaphraftes* writ his Life, as alfo the glo-
' rious Martyrdom of S. *Aretus*, whom the *Abyffines* call *Eruck*, and
' of 340 of his Companions, put to Death by *Dunaan*, the *Jewifh*
' King of the *Homerites*, which Life is in the 5th Volume of *Surius*,
' on the 24th of *October*; and Cardinal *Baronius* in his Annals,
' in the Year of our Lord, 522.

' The fame Story tranflated litterally from *Simeon Metaphraftes* is
' in the *Ethiopian Sanquazar*, which is their *Flos Sanctorum*, or Lives
' of Saints; and King *Kaleb*'s Life is alfo by it felf, and agrees in all
' points with that of the Holy Martyrs, without any other dif-
' ference, fave only in the Names of the Kings, for they call him
' *Kaleb*, whom we Name *Elesbaan*, and him we call *Dunaan*,

' they

' they Name *Phineas*, or *Phinees*; but all we write of *Elesbaan*
' and *Dunaan* they lay of *Kaleb* and *Phineas*.

Several
Names given
to one Person.
  ' Nor is this to be look'd upon as an Objection, becaule, a-
mong the *Abyffines*, there is a great diverfity and multitude of
Names, efpecially among their Emperors, who have two at leaft
' the one given in Baptifm, the other at their Coronation. And
' not to mention the Queen of *Sheba*'s Son, who we have already
' fhow'd had three Names; that King who fent the firft Embafly
' to the *Portuguefes*, when he heard of their being come into *India*,
' was firft call'd *David*, afterwards *Lebna Dangil*, fignifying, the
' Virgin's Incenfe, and laftly *Onag Segued*. His Eldeft Son was
' nam'd *Claudios* and *Afnaf·Segued*; his Son *Sarza Danguil*, and
' *Malac Segued*, the Emperor who fent for the Fathers of the
' Society, and receiv'd them with great Honour, *Socinios* and *Sul-*
' *tan Segued*; his Son, who cruelly perfecuted and expell'd them
' *Faciladas*, or *Bafilides*, and *Sultan Segued*.

  ' Hereof there are alfo many Examples in Scripture, as *Jacob*
' and *Ifrael*; *Jefus* and *Jofhuah*; *Raguel* and *Jethro*; *Hobab*
' and *Cin*, and many more. In all other Refpects there is a
' wonderful Agreement, between our Books and thofe of *Ethi-*
' *opia*, which I compar'd together, with all poffible Care and
' Exactnels; and theirs begin precifely as ours do with thefe

Ethiopian
and Europe-
an Hiftories.
agree.
  ' Words, which may be feen in *Surius*, Tom. 5. Octob. 24.
' and in *Baronius*, Tom. 7. An. 522. lit. n. *It was now near the*
' *the 5th Year fince* Juftin *wielded the Scepter of the* Roman *Em-*
' *pire, at which time* Elesbaan *was Emperor of the* Ethiopians
' (they call him *Kaleb*). *A Man, who univerfally ob:ain'd a great*
' *Name for his Piety and Juftice. He had built a Palace in the*
' *City* Auxume, *&c.* The 5th Year of the Emperor *Juftin*, is of
' CHRIST 522; for he began his Reign in 518, according to the
' Calculation of the Cardinals *Baronius*, and *Bellarmin*. Now
' the Emperor *Kaleb* living in the Year 522, it follows, that
' then alfo liv'd *Abba Pantaleon*, one of the 9 Monks, which is
' prov'd by the fame Hiftory, as clear as the Light of the Sun.

340 Mar-
tyrs.
  ' For towards the end of it we find, both in the *Latin* and E-
' *thiopick* Copies, that the wicked *Dunaan*, or *Phineas*, having
' put to Death S. *Aretas*, or *Eruth* and his 340 Companions, in
' the City of *Nagran*, and the moft Pious Emperor *Juftin* being
' acquainted with it, he full of Holy Zeal writ to *Afterius*, Pa-
' triarch of *Alexandria*, to exhort by Letter King *Elesbaan* to
' take upon him the Revenge of the Blood of the Innocent Mar-
' tyrs, and the chaftizing of the Perfidious *Jew*. The Patriarch,
' whom *Simeon Metaphraftes* calls *Afterius*, is in the *Ethiopian* Hi-
' ftory nam'd *Timothy*. And the Truth is, there were both thefe
                                          ' Patriarchs

' Patriarchs in *Alexandria,* at that Time; but *Asterius* was the
' Catholick, and *Timothy* the Heretick; which continu'd, for the
' most part, after the Schism of *Dioscorus,* as we prove by many
' Examples in a considerable Volume, we have compos'd, En-
' titled *Branhaymanot,* signifying, the light of the Faith, or an
' *Ethiopian* Catechise, divided into 12 Books, where we confute
' all the Errors of *Ethiopia* and the Eastern Church; *lib. 7. cap. 24.*
' and it is likely, that he who translated that Story into the E-
' *thioptick,* was a Heretick, and for the Honour of *Timothy,* a
' mischievous Heretick, and condemn'd in the 6th General Coun-
' cil, feigns that the Emperor *Justin* recommended to him this
' Affair, whereas he committed it to *Asterius,* the Catholick, as
' *Simeon Metaphrastes,* an Author renowned for Sincerity and
' Sanctity, writes.

' The Holy King *Kaleb* having receiv'd the Patriarch's Letters *King* Kaleb
' and Recommendations from the Emperor *Justin,* was so inflam'd *Victorious,*
' with the just Desire of Revenge, that he rais'd an Army of *becomes a*
' 120000 Men, and gather'd a Fleet on the Red Sea of 133 Sail, *Monk.*
' to attack the Tyrant by Sea and Land. But he would not set
' out, before he had advis'd with, and receiv'd the Blessing of a
' Holy Old Man, to whom God reveal'd many Things that were
' to come; and who had been 45 Years shut up in a little Tower,
' doing extraordinary Penance and conversing only with God.
' The King laying aside all his Royal Robes, and putting on a
' mean Habit, went to the Holy Monk, carrying him a little
' Basket full of Frankincense, with several Pieces of Gold hid a-
' mong it: The Old Man perceiving the Fraud, and rejecting the
' Present, said to him, *God be with you, and with your Queen; go*
' *to the War with Confidence, arm'd with the Sacrifice of the Martyrs,*
' *which God has receiv'd as a sweet Odour; and with the Prayers of*
' *the Patriarch of* Alexandria, *and the Tears of the Emperor* Justin.
' *Blessam* hearing these Words, went away well satisfy'd, and
' fell upon the Tyrant, whom he slew, burning his Royal City,
' and restoring *Nagran* to the Christians. Then returning in
' Triumph to *Auxum,* he sent his Crown to *Jerusalem,* and go-
' ing out of his Palace at Night, cloath'd in Hair-Cloth, went
' up to the top of a Mountain, where he shut himself up in a little
' Room, and liv'd a long time, like a Monk; having nothing of
' his own, but a Mat, and a Cup to drink Water out of.

' This is in short what is more largely related, both in ours
' and the *Ethiopian* Histories; but in these and all their Books,
' and in the Mouths of them all it is agreed; that the Holy Old
' Man, King *Kaleb* went to advise with, and who had confin'd
' himself 45 Years to a Tower, was *Abba Pantaleon,* one of the

' Nine Monks, no Man being able, or daring to contradict it ;
' for besides that all the Books of *Ethiopia* unanimously deliver it,
' the very Place, which we have seen several times confirms it ;
' for two Miles East of *Auxum* stand the Church and Monastery,
' built by *Abba Pantaleon*, and call'd *Beth Pantaleon*, that is,
' *Pantaleon's* House; and about a Musket-shot from it is still
' standing the little Tower, in which he was shut up, and where
' he was visited by the Emperor; and in the mid way, between

Remarkable   ' *Auxum* and *Beth Pantaleon*, there are three Caves, within one
Caves.   ' another and hew'd out by Hand in the Rock, one of which is
' the Entrance, and has the Door to the West, being 15 Cubits
' long and 4 in Breadth; and at the end of it are two other
' little Rooms, in the nature of a Cross, to the Entrance, each
' of which is 10 Cubits long, and that on the Right Hand, or
' to the Southward is 4 Cubits wide, and that opposite to it 6.
' All the Ground lying under these Caves has a square Wall
' about it.

  ' This is the Place, whither King *Kaleb* withdrew, and it is
' honour'd as such. His Tomb and that of the Abbot *Pantaleon*
' are in the Church of *Beth Pantaleon*, which being laid open by
' a great Earthquake that hapn'd in the Year 1630, we recom-
' mended it to the Monks to have them speedily made up. All
' these Places we visited devoutly, and caus'd them to be exactly
' measur'd.

  ' Since thus it appears, that *Abba Pantaleon* was shut up in the
' little Tower, in the 5th Year of *Justin*, and in 522 of CHRIST,
' it follows, that he went into it in the 477; and since of course
' he must have been some Years before in *Ethiopia*, we may con-
' clude he came thither, with his Companions, between 470 and
' 480, and liv'd in it, during the Reigns of *Amiamid*, *Tacena* and
' *Kaleb*. Thus it must be allow'd, that those Nine Monks, so
' famous in *Ethiopia* were *Greeks* and not *Latins*, and went thi-
' ther in the 5th Century. Thus far the Patriarch *Don Alphonso*
' *Mendez*.

C H A P.

C H A P. XVII.

At what time Tecla Haymanot *flourish'd, who much dilated the Monastical Life in* Ethiopia ; *of the manner of living of these* Ethiopian *Religious Men, and particularly of the Habit they wear* ; *and an Account of some Monasteries.*

THE most remarkable Thing in this *Ethiopia*, relating to these Religious Men of theirs, is the Life of *Tecla Haymanot*, who, according to their Relations, was a great Saint: and Worker of Miracles, and very much dilated, and by his Example and Doctrine reform'd the Monastical Profession in *Ethiopia*; and in regard that some Modern Authors will needs make *Tecla Haymanot* to be of other Orders, I will here set down, what the aforemention'd Patriarch of *Ethiopia* writes of him.

‘ Altho' those Fathers, says he, who enter'd *Ethiopia*, about the
‘ Year of our Lord 470, in the Days of King *Amiamid*, much
‘ increas'd the Monastical Discipline ; yet it extended not beyond
‘ the Kingdom of *Tigre*; where each of them founded but one
‘ Monastery, which retains their Names till this Day. But *Abba*
‘ *Eustatheos*, and *Abba Tecla Haymanot*, who descended from them,
‘ were Heads of great Companies of Monks, and erected many
‘ Monasteries, throughout all the Provinces. Of these *Abba Tecla*
‘ *Haymanot*, which signifies, Plant of the Faith, has a more nu-
‘ merous and renowned Family. The Head of them was for-
‘ merly *Debra Libanos*, which signifies, Mount *Libanus*, in the
‘ Province of *Xaoa*, where their General resided, whom they
‘ call *Ichegue*, and he afterwards remov'd it to the Kingdom of
‘ *Begameder*, on Account of certain Barbarians call'd *Gallas*,
‘ possessing themselves of all those Lands.

‘ It is no difficult matter to discover the time, when *Tecla*
‘ *Haymanot* flourish'd, as well by what has been said, as by the
‘ rest we find writ in his Life, which we have in our Custody,
‘ faithfully translated out of the *Amara* Language into *Portuguese*,
‘ wherein is said as follows. *The Pedegree and Genealogy of our*
‘ *Fathers is this which ensues. The Angel* S. Michael *gave the Succession of*
‘ *Habit of a Monk to* S. Antony ; S. Antony *to* S. Macarius ; *he Monks.*

Tecla Haymanot, a Holy Monk:

N 2 *to*

' *to* S. Pachomius, *and he to* Abba Arogavy, *who was one of the Nine*
' *that came into* Ethiopia. *He gave the Habit to* Abba Christos
' Bezana, *and he to* Abba Mascalmoa; *he to* Abba Joanni; *he*
' *to* Abba Jesus; *he to* Abba Tecla Haymanot; *and then* Abba
' Tecla Haymanot *gave the* Asquema *to* Abba Jesus, *as has been*
' *said,* &c. Thus far the Book of the Life of *Tecla Haymanot.*
' *Asquema* is a fort of Scapular; and it seems thole Monks, be-
' ing *Greeks,* call'd it *Asquema,* because it was as much as the
' *Schema Monachismi,* or the Badge of a Monk; for most of the
' Monks of *Ethiopia* are clad as every one can, or fansies, but if
' they wear that Scapular, which is made of soft well drest'd
' Thongs of Leather, they are reeken'd as Holy as *Pachomius,* or
' *Macarius.* It plainly appears, that in this Tree, or Genealogy,
' there are but 3 Lives between *Abba Arogavy,* (who came with
' *Abba Pantaleon*) and *Abba Tecla Haymanot,* which are thole of
' *Christos Bezana,* Mascalmoa and *Joanni;* for tho' it mentions
' *Abba Jesus,* yet *Tecla Haymanot* took the Habit from *Abba*
' *Joanni.*
   ' Now *Abba Arogavy* being very Old, when he came into *E-*
' *thi*pia, about the Year 470, let us suppofe he might live till
' 500, and let us allow 120 Years to the other three that suc-
' ceeded, and it will follow that *Tecla Haymanot* was born about
' 515, or 520, little over or under, which is prov'd by an un-
' deniable Argument drawn from his Life, in which it is written,
' that he being 15 Years of Age, was carry'd by his Parents to
' the *Abuna Kirilos,* who was Patriarch in *Ethiopia,* when *Abba*
' *Benjamin* was lo at *Alexandria.*
   ' This *Benjamin* was an *Eutychian* Heretick and *Monothelite,*
' as appears by an Epistle of his, which is in the *Haymanot Abbau,*
' being their Book, of the Faith of the Fathers, wherein he im-
' pugns the Belief of the two Natures of CHRIST, our Saviour,
' and the Council of *Chalcedon,* and he liv'd about the Year of our
' Lord 630, being the fame when S. *Sophronius,* Patriarch of *Je-*
' *rusalem* liv'd, as may be feen in Cardinal *Baronius,* Vol.8. An. 634,
' and in *Bellarmin de Script. Ecclef. an.* 634. For S. *Sophronius* in
' that excellent Epistle he writ to *Sergius,* Bishop of *Constantinople,*
' which is all preferv'd at length in the 6th General Council,
' *Action* 11. after having excommunicated all the ancient Here-
' ticks by their Names, towards the end adds, *With them also he*
' *cover'd and cloath'd with Anathema and Catathema* Benjamin *of*
' Alexandria, *and* John *and* Sergius, *and* Thomas, *and the Ser-*
' *vant of the* Syrian, *who still lead an execrable Life, and cruelly*
' *oppofe Piety.* If *Benjamin* liv'd in the Days of S. *Sophronius,*
                                                     ' and

' and S. *Sophronius* writ about the Year 620, or 630, it is plain that
' *Tecla Haymanot* was then a Child.

Thus far the Patriarch *Don Alfonso Mendez*, whence it follows,
that the first Monks enter'd *Ethiopia*, together with S. *Frumentius*,
in the 4th Century; and that in the 5th Century, the other Nine
came, as a Supply; and that *Tecla Haymanot* regulated his Company of Monks, who follow'd his Institute in the 6th Century.

All *Ethiopia* in general looks upon *Tecla Haymanot* as a great
Saint, and in his Life, which is writ in several Books, they tell
us what extraordinary Penances he perform'd, the singular Graces
he receiv'd from God, many Apparitions and Miracles, and how
he went several times to *Jerusalem*, as Leader and Guide of a
vast Number of Monks; and if he was not their Founder, he was
at least the Increaser and Ennobler of their Religious Profession,
which flourish'd very long in *Ethiopia*, after an extraordinary
manner in number, Heroick Virtue and Learning.

My good Opinion of this great Saint of the *Abyssines*, is nothing lessen'd on account of the many Apocryphal Stories told of
him in his Life; as for Instance, that our Saviour once appearing
to him, said, That whosoever should kill a Snake, upon *Thursday*,
or *Sunday*, should have all the Sins he had committed in 40 Years
remitted him; and others as unlikely. For even among us many
Apocryphal Tales are written of S. *George*, and many other Saints,
and of the Apostles themselves, and yet we do not the less look
upon them as great Saints; for we believe the Truth that is told
of them, and not what is groundless.

I will here briefly describe the Course of Life of these Religious *Religious*
Men, as well those of *Tecla Haymanot*, as those of *Abba Eustateus*, *Habit.*
who was another Reformer among them, of the same Order of
S. *Antony.* Of these, *Tecla Haymanot* was a Native of *Ethiopia*,
and *Eustateus* of *Egypt.* In the first place the Habit of them all
is the same, unless we say it differs in each of them; for they are
alike in their *Asquema*, among such as wear it, and that is a little
Brede, of three slips of ordinary Red Leather, which being put
about the Neck, are fasten'd to a little Iron, or Copper Hook,
they have on a Thong they gird themselves with. In all other respects, every one cloaths himself as he can afford, or fansies. Many
of them wear a Hood, others a Cap, and others a Cloth on their
Head, and others nothing at all, being apparell'd like all other
People.

Many of those who profess the Eremetical Life wear Skins hol- *Monks.*
low'd about the Neck, and dy'd Yellow, or else Cloth of the
same Colour; and every one goes into the Desert, when he pleases,

and

and fo returns, when he thinks fit. Thofe who go more Re-
ligioufly clad, wear Black Cloth, which is like a Mantle, and under it, one they call a Shirt, but it is like a Caffock, or white
Habit girt with a Thong. Others wear a black Habit, and look
like our Clergy-Men, efpecially if they ufe Caps, and not Hoods.
Both Clergy-Men and Monks carry in their Hand a Crofs of Wood,
or Iron, or Brafs; and if they are Mafters, fo they call the Priors,
or Abbots of Monafteries, their Crofs being large, and having no
Foot, tho' well fhap'd, is carry'd by a little fort of Brother, who
is like a Knight's Squire to carry his Spear; and the Crofs is a
Token, not only of their Profeffion, but the Dignity they enjoy.

Their Rules.   They were all oblig'd to faft all the Year, till Three in the
Afternoon. They had their Canonical Hours, to fay and fing, the
which they met at Mid-Night, and feveral times in the Day;
and generally fpeaking, the People of *Ethiopia* are much inclin'd
to Penance, wherein thefe Religious Men fignaliz'd themfelves,
going into Water in cold Weather, and continuing in it feveral
Hours. It is faid of fome of them, that they fhut themfelves into
very large Trees, cutting open a place in them, which would contain their Body, till the Wood growing on both fides, prefs'd and
bury'd them in it felf, which feems incredible; but fo *F. Emannel*
Fafting.   *de Almeyda* relates it. In fafting particularly they are very con-
ftant, many of them did never eat but once in two Days; and
this fome ftill obferve in *Lent*; others would only eat on *Sundays*,
and many fpent all the Holy Week, without eating or drinking.

I will now fay fomething of thofe they call Monafteries, and
fuch Habits as we have here mention'd, deferve fuch built Mona-
Monafteries. fteries as we fhall defcribe, they being very different from thofe
of *Europe*. Perhaps when they were under their Primitive ftrict-
nefs, they might have fome more Form of a Community, but
what is known to have been practis'd almoft Time out of mind is,
that there was no fort of Enclofure among them, fo as every Monaftery fhould be within it felf, under Locks and Keys, and fhut
up with Walls; but each of them is like a Village, or little Town,
near a Church, and every one of thofe Monks has his little Cell,
or Cells of Timber, or Stone, and Clay, Thatch'd, Inclos'd or
Hedg'd in, with its Land, and all other Neceffaries, like any
Country Farmer; and at prefent they have all of them Houfes
and Families, unworthy their Profeffion, and the moft reform'd of
them are Marry'd; but the Mafters, or Chiefs muft not be Marry'd, and live fomewhat more referv'd.

So that a Monaſtery is like a Country Pariſh, and as the Lands of a Pariſh belong to ſeveral Farmers, ſo it has always been the Cuſtom to divide among them the Lands of ſuch a Monaſtery; always leaving the Maſter a good Lot, which is like the Allowance for the Abbots Table; and every Man maintains himſelf on his Share of Land, and ſome other Gifts or Charity of Kindred and Friends; and when any of theſe Monks dy'd, if he had any thing acquir'd by his own Induſtry, and not belonging to the Monaſtery, he could leave it to whom he pleaſed; but his Lands return'd to the Monaſtery.

But if any of them be very Young, and the Maſter cannot or will not give them Lands, he maintains them, and they Eat in his Houſe, but not at the ſame Table, for he always Eats by himſelf, and there is a Curtain drawn between his Table and theirs, that they may not ſee him Eat.

Such a Community deſerves ſuch Obedience as they pay to their Superiors. Every one of thoſe Religious Men, or rather Peaſants, goes whither he pleaſes, when he pleaſes, and does what he liſts, following the Dictates of their own Will, without Submiſſion to anothers. Thoſe of *Tecla Haymanot* have a ſort of General, whom they call *Ichegue*, who makes a ſort of Viſitation among them, either in Perſon or by his Deputy, whom he empowers to that purpoſe, and ſuch as he finds faulty, which he ſeldom miſſes of, have ſome Penalty inflicted on them, which is generally the Payment of ſome Goods by way of Fine.

Thoſe who follow the Rule of *Abba Euſtateus*, have no Supream Head, but every Maſter is Chief in his own Monaſtery, and the Reaſon they give which pleaſes them, is becauſe the ſaid *Abba Euſtateus* went away into *Armenia* and dy'd there, without appointing any one to ſucceed him. The Maſter of each Monaſtery is choſen by Plurality of Votes. It is to be obſerv'd, that the Superiors of the Monaſteries of the Order of *S. Antony* in *Portugal*, had the Title of Maſters.

There were many of theſe Monaſteries formerly in *Ethiopia*, whereof there are ſtill great Remains. They were extraordinary great, not ſo much for their Structure as for the Lands they poſſeſs'd, and the multitude of Monks living on and tilling them. Some of the Churches were large, even thoſe thatch'd; but all well lin'd with good Timber, with Cedar Beans very cloſe to one another, ſupported by many Columns of the ſame Wood, very beautiful and coſtly. Almoſt all theſe Churches of theirs were round, but had in the middle a ſquare Chappel; and this in the chief Monaſteries was of ſquare Stone, and had four Gates, whoſe Portals and Windows were of curious Wood; the Roof within

General of Monks.

Their Churches.

was

was in the Nature of a Cupula, always very dark, as having no firſt Light. Without this Square, between it and the round Wall, was the Body of the Church, which look'd more like a Cloiſter, and the Columns were in this Space, helping to ſupport the Roof and the Beams, which came down from the Top of the Chappel, and fell upon the round Wall ; for there being a conſiderable di-ſtance betwixt it and the Wall of the Chappel, the Roof could not be ſupported without the Aſſiſtance of the ſaid Columns.

Famous Mo-
naſteries.

The greateſt Monaſteries in *Ethiopia* were that of *Biſan,* which is a Days Journey from *Mazua,* among vaſt high Mountains, and belonging to the Monks of *Abba Euſtateus* ; but there are others yet more famous, as is that of *Debra Libanos,* ſignifying the Monaſtery, or Mount *Libanus* ; for *Debra* ſignifies both a Monaſtery and a Mountain, and their Monaſteries being generally founded on Mountains, the *Abyſſines* give them both the ſame Name. They call'd that Mountain *Libanus,* becauſe it is very uſual among them to give their Mountains Names of *Paleſtine,* and ſo there are others they call *Debra Sinay, Debra Tabor, Debra Zeyte,* ſo they Name Mount *Olivet.*

Debra Liba-
nos Mona-
ſtery.

Debra Libanos is in the Province or Kingdom of *Xaoa,* and be-cauſe the Bones of *Tecla Haymanot,* who among the *Abyſſines* is look'd upon as a Saint, were in it, the Emperors beſtow'd abundance of Lands on it. The Buildings of this Monaſtery neither are nor ever were any better than thoſe above mention'd. It had a Church like the reſt, and on the ſame Mountain a ſort of Village or Coun-try Town, of thatch'd Houſes, in which the Religious Men liv'd. The *Gallas* have taken away moſt of the Lands belonging to this Monaſtery, as being poſſeſs d of the greateſt part of the Province ; only ſome few Chriſtians live on thoſe ſtony Mountains they call *Ambas,* and in the ſaid Monaſtery there remain'd under 40 Monks. The Number of them formerly, all Men ſay, was very great, and that including the Churches and little Monaſteries there were in the Country about, all of them ſubject to *Debra Libanos,* they might be about 10000.

Debra Al-
lelo.

There is another Monaſtery very much celebrated by ſome Au-thors, call'd *Debra Allelo,* or *Allelujah,* belonging to the Monks of *Abba Euſtateus,* ſeated in the Kingdom of *Tigre,* a Days Journey from *Auxum* on a Mountain, amidſt great Woods. The Ruins of the ancient Church ſhow it has been one of the beſt in *Ethiopia.* It was 99 Foot in length, and 78 and a half in breadth, and about it are to be ſeen the Remains of abundance of round Cells. The Fathers of the Society often ask'd the Eldeſt Monks of that Mona-ſtery, what number there was of them formerly in that Place, ſome of them anſwer'd 12000, others 40000, and it may be ſup-
poſed

pos'd the firſt of them ſpoke of thoſe who dwelt near the Church, and the others meant all that were ſubject to the Monaſtery in the Country about, in which it is confidently affirm'd, there were formerly 90 Suffragan Churches, and that when the Maſter or General went to Court upon any earneſt Buſineſs, he was attended by 150 Reverend Monks on good Mules, and wearing a ſort of looſe Coats cloſe before, with only a Hole to put their Heads through over their Habit, without Sleeves.

Of all this former Grandeur, nothing now remains but ſome Ruins, and inconſiderable Footſteps, not of what it was, but what it ſeems to have been; for in the midſt of that fallen Church, there ſtands now a very little one, near which and about the *Suffragan* Churches, there are only 10 or 12 Monks left, who ſeem rather to continue there to keep up the Memory of what is loſt, than to imitate their Perfection of Life. The Founder of that Monaſtery, they ſay, was a Monk, reputed a Saint, and call'd *Samuel*, ſo great a Penitent, that he is reported to have ſpent ſome Nights in a Well, where the Water came up to his middle, and with a great Stone on his Back, which was a very uneaſy Bed.

CHAP. XVIII.

At what Time the firſt Innovation in Religion happen'd in Ethiopia, *and of the many Errors and great Schiſm of the* Abyſſines.

THE Holy Fathers call'd *Egypt* the Forge of Idols, and Sink of Abominations, on Account of the multitude of Deities that Nation ador'd, and their many Errors in Relation to the True God. Their Neighbours, the *Abyſſines*, are not at all unlike them in this ſort of Deliriums, concerning the True Catholick Religion, for among them there was an Inundation of Errors, of Schiſms, of Hereſies, and of deprav'd Cuſtoms, without any more than imperfect Shaddows, not to call it downright Darkneſs of Chriſtianity.

F. *Emanuel d'Almeyda* fills up the greateſt part of a Book, in laying open very learnedly, many of the Helliſh Abuſes and Diabolical Superſtitions of the *Abyſſines*; but the moſt Reverend Patriarch *Don Alfonſo Mendez*, for whoſe ſake I undertook this Work, writing to me from *India* in the Year 1654, tells me he is of Opinion, that all thoſe Chapters, wherein the ſaid Father ſets down and confutes thoſe Errors, may be reduc'd to leſs than one, and therefore I will contract them the moſt I can.

In

Schism of
Ethiopia.

In the firſt Place it muſt be allow'd to be no leſs certain, that the *Abyſſines* have been Schiſmaticks for many Ages, than it is now that the *Nile* has its Source in *Ethiopia*, in the Kingdom of *Gojam*. But notwithſtanding that in the Days of the wicked *Dioſcorus*, who liv'd about the Year 444, there were preſently Errors introduc'd into *Ethiopia*, which came from *Alexandria*; yet, as long as the Catholick Party prevail'd in *Alexandria*, which we find was till the Year 610 or 620, when the Holy Men S. *Elogius* and S. *John* the Almsgiver, were Patriarchs of *Alexandria*, we ſuppoſe that the greateſt part of *Ethiopia* was ſubject to the See of *Rome*, always following the Doctrine of the Teachers ſent into it. A good Proof hereof is, that S. *Gregory* the Great, who flouriſh'd about the Year 600, is highly honour'd in *Ethiopia*; as is alſo S. *Ildefonſus*, whom they call *Deeios*, and who liv'd about 650, and was Diſciple to S. *Iſidorus*, Archbiſhop of *Sevil*, contemporary with S. *Gregory* the Great. A farther Proof hereof is, that when *Juſtin*

How long it continu'd Orthodox.

was Emperor in *Europe*, about the Year 523, *Kaleb* or *Eleſbaan* reign'd in *Ethiopia*, who we know was a Saint, and Obedient to the Catholick Patriarch the Emperor *Juſtin* had plac'd in *Alexandria*. *Baronius* treats of theſe matters, *Tom.* 7. *anno* 523.

But when Hereſy had prevail'd in *Alexandria*, and throughout all *Egypt*, the *Abunas* coming from thence, the Water could not but run very foul, ſince the Spring it proceeded from was infected. This appears by many ancient Books there are in *Ethiopia*, writ on Parchment, for they have no printing; beſides, other evident Tokens there are of Schiſm and Hereſy; for at this very Time the Hereticks call the wicked Apoſtate *Dioſcorus* a Saint, who being Patriarch of *Alexandria*, with the Aſſiſtance of the vile Abbot *Eutyches*, in the Year 444. infected *Greece* with that Hereſy, of there being but one Nature and one Will in *CHRIST* our Lord. For this Reaſon the *Abyſſines* do not reckon Pope *Leo* the Firſt as a Saint, but rather abhor his Name, worthy of eternal Veneration; becauſe he approv'd the Council of *Chalcedon*, wherein 630 Biſhops met, and condemn'd the two Hereticks *Dioſcorus* and *Eutyches*.

Firſt Reunion of theirs to Rome.

True it is, that in the Days of Pope *Eugenius* the IV. who held the Council of *Florence* about the Year 1439, ſome thought the Schiſm of *Ethiopia* was at an end, becauſe about the concluſion of that Council, there came to *Rome*, together with the *Armenians*, ſome *Ethiopians* or *Abyſſines*, ſent by the Emperor *Zara Jacob*, who made Profeſſion of the *Roman* Faith, and receiv'd and carry'd with them Letters of Union with the *Roman* Church, as may be ſeen in Cardinal *Baronius* in that Year, and in *Illeſcas p.* 2. *lib.* 6. *cap.* 23. *anno* 1438, and the Life of Pope *Eugenius* the IV. on whoſe

Tomb

Tomb there is an Epitaph, and among the rest one Distich alluding to the Conversion of these *Abyssines,* which runs thus.

> Quo Duce & *Armenij, Graiorum* Exempla secuti,
> *Romanam* agnorunt, *Æthiopesque* Fidem.

Besides, the Emperor *David* writ two Letters to the Pope, in the Year 1526, which were carry'd by *F. Francis Alvarez,* Chaplain to King *Emanuel* of *Portugal,* and deliver'd to Pope *Clement* the VII. at *Bologna,* and are now publish'd in *Latin* by *Paulus Jovius.* In them the said Emperor *David* said, he would pay Obedience to the Pope of *Rome;* and he also sent *Don John Bermudes* to *Rome,* desiring of the Pope, that he would confirm him Patriarch of *Ethiopia,* as we shall see hereafter. All this that Emperor did, without the Approbation of his People, and when *Don John Bermudes* return'd, the Emperor *David* was Dead, and his Son *Claudius* receiv'd him with an ill Will, and seem'd to comply with the Promise made by his Father, only as long as he had some dependance on the *Portuguezes,* who assisted him against the *Moor Granhe;* but as soon as that Infidel was kill'd, he sent for the *Abuna Joseph* from *Alexandria,* and from that Time we shall see how they treated the Patriarchs of the Society sent thither. *The second.*

If therefore we date the Errors and Schism of the *Abyssines* from the Days of the wicked *Dioscorus,* till the Reign of the Emperor *Sultan Segued,* when he and his People for some time embrac'd the Catholick Faith, in the Year 1626, they had been Schismaticks above 1200 Years: But if we say the Catholick Faith held out in *Ethiopia* as long as they in some measure were subject to the Catholick Patriarchs of *Alexandria,* which was till the Year 610 or 620, then must we say, that the Schism of *Ethiopia* lasted 1000 Years, little more or less, and God knows when it will cease; for we shall see hereafter, how short a time that Country continu'd in its Reunion. *How long the Schism lasted.*

Besides the Antiquity of their Errors, there is a profound Ignorance in *Ethiopia;* for having no Schools, no Knowledge of Philosophy and Divinity, nor any more than some imperfect Books, with pieces of Homilies and Councils very full of mistakes, and their Bible very much deprav'd, they are so very unlearned, tho' they have good Wits, that they can neither argue in Form nor defend their wrong Notions Syllogistically; but blindly cleave to what their Forefathers taught them, and so, tho' they believe in CHRIST our Lord, it is after their own manner, and with a Thousand Follies as to the Mysteries of his Holy Life. *Ignorance of Ethiopians.*

They

Errors as to Baptism.

They have no manner of Knowledge of the Sacraments of Confirmation and Extream Unction: The other five they admit, but very ignorantly as to the Matter and Form; for in the Sacrament of Baptism some said, *I Baptize thee in the Name of the Holy Ghost*; others, *I Baptize thee in the Water of* Jordan; others, *God Baptize thee*; and others, *May the Baptism reach thee*. Besides this, there was a notable Abuse of Rebaptizing themselves several Times, upon any Occasion, and many Men and Women baptiz'd themselves most indecently many times in the Morning, by some Monk they kept for this purpose in the House, besides the general Baptism they celebrated every Year on the Day of the Epiphany, with abominable Superstitions, and such Ceremonies as rather seem'd to be invented by Sensuality itself, than to be the effects of true Christianity. Yet all this Baptizing and Rebaptizing did not amount to a real Baptism, and therefore the Fathers of the Society and the Patriarch *Don Alfonso Mendez* were of Opinion, that it was requisite conditionally to Baptize all those who were converted to the Faith, because in *Ethiopia*, either they knew not the Form of Baptism, or at least did not use it.

As to Penance.

As to the Sacrament of Penance, tho' they knew, that in order to obtain Pardon of Sins committed after Baptism, it was requisite to confess them to a Priest, and receive Penance at his Hands; yet they had very gross Errors, both as to the Form, and in other Respects; for no Man went to Confession till about 25 Years of Age, little more or less, believing themselves to be Innocents till then, and calling all such Children; and hence it is that when any one Dies between 17 and 20 Years of Age, they say, *My Soul be with that Innocent's*. They confess their Sins in General Terms, and by the gross, saying, *I have sinn'd, I beseech you to absolve me*. And if the Confessor happens to bid them express their Sins, they do so, if they be guilty of any of those three, which they only look upon as Sins, which are taking another Man's Wife, Murder and Theft. And the worst is, that the Confessors do not absolve in the Catholick Form; but only utter some Words, and touch their Backs with Rods of Olive-Tree, which therefore they always use to have ready at the Church Gates, that there may be no want of Absolutions, for want of Rods.

They believe the Real Presence.

The *Abyssines* believe and confess, that CHRIST our Saviour is in the Consecrated Host, and they receive this Sacrament in both Kinds; yet we are of Opinion, that there is no true Consecration among them through the Defect of the Ministers because they are no true Priests; and there is an Essential Error as to the matter, because they generally do not Consecrate in Wine, but in Water, for they only take Four, or Six Raisins, which are

very

very like thofe among us of the Reddeft Grapes, and thofe they fqueeze into a Cup of Water, and as foon as 'tis difcolour'd, they fay Mafs with it. They alfo commit abundance of Irregularities in the Sacrament of Holy Order, for in conferring it they do not ufe thofe Ceremonies, which the Canons have declar'd Effential.

It would be tedious to run through all the Errors of the *Abyffines*, relating to the Sacraments and the Commandments; and tho' they had fo many abfurdities brought them from *Alexandria*, yet they fetch'd others as far as *Jury*; for they precifely keep to Circumcifion, and many other *Judaical* Superftitions, like true Defcendants of *Solomon's* Son, and the other *Ifraelites Circumcifion* that came with him, who alfo taught them to keep the *Jewifh and Sabbath* Sabbath, or Saturday, and many other of their Ceremonies, *obferv'd*. making a mixture of the Law of CHRIST and that of *Mofes*, which is joining Light and Darknefs, or God and *Belial*. And amidft fo many Errors they eafily admitted thofe which beft fute with deprav'd Nature, and are moft repugnant to Catholick Purity. But when the way of Truth is once loft, there follow of Courfe the moft dreadful Precipices, till Men come to fall into the worft Abyfs of Wickednefs. However the *Abyffines* generally pay great Devotion to the Virgin *Mary*, and fo we will forbear telling any more of their Errors, all which came from *Diofcorus* and *Eutyches*, and therefore they are call'd *Eutychians* and *Neftorians*.

C H A P. XIX.

An Account of the Abuna, *who is the* Ethiopian Bifhop. *Of what fort of Clergymen they have; and of their Veftments, and Ceremonies of the Mafs.*

THE *Ethiopians* never had any more than one Bifhop of all *Abyffinia*, fince they receiv'd the Faith of CHRIST, and him they call *Abuna*, which fignifies, Our Father. The firft of them was S. *Frumentius*, of whom we have fpoken above, and as this Saint was fent from *Alexandria*, by S. *Athanafius*; fo ever after all the other Bifhops, or *Abunas*, were fent into *Ethiopia* from the

Only one Abuna, or Bifhop in Ethiopia.

fame

same Patriarchal Chair of *Alexandria*, till our Days, when *Rome* sent some Patriarchs, as we shall see hereafter. So as long as *Alexandria* had Catholick Patriarchs, the *Abyssines* had Catholick Bishops; but when *Greece* and *Egypt* separated from *Rome*, they sent Heretick Bishops, or *Abunas* into *Ethiopia*, who are generally most ignorant Persons, whereas it is so proper for Bishops to be Learned, that S. *Paul, Ephes.* 4. 11. calls them both, *Pastors* and *Teachers*.

His Ignorance, and Function.

Hence it is that several Fathers of the Society affirm, they knew, three, or four *Abunas*, none of whom they ever heard Preach, or Teach, and they seem to be of the number of those of whom the Prophet *Isaiah,* 56. 10. says, *They are all dumb Dogs, they cannot Bark.* F. *Francis Alvarez*, who was Six Years in *Ethiopia*, and relates very minute matters relating to it, does not mention, that ever he heard the *Abuna Marc* Preach; but only affirms, that when he conferr'd Holy Orders, he bid those not receive them, who had been twice marry'd, with a few other Instructions, wherein it is likely he declar'd some other Causes of Irregularity, passing by other matters very obvious. He farther says, he gave Priestly Orders, to the Blind, Lame, and Halt, and herein consisted all the Office of the *Abuna*. Accordingly the Orders are like him that Administers them; for they give them only by Imposition of Hands, with some Words, without delivering to those ordain'd the matter of Bread and Wine; whence it was always dubious, whether the Orders they gave were valid; besides the aforesaid doubt as to Baptism, which was common to all.

His manner of giving Absolution.

The better to show the great Ignorance of these Pastors of the *Abyssine* Souls, I will relate one particular, that by it we may come to the Knowledge of others like it. It is customary for the *Abunas* to appear sometimes in publick, sitting on their Chair, and, the *Abyssines* being naturally addicted to Piety, many of them presently flock together, encompassing their Pastor, to gain the Indulgences he uses to bestow among them. Thither repair'd such as would confess their Sins in publick, believing they that way obtain'd fuller Absolution. Then coming before the *Abuna* they discover'd one or two Sins, being generally of those three, I said above, they look upon as the most heinous. This done, the *Abuna* stood up, and with his Staff began to give the Penitent a disagreeable Absolution, of three, or four good Strokes, saying to him, at the same time, in a great Passion; *Have you done so? Do not you fear God? Well go thither; give him 30, or 40 Lashes.* Then the *Mazares*, who are a sort of Officers attending the *Abuna*, the Emperor, and the Viceroy, being like our Yeomen of the Guard, begin to Lash the poor Penitent, with a sort of Thongs they

carry

carry in their Hands, to keep off the People, and being long, gird
about the Body. This whipping is generally very fevere and the
Abuna for the moft part order'd 30, or 40 Lafhes; but as foon as
the Penitent has receiv'd 6, or 7, the Company intercedes for him
and interpofes; and after this unfavory Abfolution, the Penitent
withdraws, glad with all his Heart, that he is deliver'd from the
Abunas Staff and the Thongs of the *Mazares*.

Now to come to our Story, it happen'd, not many Years fince, *An inftance* that the *Abuna* being bufie hearing thefe publick Confeffions, one *of Confeffing* of thofe who came for Abfolution drew near, and being unwilling *to him.* to declare his Sin in publick, as fearing perhaps that which afterwards hapned, he ftepp'd up to the *Abuna,* and defir'd, he would
hear the Sin in private, for which he begg'd Abfolution, he anfwer'd, *How fo? Will not that Sin be made known before all the
World at the Day of Judgment? Then declare it here in publick
immediately.* The poor Penitent had no way to come off, after
that Anfwer, and, tho' much againft his Will, at length fpoke
it out in publick, and it was that he had Stolen a certain number of Cows. It was the Penitents Misfortune, that the Owner
of the Cows hapned to be prefent, who went that Moment and
accus'd him before the Judge, and there being fo many Witneffes,
who had heard him Confefs the Fact, he was immediately order'd to reftore the Cows, and they laid a farther great Penalty on
him, which was more grievous, than the Lafhes the *Mazares*
gave him. Thus, if the poor Penitent was abfolv'd from the
Guilt by his Confeffion; yet he efcap'd not the Punifhment,
which the Judge laid on him to his Coft, that he might be free
from all Satisfaction in another Life.

It is here fit to be obferv'd, that unlefs fome of the many *Reftitution* Thefts committed in *Ethiopia* is not thus made good, there is ne- *not enjoin'd* ver any Reftitution; for neither the *Abuna,* nor any of the other *in Confeffion.* Confeffors oblige the Penitent to it, this being a Point never
taught, nor practis'd in *Ethiopia.*

Anfwerable to their Ignorance was the ill Life of thefe *Abunas,* Abunas ill who never remember'd the Advice S. *Paul* gave to *Titus,* bid- *Livers.* ding him in all Refpects be a living Example of Virtuous Actions.
It is faid of many of them, that they liv'd publickly in a fcan-
dalous manner. Neither did they vifit their Cnurches in Perfon;
but now and then fent a fort of Vifitors, who were more like
Shearers of their Flock, than Cenfors of ill Lives.

It is very much doubted, whether any of thefe *Abunas* be real *No Bifhops.* Bifhops, or only plain Priefts, or rather not fo much as Priefts,
but bare Lay Monks. When the Patriarch *Don Alfonfo Mendez*
was in *Ethiopia,* a Monk of *Alexandria* liv'd there, who came to
fucceed

succeed the *Abuna Simon*, of whom we shall speak hereafter, and as such was immedrately receiv'd by many and complimented; but the Emperor *Sultan Segued*, having at that time the Catholick Faith in his Heart, which he soon after profess'd, he caus'd that Monk to be depos'd from the Office of *Abuna*, and he conversing with the Fathers of the Society, soon embrac'd the Catholick Faith, and confess'd he was no Bishop, but only a Lay Monk. He afterwards Marry'd, and liv'd upon making of Mills, and we believe he understood that Trade better than the Duty of an *Abuna*.

Their Revenues. The Revenue belonging to this their sort of Patriarchs consists in some Lands in the Kingdom of *Tigre*, which yield about 40, or 50 *Oqueas* a Year, worth 4, or 500 Pieces of Eight. They have other Lands in *Dambea*, which afford a great Quantity of Provisions, and serve for their Table; others in *Gojam* of less Value, and they themselves use to be their own Farmers. Besides this they have an Understanding with those they ordain, for all of them carry their Offerings, which I will not now go about to condemn as Simony.

It is here to be observ'd, that there neither is, nor ever was, any other Bishop, Patriarch, or as they call him *Abana*, in all *Ethiopia* but this one; this is most certain, and testify'd by all the Fathers of the Society, who liv'd so many Years in *Abyssinia*, by which we see how much that great Historian *Illescas* was misinform'd, when in the second part of his Pontifical History, *lib.* 6. *in Vita pag.* 3. *fol.* 257. he says, *Ethiopia* is divided into great Patriarchships, each of which has, at least, two Bishops; and the same Author, in the aforesaid Place, assigning to *Ethiopia* 60 very rich Kingdoms, it is no wonder, he should also allow them such a numerous parcel of Bishopricks; but what we have deliver'd is most certain; and it is generally very requisite to keep a strict Eye upon what has been writ concerning this *Ethiopia*, because it has been represented very great, and is found in reality to be but inconsiderable. And I wonder that the said *Illescas* should deliver such things, whereas he says he read *F. Francis Alvarez's* Book, tho' he there sometimes also calls him *Francis Fernandes*, and I could better excuse changing the Name of *Alvarez* into *Fernandez*, than making so many Patriarchs of one single *Abuna*.

They have no particular See. The *Abunas* have no particular See, or Cathedral in *Ethiopia*, because, as has been said, there is no City there, nor settled Court, only the *Portuguese* Patriarch *Don Alfonso Mendez* was building a stately Church of Lime and Stone, at *Dancas*, for a Cathedral. The Churches of the Camp are under the Direction of the *Debarod Goyta*, so they call the Chief, or Superior of the *Depteras*, who

who are the Chanters and Prebends of the principal Churches, and they take their Name from the Tabernacle *Moses* order'd to be made, which in the Language of their Book they call *Deptera* ; and these are in *Ethiopia*, the Persons who pretend to be best read in what Books they have, and yet they are not oblig'd to be Clergymen nor Monks, but seem to be equivalent to the *Levites*.

The proper Duty of these Men is to sing, and to beat a sort of Drums or little Tabors, during the Divine Office, and at the same time to Dance and Skip, with such terrible Noise as if the Church were falling ; so that our madest Antick Dancers could not outdo them. This noisy and tiresome Solemnity, begins on their greatest Festivals, long before Day, and they hold it on till near Noon, without ever giving over their joyful and unharmonious Exercise. This they value themselves so much upon, that the Emperors own Brother *Raz Sela Christos*, of whom we shall have much to say, was very proud of keeping Time for them, tho' the Dancers would have sav'd him the Labour. His own Cousin *Melca Christos*, Lord Steward to the Emperor, was very glad when he had the good Fortune to play upon the Tabor: Nay, they rattle and shake it for many Hours, and herein they say they imitate King *David*, when he went dancing before the Ark of the Covenant, and that they observe what he recommended, *Psalm* 150. *v.* 4: *Praise him with the Timbrel and Dance ; Praise him with string'd Instruments and Organs ; Praise him upon the high sounding Cymbals.* *Depteras their Mad Ceremonies.*

Besides these their *Levites*, they have Clergymen, who in *Ethiopia* were always marry'd, and marry'd after they had receiv'd Deacons Orders ; for as to those of Sub-Deacon their *Abunas* do not use to give them, but the Degree of Deacon they bestow on very small Children, and sometimes on sucking Infants, especially if they be the Sons of great Men, that they may have the Priviledge of going into the Chappel to receive the Sacrament with the Clergy, and not without it, or at the Church Gate, as those do who are not in Orders. And these are the Orders so much talk'd of the pretended *Prester John* had, being only those of Deacon, as has been said. *Priests and Deacons.*

The Clergy in *Ethiopia* marrying, they have for the most part considerable Families, and tho' the Sons succeed their Fathers in their Churches and Benefices, yet they are generally Poor, and live upon the Labour of their Hands, tilling the Land as Lay-Farmers do. They wear no Clergymans Habit, nor are they Shorn, or have any other Mark of Distinction, but only a little Cross in their Hand, and a small Cap of any Colour, and accordingly are very little respected ; and there being no Priviledges of the Church among them, their Ordination does not free them from being punish'd by the Lay-Magistrate, like other Secular Persons. *Clergy marry'd and Poor.*

P.   Such

Vestments at Mass. Such as the Ministers of the Altar, such are their Vestments, and other Necessaries for celebrating their Mass. Every time they are to say Mass, they say some Prayers over and bless the Sacerdotal Vestments, and indeed they need a daily Blessing, being so indecent for that use, that all their Benedictions are little enough to sanctify them; for instead of an Alb they generally use an old Tunick bought of the *Turks*, well worn, which they put on without any other Fashioning or Alteration, only relying on their Blessings. That which answers to the Chasuble is very narrow, but behind it drags about half a Yard, and this they call *Motat*. As for the Amice, Girdle, Stole and Maniple, they use none, and much less might serve, considering how easily they content themselves as to this their Mass, which consists of many Prayers, the Priests and Deacon say each apart, several whereof are in themselves devout and well worded.

Mannner and Hours of saying it. There is no Image on the Altar, only some one they place when they are to say Mass. Behind the East end of the Church there is always a small Room, which is for the Hosts, and in it all Necessaries for making of them, and the Host is a leaven'd Cake, which is not kept till the next Day, and they wonder we do not make Hosts every Day. They go from thence praying to say their Mass, and only one is said, with this variety as to the Hours, that on *Sundays* and other Days which are not Fasts, it is said in the Morning. On Fasting Days they say it, at the time they are to Eat, that is, at Three in the Afternoon, on *Wednesdays* and *Fridays*, and at Sun-setting in Lent.

Wine and Communion. The Wine they prepare for Mass is thus made; they bring 4 or 5 Raisins, as has been hinted before, which they keep on purpose, and squeeze to pieces with their Fingers in a Cup of Water, bigger or less, according to the number of People that are to Communicate; for they all receive under both kinds, or to say the Truth under neither, it being most certain that the Matter here is not Wine but Water, since a Cup of Water cannot be converted into Wine by 5 or 6 Raisins. I also question their Form of Consecration, for their Words for the Body of CHRIST are these: *This Bread is my Body*; and for the Blood, *This Cup is my Blood*; which Words seem to make an essential Alteration in the Sense, as *F. Layman* expresly declares in *Theolog. mor. lib. 3.* and may be seen in the Learned *F. Francis Suarez, Tom. 3. in 3 par. disput.* 58. *Sect.* 7. *and disp.* 59. *Sect.* 5.

Hallelujas always us'd. In the Mass they say all by Heart, only reading the Gospel in the Book the Priest carries on his Left Shoulder, and going without the Chappel Door, there reads the Gospel of the Day. They do not vary the Gospels as we do, according to the several Festivals;

vals; but they read one Evangelist one whole Year, and the next
Year another, and so in four Years run through them all.   They
always say *Hallelujas*, even in the Masses for the Dead, as we
shall see in the second Book.

The Priest gives the Sacrament at the Chapel Door to Men and
Women, saying, *The Holy Flesh of* Emmanuel *our God of Truth,
which he took of the Lady of us all*; and the Communicant says,
Amen, Amen.   Then the Deacon gives the Blood with a Spoon, *The Sacra-*
saying, *This is the Blood of JESUS CHRIST, for the Life of the ment how*
Flesh and Soul, and for Life everlasting.   Then one who represents *given.*
our Sub-Deacon, pours a little Water into the Palm of the Communicants Hand, with which he rinses his Mouth and Drinks it.
All the Communicants stand, and this may suffice as to the Ceremonies of the *Abyssine* Mass.

Thus we have given a brief Account of the Affairs of this *Ethiopia* or *Abyssinia*, which may improperly be call'd the Empire of
Prester John.   We have seen the Original of the Catholick Religion there; we have discover'd who were the first Religious Men
that enter'd into it; we have related the Occasion they had to leave
the true Faith; and we have writ what is most requisite to be
known of their Customs and Errors, and of their *Abunas*, who
ever since their first Revolt, always came to them from *Alexandria*, till the Days of their Emperor *Zara Jacob*, before spoken of,
who was Ten Years without any *Abuna*, endeavouring to get one
from *Rome*, and after his Death continued so 13 Years longer, till
perceiving the Impossibility of having one from *Rome*, they brought
one from *Alexandria*, which was the *Abuna Marc*, who was living in *Ethiopia* at the time when *F. Francis Alvarez* came thither, sent by King *Emanuel* of *Portugal*, with his Ambassador, as
we shall see, with many other remarkable Accidents, in the en-
suing Book.

The End of the first Book.

THE
TRAVELS
OF THE
JESUITS
IN
ETHIOPIA.

BOOK II.

CHAP. I.

Of the first Discoveries of Ethiopia *by Land and Sea;
of the Empress* Helen, *and a Magnificent Church she
built*; *Embassies between* Ethiopia *and* Portugal, *and
some other Particulars.*

PRINCE *Henry*, Son to King *John* the first of *Portugal*, having before any other sent out Ships to make new Discoveries along the Coast of *Africk*, and they successfully passing
beyond any that had been before them, the Kings his Nephews
prosecuted what he had so happily begun, till their Adventurers
pass'd that, ever since so famous Promontory call'd the *Cape of
Good Hope*. So far had King *John* the II. proceeded, when he
pitch'd upon two of his Subjects well skill'd in the *Arabick* and
other

other Languages, to travel by Land into *India,* and there endeavour to find out a Christian King, vulgarly call'd *Prester John,* and enquire whether the Spices and other Commodities brought from those Eastern Parts up the *Red Sea,* and thence by Land to *Grand Cairo* and *Alexandria,* and so to *Venice* by the *Mediterranean,* might not at once be convey'd to *Portugal* upon the Ocean. These two Men were *Peter de Covilham* and *Alfonso de Payva.* Both of whom after long Travels went into *India* and *Ethiopia,* but neither return'd into *Portugal ;* for *Payva* in his Return dy'd at *Grand Cairo,* and *Covilham* was not permitted to depart *Ethiopia* by the Emperor then reigning : But before he went into that Empire, he writ to King *John* from *Grand Cairo,* by means of two *Jews* sent after them by the same King *John,* giving him a particular Account of his Travels, how he had been in *India,* and found that the *Portugueze* Ships might by the way of the Ocean Sail thither, and that his Companion had been in an Empire call'd *Ethiopia,* and at the Court of that Monarch, who was a Christian, and in all likelyhood the famous *Prester John,* his Highness was so desirous to find out ; and for as much as his Highness order'd a Letter to be deliver'd to the said *Prester John,* since his Companion was Dead, he was going to carry it himself. This was the Substance of *Covilham's* Letter, and his Account was extraordinary pleasing to King *John,* and it was generally concluded throughout all *Portugal,* that the so much sought for *Prester John* was now found out ; whereas the real Prince of that Name must be in *Asia,* and this here was in *Africk ;* for the *Prester John* they were sent to find out, was a Christian Prince reigning in the Inland of *Asia,* at the time when *Marcus Paulus Venetus* travell'd through *Asia,* as he affirms, and the extraordinary Account he gave of that Monarch having fill'd all *Asia* with his Fame, the greatest Christian Princes conceiv'd an ardent desire of finding him out. This Discovery of *Covilham* and *Payva* happen'd in the 1490, and was follow'd by *Vasco de Gama's* sailing round into the East in 1497. In 1505 *Alfonso d' Albuquerque* was the first *European* that enter'd the Mouth of the *Red Sea,* and by that means the *Ethiopians* came to hear of the great Exploits of the *Portuguezes* in *India,* confirming the mighty Things they had been told of that Nation by *Peter de Covilham,* who was still living among them. The great Empress *Helen,* Dowager to the Emperor *Beda Mariam,* at that time governing *Ethiopia,* during the Minority of her Son *David,* and desiring to settle a Correspondence with the King of *Portugal,* writ to him, and sent a sort of Embassy by one *Matthew* an *Armenian,* and with him, as a Token of the Faith she profess'd, a Piece of the Holy Cross. [1] This Messenger was nobly entertain'd by *Alfonso.*

Covilham and Payva in Ethiopia.

Helen, Empress of Ethiopia.

[1] through from Jerusalem during the reign of David I (1382–1411) Bruce I p. 500

fonso d' Albuquerque, who order'd a Gold Box to be made to carry the Holy Wood, with the greater Honour. *Matthew* coming to *Lisbon,* found an honourable Reception from King *Emanuel,* who sent him back well satisfy'd into *Ethiopia,* as shall be mention'd more fully hereafter. This was the beginning of the following Friendship between the *Portuguezes* and the *Abyssines,* and hence ensu'd all those strange Accidents, which we shall speak of hereafter.

Alexander Nahod *and* David, *Emperors.*

When *Peter de Covilham* enter'd *Ethiopia,* which was in the Year **1490,** as was said above, the Emperor *Scander* or *Alexander,* being the only one of that Name reign'd there, who the Natives affirm was a true *Alexander* in Generosity, as well as by Name. *Nahod* succeeding him in the Throne, would never give *Covilham* leave to depart, both because he had a great value for him, and in Regard it was the Custom of the Nation to detain all Strangers that came into it. *Nahod* reign'd 13 Years, and left the Crown to his Son *Lebna Danguil,* otherwise call'd *David,* then an Infant, and during his Minority the Empire was govern'd by his Mother *Magueza,* and the Empress *Helen,* who had been Wife to the Emperor *Beda Mariam,* much respected by all Men, for her singular Gravity and Wisdom.

This Lady had neither Son nor Daughter, but enjoy'd many Lands left her in the Kingdom of *Gojam* by her Husband, was very Rich, and perform'd extraordinary Works. The most famous of them all was the building the stately and magnificent Church, that had been till then in *Ethiopia,* whereof some considerable Remains were afterwards to be seen. In order to raise this Structure, she caused the ablest Architects to be brought out of *Egypt.* This Pile was erected in the middle of the Kingdom of *Gojam,* in a Territory call'd *Nebesse,* water'd by the River *Nile.* There at the Foot of a Hill was an Enclosure made of Stone and Clay square, and each side of it about 200 Fathom long, the Wall about 2 Yards thick, and above 5 in Height; the whole Work as was said of Clay and Stone, but so strong, that *F. Emanuel d' Almeyda* testifies it requir'd much Strength to break off any Stone.

A Church built.

Within this Enclosure the Church was built, all of it square, not only in the inner Part, which is like a Chappel, but in the outward Walls, contrary to the manner of all other *Ethiopian* Churches, which are round, as has been said before. *F. Emanuel d' Almeyda* saw a considerable part of these Walls still standing, and says they were about 104 Feet in length, and tho' much of it was fill'd up with the Stones that had fallen, he says the Chapel might be about 60 Foot long, and all the Stones, as well those standing as the others, fallen down large, smooth, fmooth, and moft artificially polifh'd, and on each of them were carved Rofes, Pinks, Lilies and feveral other Flowers, one upon each Stone ; and tho' very many had every one a different Flower on it, which was wonderful to fee, what variety of feveral Flowers the Artift could fanfie, and all of them fo curioufly cut, that it was impoffible to outdo them in Gold, Silver or Wax, or even with a Pencil. And the People told the Fathers, that feveral of thofe Rofes were cover'd with Gold and Silver, the Workmanfhip exceeding the value of the Metals, many of them ftill to be feen.

It was not only the Structure of this Church that coft fo much, for it was nobly endow'd and adorn'd, as having moft precious *Its Wealth* Veftments, and Gold Chalices and Patens of extraordinary value. *and Beauty.* F. *Emanuel d' Almeyda* affures us, that even in the Days of the Emperor *Sultan Segued,* he faw two Altar Stones belonging to it all of Solid Gold, the one weighing 800 and the other 500 *Oqueas.* However, there was one great defect in this noble Structure, which was want of light ; but perhaps not the Fault of the Architect, who might likely comply with the Cuftom of the Country, where, as has been faid, all the Churches are very dark. Now there being no other covering in *Ethiopia* but Thatch, and nothing to be done in this Church, either by Day or Night, but by Candle-light, we may eafily guefs how much it was expos'd to danger of Fire ; and before this ftately Work had ftood 20 Years, the *Mahometan Granbe,* invited by the Fame of the Wealth it contain'd, came, and after plundering fet Fire to it, fo that all was reduc'd to Afhes but the Stones. Out of thefe Ruins a *Roman Jefuit,* with the Affiftance of the Emperor *Sultan-Segued,* undertook to raife a more lafting Pile, which was call'd *Mertola Mariam;* that is, the Lodging of *Mary*; and F. *Jerome Lobo,* who was then prefent, fays, that when they came to dig up the Foundation of the Chappel to build the new one, they found four Gold Plates about the bignefs of the Palm of a Man's Hand, with the Name of one of the Evangelifts cut on each of them, as if the Chapel were founded on the four Evangelifts.

During the Reign of the aforefaid Emperor *Lebna Danguil, David,* or *Sultan Segued,* for he had all thefe Names, King *Emanuel*'s Ambaffador arriv'd in *Ethiopia,* which was in Return for the above mention'd *Matthew* the *Armenian,* fent into *Portugal,* at which Time the Affairs of *Abyffinia* being in a better Pofture than they prov'd afterwards, that Emperor's Letter bore feveral magnificent Titles, as *David, the beloved of God, Pillar of the Faith,* *The Empe-* *Kinfman to the Race of* Juda, *Son of* David, *Son of* Solomon, *Son of* *ror's Titles.* *the Pillar of* Sion, *Emperor of the Great and High* Ethiopia, *and of*
iti

its great Kingdoms and Provinces. &c. Hereupon King *Emanuel,* immediately order'd a Solemn Embaſſy in anſwer to this, and choſe for it *Edward Galvam,* a Perſon of ſingular Capacity, who had been Secretary to the Kings *Alfonſo* the V. and *John* the II. and Ambaſſador at *Rome,* in *Germany* and *France,* with whom he ſent one of his Chaplains call d *Francis Alvarez,* a Virtuous and Diſcreet Man. By them he ſent coſtly Preſents to the Emperor *David,* and his Protectreſs the Empreſs *Helen.* But the Ambaſſador *Edward Galvam* being above 70 Years of Age, dy'd in the Iſland of *Camarane,* which is within the *Red Sea;* ſo that the Embaſſy was diſappointed at that time. Afterwards *Lope Vaz de Sequeira* entering upon the Government of *India,* and ſailing into the *Red Sea* againſt the *Turks,* happen'd to put into the Port of *Mazua* in *April* 1520, which Iſland was then ſubject to the *Abyſſine* Emperor, and being there viſited by the Chriſtians of the Country, the *Bahar Nagays,* who is Governor of the Sea Coaſt, and the Monks of *Bizam,* and obſerving how joyfully they all receiv'd *Matthew* the *Armenian,* whom he brought back from *Portugal,* he reſolved to put his Prince's Commands in execution.

To this purpoſe he made Choice of *Don Roderick de Lima* to go Embaſſador, and with him went *F. Francis Alvarez,* and ſome

Portugueze *Embaſſy.*

other *Portuguezes,* and tho' they ſuffer'd much by the way, they all came ſafe to the Emperor's Court, who receiv'd them with great Pomp, and Expreſſions of Affection, ſignifying his Satisfaction for that Embaſſy, and entertaining them with all the Magnificence *Ethiopia* could afford, diſmiſſing them at laſt after many delays, either becauſe it is the Cuſtom of the Country, or for the more State. But the main Thing that kept them there 6 Years was the want of Shipping; for if any happen'd to come from *India,* it was at a time when they were very far from the Sea. At length they departed *Ethiopia* in the Year 1526, and the News of the Death of King *Emanuel,* and King *John* the III'ds. Acceſſion to the Crown

Ethiopian *Embaſſy.*

being brought before they were gone, the Emperor *David* ſent him a Letter, which may be ſeen at large in *F. Francis's* Hiſtory, *Chap.* 135, and with it his Crown of Gold and Silver, and as an Ambaſſador a Monk of his call'd *Zagaza Ab,* a Man in great Authority among them, and well read in their Books; by whom he alſo ſent a Letter to Pope *Clement* the VII. earneſtly intreating *F. Alvarez* that he would go with his Ambaſſador to *Rome.* Thoſe Letters are elegantly tranſlated into *Latin* by *Paulus Jovius,* and in them the ſaid Emperor acknowledges the Pope to be CHRIST's Vicar upon Earth, and Supream Head of the Church. The Ambaſſador was honourably receiv'd at *Rome,* and all this may be ſeen at large in *James de Conto, Dec.* 4. *lib.* 1. *cap.* 10. *John de Barros, Dec.* 4 *cap.* 4.

and

and in the faid *F. Francis Alvarez*'s Hiftory of *Ethiopia*. This Hiftory of *F. Alvarez*, has been tranflated into *Spanifh* and *Italian*, and may very fafely be credited, as *F. Emanuel d' Almeyda* obferves, in all things he fays, he faw, becaufe befides his being a Man of undoubted Reputation,there has been nothing fince found in *Ethiopia* to contradict what he affirms. However great Caution is to be us'd as to all thofe Affairs he took upon hearfay, becaufe the *Abyffines* are very much given to magnifying of all that belongs to them to Strangers, whom they delight to impofe upon, as the faid *F. Alvarez* found by Experience, in the difficulty they had of obtaining Audiences from the Emperor, whofe Treafures, tho' much greater at that time than fince, were nothing like what they pretended; and may much more eafily be fet down in Paper, than found in his Country.

The Ceremonies he tells us were us'd in conducting them lei-furely through the Doors, and the ftops they made in the Chambers of the Palace, were all Tricks they put upon the *Portuguefes*, as being Strangers. The Stage, or Throne, he fays, they faw the Emperor on, the firft time, was doubtlefs made only for that oc-cafion, his Throne being no other than a Couch after their Fafhi-on, but now he has one made in *China*, which the *Portuguefes* prefented him; and this, or thofe they had before, are generally well adorn'd, as has been already fignify'd.

Zagaza·Ab, the *Abyffine* Embaffador, who came into *Portugal*, *Declaration* with *F. Francis Alvarez*, compos'd a Treatife there, wherein he *of the* Ethi-declares the Faith of the *Ethiopians*, which was tranflated into *opian* Faith. *Latin* by *Damian de Goes*, and is to be feen in *Hifpania Illuftrata*, among the Affairs of *Portugal*; but we are to be very cautious in reading this Book, becaufe that *Abyffine* being in a ftrange Coun-try, fo remote from *Ethiopia*, where no body could contradict him, faid many things that were groundlefs, and fpoke not fo truly as he ought to have done concerning their Errors, faying there were none among them, whereas we are convinc'd there are very many.

Q CHAP.

Chap. II.

The great Havock made in Ethiopia *by the* Moor
Granhe; *the Emperor* David *craves Aid of the
King of* Portugal; David *dies, and is succeeded by*
Claudius; *Don* Christopher de Gama *comes to
his Assistance with* 400 *Men, and twice defeats the
Infidels.*

THE Emperor *David* above mention'd, who at the beginning
of his Reign had been extraordinary successful against his
Enemies the *Moors,* suffer'd very much in his latter Days, from
an Irruption made into his Dominions by *Ahamed,* the *Moor,*
who had the bye-Name of *Granhe,* signifying, Left-handed, because he was so. This Infidel being assisted by the King of *Adel,*
in Revenge for the Havock the Emperor *David* had made in his
Country, enter'd *Ethiopia* with a mighty Army, over-ran the
Kingdom of *Fategar,* destroy'd many Towns, burnt Villages,
took abundance of People, and had Thoughts of conquering all
Ethiopia, encourag'd by his first successes.

Granhe the Moor Invades Ethiopia.

The Emperor having such an Enemy within his own Dominions, gather'd all his Forces, consisting of 3000 Horse, and a
great multitude of Foot, and meeting *Granhe,* who had then but
300 Horse, and a much smaller number of Foot, was overthrown,
and abundance of his Men taken. Two Years after, the Emperor led on a greater Army, and tho' he obtain'd a considerable
Victory over the *Moor;* yet from the Year 1528 till 1540, when
David dy'd, the *Moors* of *Adel,* commanded by their General
Granhe, for he was neither King of *Zeila,* nor of *Adel,* nor is
Zeila any more than a Sea-Port of *Adel,* over-ran the best part
of the *Abyssine* Empire, routing all the best Commanders that
offer'd to oppose them, destroying all they met with, and plundering the Churches, which were then very rich.

Abyssines easily re- nounce their Faith.

Among the other Prisoners taken by the *Moors,* was one of
the Emperor's own Sons, call'd *Minas,* who succeeded *Claudius,*
his Elder Brother, in the Empire; besides many great Men of the
Abyssines went over and took part with *Granhe,* and what is worse,
immediately

immediately became *Mahometans*; but as *F. Francis Alvarez* observes they make no difficulty of changing their Religion; for as
soon as it goes ill with *Mahomet*, they again turn Christians, and
being rebaptiz'd, fansie they are as Innocent as new born Babes;
nor do they afterwards look upon it as any shame, that they renounc'd their Faith.

  The unfortunate Emperor perceiving the Ruin of his Empire,
and that the *Moorish* General bore down all before him, like an
impetuous Torrent, thought of sending to *India* to crave Succour
of the *Portuguese*, and at the same to *Portugal* to King *John* the
3d, and even to *Rome* to submit himself to the Pope again, so the
more to oblige him. To this purpose he pitched upon one Master
John, a *Portuguese* of the Embassador *Don Roderick de Lima*'s Re- *A Portu-*
tinue, who had stay'd behind, to go as his Envoy to crave Succour, *guese Pa-*
and the more to oblige him, order'd he should be created *Abuna*, *triarch.*
or Patriarch of *Ethiopia*, because he was a Catholick, by this good
beginning to show his Resolution of submitting to the See of *Rome.*
The *Abuna Marc*, was still living at that time, and enjoy'd that
Dignity in *Ethiopia*, being as *F. Francis Alvarez* writes, very well
affected towards the Catholick Faith, and readily comply'd with
the Emperor's Desires, naming the said Master *John* for his Successor, who from that time forwards was call'd *Don John Bermudes*,
and receiv'd Holy Orders there, for he was a Lay-Man before,
which Dignity the said *Don John* tells us in his History of *Ethiopia*
he receiv'd upon Condition that he was to go to *Rome* for the Pope
to confirm it.

  Having receiv'd the Emperors Letters, and taken Orders from *Confirm'd at*
the *Abuna*, he set out by Land, and after many Hardships ar- *Rome, and*
riv'd at *Rome*, in the Year 1538, *Paul* the 3d being Pope, who *sent back.*
receiv'd him with his usual Courtesie, and having dispatch'd him
with Bulls not only to be Patriarch of *Ethiopia*, but of *Alexandria* he came to *Portugal*, and was as well receiv'd by King *John*
the 3d, who honour'd him both as the Emperor's Embassador,
and Patriarch of *Alexandria*. He dismiss'd him with Orders to
be furnish'd with 450 Musquetiers in *India*, whither he sail'd in
the Year 1539, was honourably treated at *Goa*, by the Viceroy
Don Garcia de Noronha, who dying before he could put the Kings
Orders in Execution, was succeeded by *Don Stephen de Gama*,
who, as we shall see, convey'd the aforesaid supply into *Ethiopia*,
together with the above mention'd Patriarch *Don John Bermudez.*

  Whilst the Succours were preparing in *Portugal* and *India*, the
Emperor *David* declin'd daily, and at last retir'd to an inaccessible
Mountain, call'd *Damo*, most of the others being already subdu'd,
Q 2 where

Ethiopia
distress'd.

where he defended himself, with some brave Men that stuck to him, barely supporting the Name, tho' not the Majesty of an Emperor; but in this invincible Fortress he was conquer'd by Death, for there he ended his Days, at 42 Years of Age, whereof he reign'd 33, the first 20 prosperous, the last 13 full of Adversity. His Son *Glaudios,* or *Claudius* succeeded him, at 18 Years of Age, under the Direction of his Mother *Cabelo Oanguel.* The first Action of his Reign was successful, for having gather'd some Forces, he overthrew the *Moor Amiroxman;* but was soon after defeated by him, and forc'd to retire to *Xóa,* with only 60, or 80 Men, with whom he winter'd there. How the Emperor was reliev'd by the *Portuguefes* in this Diftrefs, we will now deliver out of *F. Peter Pays* his Account of the Affairs of *Ethiopia,* he having liv'd 19 Years in that Country, and known many of the *Portuguefes* themselves, or the Sons of those, who were concern'd in those Actions, which is thus.

400 Portu-
guefes *sent to*
succour Ethi-
opia.

In the Year 1541. *Don Stephen de Gama,* then Governor of *India,* enter'd the Red Sea with a confiderable Fleet, and having done much Harm to the Infidels on the Goaft of *Arabia,* came to an Anchor at the Ifland of *Mazua,* whence he fent his Brother *Don Chriftopher de Gama,* with 400 Men to the Affiftance of the Emperor of *Ethiopia.* Thefe Men met with extraordinary Difficulties in paffing the uncouth Mountains, over which it was almoft impoffible to draw their Canon, but having overcome them, and being met every where by the Country People, who look'd upon them as their Deliverers, they brought down the Emprefs *Cabelo Oanguel* from the Mountain *Damo,* to which fhe was retir'd for Safety, there being no way to get up it, but being hoifted in Baskets. In *December* they departed from *Debaroa,* where they had receiv'd the Emprefs, and with her march'd to join the Emperor, who was in another Place naturally impregnable. On the firft of *February* 1542. they came to a very ftrong Mountain, which the *Moor Granbe* had made himfelf Mafter of by Treachery, and pofted on it an Officer with 1500 Men. This Mountain is but Three Days Journey from *Debaroa* the right way, but they fpent fo much time becaufe they took a great Compafs about to reduce other Parts. *Don Chriftopher* refolv'd to attack the Mountain; becaufe fhould he leave the *Moors* poffefs'd of it, all that Country he had recover'd muft fubmit to them again, and they might cut off his Provifions. The Emprefs would have diffwaded him, reprefenting the Impracticablenefs of the Attempt, but his Refolution prevail'd.

On

On the Top of the Mountain is a Plain about a League over, *Impregnable* with Water enough to ferve Abundance of People, and tho' there *Mountain.* are Three Afcents, they are fo ftrong, that it appear'd impoffible to force them, had they been guarded but by a very fmall number. The chief of thefe Afcents is call'd *Amba Zanet,* which Name is given to all the Mountain. At the Foot of this Afcent was a ftrong Stone-Wall, with a Gate in it, whence the way up was very ftreight and fteep, and at the top another Gate in the Rock it felf. The 2d Afcent they call *Amba Xembut,* not fo difficult, tho' bad enough. The 3d is *Amba Gadabut,* ftronger than both the others, being all hew'd out of the Rock, and may be eafily kept with Stones from above. They are about a Mufquet-fhot from one another, and each of them defended by 500 Men with Bows, Arrows, Lances, and Bucklers. *Don Chriftopher* having obferv'd all this, order'd three falfe Attacks to be made that the *Moors* might fpend their Arrows, and having perform'd it, without coming too near, upon a Signal given all his Men drew off, the *Moors* giving great Shouts for Joy. The next Morning, by break of Day, he attack'd the three Paffes in Earneft, and forc'd them all, the Infidels flying to the top, where being purfu'd by the *Portuguefes,* they were every Man of them kill'd. Of *Gain'd by* the *Portuguefes* Eight were Slain, and 40 wounded. The Place *the Portu-* was deliver'd up to the *Ethiopians,* who plentifully fupply'd the *guefe.* *Portuguefes* with Provifions, during all the Month of *February* they ftay'd there, admiring that Action, which they had thought Impracticable.

Intelligence being brought that Five *Portuguefe* Veffels were arriv'd at *Mazua, Don Chriftopher* fent a Captain of his own, with 40 Men to get fome fupply of Ammunition, and carry Letters for the Viceroy of *India,* and fet forward himfelf, with his Forces towards a Country, where a Chriftian *Abyffine* had been compell'd to fubmit to the *Moors,* and now fent to inform him, that if he would come to him, he would find no oppofition. He had not gone far before he receiv'd an Exprefs from the Emperor, defiring he would make hafte to join him, becaufe the *Moor Granhe* was advancing towards them, and each apart would be too weak to withftand him. Being come to thofe Lands, whither the *Ethiopian* Commander above mention'd, had invited him, he was met and prefented by him with Eight fine Horfes, and inform'd the Enemy was fo near, that he could not advance without meeting them. It troubled *Don Chriftopher* that he could neither join the Emperor, nor ftay for thofe Men he had fent to *Mazua,* however he refolv'd to Fight, and encouraging his Men, they all approv'd of his Refolution. The next Day the Enemy being at
                                   hand.

Their first
Victory.

hand he incamp'd on a Rising Ground, where *Granbe* having taken a View of his small Forces, enclos'd him with 15000 Foot, arm'd with Bows, and Arrows, Darts, and Bucklers, besides 1500 Horse, and 200 *Turkish* Musquetiers, thinking to starve him out. *Don Christopher* understanding his Design, after some small Skirmishes drew out all his Men with the Empress in the Center, on the 4th of *April*, 1542. The Canon and Muskets made the Infidels keep off, but the *Turks* advanc'd and did some harm with their Shot, and *Granbe* himself coming on with 500 Horse, the *Portuguefes* began to be hard press'd, but that the Canon being well play'd kill'd many of the Horse and made the rest slacken. Many of the *Portuguefs* were now wounded, and *Don Christopher* shot through a Leg, yet left not the Battle, but encourag'd his Men. *Granbe* on the other side thinking his Men gave way, came up so close, that he was also shot through the Leg, and his Horse kill'd under him, whereupon his Men struck their Colours, and carry'd him off, the *Portuguefes* pursuing them till they were all so spent that it was thought a rashness to go any farther, and therefore they return'd victorious to their Camp, where they found the Empress and her Women, dressing the wounded Men and binding their Hurts with their own Linnen, for want of other. Of the *Portuguefes* Eleven were kill'd, among the Infidels slain the *Abyssines* knew four of *Granbe*'s Commanders of Note, and 30 *Turks*, *Don Christopher* sent that very Night, to acquaint the *Portuguefes*, who were gone to *Mazua*, with his Success and hasten them back.

Twelve Days after the Defeat of *Granbe*, the *Portuguefes*, who had been wounded, being pretty well recover'd, and the Infidels recruited and grown strong by several Parties, that join'd them, *Don Christopher* resolv'd to give Battel again, and marching towards them was receiv'd with great Shouts and Cries of those *Barbarians*, much encourag'd by their fresh Accession of Forces, and particularly that of a famous Commander call'd *Garac Amar*, who had brought them 500 Horse and 3000 Foot. This Man took the van, and charg'd the *Portuguefes* with such Fury, that had all his Men been like him, he must doubtless have over-run them, but the damage the Canon did prevailing with them to keep very open, he and Four or Five others, who follow'd him close breaking into the *Portuguefes* Battel, were kill'd fighting bravely. *Granbe*, who was carry'd on Mens Shoulders, because of his Wound, order'd all the rest of his Horse to Charge on all sides, which made the Fight very hot. Only Eight *Portuguefes* had Horses, and did wonders, but being so few durst not go far from their Foot, who made a great Slaughter of the Enemy.

The second.

In

In the Heat of the Action the Powder of the *Portuguese* unfortunately took Fire and blew up, killing two of them and hurting several others; yet had this good Effect, that the noise so terrify'd the Infidels Horses that they ran away in spight of their Riders, and the *Portuguese* improving that Advantage, charg'd the Foot so vigorously that they were put to flight, and pursu'd about half a League, which was the farthest the Victors were able to follow for mere weariness. The Enemies Tents were all taken standing with much Booty. Of the *Portuguese* 14 were kill'd, and 60 wounded, whereof 4 dy'd of their Wounds. That ground being unfit to encamp, they march'd thence to a pleasant River side, where they saw many *Moors* with their General *Granbe*, who perceiving they were discover'd, fled with all speed, for Eight Days together to a strong Mountain, many of them perishing by the way.

Don Christopher having lain in that Place two Days to cure the Wounded Men, was there join'd by the *Portuguese*, who had been sent to *Mazua*, and by the *Babar Nagays* with 30 Horse, and 500 Foot. Being thus reinforc'd, he resolv'd to pursue *Granbe* immediately, and therefore leaving 14 of his Men, that were most Wounded on a strong Mountain, under the Care of the Governor of the Country, who was extraordinary kind to them, he march'd on Ten Days, till he came to the Mountain *Granbe* had fled to, which was very large, and strong. The Winter now beginning with much Rain, *Don Christopher* was perswaded to take up Quarters during it, at the Foot of another Mountain opposite to that where *Granbe* lay, convenient for cutting off his Provisions. The Country People built the Men Huts, and brought them plenty of Provisions with great readiness and good will.

In this Place a *Jew* inform'd *Don Christopher*, that he might easily make himself Master of a strong Mountain, call'd *Oaiy*, in the Province of *Cemen*, which was near, and where there were many Horses; besides that the Emperor, who had but small Forces, could not come to join him any other way. He set out at Mid-Night with 100 *Portuguese*, and coming to the Mountain went up it the way the *Jew* led, but on the top found 3000 *Moorish* Foot and 400 Horse, whom after a sharp Dispute he routed with much Slaughter, and of those that fled many were kill'd by the *Jews*, who inhabited that Mountain. Not one *Portuguese* was kill'd in this Action, which amaz'd the *Jews* of the Mountain, and particularly him that guided them, who thereupon became a Christian, and having been always Loyal to the Emperor was left Governor of the Mountain, as he had been always before the *Moors* took it. The Booty was very considerable,

[marginal notes:] Don Christopher de Gama blocks up Granhe.

Gains a strong Mountain.

siderable, and among the rest 300 Mules, and 80 choice Horses, which *Don Christopher* valu'd most, and return'd to the Camp with all speed, for Fear the Infidels knowing of his Absence, should attack it; leaving 30 *Portuguese* to follow with the Horses because the way being very bad, they travell'd slowly.

Granhe *reinforc'd.* During the time the *Portuguese* winter'd, the *Moor Granhe* labour'd to gather new Forces, and especially to get some *Turks*, and sending a considerable Present to the Bassa of *Zebid*, in *Arabia*, was by him supply'd with 700 Musquetiers, 30 of them Horse, and 10 Field Pieces; besides a number of *Arabs*, to whom a considerable number join'd themselves out of *Ethiopia*. The *Turks* arriv'd the same Night that *Don Christopher* return'd to his Camp, and the next Day *Granhe* came down from the Mountain, covering the Plain with his Men, and encamp'd so near the *Portuguese*, that their Field-Pieces reach'd their Intrenchments. *Don Christopher* seeing what a strong supply *Granhe* had receiv'd, consulted with his Officers, among whom it was resolv'd, that it was impossible to retire, and therefore they must Fight; but would make the best Defence they could in their Camp, till the other *Portuguese* came up with their Horses. They therefore sent to hasten them, and spent the Day in preparing to receive the Enemy, yet could not hold out till the Horses came, as we shall see in the next Chapter.

CHAP.

C H A P. III.

The laft Battel, in which Don Chriftopher *was defeated* ; *his Death* ; *the* Portuguefes, *who efcap'd
the Slaughter, join the Emperor* Claudius, *and rout
fome of* Granhe's *Commanders* ; *how that Infidel
was routed, and kill'd* ; *what happ'ned after this
Victory, and how the Emperor flighted the* Portuguefes.

THE *Moor Granhe* finding himfelf fo ftrong, refolv'd to lofe ne
Time, and therefore the next Morning, being the 28th *Au-
guft* 1542, by break of Day he advanc'd towards the *Portuguefe*
Camp with all his Men, the *Turks* leading the Van, with 10
Pieces of Cannon. *Don Chriftopher* on the other fide, affign'd his
Men their Pofts, with Orders only to make them good, without
fallying upon the Enemy, till the Horfes were come up. When **Gama at-**
they were within Mufquet-fhot, both fides began to play their **tack'd.**
Cannon and fmall Arms with great Fury, which lafted fome
Hours, the Infidels ftill advancing ; fo that *Don Chriftopher* perceiving his Intrenchments were not ftrong enough to oppofe fuch
a Power, fally'd out with 50 *Portuguefe* Mufquetiers, and falling
on 100 *Turks*, and a number of *Moors* drove them for a confiderable fpace, with much flaughter, but a greater multitude coming
upon him, he retir'd again, with the lofs of four of his Men kill'd,
and moft of the reft wounded, as was he himfelf with a Mufquet-
Ball in his Leg. The other *Portuguefe* Commanders, in their turns
made Sallies, and drove the Enemy a confiderable fpace, but in
the Retreat, they ftill loft Men, and had many wounded. Thus
they held on till Noon, when the Emprefs's Houfe was fo full
of wounded Men, that it could hold no more, and the Enemy
drew fo near, that two of her Women were hurt within it.
Captain *Franfis de Abreu* fallying with his Men, and having beat
back the *Turks*, in his Retreat was fhot Dead, and his Brother
Humphrey, who fuftain'd him with another Body, underwent the
fame Fate. *Don Chriftopher* having loft fo many brave Men, and
feeing the reft either wounded, or much tir'd, fally'd out himfelf

R   with

with the Royal Standard fo furiously, that he drove the Infidels before him with great Slaughter; and it is thought would have certainly got the Day, had the Horfes been come up, but there were only Eight with him, which fought all the Day. Yet he purfu'd the *Moors* a confiderable way, and then his Men being fpent retir'd. The *Turks* then rally'd, firing after the *Portuguefes*, fome of whom they kill'd, and broke *Don Chriftopher's* Right Arm.

Diftrefs'd. Captain *Emanuel de Acunha* came in at this time, with his Men, and brought them off, but many wounded, and the reft fo fpent, that they were not able to make ufe of their Arms. However they twice repuls'd the *Turks,* who had broke into their Trenches, and the Day being far wafted, compell'd *Don Chriftopher* by main Force to retire towards the Mountain, the Patriarch, and the Emprefs going before. Many of thofe who could not keep up, be-

Routed. caufe of their Wounds, were kill'd in the Purfuit; but Night coming on, and the Mountain being very woody, the greateft part efcap'd, efpecially thofe who follow'd the Patriarch and the Emprefs. The *Turks* enter'd the Camp, and butcher'd Forty *Portuguefes* they found fo defperately wounded, that they were not able to ftir.

    Don Chriftopher efcap'd that Night, with 14 wounded Men; the next Day they were all but one taken by a Party of Infidels, who carry'd them to their General *Granhe*, before whom lay 170 Heads of the *Portuguefe* flain, which he had gather'd, giving a Reward

Barbar oufly us'd and beheaded. for every one. The Barbarian caus'd *Don Chriftopher* to be cruelly Scourg'd in his Prefence, and buffeted, with his Slaves Slippers, and after leading him about the Camp with much Cruelty, he was return'd to *Granhe*, who twifted his Beard with Wax, fet Fire to it, pull'd off his Eye-Brows, and Eye-Lafhes with Nippers, and after many more Inhumanities ftruck off his Head, with his own Hand. The *Turks* hearing of his Death, were in a great Rage, for they defign'd to have fent him to *Conftantinople*, and therefore after upbraiding the *Moor* for prefuming to kill him without their Knowledge, they went away, to return to *Zebid*, with *Don Chriftopher's* Head, and the *Portuguee* Prifoners, yet left him 200 *Turks*, as they had been order'd, in Confideration for the Tribute he paid them. A *Portuguefe* who made his Efcape from them gave this Account.

    The *Portuguefes* during that difmal Night after their overthrow wander'd about the Mountain, not knowing whither they went, only thofe who follow'd the Emprefs had the better, becaufe there were *Ethiopians* to lead them, who knew the Country. She had fent People every way to conduct fuch as were aftray. The next Day, thofe who had been left with the Horfes join'd her, but

but knew nothing before of the Defeat. Soon after came the *Portuguese*, who escaped, when *Don Christopher* was taken, and then the other that fled from the *Turks*, and having told the manner of his Death, it renew'd their Sorrow. The Empress with all the Women lamented him for 8 Days, as if he had been her own Son. *Scattered Portuguese assemble.* On this Mountain they continu'd some Days to rest themselves, and cure the wounded, as also to pick up those that were scatter'd till about 120 came together, and they receiv'd Intelligence, that the Captain *Emanuel D. Acunha*, with 50 *Portuguese* had got safe into the Country of the *Bahar Nagays*, without knowing which way they went, and where there very lovingly entertain'd. Some time after, the Empress with the *Portuguese*, and all that follow'd her, went to the *Jews* Mountain, which *Don Christopher* had gain'd, because besides its being almost impregnable, there are large Corn Fields on it, Abundance of Grass for Cattel, and Plenty of Water, which never fails. They were well receiv'd by the Commander *Don Christopher* left there, who supply'd them with all they wanted, or could ask of him.

Ten or twenty Days after their coming to this Mountain, the Emperor arriv'd at the Foot of it, with very few and those sorry Men, whom the *Portuguese* went down to receive, and he, tho' highly concern'd for their Loss and the Death of *Don Christopher*, did them much Honour, bidding them not to think they were in a strange Country, since it should be as their own, and immediately furnish'd them all bountifully with Cloaths, Tents, Mules, Servants, and all other Necessaries. He stay'd on the Mountain some Months, till his Forces came together, and he had assembled 500 Horse, and 8000 Foot, when the *Portugueses*, thinking they were strong enough to fight the *Moors*, begg'd of him, that he would assist them to revenge *Don Christopher*'s Death. He question'd the doing of it with so small a Number; but understanding that the *Turks* were gone home, and only 200 of them left, he consented. He sent to the 50 *Portugueses*, that were gon to the Land of *Bahar-Nagays* to come to him with all possible Speed, and to bring with them the spare Arms *Don Christopher* had left on the Mountain *Damo*, where he found the Empress, that being a Place of Safety. When the Emperor's Messengers came they found not the *Portugueses*, who believing that all the Rest of their Countrymen were cut off, and it was impossible for them to come to the Emperor, were gon towards *Mazua*, to expect some Vessels, to carry them back to *India*. The Emperor's Servants return'd with the Arms, which were of great use, because those who had escap'd from the Battel were very ill provided. *The Emperor whom the Portugueses joins them.*

The

The Emperor perceiving it was in vain to expect thofe *Portuguefes*, who were too far off, fet out from that Place on the 6th of February 1543, with 120, or 130 *Portuguefes*, who refuſ 'd to be commanded by any Man, but the Emperor himfelf. With thefe, and his own 500 Horfe and 8000 Foot, he mov'd towards the *Moor Granbe*, leaving the Emprefs his Mother on that Mountain. In the Province of *Ogara* he found a *Moorifh* Commander, with 300 Horfe, and 2000 Foot, whom he attacked by break of Day, 50 *Portuguefe* Horfe leading the Van and flew the Commander, with moſt of his Men, taking fome Prifoners, who jnform'd him that *Granbe* was not far off in the Kingdom of *Dambea*, at a Place call'd *Darafquea*, near the Lake the *Nile* croffes, with his Wife and Children, who having been long from him, came thither foon after he overthrew *Don Chriftopher*.

Granbe underftanding that the Emperor was advancing towards him, mufter'd his Forces, and found 13000 Horfes and Foot, befides 200 *Turks*. The Emperor came and incamped in Sight of the Infidels, at a Place call'd *Oinadaga*, where there were feveral Skirmifhes, before they came to a Battel; in one of which 70 *Portuguefe* Horfe charg 'd 200 of the Enemy, killing their Commander, with 12 of his Men, and putting the Reſt to flight. The *Abyffine* General was a notable Soldier, and did the Enemy much Harm, who therefore drew him out treacheroufly, on Pretence of a Conference, and fhot him dead, which much difcourag'd his Men, and therefore the Emperor refolv'd to fight immediatly for Fear they fhould deferthim· At Break of Day the Army drew out, the *Portuguefe* leading the Van, with 250 *Ethiopian* Horfe, and 350 Foot. The Emperor brought up the Rear with 250 Horfe more, and 4500 Foot. In this Pofture they advanc'd towards the Enemy, who mov'd in two Lines alfo, *Granbe* leading the firſt, with 200 *Turkifh* Mufqueters, 600 *Moorifh* Horfe, and 7000 Foot, the fecond was commanded by another General, and confifted of 600 Horfe, and 6000 Foot. Both Armies charg'd with great Fury, and the *Turks* began to drive the *Ethiopians* before them, which they *Portuguefes* perceiving they turn'd that way and made them retire to the Main Body of the *Moors*, whither they purfu'd them with many of the braveſt *Abiffines*, and oblig'd them to turn their Backs. *Granbe* perceiving their Diforder came up in Perfon, but the *Portuguefes* knowing him he was foon fhot through the Body, and dropt upon his Horfes Neck. His Men feeing it, Made no longer Refiſtance but fled immediatly. Only the Commander of the *Turks* would not condefcend to fave himfelf by Flight, but attack'd 5 *Abyffine* Horfemen, wreſted a Spear out of one of their Hands, and houghed his Horfe, cut a *Portuguefe* over the Knee, and laid hold of his

Lance

(margin note left, upper) Defeats a Party of Moors.

(margin note left, lower) Granbe defeated and kill'd.

Lance, but was kill'd by him with his Sword. The Emperor's Men purfu'd the flying *Moors* with great Slaughter, but the *Portuguefes* apply'd themfelves fo entirely to the *Turks,* That of 200 only 14 efcap'd, to *Granhe's* Wife, who hearing of the Rout, got away with 350 Horfe, that guarded her, and all the Treafure her Husband had fcrap'd together; the Conquerors being all bufy deftroying their Enemies, and taking the Plunder of the Camp, where they found a confiderable Number of Captives,to their great. Joy, fome meeting with their own Children, others their Wives, and others their Brothers, or Sifters. They all acknowledg'd the great Affiftance receiv'd from the *Portuguefes,* and the Emperor did them extraordinary Honour, and it was very remarkable, that, tho' they fought with fuch Bravery, not one of them was kill'd.

Thus far *F. Peter Pays,* who had the whole Account, from creditable Perfons, who were Eye-witneffes. The Emperor after returning Thanks to God, for fo great a Victory, coming down from the high Grounds of *Oinadaga,* incamp'd near the great Lake they call the Sea of *Dambea,* before defcrib'd. Being ftill dubious, whether *Granhe,* was dead of his Wounds, an *Ethiopian* Commander brought him that Infidels Head, pretending he had kill'd him; but a *Portuguefe* Soldier producing an Ear he had cut off, when he fell prov'd the Fact was his own. The Head was firft fhown to the Emprefs, and afterwards fent to all Parts of the Empire, to be feen by the People, who made great Rejoycings, for being deliver'd from fo barbarous an Enemy. The 50 *Portuguefes,* who we faid went for *Mazu,* after the Defeat of *Don Chriftopher,* in order to embark for *India,* hearing the News, turn'd back immediately, and taking the Emprefs along with them, came to he Camp, and joint'd the others, that were there before The Emperor continu'd in that Place two Months, during which time the Fame of the Victory fpread it felf all over *Ethiopia,* confirm'd by the Sight of *Granhes* Head, the *Moors,* who were in feveral Garrifons flying, and whole Kingdoms and Provinces returning to the Emperors, Obedience, as did moft of the great Men, who had rebell'd and join'd the *Moors,* renouncing their Faith, all whom the Emperor admitted to Grace, it being no new Thing with thofe People to change their Party and their Religion, according to Succefs. Among thefe was *Raz Adeguna,* Father to *Ifaac* the *Bahar Nagays,* who, tho' a great Offender was pardon'd for the Sake of his Son, that had continu'd Loyal, and brought in the *Portuguefes.* Another came and fubmitted himfelf, who was faid to have been the Caufe of *Don Chriftopher's* Death; whom alfo the Emperor forgave at the Requeft of many great Men, which the *Portuguefes* remonftrating againft, he anfwer'd, That having given his word, he could not depart

part from it. Hereupon two *Portuguese* went into that *Ethiopian's* Tent, and ftabb'd him in many Places with their Daggers. [*This was certainly a great Piece of Infolence in those Men; tho' it went unpunish'd, in regard of their late Merit, and was doubtlefs an Incouragement to them to commit other Villanies, for which it is likely they were afterwards fo hardly uf'd as they complain of.*]

Funeral Obfequies.

The Month of Auguft coming on, towards the End whereof was the Anniverfary of *Don Chriftopher's* Death, which the Emperor refolv'd to commemorate, after their Manner, he fent to all the Country about, for the Clergy, and Poor to repair to his Camp. The Number of the latter amounted to above 6000, to all whom he gave bountifull Alms, and a noble Entertainment to about 600 Monks, and a great number of Clergy-men; this Treat being the Principal Invitation to the Funeral Obfequies, which they perform their Way, faying over all *David's* Pfalter entire, without any Leffons, Antiphons, or Verfes, or any other Diftinction, but only Abundance of *Hellalujahs*, fo often repeated, that they make fufficient Amends for the want of Leffons, for they are no lefs free of them upon forrowfull Occafions, than upon the Joyful.

The *Ethiopians* had promis'd, under their Diftrefs, to fubmit themfelves to the See of *Rome*, as appears by the Embaffies above mention'd, the Emperor *David* fent to that City, and to *Portugal*. They alfo ingag'd to give the *Portuguefes* the third Part of their Empire, in Cafe it was recover'd by their means from the *Moors*; but when deliver'd they perform'd neither. The Partriarch *Don John Bermudez* feeing the fuccefs of the *Portuguefe* Arms, put the Emperor *Claudius* in Mind of his Father's Promife to fubmit himfelf to the See of *Rome*, and requir'd his Performance, to which the Emperor return'd a very haughty Anfwer; where-

Ethiopians exafperated by the Portuguefe Demands.

upon, the Patriarch after feveral Admonitions, excommunicated the faid Emperor, and threatned to do the fame by the *Portuguefes* if they ferv'd him any longer. The Emperor valu'd not the Excommunication, but perceiving the *Portuguefes*, of whom he ftill ftood in need defign'd to return to *India*, he alter'd his Tone, pretended to repent, honour'd the Patriarch, renounc'd his Errors, and folemnly fwore to embrace the Catholick-Faith, commanding all Perfons by found of Kettle-Drums to own the Pope as Head of the Church; but all this was counterfeit, and happen'd before the Death of the *Moor Granhe*. As foon as he faw that Infidels Head he difcover'd himfelf, defpifing the Patriarch, fending to *Alexandria* for another *Abuna*, and mifufing the *Portuguefes*. Not fo fatisfy'd, he commanded his Army to deftroy them all, yet they ftanding together, made their Party good againft 20000 *Ethiopians*, killing many, and obliging the Reft to defift.

Th

The Emperor thus difappointed of his Aim, the better to bring it about, fell again to his Diffimulation, pretending to repent, that he might with lefs Danger take them in the Snare; yet could not but fhow his Deceitfulnefs; for being inform'd, that the new *Abuna Jofeph* was come from *Alexandria,* he went away to receive him at *Debaroa* with great Solemnity. The Patriarch *Don John Bermudez* immediately follow'd and the Emperor hearing of it, order'd him to be fecur'd, and put into one of thofe natural Fortreffes we have fpoken of call'd *Ambas.* As foon as the *Portuguefes* were inform'd of it, they forc'd that Place, and refcu'd him. The Patriarch perceiving how little good he was like to make of that Dignity, refolv'd to withdraw himfelf into *India,* before the Emperor brought him into fome greater Inconveniency. Accordingly he privately retir'd into the Kingdom of *Tigre,* and to *Debaroa,* where he lay conceal'd about two Years, and in the Year 1556 went over to *Goa,* and thence to *Portugal,* where King *Sebaftian,* who had fucceeded King *John* the 3d, allow'd him an Honourable Maintenance.

The Portuguefe Patriarch withdraws.

C H A P. IV.

How the Portuguefes *liv'd in* Ethiopia, *after what has been faid above;* King John *the 3d is for fending a Patriarch thither, fome* Jefuits *fet out for that Miffion; an Embaffy fent into* Ethiopia *proves unfuccefs full.*

OF *Don Chriftopher de Gama's* Men, about 170 remain'd, to whom the Emperor *Claudius* gave confiderable Lands, on which they liv'd plentifully, after the Country Fafhion, moft of them having Horfes, Mules and Servants to attend them both in Peace, and War, as all the Fathers who were in *Ethiopia* about that Time do teftify. But under the fucceeding Emperor *Adamas Segued,* they fuffer'd very much; and in the Reign of his Son *Malac Segued,* who rul'd 34 Years. tho' they were not altogethet fo hardly us'd yet they found not the Kindnefs they deferv'd; for the *Abiffines* never truly affected them. I do not deny, but that they gave them

Portuguefe well rewarded.

                                                            fome

fome Occafion at firft, as undervaluing the *Ethiopians*, and taking too great Liberty, as is uf'd among Soldiers, in ftrange Countries. [*We fee here, as was obferv'd before, that the* Abyffines *were not altogether to blame, being much provok'd by the Pride, and intolerable Crimes of thofe, who pretended to defend them, fo that perhaps they knew not whether the* Moors *were worfe Enemies, than thefe Auxiliaries.*]

It is ufual in *Ethiopia* for the Emperors to take away, and change the Lands of their Officers and Soldiers; which they after practis'd upon the *Portuguefes*, always allotting them fuch as were on the Frontiers, where they muft be continually upon their Guard, and obtain'd fignal Victories, under their Commander *George Nogueyra*, who was fucceeded by *Francis Jacome*; and the Lands they gave them being the worft and moft expof'd, which they took away when improv'd, and better fecur'd, the Soldiers fuffer'd much Want, efpecially the old Men, Widows, and Children, who had no Allowance, and therefore the others Charitably fhar'd what they had with them, whether little or much. The *Portuguefes* labouring under thefe Difficulties, wrote often to the Kings of *Portugal*, and Viceroys of *India*, begging Relief, fome of which Letters I have feen, writ on Pieces of Parchment, and Slips of Paper, by their Captain *Francis Jacome*, and *Gafpar de Mez-*
Viciffitudes in *quita* and others whofe Names are not now legible. However
their Fortune. they were never brought away, but that they might not feem to be wholly neglected, it was order'd, that they fhould have every Year 1200 *Pardaos* of *Mamudes*, being fo many Pieces of Eight, return'd them, out of the Cuftom-Houfe at *Diu*, which has been accordingly practis'd, but is a very fmall Support, confidering the Number of thofe defcended from the *Portuguefe*. The Kings of *Portugal* alfo ordain'd, that *Jefuits* fhould be fent into *Ethiopia* to confirm the *Portuguefes* in the Faith, and convert the *Abyffines*; and as long as thofe Fathers had any Intereft with the Emperors, they always favour'd the *Portuguefes*; efpecially, when the Patriarch *Don Alfonfo Mendez* was there, in the Reign of the Emperor *Sultan Segued*, who affign'd many Lands for the Refidences of the Fathers, and the Maintenance of the *Portuguefes*. Befides *Raz Sela Chriftos*, that Emperor's Brother, call'd many of them to his Army, and gave them good Lands, fo that no *Ethiopians* made a better fhow at Court, or in the Camp, yet afterwards when Things alter'd, as fhall be fhown they came to want Neceffaries, and endur'd great Hardfhips, having only the Comfort of wifhing, or hoping to be carry'd away into *Portugal*; but there they ftill remain in Servitude, wholly forfaken, and abandon'd.

This was the Pofture of Affairs in *Ethiopia*, when at *Lisbon* they imagin'd it was wholly reduc'd to the Obedience of the See of *Rome*,
and

and that for perfecting its Conversion there only wanted the King A Patriarch of *Portugal*'s sending a Patriarch, and Missioners, which the King *and Bishops* presently resolved to do after having sent the 400 Soldiers, above *chosen for* mention'd. If any rightly remark that the Patriarch Don *John* *Ethiopia.* *Bermudez* being still living, it looks unlikely that another should be sent, without taking notice of him, we shall satisfy them by declaring that the Pope consecratd him Patriarch of *Alexandria*,and Don *John Nunez Barreto*,was now sent as Patriarch of *Ethiopia.* King *John* the 3d of *Portugal* having propos'd his Design to Pope *Julius*, the 3d, and to *S. Ignacius*, they pitch'd upon *F. Nunez Barreto* to be Patriarch of *Ethiopia*, *F. Andrew de Oviedo* for Bishop of *Hierapolis* and *F.Melchior Carneyro* of *Nice.*

Whilst all Things were disposing for their Consecration, and Departure, 12 Religious Men were immediately sent for *Ethiopia* by the Founder of the Society, and these were *F. Antony de Quadros,* *F. Emanuel Fernandez,* *Micer John* a *Fleming*, *Michael Calatayud,* 12 Jesuits a *Catalonian*, and *Jerome de Cuenca*, with the Brothers *John Gon-* sent. *zalves*, *Bartholomew Carrilo*, *Francis Lopez*, *Gonzalo Cordero*, *Anto-* *ny Fernandez*, and *John de Bustamante*; besides three other Religi- ous Men of the Province of *Castile*, call'd *F. Andrew Gonzales,* born at *Medina del Campo* ; *F. Pascual*, a *Catalonian*, and Brother *Alfonso Lopez*. These sail'd from *Lisbon* aboard the *India* Ships, on the first of April 1555, but one of the Ships, in which were the 3 last Fathers above mention'd was cast away 500 Leagues from *Goa*, on the Flats call'd of *Pero dos Banhos*. The others arriv'd safe in *India*. At *Lisbon* the Patriarch and Bishops were soon after con- secrated, and the King generously furnish'd them with Vestments, Plate for the Service of the Altar, Books, and all other Necessa- ries. It is to be observ'd, that the two Bishops were appoint- ed Coadjutors to the Patriarch, and to succeed him, one after another in the said Dignity, with full Power to Consecrate other Bishops, ordain Priests, and use all Patriarchal, and Episcopal Jurisdiction.

Considering the great Distance betwixt *Portugal*, and *Ethiopia*, and the Instability of human Affairs, King *John* had order'd *Don* *Peter Mascarnehas*, the new Viceroy of *India* to sound the Minds of the *Ethiopians* touching their receiving the new Patriarch, for Fear of any Change in them. The Viceroy accordingly made Choice of one *James Diaz*, a Priest, to go in the Quality of En- F. Gonzalo. voy, or Embassador, into *Ethiopia*, and with him sent a very able Rodriguez and religious Father of the Society, call'd *Gonzalo Rodriguez*, with *in* Ethiopia. the Lay-Brother *Fulgenocio Freyre*, who had serv'd the King well in *India*, and afterwards led a very pious Life in the Society. These had the King of *Portugal*'s, and the Viceroys, Credentials, S   and

and fail'd from *Goa* with a good Convoy of Men of War and other
Veffels on the 7th of February 1555, and in 30 Days came to an
Anchor at *Arquico*, a Port then belonging to the *Abiffine* Emperor.
Having refted a few Days, they continu'd their Journey by Land,
and being come to the Place where the *Bahar Nagays*, or Governour of the maritime Provinces, was, were by him favourably receiv'd, with Expreffions of Affection. Thence they proceeded
to the Place where the Emperor was. We will now deliver the Account of their Journey and Proceedings from a Letter writ by the
aforefaid Father *Gonzalo Rodriguez* out of *Ethiopia* to the Fathers of
the Society in *Portugal*, and dated the 13th of September 1556,
where we fhall find many Particulars concerning that Empire of unqueftionable Truth, and well worth our Knowledge.
He writes to this Effect.

His Acount
of Affairs
there.

'On the 17th of *May* we arriv'd where the Emperor of *Ethiopia*
'was, whom we found incamp'd, with Abundance of Tents a-
'bout him; he order'd us to be receiv'd, and the next Day we
'had Audieance of him. He fate on a Couch, with Curtains about
'it, and all the Tent adorn'd with Silk Hangings, and Carpets.
'*James Diaz* deliver'd him his Letters, which he order'd to be
'read, in the prefence of all the *Portuguefes*. In them our King
'inform'd him, that, the next year, he would fend one of his own
'Houfehold, with a Number of religious Men of holy Lives, and
'fingular Learning. He look'd much out of Countenance, and
'was fo diforder'd, that when we fpoke to him, he anfwer'd no-
'thing to the Purpofe, and fo we took our Leave, and 2, or 3
'Days after he went away to vifit a Grand-mother of his, 8, or 10
'Days Journey off, leaving us in an open Field wholly unprovid-
'ed, without any Body fo much as to compliment us in his
'Name. An honeft *Portuguefe* made amends, carrying us to his
'Houfe, which was 2, or 3 Leagues off, where we were entertain-
'ed, and he return'd to the Emperor. Here we continu'd about a
'Month, the Emperor fpent in his Journey, and I compos'd a
'Treatife of the *Ethiopian* Errors, and the Infallibility of our holy
'Faith, to prefent it to the Emperor; and was at the fame time
'inform'd by a *Portuguefe*, who was much in his Favour, that
'he faid, he had no Occafion for the Fathers, and would not fub-
'mit to the See of *Rome* ; and others affur'd me, that feveral great
'Men declar'd, they would rather be fubject to the *Moors*, the
'leave their ancient Cuftoms for ours. This confirm'd me in
'the Refolution of giving him all in Writing, that I might have
'fpoken by word of Mouth, had I known the Language, that by
'his Anfwers, I might fully know his Defigns, which he had fo
long

' long Difguis'd. I therefore defir'd the Emperor would affign
' me two learned Monks to tranflate what I had writ, and alfo
' let me fee a Book, which they call, the *Adultery of the Francs*,
' compos'd by the Schifmaticks of *Alexandria*, from whom they
' receive their *Abuna*, and therefore Pay Tribute to the *Turks* ;
' and the faid Book rejects the Councill of *Chalcedon*, pretending
' that it made four Perfons of the Bleffed Trinity, and charging us
' with many more Errors.

 ' He refus'd the Book, and was very angry that we knew the
' Contents of it ; but appointed the Monks, yet they would not
' put their Hand to tranflating, either for Fear of the Emperor, or
' becaufe he had fo order'd. However with the Affiftance of the
' Captain of the *Portuguefes* I got it done, an honeft *Portuguefe*,
' who underftood the Language well, being my Interpreter. Then
' having ask'd a Monk to write it out fair, the Emperor after ap- *Controverfy*
' pointing one, fent us Word, we might fhow it him as it was, or *about Religi-*
' elfe talk no more of that Bufinefs. That he might have no Ex- *on.*
' cufe we did fo, on the Day he appointed'd, being the 20th of Au-
' guft, when we went to him, attended by the Captain of the *Por-*
' *tuguefes*, and 7, or 8 others. Being come into his Prefence, I
' began to make a fhort Speech, declaring what I came about, but
' he cut me off fhort, and talk'd of fomething elfe, as being pre-
' par'd againft all I defign'd to fay. He look'd upon the Treatife
' I gave him, defended his Opinions, and made Slight of all I
' could fay, till I asking him pofitivly, whether he would fubmit
' himfelf to the See of *Rome*, and receive thofe learned Men the
' King of *Portugal* was fending. He faid he had learned Men e-
' nough of his own, and would never obey any but the Patriarch
' of *Alexandria*, as he had always done. Finding him pofitive, I
' withdrew, and then he commended me very much to the Captain
' of the *Portuguefes*, read the Treatife I left him very often, and
' fhow'd it to his Mother, Brothers, and great Men, whereupon
' the *Abuna* excommunicated any that fhould read it, and the Emperor
' asking his Leave fo to do he deny'd him, for which Reafon the
' faid Emperor call'd him *Moor* and Heretick, who would read the
' *Alcoran*, and forbid the reading of fo excellent a Chriftian
' Writing ; and therefore fince he was Prelate and *Abuna* bid him
' anfwer, what a plain Clergyman propos'd.

 ' This affair being now the only Talk at Court, and Parties di-
' vided about it, the Emperor refolv'd to confult certain Monks,
' look'd upon as holy Men concerning it, and order'd my Treatife
' to be fair copy'd, tho' I fear'd he might caufe fome Paffages of it
' to be left out. When the Emperor was to give me his pofitive An-
' fwer, he put me off with Delays, whereupon I went to take my

         Leave

' Leave of him, in Order to return into *India,* when he defir'd I
' would give him a Month longer. A few Days after he decamp'd,
' and remov'd two Days Journey from that Place. We follow'd
' him, and in this new Camp came to me three Monks, one of them
' a learned Man who had a mind to difcourfe me upon Matters of
' Faith. He told me he approv'd of all our Doctrine, except only,
' not keeping the Saturday, and eating Swines Flefh, and Hare ;
' but proceeding difcover'd many of their Errors ; *viz.* That the
' Souls of Men, departing this Life, could not immediately fee the
' Face of God, but went to the Terreftrial Paradife ; that the Holy
' Ghoft did not proceed from the Son, but only from the Father ;
' that the Son, as Man, was equal to the Father ; that only the
' *Moors* and Infidels were to be in Hell for ever. I fatisfy'd
' him fo well, as to all thefe Points, that whifpering me in
' the Ear, left the other Monks, who were ignorant, might hear, he
' faid, that was the Truth, and he would preferve it in his Heart.
  ' The Time appointed being come, I took leave of the Emperor,
' who gave me free Liberty, and faid he had fent a Man to receive
' the Fathers the King of *Portugal* was to fend him, and defign'd to
' hear them. In my way I adminifter'd the Sacraments to the *Por-*
' *tuguefes* and Marry'd feveral of them, who liv'd with *Abyffine* Wo-

F. Rodrigu-
es *returns to*
India.

' men. At one of their Manfions I receiv'd a Compliment from
' the Superior of the greateft Monaftery of Monks, and another of
' Nuns call'd *Debra Libanos,* and therefore went to vifit him, ac-
' company'd by all the *Portuguefes.* We found not the Superior
' at home ; but faw the Monafteries, which are not like ours in
' *Europe,* for every Monk lives in a Houfe by himfelf, and works
' for himfelf, fo that the Monaftery is like a Village of thatch'd
' Houfes, the Monks on the one Side, and the Nuns on the other,
' and they fay, they get many Children among them. Thefe are
' not *Francifcans,* nor *Auguftinians,* but of *Tecla Haimanot,* which
' in their Language fignifies, Plant of the Faith, and he was of
' the Order of *S. Anthony.* This Man the *Abyffines* reckon a great
' Saint, and fay, the notableft Miracle he wrought was the killing
' of a great Serpent, ador'd as a God by the Heathens, whom he
' converted to the Faith they now hold in *Ethiopia.*

  Thus far *F. Gonzalo Rodriguez*'s Letter, who refolv'd to get a-
way into *India,* before the Emperor chang'd his Mind and ftop'd
him, fome Perfons having perfwaded him, that the King of *Por-*

Politick
Fear of the
Abiffines.

tugal intended to make himfelf Sovereign of *Ethiopia,* and him
Tributary, as he had done by feveral Kings in *India* ; adding, that
the King of *Portugal* already ftil'd himfelf Lord of the Conqueft,
and Commerce of *Ethiopia* and *Arabia,* and therefore fince fo few
Portuguefes as came with *Don Chriftopher de Gama* had done fuch
                                                        great

great Feats, what must they expect if a greater Number should come and joyn those who were there and knew the Country ; for which Reason they might justly suspect, that the Father, and the rest that came with him were no better than Spies, under pretence of Religion. These Considerations render'd the Emperor averse to the *Portuguese*, and therefore *F. Gonzalo Rodriguez* went away to *Baroa*, there to expect Shipping, where he found *Don John Bermudez*, who, as has been said, was also withdrawn out of *Ethiopia*. *John Peixoto* coming to *Mazua* with two small Vessels, the Patriarch and his Fathers went aboard him, and arriv'd safe at *Goa*.

C H A P. V.

Don John Nunez Barreto, *the new Patriarch, arrives at* Goa, *and the Bishop* Don Andrew de Oviedo *goes into* Ethiopia *; how he was receiv'd by the Emperor* Claudius *; the Death of that Monarch ; Adamas* Segued *succeeds, his Tyrannical Government, and Overthow.*

THEY little thought in *Portugal*, that the Affairs of *Ethiopia* were in the Posture we have here represented, and therefore for the more Grandeur the King appointed *Ferdinand de Sousa de Castello Branco* to go along with the Patriarch as his Embassador to the *Abyssine* Emperor. They sail'd from *Lisbon*, with the Bishop *Don Andrew de Oviedo*, *F. Gonzalo de Sylveira*, and others, on the 15th of *March* 1556, and arriv'd at *Goa* on the 13th of *September* that same Year, where they found *P. Gonzalo Rodriguez*, newly return'd from *Ethiopia*, who gave them a far different Account of that Country than they expected. However, the Patriarch and his Companions consulting together, resolv'd to proceed ; but the Governor of *India*, *Francis Barreto* and his Council were of another Opinion, not thinking it fit to expose the Patriarch and the Embassador to any Affront, and therefore only sent the Bishop *Don Andrew de Oviedo*, with some Companions, in Four small Vessels, who landed at *Arquico* about the latter end of E-

Portuguese Embassador and Bishop.

The Bishop in Ethiopia.

of *March* 1557, and thence travell'd by Land to *Debaroa*, where
the *Bahar Nagays*, or Governor of the Coast resided. The second
Days Journey they met Four of the *Portuguefes* who liv'd in E-
thiopia, and came to the Coast to fee whether any Supply was
fent them, according to what has been mention'd before. They
were all overjoy'd to meet, and travell'd together to *Debaroa*,
where that *Ifaac* was still *Bahar Nagays*, who brought *Don Chriftopher de Gama*, and the *Portuguefes* into *Ethiopia*, in the Year
1541. He receiv'd the Bishop and his Company very courteoufly, and from thence the faid Bishop immediately fent a Letter
to the Emperor, acquainting him with his Arrival at *Debaroa*, the
Patriarchs being ready in *India* to come over, and his own Defign
to repair to his Court. What happen'd to the faid Bishop in this
Place, on the way and at Court, shall be briefly deliver'd out of
of a Letter written by *F. Emanuel Fernandez*, Superior of that Miffion, to *F. James Laynez*, General of the Society, in the Year
1562; for there was no poffibility of writing fooner, by reafon of
the *Turks* coming to conquer that Coast of *Tigre*; fo that no Letter could be fent to *India*, much lefs into *Europe*, for Six Years.
The aforefaid *F.* Superior's Account abftracted in fhort is as follows.

*His Recepti-
on at Deba-
roa.*

‘ We came to *Debaroa* on the 25th of *March* 1557, where the
‘ Bishop was honourably receiv'd by the *Bahar Nagays*, and the
‘ People all kifs'd his Hand with extraordinary Refpect, which
‘ we look'd upon as a good Omen. There we stay'd 20 Days,
‘ performing the Office of the Holy Week the beft we could, and
‘ the People reforted to our Church with great Devotion, the Bi-
‘ fhop adminiftring the Sacraments to the *Portuguefes*, and re-
‘ ceiving Vifits from the *Bahar Nagays*, and other great Men.
‘ Winter coming on, and the *Turks* advancing up the Country,
‘ we fet out for the Emperor's Camp, and came in 50 Days to
‘ him, as fhall be faid. Having mention'd the coming of the
‘ *Turks*, I muft inform your Reverence, that when we came to
‘ *Mazua*, an Ifland on the Coast of *Ethoipia*, and the anchoring
‘ Place of all Ships trading hither from *India* and *Arabia*, we there
‘ found a *Turkifh Baffa*, with 500 or more Men, defign'd to con-
‘ quer *Ethiopia*, and expected the Arrival of our Ships; when fee-
‘ ing thofe that came could do him no harm, he landed, and that
‘ oblig'd us to depart haftily from *Debaroa*, and tho we have been
‘ here above 5 Years, we do not know that any Letter of ours is
‘ paft into *India*, notwithftanding we have try'd fo many ways,
‘ that we fear three Men fent by us are kill'd. Thefe *Turks* I
‘ fpeak of, tho' they have done much harm in the Country, and
                                                    ‘ taken

' taken abundance of Captives, have fail'd in their Enterprize,
' lofing moft of their Men and much Treafure, being beaten out,
' and could never have return'd, were it not for what fhall be
' mention'd hereafter.

  ' In our way to the Court, we adminiftred the Sacraments to
' many *Portuguefes*, which took us up feveral Days. About 8 *At the Em-*
' Days Journey fhort of the Emperor's Camp, he fent a Nobleman *peror's Court.*
' to Compliment the Bifhop, who brought many Mules to carry
' us and our Baggage. At the laft Days Journey, he fent us an
' Order to ftop till we heard from him. Two Days after he fent
' to call us, and when we were within a Musket-fhot, another
' Meffenger came with Orders for us to pitch our Tents, which
' now made a good Show, we being joyn'd by many *Portuguefes*. '
' There we continu'd that Night, and the next Day at Noon
' many of the Emperor's Kindred, and principal Officers well
' mounted and accouter'd, came to the Bifhop's Tent, and two
' of the greateft going in, deliver'd their Meffage, that the Empe-
' ror fent for him. We went immediately, where he with his
' Mother and Brothers was looking out from a high Place, and
' tho' it was not ufual, would have all Ride into the firft Court,
' he feeing all from another within. After ftaying there a while,
' he commanded us to alight and go into the fecond Court, in
' which the Tent he liv'd in ftood, and made us ftand there a
' while again, whilft he look'd at us through Silk Hangings.

  ' On both fides the Entrance of his Tent ftood a great number
' of Old Men and Perfons of Quality, with Truncheons in their *His Atten-*
' Hands, very orderly. As we all ftood thus filent, two of his *dance.*
' Servants came out of the Tent, one whereof was the *Bahar Na-*
' *gays*, and making Obeyfance to the Bifhop, conducted us in to
' the Emperor, who receiv'd us very courteoufly and lovingly ;
' and after fome fhort Difcourfe, the Bifhop deliver'd him the
' Letters from the Governor of *India*, our Patriarch, and others,
' which having receiv'd, he prefently began to look difpleas'd,
' being far from any Thoughts of a Reconciliation with the Church
' of *Rome* ; yet being Noble, Difcreet, and a Lover of the *Portu-*
' *guefes*, he endeavour'd to conceal it, tho' not fo much but that
' double Dealing might be perceiv'd.

  ' However, he always behav'd himfelf civilly towards the Bi-
' fhop, and whilft he liv'd none durft fhow him Difrefpect ; be- *His Good*
' fides that he furnifh'd us plentifully, becaufe he was naturally *Qualities.*
' Generous, efpecially where the King of *Portugal* was concern'd,
' as owing an Obligation to him. He was fo good natur'd, and fo
' much concern'd for the Sufferings he apprehended the Bifhop
' might be expos'd to, that going to engage the *Moors*, by whom
                                                 ' he

‘ he was kill'd, he faid,. *Alas, poor Bifhop ! What will become of*
‘ *him if I die ?* This Emperor *Claudius* was fo well qualify'd, ba-
‘ ting his Obftinacy in Religion, that I am pofitively of Opinion
‘ there was not a wifer Man in the Empire, or fo fit to Govern.
‘ He was very well inftructed in the *Portuguefe* Manners and
‘ Cuftoms, and us'd fo much Courtefy towards the Bifhop, that
‘ in the Height of his Obduracy, we ftill hop'd for fome good
‘ of him.

Thus far the Fathers Letter, the remaining Part we fhall infert
below, after mentioning fome Things that happen'd to make it
more plain. After the firft Interview, the Bifhop began to Difcourfe the Emperor about the main Point of forfaking his Errors,
and fubmitting to the Pope, who anfwer'd, That his Forefathers
had always own'd the Chair of S. *Mark* at *Alexandria*, and he
could fee no Occafion to difquiet the People, who were peaceable,
and fatisfy'd with their *Abuna*; yet fince he came fo far to *Ethiopia*, whither never any Perfon of fuch Quality came on the like
Embafly, he would advife with his Council and learned Men,
Religious　in order to give him a final Anfwer. The Bifhop perceiv'd this
Controverfies. was only to delay Time, and excufe himfelf on the Opinions of
others, who he knew were harden'd in their Errors, and therefore fent him a long Letter in their learned Language, to endeavour to move him to fome better Difpofition. At the Bifhop's
Requeft there were feveral Meetings of the learned Men, all whom
the faid Bifhop eafily confounded, and then the Emperor would
take up the Argument, and manage it fo dexteroufly, that he
fometimes fet the Bifhop hard; and tho he ftill ran them all down,
yet they gave out, that they had got the better; fo that all came
to nothing. This put the Bifhop upon Writing againft all their
Errors, and delivering it to the Emperor, who return'd an Anfwer in the fame manner, refolving never to fubmit to the See
of *Rome*. Thefe Things happen'd about the latter end of *December*
1558. when the Bifhop thought fit to withdraw himfelf from
Court, as he did about the beginning of *February*, and publifh'd
Too hotly　a Circular Letter advifing the *Portuguefes*, and fome other Catho-
purfu'd.　licks there, to be cautious in converfing with the Schifmaticks, and exhorting the *Abyffines* to forfake their Errors; and at
the fame time condemning them as refractory, and obftinate a-
gainft the Church.

Let us now fee what became of the Emperor. After the Death
of the *Moor Granbe*, another Infidel call'd *Nur*, Chief Governor
of the Kingdom of *Adel*, burning with the Defire of revenging
his Father's Death, who had been kill'd with *Granbe* at *Ogara*,
watch'd

watch'd all Opportunities, and sent Spies into *Ethiopia* to give him
an Account of the Posture of Affairs there; by whom he was *The Emperor*
inform'd, that tho' the Emperor *Claudius*'s Forces were numerous, *routed and*
yet they were undisciplin'd and unfit for Service. Upon this In- *kill'd.*
telligence he gather'd a great Army of Foot, and 1700 Horse, with
which he enter'd *Abyssinia*, destroying all before him, and marching directly towards the Emperor, who boldly set forward to meet
him, as they did in a spacious Plain, fit for their purpose. Both
Parties being bent upon engaging, they presently fell on; but the
Abyssines wanting Discipline, as soon as they felt the Fury of the
Enemies Onset, threw away their Arms and turn'd their Backs,
forsaking their Sovereign, who behav'd himself with the utmost
Bravery, in the midst of the Infidels, killing several of them with
his own Hand, assisted only by 18 *Portuguese*, who tho' they did
all that Men could do, yet being encompass'd by a multitude of
Moors were overpower'd, and fell all of them with the Emperor.
The Victors pursuing their Advantage, slew many, took abundance of Prisoners, and made themselves Masters of the Camp,
where they found a considerable Booty. The *Moor Nur* returning home Victorious, enter'd the City riding on a little Ass in
humble manner, amidst the Acclamations of the People, giving
for his Reason, That God alone had given the Victory, and therefore all the Glory ought to be his, since he fought and conquer'd
for him. A wonderful Example of Moderation in an Infidel, fit
to confound Christians, who are puff'd up with Vanity upon e-
very little Success. Thus ended the unfortunate Emperor *Claudius*, or according to the *Abyssines Glaudios*, which was his Christian Name, tho' often call'd *Afnaf Segued*, being the Name he took
at his Accession to the Crown.

After the Death of *Claudius*, his Brother *Minas*, which signifies Faithful, succeeded him in the Throne, and at his Inaugura- *Minas suc-*
tion took the Name of *Adamas Segued*. He was of a perverse and *ceeds Clau-*
cruel Disposition, whereof he had given some Instances in his *dius.*
Infancy; and having been Prisoner, and bred up among *Moors*
and *Turks*, he had their Native Insolence instill'd into him, with
their Falshood and Fierceness. In short, he behav'd himself so
Tyrannically, not only towards the *Portuguese*, but his own People, that they had all Reason to lament the loss of his Brother
Claudius. F. *Emanuel Fernandez* gives us an Account of his Barbarity towards the Bishop and other Catholicks, in the same Letter we gave part of above, and he being an Eye-witness of undoubted Reputation, we will here abridge the rest of it.

Persecutes the Catholicks.

'Claudius dying without Issue, says this Father, was succeeded
'by a Brother, who at the Time when the Portuguese deliver'd
'those Kingdoms from the Oppression of the Moors, was Prisoner
'in Arabia; but when Claudius at the Expence of the Blood of
'our Men had recover'd his Dominions, he ransom'd him; so
'that he might be said to have been bought with the Blood of the
'Portuguese, rather than Gold: Yet all the Gratitude he show'd,
'was, that being come to the Crown, he seem'd to aim at no-
'thing more than the utter Destruction of those few Catholicks
'that remain'd in his Kingdom. The Emperor Claudius had gi-
'ven free leave to all Ethiopian Women that marry'd Portu-
'guese, to embrace, if they thought fit, the Doctrine of Rome,
'and the same to all their Slaves and Families: But the first
'Thing Adamas Segued did, was forbidding all Native Ethiopians
'whatsoever, repairing to the Portuguese Churches, upon severe
'Penalties, alledging, that his Brother came to that untimely
'End, for permitting the Exercise of the Catholick Religion in
'his Dominions. This was so vigorously executed, that a Wo-
'man was publickly whipp'd only for being a Catholick, two
'Wives of Portuguese were imprison'd on the same Account, and
'many of their Children taken from them, which made several
'renounce their Religion, for fear of his Threats. Nor did he
'stop there, but because two Armenians had been converted, he
'banish'd the one and beheaded the other; besides that, he con-
'tinually took from the Portuguese those Lands they had receiv'd
'from his Brother Claudius, as a Reward for their Faithful Ser-
'vices. He kept the Bishop Prisoner six Months, and threatned
'to burn the other Fathers; besides many other Wrongs too tedi-
'ous to relate. But God making use of him only to chastise the
'Insolencies some Portuguese committed in Ethiopia, he went

His Subjects Rebel,

'not himself unpunish'd; for he being inhuman towards his
'own Subjects, about the latter end of the Year 1560, most of
'the Nobility of Ethiopia rebell'd against him, and gave the
'Crown to a Youth call'd Habitacum Tascaro, Bastard Son to an
'Elder Brother of his, deceased. This Prince was joyn'd not
'only by the Prime Men of the Kingdom, but by the Captain of
'the Portuguese with 30 of his Men, the rest being at that time
'too far off. The Emperor hearing of this Conspiracy, march'd
'first against the Bahar Nagays Isaac, a Man noted for Martial
'Affairs, and who had deliver'd the Empire from great Misfor-
'tunes. He was then towards the Sea Coast, executing some
'Orders he had receiv'd from Tascaro. At the first Encounter
'Isaac had the better, but in the second was forc'd to fly. This
'done, Adamas turn'd back against Tascaro, and on the 2d of
                                                              July

' *July* 1561. routed and took him Prisoner. In the mean while,
' the *Bahar Nagays*, who had escap'd out of the Battel, and
' waited about the Sea, in hopes of some *Portuguese* Supplies that
' were expected from *India*; failing of them, and fearing to be
' surpriz'd by the Emperor, concluded a League with the *Turks*
' above spoken of, and being joyn'd by them, proclaim'd another
' Brother of that *Tascaro*, who had been put to Death. The Emperor
' *Adamas* march'd against *Isaac* and the *Turks* to *Tigre* with nume-
' rous Forces, and on the 20th of *April* 1562, was routed with- *And rout*
' out fighting; for both he and his Men being terrify'd with the *him.*
' Cannon fled, and left their Camp to the Enemy. All this while
' we had been in the Emperor's Camp, so hardly us'd, that we
' durst not pitch our Tents without his Directions.

' Upon this Defeat we were made Prisoners by *Turks* and
' *Abyssines*, who fought against the Emperor, and God sav'd
' our Lives by means of the *Portugueses* that were there. We
' had been before robb'd four times, and were now reduc'd to
' Extremity, only the *Bahar Nagays* gave us our Chalice and some
' small Things, the rest we ransom'd the best we could. Your
' Reverence may guess what a miserable Condition we are in,
' being Forty in Family, and forc'd to relieve, when we are able,
' the *Portuguese* Widows and Orphans, and no body to ask an
' Alms of; for the *Portugueses* have more occasion to beg than
' give, and the Natives are more inclin'd to take and steal than
' to part with any thing. For our Table, we have scarce a Belly
' full of parch'd Barley. The Bishop is not fit to be seen. We
' beg your Blessing, and the Prayers of all the Society, and ha-
' ving no way left to write, your Reverence may take this, if
' it comes to your Hands, for the last. *Ethiopia, July* the 29th,
' 1562.

> *Emanuel Fernandez,*   *Francis Lopez,*
> *Antony Fernandez,*   *Gonzalo Cardozo.*

T 2   CHAP.

C H A P. VI.

Persecution under the Emperor Adamas Segued; *Brother* Fulgentius Freyre *sent from* India, *taken by the* Turks; F. Andrew Gualdames *attempting to go to Ethiopia kill'd by those Infidels; the Death and Character of the Patriarch and his Companions.*

He insults the Bishop.

F. *Emanuel Fernandez* was very brief in relating the Sufferings of the Catholicks in *Ethiopir,* under the cruel Emperor *Adamas Segued,* their mortal Enemy, whereof a particular Information was afterwards taken in *Ethiopia* from the Depositions of Eye-witnesses. Among the rest of his Extravagancies, he once sent for the Bishop, and bidding him never more to presume to teach his Doctrine in that Empire: That Prelate answer'd, he could never forbear Preaching the Word of God. At this the Emperor was so enrag'd, that he drew his Sword, and ran at him; but the Sword droping out of his Hand, he fell upon him with his Hands, striking and tearing his Cloaths, and laying hold of the Sword again, like a raving Mad-man, would have kill'd him, had not the Empress and several Noblemen interpos'd. After this he banish'd the Bishop, and his Companion F. *Francis Lopez* to a barren Mountain, where they suffer'd very much, this being the 3d time he had been banish'd.

Br. Freyre *sent to Ethiopia.*

It was no small Addition to the rest of their Afflictions, that they could receive no News from *India* or *Portugal,* for in the Year 1557, the *Turks* possessing themselves of all the Sea Ports, cut off all Communication betwixt *India* and *Ethiopia.* This very much perplex'd the Patriarch *Don John Nunez Barreto* at *Goa,* who never gave over importuning the Vice-Roys of *India,* either to set him ashore on the Coast of *Abyssinia,* or to send some Ships that might bring him News of the Bishop, and how Affairs stood in that Country. At length, in the Year 1560, the Vice-Roy *Don Constantine de Braganza* fitted out three Ships, in which the Provincial of the *Jesuits,* at the Request of the Patriarch, sent Brother *Fulgentius Freyre,* who had before been in *Ethiopia,* and return'd thence with F. *Gonzalo Rodriguez,* as has been said. These

Ships

Ships set sail in February 1560, but the *Turks* being Masters of *Maz̄ua*, the Commander would not suffer Brother *Fulgentius* to be set a shore; yet he found Means to give Letters to a *Moor*, who going away to the Port of *Arquico* deliver'd them to the Servants of the *Portuguese*, that were come thither to hear News from *India*, and they carry'd them to the Bishop.

As the Commander was making off he was pursu'd by four *Turkish* Gallies, well mann'd, which falling upon his Vessels, took it, whilst the two others that attended him fled, and made their Escape to *Goa*. Brother *Fulgentius Freyre* was taken on Board this Vessel, very much wounded, and sent to *Gran Cairo*, where he continu'd in Slavery two Years, under very great Hardships. The Brother was *Taken by the* there till Pope *Paul* the 4th sent two Fathers, of the Society to *Turks. and* *Egypt*, to reduce the *Coptis* into the Bosom, of the Church, who *ansome'd.* finding him there writ over immediately to *Rome*; by Order from whence, he was ransom'd and sent thither, thence to *Portugal* and venturing back again to *India*, in his old Age, dy'd at Sea.

The Bishop, and Fathers in *Ethiopia* were no less desirous to hear News from *India*, than the Patriarch, and others there to know how matters stood with them. Besides that they would fain perswade King *John* to send 5, or 600 *Portuguese*, who might easily make themselves Masters of the Sea Ports, rescue the other *Portuguese*, and compel the *Ethiopians* to submit to the See of *Rome*, as they had promis'd. To this Purpose it was thought absolutely necessary that one of the Fathers should attempt to get over into *Ethiopia* and F. *Andrew Gualdames* was pitch'd upon. He being come in Sight of *Mazua*, with a *Portuguese* that offer'd to bear him Company, and understanding there was a Ship of *Banaens* there bound for *India*, for want of a better Messenger, entrusted a *Moor*, upon *Another Je-* Promise of Reward to go to the Captain of the *Banean* Ship, and *suit taken,* agree with him to take them in privately, for a considerable Sum *and murder-* to be paid in *India*. The Perfidious Infidel, instead of treating *'d.* with the *Banean*, betray'd them to the Bassa of *Mazua* by whom they were taken that Night, and immediately cut in Pieces. This good Father was a *Spaniard*, born in the Town of *Xeres de la Frontera*, and is said, to have learnt the *Abissine* Tongue in six Months.

Don John Nunez Barreto, the Patriarch, having been six Years at *Goa*, without any News from *Ethiopia*, or possibility of going thither in Person, dyed there on the 20th of December 1562. By his death the Bishop *Don Andrew de Oviedo* came to succeed in the Malac Se- Patriarchship, as had been appointed by the Pope. We said before gu'd *Emperor.* how the Emperor *Adamas Segued* was routed by the *Bahar Nagays Maac*, and the *Turks*, but his early Flight avail'd him not, for he was kill'd in the Pursuit, and in his Stead, his Son *Sorfa Danguit* was

was set upon the Throne, and took the Name of *Melchi*, or *Malac Segued*, whose Life was continually aim'd at by treacherous Contrivances, and he obtain'd many Victories. He was crown'd and anointed at *Auxum*, with great Solemnity, according to the ancient Custom, which had been quite out of Use, for many Years, by Reason of the Wars. This Emperor was generally fortunate in in his Wars, for he drove the *Turks* out of the Kingdom of *Tigre*, and attack'd their Fortress at *Arquico*; he was zealous for Christianity in his way, and neither encourag'd, nor persecuted the Fathers, nor the Catholicks, being wholly taken up with his Wars, without ever admitting any Discourse of leaving his Errors. He reign'd almost 33 Years, and tho' he seem'd to respect the Father's looking upon them as holy Men, yet he made no Account of their Doctrine.

All this Emperor's Reign being infested with Wars, and he not caring to hearken to religious Matters, the Fathers stay'd in the Kingdom of *Tigre*, with *Isaac* the *Bahar Nagays*, with whom also kept most of the *Portuguese*, and settled on a Mountain they call *Maegoga*, at a Town nam'd *Fremona*, often mention'd by us. Some Knowledge they had in *India*, in *Portugal*, and at *Rome* of the Difficulties the Patriarch, and his Companions labour'd under in *Ethiopia*, how little good they were able to do, and how far the Emperor *Claudius* had been from performing what he promis'd. Nor were they Ignorant that the Emperor *Adamas Segued* had persecuted the Fathers, and oppress'd the *Portugueses*, who deliver'd him from the Captivity of the *Moors*. These Things mov'd Prince *Henry*, who govern'd *Portugal* during the Minority of King *Sebastian* to ask leave of Pope *Pius* the 5th for the Patriarch to leave *Ethiopia*, which his Holiness readily granted, by his Bull, sign'd the 1st of *February* 1566, and directed to the said Patriarch. He receiv'd a Copy of this Bull in the Year 1567, and after declaring his Readiness to comply with it, and depart for *Japan*, or *China*, acquainted the Pope, that there might be still Hopes of converting *Ethiopia*, were the Preachers supported by 5, or 600 *Portugueses*, alledging the good disposition of many of the People to embrace the Catholick Religion, who were withheld from it by Fear of Punishment. Besides he added, there were Multitudes of Infidels easy to be brought into the Church, being well meaning People, and, not much addicted to Idolatry. He further alledg'd, he was inform-ed there were many of those in some Parts of the Empire, who had desir'd of the Emperor to be made Christians, which he had re-fus'd for Worldly Interest, because they made many of them Slaves, which they thought they might not do with Christians. The People who made this Request, inhabit the Kingdom of *Damut*, which is

Preaching propos'd with Force of Arms.

a very large Country. The Gentiles of another Country call'd *Sinaxi*, where there is much Gold, about three Years since intreated a Kinsman of the Emperor's, who made War on them, to desist and they would pay him Tribute, and become Christians, which he would not grant them. Of these Pagans, especially those of *Damut*, the *Moorish* Merchants, whereof there are great Numbers among the Christians, buy Multitudes, whom they carry down to the Sea, and sell them to the *Turks*, and *Moors*, and I am of Opinion there are above 100000 of them thus sold to those Infidels. Who afterwards become *Mahometans*, and good Soldiers, doing much harm to the Christians, &c.

It cannot but be observ'd here, that the Insolencies of the Portuguese above hinted at, and now these demands of Men to convert Ethiopia *by Force, together with the Demand of one third Part of the Abissine Empire for the Assistance given against the Moors ; these Things, with many other Circumstances of the same Nature must of Necessity give the* Ethiopians *an Aversion to the* Portugueses, *and a dislike to all they propos'd ; as concluding that under the Colour of Religion they came to subdue them, and to take that Crown from the Infidels for themselves ; especially since as the* Ethiopians *observ'd, the King of* Portugal *already took upon him the Title of Lord of the Commerce of* Ethiopia *and* Arabia. *Those Religious Men who endur'd so many Hardships, may be allow'd to have acted out of a true ReligiousZeal,but perhaps they had done more good, had all those dissolute* Portuguese *Soldiers been carry'd away, and only they left to preach, and Teach, which yet ought to be done with much Mildness, and Patience without expecting to compel all the Nation at once to a Compliance, of which we shall see more hereafter, and therefore thus much may suffice in this Place.* Note of Iregular Proceeding.

There is another Letter of *Emanuel Fernandez*, wherein he gives a particular Account of all that befel him, and his Companions, but being more full of Religious than other Matters, I shall only pick out of it some few Remarks worth knowing. He says. The *Turks* enter'd *Ethiopia* in the Year 1572, which was the 4th Time, after the Fathers were there. They took many Captives, and went as far as a Town where the *Portugueses* resided, who made their escape but the Town was burnt, whence they return'd to *Debaroa* nearer the Sea, built a Fort, and continu'd making Excursions. This oblig'd the Catholicks to abandon those Places, and withdraw into the Kingdom of *Dambea*, and other Parts. Only the Patriarch, and some few with him, continu'd amidst those Dangers to endeavour to send Advice over to *India*, and in Hopes of Succours from thence. With the Catholicks that went away, the Patriarch sent *F. Gonzalo Cardazo* ; and *F. Francis Lopez*, the first of which was murder'd on the way by Robbers, and the latter wounded in the Arm, Turks entering Ethiopia

Arm, yet went on with his Company, and settled with them in *Dambea*. In the rest *F. Fernandez* declares the good Disposition there is among many of the Natives, and especially the Gentiles, to embrace the Catholick Religion, could they be protected in it, and says, several Persons of Note were privately converted, but kept it to themselves for fear of suffering Persecution. In another Letter dated December the 20th, 1557, the same Father complains that the 5, or 600 Men so often desir'd, are not sent, bewailing the Loss of so many Souls, for want of them, and alledging, to justify the making Use of that Force, that even in Christian Countries the Prelates would have no Authority were they not supported by the Lay-Magistrates. He urges, that God punishes the Obduracy of the *Ethiopians*, as he did the Egyptians, with Flies, for such he calls the Barbarous *Galas*, as being a naked unarm'd People ; and yet the

The Patri- *Abyssines* well arm'd and mounted, are not able to withstand them
arch's Life. which indeed looks more like a Judgment, than any thing natural.

The Patriarch continu'd several Years at *Fremona*, without ever receiving any Succours from *Portugal*, or *India*, or any Fleet coming to carry him off. All this while his Life was so holy, and exemplar, that one of the greatest Men in the Kingdom of *Tigre*, tho' himself a Schismatick, was wont to say ; That none of the ancient Saints in the Desert attain'd to more Perfections than the said Patriarch did in *Fremona*. His Palace was a thatch'd Cottage, his Diet a thin Cake of *Tef*, a Grain before mention'd, his other Dainties were Cabbage, or Linseed, without any other seasoning, but Salt and Water ; and even these he was to sow, and bring up himself. His Poverty was such, that he was reduc'd to tear the first white Page out of his Breviary to write a Letter on. Another he afterwards writ to the Pope, and wanting even such a Leaf, he cut off the Margents of the Breviary, and sow'd them together, to write it on. In the midst of his Sufferings he spar'd no Labour, attending the Poor of all Sorts, which was the Occasion of converting many Schismaticks. At length it pleas'd God to take him out of this World, in the Year 1577, when he had been above 20 in *Ethiopia*, and was not only Lamented by the *Portuguese*, but by all that knew him, and the Viceroy of *Tigre*, when he receiv'd this News beat his Face with both Hands, as is usual among those People in extraordinary Afflictions, often crying in a dismal Tone, *The Patriarch is Dead, the Patriarch is Dead, we are all undone.* This great Man was a *Spaniard*, born at *Illescas*, a Town between *Madrid* and *Toledo* in the Kingdom of *Castile* , his Sanctity of Life wonderful, and to pass by many other prodigious Passages well attested, all *Ethiopia* still own that the Town of *Fremona* was particularly protected by Heaven for his Sake, against all Enemies, for tho' the Barbarous *Gallas* ravag'd all the Country about it, yet they

never

never did the least Harm in that Place, notwithstanding many of them came into it, and it had no human Defence.

Five other Fathers came into *Ethiopia* with the Patriarch, two whereof we have already declar'd dy'd by the Sword; the first *F. Andrew Gualdames,* kill'd by the *Turks,* near *Arquico;* the other *Gonzalo Cardezo,* by the Robbers, on the way to *Dambea.* There remain'd three, the first of these that dy'd was *F. Emanuel Fernandez* Superor of the Mission, who after enduring infinite Hardships for his Flock, at length departed this Life, spent with overmuch Labour. *F. Antony Fernandez,* born at *Braga* living till the Year 1593, labouring indefatigably for the good of Souls, and travelling in his old Age an hundred Leagues, only to assist one wounded *Portuguese* at his Death, had scarce Strength enough left him to return to *Fremona,* where he soon after departed this World. Only *F. Francis Lopes* remain'd to take Care of all the Catholicks, which was an immense Labour, and he quite spent with Age and Fatigues. He foretold he should dye within 15 Days, that within a Year another Father would come from *India,* and others after him; all which hapened as he had said. He dy'd at 80 Years of Age. The Bodies of the Patriarch and his Companions, were all bury'd in the thatch'd Church at *Fremona,* and afterwards translated to *Goa* by Order of the Patriarch *Don Alfonso Mendez.* Thus ended that Mission of *Ethiopia* which had lasted 40 Years, *viz.* from 1557 till 1597, when *F. Francis Lopes* dy'd.

Death of the other Jesuits

U   CHAP.

C H A P. VII.

The Fathers Antony de Monferrate, *and* Peter Pays
appointed at Goa *to go into* Ethiopia; *they are ta-
ken at* Dhofar *and sent Prisoners to the King of*
Xael *then to the* Baſſa *of* Yemen, *in* Arabia Felix.
*An Account of what they saw in that Country, and their
Captivity.*

Revolutions.
in Portugal
WHILST thoſe Things we have ſpoken of in the laſt Chapter
happened in *Ethiopia,* King *John* the 3d of *Portugal,* who encourag'd that Miſſion, dy'd, in the Year 1557, King *Sebaſtian,*
his Succeſſor, being wholly bent upon the unfortunate Expedition
into *Africk,* little regarded the Affairs of *Abyſſinia,* and the Cardinal *Henry,* who reign'd after him liv'd not long enough to effect the good Intentions he had that Way. *Philip,* the 2d of *Spain*
aſcending the Throne after him, charg'd *Don Duarte de Menezes,*
Earl of *Tarouca,* and Viceroy of *India,* to ſpare no Labour, or
Coſt, for the Promoting of the Converſion of *Ethiopia.* This Order
came to *Goa* when that Viceroy was Dead, and the Goverment
devolv'd upon *Emanuel de Souſa Coutinko,* who no ſooner receiv'd
it, but he acquainted the Provincial of the *Jeſuits,* by whom he
was offer'd as many Fathers as he ſhould think fit. The Governour
F. Monſer-
rte and F.
Pays, deſign-
'd for Ethi-
opia.
thought two ſufficient for the preſent, and *F. Antony de Monferrate,*
a *Catalonian,* and *F. Peter Pays,* a *Caſtilian,* were pitch'd upon, this
being in the Year 1587. *Lewis de Mendoza,* who liv'd at *Dia,*
undertook to ſend them in ſome Ship of *Indian Baneans,* that traded to *Maxua.* The two Fathers embark'd for *Diu* in *February* 1588.
and being forc'd by a Storm into the Bay of *Babaos,* ſent thence to
acquaint *Lewis de Mendoza,* who brought them into the City by
Night, clad like *Armenians,* for Fear leſt any *Mooriſh* Sailers, belonging to the Red Sea ſhould know, and betray them to the *Turks.*

They ſtay'd long at *Diu,* whilſt *Lewis de Mendoza* endeavour'd to
prevail with any *Banean,* or *Mooriſh* Merchants, to take them
aboard, which none of them would venture, fearing their Ships,
and Goods might be ſeiz'd, for carrying white Men they could
give no Account of. Being thus diſapointed, the Fathers themſelves never gave over, till they found an *Armenian* belonging to *Alep-
po*

po, who undertook to carry them by the way of *Bazora*, to his own Country, and send them thence to *Grand Cairo*, where they would find Caravans, to carry them safe into *Ethiopia*. This was a tedious way about, yet their Earnestness made it appear easy, and therefore they imbark'd on board the *Armenian's* Ship, putting into *Mascate* for Water, where *Belchior Calaxa*, a Man well affected to the Society commanded, he show'd them the way they went was not likely, and undertook to send them aboard a *Moor*, who was his *They came to* Friend to some Port of *Abyssinia*. Whilst the *Moor* made ready, they *the Islands of* went over to *Ormuz*, were they were charitably entertain'd in the Curia Mu- Monastery of the *Augustin* Friars, and forc'd to continue till the ria. 26th of *December*, the aforesaid Year 1588, when the *Moor* took them aboard, designing they should land at *Zeyla*; but a violent Storm having much shatter'd the Ship, and broke off the Rudder, he was oblig'd to put into one of the Islands of *Curia Muria*, call'd *Suadie*, near to another they name *Asquie*, on the Coast of *Arabia Felix*.

All these Islands are small, and inhabited by a poor miserable People, covering their Houses with the Weeds the Sea casts upon the *Description* Shore, and feeding on Fish, whereof they have Plenty, but want *of those I-* Wood to dress it, and therefore eat it raw, only dry'd in the Wind. *lands.* The Sea casts up much Amber Greese there, for they offer'd the Fathers some at a very small Price, which they valu'd as little. Here they continu'd 7 or 8 Days, fitting out a small Vessel the *Moor* hir'd, because his Ship was disabled. After much strugling with contrary Winds they were spy'd from the Shore, tho' they endeavour'd to avoid it, and taken by two light Vessels well arm'd, which came out in Quest of them. The Reason of their being so watchfull upon the Coast, was because the *Moor*, who carry'd the Fathers, had intrusted another *Moor* with the Secret, that he was to carry *Portugueses* to *Zeyla*, and this other Infidel gave Advice at *Dhofar*, where they were provided to take that Vessel.

After a strict Examination, the Fathers being look'd upon as *The Jesuits* Spies, tho' telling the downright Truth of their being bound for *taken by* *Ethiopia*, were stripp'd almost naked, and shut up in an old House *Moors.* of Mud Walls, where they had little to eat by Day, and abundance of Vermin to break their rest at Night. At last the Commander of *Dhofar* resolv'd to send them to his Master, the King of *Xael* in *Arabia Falix*. They were put aboard a small Vessel, which carried them 5 Days along the Coast, till they landed on *Sent to Xael.* an open Shore, and began to travel by Land, with much trouble afoot, being ill shod, but the *Moors* at length set them on their Camels, for the more Expedition. The third Days Journey they enter'd upon such a Sandy Desert, that there was no Track, but they

Large De-
sert.

Tarim City.

Heynan
City.

King of Xael
describ'd.

they travell'd by the Sun in the Day and by the Stars at Night. The Heat was exceffive, the allowance of Bread to the Fathers very fmall, and that of Water lefs, becaufe they had none but what the Camels carried. Ten Days they travell'd over that Defert, at the end whereof they reach'd *Tarim*, a large City, where the News was foon fpread abroad, that there were *Portuguefe* Prifoners, whom the People flock'd to fee, at firft gazing as if they were amaz'd. Then asking thofe who conducted them, whether they believ'd in *Mahomet*, and being told they did not, call'd them *Cafares*, and after many Reproachful Words, fpit on their Faces, and had they not been put into a Houfe, would have fton'd them to Death. The next Morning they were conducted out of the City before Day, for fear of the Rabble, and travelling through a Country well inhabited, came the third Day to a Town where a Brother of the Kings call'd *Xafer* then was, who receiv'd them courteoufly, ask'd many Queftions, and gave them *Caboa* to Drink. [*This I fuppofe is Coffee, which they were not acquainted with.*] Being difmifs'd by him, they travell'd all the Night, and by break of Day were near *Heynan*, the King of *Xael's* Court. They were carried to the Fort, where the King refided, which was lofty and ftrong, tho' of Clay, as are all the Buildings in that Country. There they put them into a fmall *Gueritte*, or Centinels Box on the Wall, where they had trouble enough from the many People that came to fee them, and could never be fatisfy'd with gazing.

Two Days after their Arrival, King *Humar*, for fo he was call'd, order'd their Cloaths fhould be given them, they being in no Condition otherwife to be feen at Court. After Dinner they were brought before him, where he was in State on the Top of the Fortrefs, fitting upon a boarded Elevation rais'd a Yard from the Ground, and cover'd with rich Brocard. He was clad in very fine Green Cloth, and on his Head a Turbant Embroider'd with Gold. As to his Perfon it was comely, and he feem'd to be about 40 Years of Age. He receiv'd the Fathers courteoufly, made them fit down, and would not let the *Syrian* Boy that came with them ferve for an Interpreter, but fent for a Renegado Woman that belong'd to the Queen, and knew the Language of the Country, and enough of the *Portuguefe*. The King fpoke to her in *Arabick*, and fhe, turning to the Fathers, faid, *The King bids you not be troubled, becaufe God has brought you hither ; but I fay your Sins have brought you hither, among fuch wicked People.* He ask'd, who they were, and whither they went. They anfwer'd, they were Fathers, and going to *Ethiopia* to live with the *Portuguefes* that went thither formerly. Many more Queftions he ask'd,
and

and spent the Afternoon in Difcourfe; and to conclude, they begg'd he would order them their Books to pray by, out of their Baggage. He anfwer'd, *Offba Alal, Offba Alla,* which is their way of granting what is ask'd, and fignifies, *It will pleafe God, it will pleafe God* ; and fo it prov'd, for the next Day they had their Breviaries, which was no fmall Comfort.

Some Time the Fathers continu'd there, without knowing what would become of them, till the Woman above mention'd coming to Vifit them, faid, The King was very willing to Ranfom them, but afraid of the *Turks,* whofe Tributary he was, and therefore fhe believ'd they would ftay long there. They ask'd her, how fhe came into that Country ? She anfwer'd, That going from *Chaul* to *Ormuz* in a very fmall Veffel, which had only 8 Men ; they were drove by ftrefs of Weather to *Xael,* where the *Moors* invited them afhore, pretending Friendfhip, and the *Portuguefes* believing them, were taken, as was their Veffel, and fhe in it. They were all fent to that City, where *Sultan Ammar's* Father then reign'd, who us'd all means to pervert them, but could never prevail, and they all dy'd, confum'd with Hardfhips. She added, that one of thefe Men, whofe Surname was *Preto,* having contracted Friendfhip with a *Moor* that traded to *Melinde,* defir'd that he would carry a Letter for him ; which the Infidel promis'd, but as foon as receiv'd, deliver'd it to the King, who having found one ito interpret it, underftood it gave Advice for a Veffel to come upon the Coaft of *Xael,* where they might eafily take fome *Moors* to exchange for him, and other Chriftian Captives. The King in a Rage order'd *Preto* to be brought before him, and ask'd him, Whether that was his Letter. He anfwer'd, it was. Then faid the King, you fhall immediately turn *Mahometan,* or Dye. *Preto* gallantly reply'd, *I am no fuch Man to turn Mahometan :* Adding much more, with fuch Chriftian Fortitude, that the King caus'd his Head to be ftruck off in his Prefence, and the Body to be thrown out at the Window. Thus he ended his Days glorioufly in Defence of the Faith, and tho' his Chriftian Name be loft to us, we may with good Reafon believe it is written in the Book of Life. The Fathers extoll'd the Bravery of that *Portuguefe,* and blam'd the Old Woman, who was of the Kingdom of *Pegu,* for renouncing her Faith, encouraging her to return to it, and make a good End. She anfwer'd, fhe only honour'd CHRIST in her Heart, but had not Courage to confefs him openly.

The Fathers continu'd four Months in Prifon, where they fuffer'd very much ; for tho' that part of *Arabia* is call'd *The Happy,* it is to be fuppos'd the Ancients gave it the Name by the Rule of

Con-

[margin notes:] Indain Woman Captive. Arabia Felix.

Hadramut Province.

Contraries, or else through a mistake, for it has no other Happiness, but many Miseries, which confume poor Captives, and from which the Natives are not exempt. That Province of it is call'd *Hadarmot,* or *Hadramut* ; the least part of it is till'd, and even that yields no great Crop. The Product is Wheat, Barley, and Millet, and this last is the main Suftenance of the People ; but the quantity of every fort is fo fmall, that there are frequent Famines. They have a few Palm-trees, whofe Dates fomewhat fweeten their Hunger. The Natives are of a Tawny Complexion, and the Cloaths they wear anfwerable to their Poverty and fhort Diet ; yet they are careful to Drefs their Hair, becaufe it is of their own Growth, and cofts no Money. They let it grow very long, and then curl it up with hot Irons, for they have learnt this piece of Vanity ; but then inftead of coftly Effences, they greafe it well with Butter that it may fhine, which is a Decoration fit for thofe who ufe it, for the Duft fticking to the Hair, it cannot chufe but look as comely as it is fweet feented.

Women there.

When the Women go abroad, they cover their Heads with white Cloths, and their Faces with black Veils like Nuns. They have fome *Jewish* Cuftoms among them, and particularly that of lamenting their Dead. One of the King's Daughters happening to Dye whilft the Fathers were there, abundance of Women, with their Hair very full of Duft, and fhrieking moft unmercifully, conducted the Queen to a Houfe that was near the Fort, where they continu'd a whole Month weeping and wailing. They went out twice every Day upon the flat Roof of the Houfe, where placing themfelves in two Ranks they beat their Breafts, and now and then threw their Arms about one another's Necks, with many doleful Expreffions and difmal Cries, expreffing Sorrow.

Yemen Kingdom.

The Kingdom of *Yemen,* or *Yamen,* begins at the Mouth of the *Red Sea,* and runs along the Coaft of *Moqua,* or *Moqba,* or *Mecca, Camarane* and *Obida,* Sea Port Towns belonging to the faid Kingdom, and many other Lands and Cities up the Inland, bordering on the Kingdom of *Xael,* whofe King pays Tribute to the *Baffa* of *Yemen,* who as foon as he heard that the Fathers were taken, fent immediately to King *Humar* to have them convey'd to him ; becaufe all *Portuguefe* Captives belong'd to the Great *Turk,* according to Articles agreed on betwixt them. The King readily comply'd, and fent 4 Horfes with them as a Gift to the *Baffa,* not out of Love but Fear, being us'd to make him great Prefents, to fave greater Extortions. He alfo furnifh'd the Fathers with Camels for the Journey, and order'd thofe that conducted them to ufe
them.

them well, and fee they wanted for nothing, becaufe thefe Fathers, faid he, ask nothing for themfelves.

On the 27th of _June_ they came to the laft ftrong Place in the Kingdom of _Xael_, where they took Provifion of Water for the _Great Defert_ Defert, upon which they then enter'd, being all Sand, without any Road, fteering by the Sun and Stars, and for fear thefe Guides fhould be hid from them by Clouds, they travell'd four Days and Nights without refting, but at Noon and Nightfall, whilft the Camels fed, who never Drank all that while. The 5th Day they found a Spring, by which they refted till the Evening, and at Nightfall fet forward again, to get out of the Defert, and efcape the Robbers thofe Solitudes are never without.

The next Day they came to a fmall Town call'd _Melquis_, where _Melquis_ they faw the Ruins of ftately Structures, and Stones with ancient _Town._ Infcriptions, which the Natives themfelves could not read; but faid there was formerly a very large City, and that the Queen of _Sheba_ had there mighty Flocks of Cattel, which, if true, verifies what I faid before, that the Queen of _Sheba_ was not only Sovereign of _Ethiopia_, but of a great part of _Arabia_. From _Melquis_ they travell'd 12 Days, through a well Peopled Country; till they came to _Canaan_, the Capital of the Kingdom of _Xiomen_, and _Canaan_, Refidence of the _Baffa_, where they were receiv'd by the _Subafhi_, _Capital of_ that is, the Governor, with abundance of Foot, and fome Horfe, _Xiomen._ who ordering the Kettle Drums to beat, made the Fathers walk afoot before his Horfe, leading them as it were in Triumph, thro' the principal Streets of the City, to the Fortrefs and _Baffa_'s Palace, as the _Romans_ drove their Captives before them to the Capitol. When they were at the Palace, down came the _Teftardar_, who is the Steward; and ask'd them feveral Queftions, for they were carry'd as Spies, to all which they anfwer'd the downright Truth. After much Examination they were carry'd to Prifon, and put into the common Side, befides which _F. Pays_ had Irons, but _F. Monferrate_ they exempted, becaufe he was very Old.

The _Teftardar_ carry'd the _Syrian_ Youth to his Houfe, and being taken with his Behaviour made him his Caterer, and he often _Charitable_ bringing him the overplus of his Money, the Mafter would fome- _Syrian_ times give it him, which he carry'd to the Fathers, and was a _Youth._ great Relief to them. Soon after meeting a _Turk_ of Note, who was his Countryman, and acquainting him with his Condition, he procur'd Liberty of the _Baffa_ for him to return to his own Country. He took leave of the Fathers, promifing to return to _India_; and to do them all the Service he could, which he faithfully perform'd; for within a few Months he made his way to

Ormuz,

Ormuz, and thence to *Goa*, where he gave an Account of what had befallen the Fathers, and the Condition they were in.

Portuguese
Captives at
Variance.

The Fathers found in the Prison 26 *Portuguese* and 5 *Indian* Christians, taken on the Coast of *Melinde*, who besides their Captivity, were at such variance among themselves, that they were ready to Murther one another. The Fathers by their good Instructions and Example, made them Friends, and wrought such a Change, that the very *Turks* were astonish'd at it. For their Comfort God order'd it, that the *Bassa*, who had been one of the Great *Turk*'s Gardiners, and still lov'd that Art, employ'd them all to work in his Garden; and the Goaler took them from the common Side below, and gave them such an Appartment above, that the Fathers had a large Room to themselves, and they were all easie, making a sort of Chappel there, and endeavouring to serve God the best they could.

C H A P. VIII.

The remaining part of the Captivity of the Fathers, till they were ransom'd; some further Account of Arabia Felix; *F.* Abraham de Georgijs *sent to* Ethiopia, *put to Death by the* Turks; *F.* Belchior da Sylva *sets safe into* Abyssinia; *a College of* Jesuits *founded for that Mission at* Diu.

Turkish re-
puted Saint.

WHEN the Fathers had been two Years in Captivity, the *Bassa*'s Wife prevail'd with him to order their Liberty; but a *Banean* Informing, that he might get 2000 Crowns for their Ransome, he recall'd his Word, and us'd them worse than before, demanding 10000 Crowns of them. An *Algierine Turks*, reputed a Saint, coming thither was a great Help to them in their want, for he would often send for, discourse with, and treat them very splendidly, commending them for good and learned Men. Another Man of Note, being a *Spanish* Renegado, us'd all his Endeavours to get them discharg'd, but all in Vain; for both these Friends at last departed the City, and left the Fathers to their Wants, and Sufferings, with only this Comfort, that they were usefull to

the

the other Chriftian Captives, fome of whom they got ranfom'd, and perfwaded 5 Renegadoes to make their Efcape to *India* as they did, and were reconcil'd to the Church.

Six Years they continu'd in Captivity in the City of *Canaan*,moft barbaroufly us'd, to extort from them the Sum of 2500 Crowns. This City had been formerly very great, as being the Capital of the Kingdom of *Yemen*, encompafs'd with ftrong Walls, and mighty Bulwarks of Earth. When the Fathers were there it contain'd about 2000 Families, 500 of them *Jews*. The Country is pleafant, and full of Gardens, and Orchards, producing almoft all the Sorts of Fruit we have in *Europe*, and is 60 Leagues from *Moca*. Thither the Fathers were fent, to fee whether the *Indian* Merchants would purchafe them. *F. Pays* went on a Camel, but *F. Monferrate* having had a Fall oft one defir'd to ride an Afs, which being joftled by a Camel gave him fuch another Fall, that he could not ftir, without being fupported by *F. Pays*, and a *Brachman* who was Captive with them. Thus they came to *Tais*, a fmall City, but has a ftrong wall, then to *Mouza*, which is fmaller,and laftly to *Moca*, where they were fhut up in a Ground Room full of Spice, which with the Heat of the Day and want of Air had like to have ftifled them, had not an *Abyffine* Youth, who was over 'em cooling his Mafter with water, told him, they muft needs perifh there with the Heat, who thereupon gave him Leave to remove them to a cooler Place.

Canaan City and Country.

Miferable Captivity.

After many Threats to extort a Ranfom from them, they were put into a Galley, where they had a very fmall allowance of bitter Millet in Grain. When they had endur'd thefe Hardfhips three Months, the *Turk*, who we faid had befriended them at *Canaan*, happened to come to *Moca*, and got them from aboard the Galley to his Houfe, where he entertain'd them very plentifully for 20 Days. Being then oblig'd to depart, he recommended them to the Captain of the Galley, defiring he would not put them to the Oar, but 5 Days after he was gone, the Captain,contrary to his Promife, return'd them to all their former Miferies. *F. Monferrate*, who was very old, falling fick, the Captain order'd him afhore, and *F. Pays* to look after him,but gave them no Allowance. In this Diftrefs, a *Banean* furnifh'd them with fome Rice, and Butter, and a Crown in Money, with which and *F. Pays* his Care *F. Monferrate* recover'd.

Charitable Turk.

They continu'd in this deplorable Condition a whole Year at *Moca* till Ships came from *Diu*, and in them Orders from *Mathias d' Albuquerque*, Viceroy of *India* that year 1595, to a *Banean*, with pofitive Orders to ranfom the Fathers at any Rate, the King of *Spain* having directed the Price fhould be paid out of his Reve-

nue. The *Banean* pursuant to his Orders, tho the Fathers oppos'd
it, alledging, that Mony might ransom many more, bought them
for 500 Crowns. Besides this they were forc'd to give 50 Crowns
to the Captain of the Galley, who exacted it, for the Time he had
suffer'd them to be ashore. At length they embark'd for *Diu*, and
arriv'd safe, after 29 Days Sail. There the Reverend Father Guar-
dian of the *Capucines* carry'd them to his Monastery, where they
had all the Entertainment that poor Order could afford; the *Jesuits* having no House at *Diu* as yet. Thence the *Dominicans* took, and
entertain'd them many Days in their Monastery. Next they
sail'd to *Chaul*, where the Brotherhood call'd *a Misericordia*, or of
Mercy, not only treated them, but order'd the Mony they said
was requisite for redeeming of the other Captives at *Canaan*. In
fine, they return'd at last to their own Monastery at *Goa*, after 7
Years Captivity. *F. Monserrate* dy'd there in the Year 1600, he
was a *Catalonian*, as has been said, and besides all his other Labours, had been two Years a Missioner in the Great *Mogol's*
Country. Of *F. Pays* we shall have occasion to speak hereafter,
when he again attempted to get into *Ethiopia*, where he liv'd many
Years, as we shall see.

When the Superiors at *Goa* receiv'd the News of the aforesaid
Father's Captivity in *Arabia*, they had also Intelligence, that only
F. Francis Lopez remain'd alive in *Ethiopia*, and therefore resolv'd
to hazard two other Fathers for the good of the Christians in that
Country. To this purpose they pitch'd upon *F. Abraham de Georgijs*, a *Maronite* by Birth, very learned, and Master of the *Arabick*,
Chaldaick Hebrew, and *Syriack*, who had enter'd himself into the Society at *Rome*, being there in the College of his Nation where-
many zealous Men are bred, who go over to instruct their Countrymen. The *Maronites* are the Inhabitants of Mount *Libanus*,
and the Country about it, who tho' subject to the *Turk*, profess
the *Roman* Catholick Religion, and some of them come over to be
educated in the foresaid Seminary at *Rome*, founded by Pope *Paul*
the 3d. They have a Catholick Patriarch, and 8, or 9 Bishops
under him. *F. Abraham* being well vers'd in the *Chaldaick* was
at this Time, on the Mountains of *Malabar*, instructing the
Christians of *S. Thomas*, whose Priests, and learn'd Men have the
Holy Scripture in *Chaldaick*, these People had been formerly *Nest-
orians*, who us'd to receive their Archbishop from *Babylon*. Upon
the first call he repair'd to *Goa*, where being acquainted with
what he was design'd for, he kept up close for a whole Year,
letting his Beard grow, and keeping quite out of Sight, to the
end that when he set out, he might not be known and discover'd by the *Moors*. When the Year was up he cloath'd himself

felf in the habit of a *Turkish* Merchant, and tho' a Companion had been appointed him, it was thought better he should go alone, only attended by one *Abyssine* Youth.

On the 6th of *January* 1595, he set out for *Diu*, where he imbark'd in a Ship of *Baneans*, bound for *Mazua*, arriv'd at that Place and was well receiv'd by *Xafar*, the *Turkish* Commander, believing him to be a *Turk*. He had his Leave to go over to the Continent, and being half Way on the Channel, that parts it from the Island, the *Banean*, Captain of the Ship that brought him thither, said to the *Bassa*, who was at a Window looking that way, Do you let that Man go so, Sir? I must tell you I know not whether he is a Christian, or a *Mahometan*. The *Turk* immediately sent a Boat after, and brought him back where upon Examination, he readily own'd himself a Christian. The *Bassa* told him he must either turn *Mahometan*, or dye; to which he answer'd, He might do as he pleas'd, for he was not a Person that would renounce his Faith. The *Abyssine* Youth that attended him, being also taken, discover'd all the Secret, and turned *Turk*. The Bassa us'd all possible Means to perswade the Father to follow the Youths Example, but finding him not to be mov'd, caus'd his Head to be struck off.

Arrives at Mazua.

Put to death for the Faith.

The News of his Death being brought to *Goa* in the Year 1595. and that of *Francis Lopez*, the last remaining in *Ethiopia* of the Missioners, in 1597 the Fathers were in great Concern for the distressed Catholicks of that Country. Those People in the Letter wherein they gave an Account of the Decease of the Fathers, advis'd, that since it was impossible for any *European* to pass into *Ethiopia* by way of the Red Sea, by Reason the *Turks* kept such strict Guard, they might send them some Priest, that was a Native of *India*, who being like the *Baneans* in Colour, and speaking their Language, and those People freely trading up the Red Sea, would be in less Danger. The Project was approv'd of, and *F. Belchior da Sylva*, a Secular Priest, pitch'd upon, being a *Brachman* by Descent, then Vicar of the Church of *S. Anne*, one of the richest in *Goa*, and a Man of Learning, and Piety. The good Priest imbark'd for *Diu*, and went thence to *Mazua*, in the Habit of a Seaman, in *March* 1596, where he found a Catholick of *Fremona*, come to look for Letters from *India*. By him he sent Word to the *Portugueses*, and setting out himself, for fear of the *Turks*, arriv'd in four Days at *Debaroa*, where he was receiv'd by several *Portugueses*, and Catholicks of *Fremona*, who conducted him thither with great Joy.

F. Belchior da Sylva arrives in Ethiopia.

F. Belchior da Sylva continu'd six years in *Ethiopia*, five before the coming of *F. Peter Pays*, who went to relieve him, and

one

one with him, expecting Shipping for *India*, all which Time he behav'd himself like an excellent Pastor, sparing no Pains to administer the Sacraments to the *Portuguese*, who were much dispers'd up the Country. He had Instructions, when he came from *India*, to endeavour to discover some way for the Fathers to get into *Ethiopia*. In the Year 1602 having consulted with the Principal *Portuguese* in the Kingdom of *Tygre*, they all came to this Resolution, that there was no Port like *Bailur*, which is just within the Mouth of the Red Sea, on the left Hand, opposite to *Moca*, 12 Leagues up the *Abyssine* Channel, and belongs to the Kingdom of *Daneali*; which tho' subject to a *Moor*, yet he so much depends upon the Emperor of *Ethiopia*, that by Virtue of a Letter from him, he would suffer them to pass. This Opinion all the *Portuguese* and *F. Belchior da Sylva* gave under their Hands, which has been here set down, tho' for the present the Fathers found a way through *Mazua*, yet because it may be of use another Time, and the Patriarch *Don Alfonso Mendez* pass'd that way, as we shall see hereafter.

Another way into Ethiopia contrived.

House of the Jesuits at Diu to that purpose.

Whatsoever way was found into *Ethiopia*, the Fathers perceiv'd it would be very necessary to have a House at *Diu*, that being the principal Port for the Trade of the Red Sea, because being there they could contract Friendship with the *Moors* and Gentiles sailing thither; for they might favour them with the Governour, and Custom-House, and those Traders, in Return, would carry them in their Ships, and procure them a safe Passage. The *Baneans* endeavour'd all they could to obstruct it, believing the Fathers would endeavour to convert the *Moors*, and Gentiles that came to trade thither, which would be a Hindrance to their Dealings, and lessen the Income of the Customs. However the Viceroy and King *Philip* the 2d positively resolving to favour the *Jesuits*, this Obstacle was remov'd, and those very *Baneans* perceiving what Kindness they receiv'd from the Fathers, grew so well affected towards them, that for several Years they gave them bountifull Alms, till their Church, and College were built.

CHAP.

C H A P. IX.

F. Peter Pays *finds Means to get into* Ethiopia. *What Emperors succeeded in that Empire, after* Malac Segued; *the Emperor* Za Danguil's *Victories.*

WE have already given an Account of the 7 Years Captivity of *F. Peter Pays*, who being well recover'd of the Hardships he endur'd in that time, set his Heart again upon attempting to get into *Ethiopia*, and in order to it went a way to *Diu*. King *Philip* the 2d had order'd six small Vessels to be fitted out to carry some Fathers into that Country, yet the Viceroy would provide but 2, and those meeting with a Storm, between *Goa*, and *Diu*, the one of them was forc'd into *Damam*, and the other reach'd its intended Port, much shatter'd and unmasted. *F. Pays* impatient of this Disappointment, set himself upon finding another way, and meeting some Servants of the Bassa of *Suaghem*, who came thither to trade and were returning home, he contracted Friendship with them, and particularly with their Chief, call'd *Razuam Aga*. The Father spoke *Arabick* perfectly well, having learn'd it, during his 7 Years Captivity, and in Familiar Discourse with the *Turk*, who took him for an *Armenian*, pretended some Desire to Return into his own Country, but that the Fear of falling again into the Hands of the *Turks* restrain'd him. The *Aga* readily promis'd to carry him safe to *Suaghem*, and thence to *Grand Cairo*, whence he might go with the Caravan to *Jerusalem*, and so into his own Country. *Father Pays* return'd him Thanks, and ask'd, whether, when they came to *Mazua*, he might not with Safety go up a little way into the Country, to seek after some Goods belonging to certain Fathers who dy'd there. The *Turk* told him, it would be very easy, and offer'd to bear all his Charges. In fine their Friendship was so closely knit, and the *Turk* show'd so much Sincerity, that the the Father embark'd with him, and they sail'd from *Diu*, on the 22d of *March* 1603. The *Aga* treated the Father all the way, with extraordinary Kindness,.

A Turk *conveys* F. Pays *into* Ethiopia.

and.

and they arriv'd at *Mazua*, on the 26th of *April*. The *Baffa* being then abfent, one *Muftadem*, a great Friend to *Raznam Aga* commanded in that Place, who was very civil to the Father for his Friends Sake, and gave him leave to go into *Ethiopia*, when he pleas'd to feek for thofe Goods he had told the *Aza* of.

He comes to Fremona. The fame Day F. *Pays* arriv'd there, he met with a Chriftian come from *Fremona*, by whom he fent *F. Belchior da Sylva* the News of his being in that Place. Some Days he was oblig'd to ftay at *Mazua* for Company, there being no travelling alone, becaufe of the many Robbers. At length meeting with 6 Chriftians, who came from *Fremona*, to enquire for News from *India*, he took leave of his Friend *Raznam*, who promis'd to ftay there for him two Months, and on the 5th of *May* 1603, began his Journey with the aforefaid 6 Chriftians, the *Shabander*, or Captain of the *Baneans*, attending him over to the Continent, and fending two *Moorifh* Servants to wait on him fome Days Journey farther. He travell'd all the way to *Debaroa*, which is 5 or 6 Days Journey, over very high and craggy Mountains, clad in an old *Moorifh* loofe Coat, with a Piece of Dimety inftead of a Cloak, for tear of the Thieves. On the 10th of *May* they came fafe to *Debaroa*, whither the next Day came the *Portuguefe* Captain *John Gabriel*, a Man of Worth, with feveral *Portuguefes* from *Fremona*, to receive the Father. They fet out from thence, and on the 15th of *May* got to *Fremona*, where they were receiv'd with extraordinary Joy, by the *Portuguefes* and other Catholicks, and they all repair'd to the Church to return Thanks to God. A few Days after *F. Belchior da Sylva* came to *Fremona*, having been 6 Months abroad adminiftring the Sacraments to the *Portuguefes*, who were difpers'd about the Empire, and was now overjoy'd to fee *F. Pays*, which fet him at Liberty to return to *India*. The *Portuguefe* Captain, *John Gabriel*, was fent to Court, to acquaint the Emperor *Jacob*, then reigning, with the Arrival of the Father, which News that Monarch receiv'd with fatisfaction, and order'd that as foon as the Winter was over he fhould repair to him. But now whilft *F. Pays* repofes himfelf, after his Fatigues by Sea and Land, let us take a view of the Affairs of *Ethiopia*.

Ethiopia. Affairs of It has been declar'd above, that at the time when the Patriarch Don *Andrew de Oviedo* dy'd, the Emperor reigning in *Ethiopia* was call'd *Malac Segued*. He by his Emprefs *Mariam Cina* had feveral Daughters, but never a Son; by others he had two Baftard Sons, the one nam'd *Za Mariam*, the other *Jacob*. Thus having no lawful Iffue Male, *Malac Segued* defign'd a long time for his Succeffor, a Nephew call'd *Za Danguil*, Son to his Brother *Leffena Chriftos*, and in order to it bred him up at Court, that the

Great

Great Men might refpect and affect him. However, a little before his Death, his Son *Jacob*, whom he had never feen, becaufe
bred far off, being brought to Court, and Fatherly Affection prevailing, he chang'd his Mind, and refolv'd to leave the Empire to
that Baftard. The Great Men perceiving his Inclination, foon
comply'd with it, and as Flatterers are want to do in all their
Difcourfes, promoted his Defign. Death put a Stop to all thefe
Practices, for the Emperor returning from his Wars with the
Galas of *Bavilo* fell Sick, and perceiving his laft Hour approach,
that being a time of impartial Juftice, he thought himfelf oblig'd
to leave the Crown to his Nephew, and accordingly made it
known to all the Great Men, charging them to enthrone *Za
Danguil*, as his Nephew and lawful Heir, the other being but a
Baftard.

Malac Se-
gued leaves
the Crown to
Za Danguil.

The Emperor was juft dying when he gave thefe Commands,
yet his Flattering Courtiers perfifted, alledging, they would have
no other Monarch but his Son. The true Reafon of it was, becaufe *Za Danguil* was then a Man grown, and *Jacob* the Baftard
but a Child, under whofe Name they thought they fhould have
the whole Power in their own Hands, without any Regard to
Juftice. Having fix'd this Refolution among themfelves, before
they made known the Father's Death, or the Son's Election, they
fent fome Troops of arm'd Men to fecure the Nephew *Za Danguil*, and others to do the fame by *Socinios*, Great Grandfon to
the Emperor *David*, who they much fear'd might call them to
Account, as being a very brave and hopeful Youth. Accordingly *Za Danguil* was feiz'd, and carry'd to a Lake call'd *Dek*, in
the Kingdom of *Dambea*, where he was kept Prifoner a long
time, and afterwards on feveral ftrong Mountains. *Socinios* getting Intelligence that they defign'd to lay him up, had the good
Fortune to make his efcape to the Frontiers of the Empire, where
he kept up in Arms, till God rais'd him to the Throne, as we fhall
fee hereafter.

The Great
imprifon him

Being rid of thefe powerful Competitors, they proclaim'd *Jacob* Emperor, at 7 Years of Age, and kept the Government in
their own Hands, with the Emprefs *Mariam Sina*, who fided
with the Confederates, fhe taking for her Affociates two of her
Sons in Law, call'd *Ras Athanateus* and *Caftuade*, Viceroy of *Tigre*,
the two Prime Contrivers of thefe Practices, the young Emperor
Jacob having nothing but the fpecious Title of Emperor. This
Triumvirate held above 7 Years, till *Jacob* being about 14 Years
of Age, began to fhow he would have a Share in the Government himfelf. Many Months were not paft fince the young
Emperor began to act of himfelf, before thofe Three who had fet

And fet up
Jacob, a Ba-
ftard.

him

him up, *viz.* the Emprefs and her two Sons in Law, *Athanateus* and *Caftnade*, at the Inftigation of *Za Sebaffe*, a turbulent Perfon, we fhall foon fpeak of, agreed to depofe him, pretending a Scruple of Confcience, for having wrong'd *Za Danguil*, whofe Right it was. This was the Colour they took to palliate their wicked Ambition, believing fince they had loft the Favour of *Jacob*, they fhould have the Power over *Za Danguil*, whom they preferr'd to the Empire. They fent to him to the uncouth Mountains, where he was Prifoner, little thinking of fuch Fortune, and being brought into the Camp, he was inftantly declar'd and honour'd as Emperor, and, what is moft remarkable, the other Emperor *Jacob* was ftill in the fame Camp.

Forfake him and fet up Za Danguil.

Jacob had barely time to efcape by the Swiftnefs of his Horfe, thinking it enough to fave his Life, and as is ufual for all Men to forfake the Unfortunate, only 8 Servants follow'd him. He took the way to *Cemen*, a ftrong Mountain Country, where many of his Mother's Kindred were, and had he got thither fafe, it would have been impoffible to take him. But there wanted not a Traitor among thofe few Friends, who, whilft the Poor Youth took a little Reft, being come near *Cemen*, went away to a Neighbouring Town, and inform'd the People, that *Za Danguil* was proclaim'd Emperor in the Camp, and *Jacob* was come thither flying, and therefore charg'd them to fecure him, under Pain of the new Emperor's Difpleafure. They all hafted out in a Body, and furprizing the unhappy Youth, carry'd him Prifoner to *Za Danguil*.

Jacob flies.

He, tho' well pleafed to have his Competitor in Cuftody, was much difpleafed with the Bafenefs of the Treacherous Servant. The Council fitting, fome were of Opinion, that *Jacob's* Nofe and Ears fhould be cut off, fo to render him incapable of governing; but *Za Danguil* being of a generous Temper, was fatisfy'd with fending him to the Kingdom of *Narea*, the fartheft of the Empire towards the South Eaft, charging the *Xumo*, or Governor, to keep a ftrict Guard over him. There we will leave him for the prefent, and fhall after a while fee this fame *Jacob* made Emperor again, and *Za Danguil* kill'd, and foon after *Jacob* Slain by *Socinios*, who took the Name of *Sultan Segued*. Let us now fee how *Za Danguil* behav'd himfelf towards *F. Peter Pays*, and in the Government.

Is taken, and committed to Prifon.

When *F. Pays* came to *Fremona*, the Emperor *Jacob* was on the Throne, but foon remov'd to make Place for *Za Danguil*, as we have feen. During that Time, the Father had the Catechifm compos'd by Doctor *Mark George* of the Society, tranflated into the *Ethiopick* by fuch as were beft acquainted with the Language, and made abundance of Children learn it by Heart. The *Ethiopians* were

Children taught their Catechife.

were so highly pleas'd to hear those Children discourse, by way of Dialogue, of all the Mysteries of Religion, that many resorted from all Parts to partake of it, and others sent for them to their Houses. The Fame of it at last reach'd the Court, and the Scholars were so highly commended, that their Master could not but partake of those Praises.

The Emperor *Za Danguil* being very affable and curious, and naturally inclin'd to hear any Thing that was new to him, especially in what related to the Doctrine of the Church of *Rome*; and being also inform'd, that the Father at *Fremona* was very Learned, a great Traveller, and could give a notable Account of what he had seen, and of the *Roman* Faith, he was very desirous *The Emperor* to see and converse with him, and to hear some of those young *sends for* Lads he had instructed. He therefore sent for the Father, and F. *Pays.* writ him a Letter, which the said Father has left us, in the Treatise of the Affairs of *Ethiopia* till his Death, which we will here insert, to give the Reader some Idea of the Stile of that Country, and is as follows.

A Letter from the Emperor *Za Danguil,* otherwise call'd *Asnaf Segued,* to F. *Peter Pays.*

MAY the Letter of the Emperor Asnaf Segued *come to the Hands of the Worthy Father, who is Master of the* Portugueses. *How is your Health? Hear these Things, and the good News of what our Lord God has done for us. We were Seven Years in Prison, and endur'd innumerable Hardships; but our Lord God taking Compassion on our Misery, brought us out of Prison, and gave us the Empire, and has made us Head of all, even as* David *says,* The Stone which the Builders refus'd, is become the Head Stone of the Corner. *Now the same Lord end that well which he has began. Hear farther; We are very desirous, that you come hither speedily, and that you bring the Books of the Justice of the Kings of* Portugal, *if you have them, for we shall be glad to see them.* Thus far the Emperor's Letter.

The next Day he dispatch'd an Express, with Orders for the Father to come with the Viceroy of *Tigre*, who was ready to *Irruption of* repair to Court. The Father was immediately ready, but the *of the Galaʃ.* Viceroy stay'd, because he receiv'd News, that the Emperor had decamp'd, to go and oppose the *Galas*, who understanding the Disorders that were in the Empire, had broke into the Country,

Y

with

with a defign to make themfelves Mafters of it. Thefe Barbarians being very numerous, had form'd 3 Armies, to the end that making fo many feveral Incurfions, they might oblige the *Ethiopians* alfo to feparate, and fo attack them the better difpers'd. The greateft Body enter'd the Kingdom of *Gojam,* whither the Emperor march'd, ordering the Viceroy of that Country to keep himfelf whole, without giving the Enemy Battel till he came: But Martial Rules being little obferv'd in *Ethiopia,* the Viceroy feeing the Enemy at Hand, and thinking it a Difcredit to lofe Time, fought and was routed.

Bravery of Za Danguil. The Emperor was concern'd at this lofs, but not difcourag'd, and therefore advanc'd fpeedily to meet the Enemy, who at firft fight offer'd him Battel, divided into three Bodies. The Imperialifts being tir'd with their march, would have defer'd fighting; yet feeing it was unavoidable, both fides fell on, the *Galas* attacking the *Abiffines* with fuch Fury, that the Emperor's Right and Left Wings both betook themfelves to Flight, and only the main Battel ftood, fupported by his Valour. The Prime Officers told him it was time to retire, before the *Galas* enclos'd him. The undaunted Youth, inftead of clapping Spurs to his Horfe to fly, alighted to fight, and taking his Buckler upon one Arm and his Sword in the other Hand, cry'd out, *I am refolv'd to dye here, you may fly from the* Galas, *but can never efcape the Infamy, if you this Day abandon the Emperor you proclaim'd but yefterday.*

He routs the Galas twice. Great is the Power of Example in a refolute Commander; they all ftuck clofe together, and rufh'd upon the *Galas* like fo many ravenous Lyons. The Barbarians amaz'd at this frefh Vigour, turn'd their Backs, and fled full fpeed. The *Abyffines* of the two Wings who had fled, were now upon a Neighbouring Hill looking on, and as foon as they faw the *Galas* run, fell into the Purfuit, and never gave over killing till Night oblig'd them to defift. The next Morning the Fields appear'd ftrew'd with Thoufands of dead *Galas.* The Emperor loft no Time, but march'd his Victorious Army as it was embrue'd in Blood, over high and craggy Mountains, to find out the fecond Body of the *Galas,* and being flufh'd with one Victory, his Men charg'd fo fuccefsfully, that they alfo overthrew them with the Slaughter of the greater part. Only the third remain'd, who thought it better to fly in Time than to ftand the bloody Weapons of the *Abyffines.* The Emperor underftanding that 400 of them remain'd on an exceffive high Mountain, to guard fome Booty they had taken, he attack'd them, and his Men climbing or flying up thofe Rocks,

the

the *Galas* were all cut in Pieces, tho' they made a good Defence. Thus the Victorious Emperor return'd to his Station, fear'd by Strangers, and honour'd by his own People.

C H A P. X.

F. Peter Pays *goes to the Emperor's Court, where he is receiv'd with great Honour, says Mass and Preaches before the Emperor; that Monarch writes to the Pope and King of* Spain, *and resolves to embrace the Catholick Faith.*

AS soon as the Viceroy of *Tigre* understood that the Emperor was return'd Victorious over the *Galas*, he acquainted Father *Pays*, that it was Time to go to Court, and they set out together in *April* 1604.

The Emperor was then at *Ondegere*, near the famous Lake of *The Empe-* *Dambea* and the River *Nile*, where it falls into that Lake. There *rors Court.* he had pitch'd his Camp, which is all the Court of *Ethiopia*, there being no other Royal City, as has been said. There were two spacious Enclosures of dry Stone, with high Hedges, and within them several Appartments, all on the Ground Floor, of Stone and Clay, thatch'd, wherein consisted all those Magnificent Structures some Authors have feign'd in *Ethiopia*, being more like Cottages than a Palace. The Emperor had here a large Room, to which there was a sort of rais'd Balcony, which many of the *Abyssines* look'd upon as a noble Building.

When they came to the Camp, the Viceroy waited at the Gate *The Fathers* of the first Enclosure, as is usual for Great Men that come from *Reception* Abroad, till the Emperor being advertiz'd, sent him Orders to *there.* come in, by one of the principal Men of his Court, who seeing the Father, saluted him courteously, and said, he would instantly acquaint the Emperor that he might come in.

The Father went up to kiss the Emperor's Hand, whom he found on his Throne, which is his Couch, well adorn'd with rich *Description* Quilts, Coverlets of Brocard, and Silk Cuttins. He seem'd to be *of the Empe-* about 26 Years of Age, tall, well shaped, and Manly. His *ror.*

Y 2   Eyes

Eyes large and bewtiful, his Nose sharp. His Lips thin, but his Complexion was somewhat tawny; and were it not for that Colour, which in *Europe* is reckned unbecoming, he would not have been inferior to the finest Men among us. In short, his Person was worthy of the Empire he held, and the Majesty he represented. The Father was withdrawing, after kissing his Hand, but the Emperor commanded, and oblig'd him, to sit Down on the rais'd Step his Couch stood on, where he discours'd him for a considerable Time, without regarding the Rest. After some Time, the Emperor made a Sign for the Father to withdraw, and order'd he should be handsomly entertain'd.

F. Pays gains Friends; The next Day he sent for him again, and there was a long Disputation about the *Roman* and the *Ethiopian* Faith, in the Presence of many Persons of Note, and several Monks: The Children also come in for a part, the Viceroy of *Tygre* desiring the Emperor to hear the Schollars, as well as the Master, with which the Emperor was so well pleas'd, that he ask'd the Father, whether he had all they said written in a Book, and being told, he had, order'd it to be sent him, and the next Sunday heard *F. Pays* say Mass and Preach.

The Emperor soon after by Proclamation forbid the keeping of the Saturday, and went on so fast in other Particulars, that the Father was oblig'd to advise him to proceed more gently. But the Emperor, *then gave him the Letters he had already writ to the Pope, and the King of Portugal*; which the Father receiv'd, and caus'd to be translated.

It is here to be observ'd, that in these Letters, the Emperor calls himself *Asnaf Segned*, which was the Name he took at his Coronation, as the Popes do at their Exaltation, tho' his Christian Name was *Za Dænguil*, as has been observ'd before. It is also to be noted, that he charg'd the Father, to write in a Letter of his own, That he then actually submitted himself to the Pope, and desir'd he would send him a Patriarch; and to acquaint him farther, that the Forces he ask'd, were to guard his own Person, against such as should oppose his settling the Faith in *Ethiopia*; for tho' he pretended they were to serve against the *Galas*, those People were entirely defeated, and would scarce return into his Dominions. But he took that Colour as not daring to trust his Secretary, nor so much as to write plain with his own Hand, for fear the Letter should be intercepted, and they might murder him. The Emperor's Letter to his Holiness, dated the 26 of *June* 1604, was as follows.

May

The LETTER.

MAY the Letter sent by the Emperor of Ethiopia Asnaf Segued, *come safe to the Honoured Father, the Humble, Victorous, and Holy Pastor* Clement, *Pope of the Noble City of* Rome. *Peace be unto your Holiness. The Peace of our Lord Jesus Christ, who partook of Poverty with the Poor, and Honour with the Honourable, preserve your Holiness's Person, and Life, like the Apple of the Eye. Amen. How does your Holiness? Hear, Sir, what we write. We being in our Empire, there came hither a Father, on whose Neck is the yoke of the Law of Christ, by Name* Peter Pays *of the House of* Jesus, *and brought us particular News, of your Holinesses Labouring to take away Sin, even to the Effusion of your Blood. The Eternal God, who is the Head, carry it on to the End. And having heard these News, that your Holiness always walks in the way of Truth, we rejoyc'd, and were well pleas'd Prais'd be God, who has given us a good Shepard to keep the Flocks with Holiness, and judge the Poor in Truth. He also told us, that you assisted Christians in all that is necessary, giving them Strength, and fulfiling their Desires, following that of* S. Paul *in his Epistle to they* Galatians, As we have therefore Opportunity, let us do good unto all Men, especialy unto them, who are of the Household of. Faith. *And therefore your Holiness chiefly assists Christian Kings in all Things. Therefore since God has given us the Empire of our Forefathers, we desire to entertain Amity with your Holiness, and with our Brother.* Don Phillip, *King of* Spain; *and to the End it may be the more lasting, we desire him to send us his Daughter, to be marry'd to our Son, and with her some Forces, to assist us, because we have in our Country certain Heathen Enemies, call'd* Galas. *If we march against these, we can not find them, for they fly, and when we return, they fall in where we are not, like Robbers; and therefore to destroy them, we desire him to send us Forces, and all Sorts of Officers, and Fathers to instruct us, that we may be all one Hart, and one Body, and establish the Faith of Christ which was lost among the* Gentiles; *so that Peace, and Love may remain among us.*

My Forefathers desir'd this before, but it did not please God; they could not compass it, because the Turks *were in the way, with Power. Now the Island, where they are, may be easily taken; we therefore intreat your Holiness to press our Brother to perform what we ask of him; and that immediately, without any Delay. We write this briefly to your Holiness, as knowing you will fulfil our Desires. Moreover let the Fathers that come be* Virtuous, *and Learned, that they may teach us what is requisite for our Souls. Few Words to the Wise.*

This

This Letter has been inferted entire, as it is exactly tranflated, to fhow the Stile of that Nation. The other Letter to King *Phillip* the 2d of *Spain*, was of the fame Form, and the Purport of it was to ask Men, and his Daughter to Marry this Emperor's Son. The Father having receiv'd thefe Letters, withdrew immediately to find out a proper Perfon to fend them by. Among the many Favours the Emperor did the Father, he order'd him 300 Ounces of Gold, which he abfolutely refus'd to accept of; and only defir'd Land to build a Church, which the Emperor granted.

C H A P. XI.

The great Men confpire againft the Emperor Za Danguil, *what Method he took ; fights the Rebels, and is kill'd ; four other Fathers arrive in* Ethiopia, Socinios *proclaim'd Emperor, takes the Name of* Sultan Sugued ; *the Behaviour of the Traitor* Za Selaffe.

Za Selaffe a Traitor.

THERE was one *Za Selaffe*, a mifchievous Villian, who had been banifh'd to *Narea*, the remoteft Kingdom of *Ethiopia*, by the late Emperor *Jacob*, for confpiring, and taking up Arms againft him; but Fortune changing, *Jacob* was banifh'd to *Narea*, and *Za Selaffe*, through the Interceffion of Friends brought to Court, by the Emperor *Za Danguil*, who made him *Xumo*, or Governour of the Kingdom of *Dambea*, and Parts adjacent, For all which Favours he prov'd fo ungrateful, that within a few Months he rebell'd againft that Soveregin, who had fo highly favour'd him. This bafe Wretch, took Occafion to rebel, becaufe he faw others in greater Favour with the Emperor than himfelf, as alfo on account of his favouring the *Portuguefes*, and the Catholick Religion. He therefore refolv'd to reftore the Crown to the Emperor *Jacob*, finding thofe very People, who had before rejected, now well affected towards him, only through their own natural Levity and Inconftancy. He imparted his Defign to *Ras Athanateus*, then the greateft Man in *Ethiopia*, next the Emperor, who

Confp'ers with others.

had before taken the Crown of *Za Danguil*, to give it to *Jacob*, and then from *Jacob*, to reftore it to *Za Danguil*, only for his own private Intereft, as was faid above. This *Athanateus* was envious

of

of the Favour the Emperor fhow'd to *Laca Mariam*, and therefore *againft the approv'd* of *Selaffe's*, Project. The Conspiracy having two fuch *Emperor.* Heads, one the wickedeft, and the other the richeft Man in *Ethiopia*, was foon efpous'd by many others, offended at the Emperors favouring the Catholick Religion, and *Selaffe* taking that for a Pretence to his Villany.

Thefe Practcies could not be long unknown to the Emperor, who tho' he fear'd *Raz Athanaus* durft not proceed to Extremities without fuller Proofs, and therefore diffembled till he found that *Za Selaffe* was the Prime Incendiary, who had already fir'd feveral great Men, and therefore it was neceffary to apply fpeedy Remedy. To this Purpofe he call'd together his Troops, and the firft among them the *Portuguefes*, being then about 200 Men, able to bear Arms, with their Captain *John Gabriel*; giving out that he *Who is for-* would march againft the *Galas*. The Danger preffing, he mov'd *faken by* his Camp, and march'd towards *Nanina*, in the Kingdom of *many.* *Gojam*, thinking in that ftrong Country he might fecure the Traitors that were about him, unlefs they ftay'd behind, knowing it was better to have open Enemies, than Traitors in his Bofom. They underftood his Defign, and therefore the 2d Day as the Emperor pafs'd a great River, *Raz Athanateus* ftay'd behind, with 300 Soldiers of his ufual Retinue. *Jonael*, another notable Perfon, and great Commander did the fame, and the Infectionhad fo far prevail'd, that every Days Journey fome great Men forfook him, and then their Followers, for very few worfhip the fetting Sun.

The Emperor having receiv'd a Reinforcement of about 200 Men *The Traitor* from the Neibouring Country, and being a Man of undaunted *Athanateus* Courage, hafted back, in Hopes of taking *Raz Athanateus* before *efcapes.* he pafs'd the *Nile*; but be having ftill Friends in the Army, they gave him timely Notice, and he efcap'd. The Emperor continu'd about the *Nile* till he had gather'd 10000 Men, and refolv'd with that Force to go meet the Enemy, who had a much greater Army; notwithftanding *John Gabriel*, the Captain of the *Portuguefes*, a brave, and experienc'd Man, labour'd all he could to perfwade him to delay Time, fince his Forces daily increas'd.

Za Selaffe at this Time rang'd about like a Fury, ftiring up the *The Abuna* People to Rebellion, telling them *Jacob* was at Hand, with a *encourag s* powerfull Army, and had the Right to the Empire, fince he held *Relellion.j* it 7 Years, and that *Za Danguil* did not deferve it, for having forfaken the Faith of his Forefathers, and ought therefore to be fhun'd as an excommunicated Perfon, and to be kill'd as a *Moor*. To crown the Work, he went to the *Abuna Peter*, and perfwaded him to abfolve them from their Oath of Allegiance to *Za Danguil*, which

which he did, and then they all thought themfelvs fufficiently authoriz'd to wage War on their Sovereign.

The Emperor in a few Days march came to *Varcha*, a large Plain, almoft in the midft of the Kingdom of *Dambea*, near which *The Emperor* the Rebels lay encamp'd, and prefently the Noife of Kettle Drums *defeated and* and Shouts of the Soldiers were heard; the Traitor *Za Selaffe* be-*kill'd.* ing fenfible, that the beft way was to fight immediately, as fear-ing that many of his Men would go over to the Emperor by Night. The Captain of the *Portuguefes* for the fame Reafon ad-vis'd to put off the Battel; but *Za Danguil* could not endure to be brav'd by the Rebels, and confided in the Juftice of his Caufe. In fine, he rang'd his Army, placing the *Portuguefes* on the Right, with fome of his own Men, becaufe there were but 200 of them, and ftay'd himfelt on the Left. It was the 13th of *Oktober* 1604, when thefe two Armies engag'd, and the *Portuguefes* falling on with the utmoft Fury, the *Ethiopians* not able to ftand the Shock fled, whom they purfu'd, killing great Numbers, till obferving they were too far advanc'd they drew back. The Emperor was not fo Fortunate on his Wing, tho' he behav'd himfelf like a Lyon, bearing down all before him; but 60 of his Horfe deferting to the Enemy, others follow'd their Example, and many more quite daunted at that Treachery, withdrew themfelves to fee the Event of the Battel. Only fome brave Men of Note, and faithful Servants ftuck clofe by their Sovereign, and his Favourite *Laca Mariam* was flain by his Side. The Traitor *Za Selaffe* feeing one of his Wings routed by the *Portuguefes*, and fearing to be to-tally overthrown if they fhould return, charg'd the Imperialifts with fuch Vigour, that he oblig'd thofe few who ftood to retire. In this Confufion one *Humardin*, of a *Moorfh* Race, who ferv'd among the Rebels, coming up with the Emperor, gave him fuch a ftroke with his Launce on the Neck, that he fell down defpe-rately wounded. He ftarted up, and defended himfelf bravely with his Sword, and kept them all off that furrounded him, till the Villain *Za Selaffe* came up with his Launce couch'd, and wounded him on the Face, and then all the reft falling on kill'd him. His Death put an end to the Strife, which was maintain'd only for his fake.

His Burial The Dead Body was ftripp'd by the Soldiers, and fome Perfons *and Tranfla-* out of Refpect having cover'd it with a Cloth, the Mifcreant *tion.* *Za Selaffe* order'd it to be taken away. Thus ended that brave Emperor *Za Danguil*, whofe Body even his Enemies attefted caft forth a fweet Odour three Days after it was Dead, when it was carry'd to be bury'd in a little Church clofe by. Ten Years after the Emperor *Sultan Segued*, his Coufin, tranflated it with great
Pomp

Pomp to a Monaſtery call'd *Duga,* in the Lake of *Dambea,* the Burial Place of many Emperors; and even then it is atteſted by
Witneſſes above Reproach, that the Body was as perfect and entire as when firſt kill'd, without any Art us'd to it, or Embalm-
ing. His Death was univerſally lamented, for he was entirely
belov'd, and the *Ethiopians* in their Hiſtories call him *The Choſen,
and ſent by God Za Danguil.*

Let us now give an Account of the two new Comers, *F. An o-
ny Fernandez,* a *Portugueſe,* and *F. Francis Antony de Angelis,* a
Neapolitan, and how they came into *Ethiopia.* Theſe two were
at firſt deſign'd to have come with *F. Pays,* but he having found
the way we have mention'd above, they ſtay'd behind at *Diu* till
another Opportunity. All things fell out as was deſir'd; for
they receiv'd Letters from *F. Peter Pays* after his Arrival in *Ethiopia,* and *Mahomet Aga,* another Servant of the *Baſſa* of *Mazua,*
came to *Diu,* encourag'd by the Favour *Razuam Aga* had
found there before. The Fathers got acquainted with this *Aga,*
and did him ſo many Courteſies with the Governor and Cuſtom-
houſe Officers, that he promis'd to carry them both ſafe into *Ethiopia.* They imbark'd with him aboard a Ship bound directly for
Suaghem, on the 24th of *March* 1604, and arriv'd at the aforeſaid
Port, where they were kindly receiv'd by the *Baſſa,* upon Information of the Favours done to his Servant on their Account. He
gave each of them a Brocard Veſt, which is the greateſt Honour
they can do any Man. Next he fitted out a *Gelva,* being a ſmall
Veſſel us'd in the *Red Sea,* and ſent his Steward with them, giving him Orders to conduct them to *Mazua,* and furniſh Horſes
and a Guard for their Paſſage to ſome Place of ſafety in *Ethiopia.*
A Storm having diſabled their Veſſel, and forc'd them back to
Suaghem, the *Baſſa* fitted out another, which carry'd them to
Mazua, where they were well entertain'd by the *Quequea,*or Commander of that Iſland and *Arquico,* and furniſh'd with a Guard
till they were met by the *Portugueſes* of *Fremona,* to whom notice
had been ſent of their coming. They came to that Place on the
13th of *July* 1604, where the *Portugueſes* and other Catholicks
receiv'd them with ſingular Joy and Affection.

The following Winter, whilſt the 3 Fathers were ſtill at *Frem-
na,* two others arriv'd there from *Diu.* They came from that
Place with another Servant of the ſame *Baſſa* of *Suaghem,* but
were in great Danger when they arriv'd at that Place, the ſaid
Baſſa being Dead, and his Succeſſor a moſt bloody covetous Villain. However, they appeas'd him for the preſent with rich Gifts,
ſo that he caus'd them to be conducted into *Ethiopia,* as the others
had been. Yet ſoon repenting, ſent after to ſtop them, and ſeize

How 2 more Jeſuits got into Ethi-opia.

Two others eſcape nar-rowly.

Z　　　　all

all they had, but it pleas'd God his Messenger came too late. The Captain of the Ship that brought them was not so Fortunate, for the Inhuman *Baſſa* laid some forg'd Crime to his Charge, for which he cut off his Head, and seiz'd the Ship and Cargo. Not so satisfy'd, he privately murther'd two *Venetians* that came in the same Ship, and took poſſeſſion of all their Effects.

Socinios *his* Deſcent. It will be proper here to give an Account how the Emperor *Socinios* came to the Crown. The Emperor *Onag Segned*, whom we commonly call *David*, had three Sons, the firſt *Glaudios* or *Claudius*, who ſucceeded him in the Empire, as we have mention'd above: The ſecond was Prince *Jacob*, who dy'd before his Brother, leaving two Sons, the one call'd *Taſcaro*, and the other *Faciladas. David's* third Son was *Minas*, who ſucceeded his Brother *Glaudios*, and was call'd *Adamas Segued*, of whom we have ſpoken, and he had Four Sons, *Serza Danguil*, who ſucceeded him in the Empire, and was call'd *Malac Segued*, *Aquieter*, *Abale*, and *Leſana Chriſtos*, and *Za Danguil* laſt ſpoken of was Son to the laſt of them. *Taſcaro*, Son to Prince *Jacob*, revolted againſt his Uncle *Minas*, or *Adamas Segued*, and being routed and taken, was caſt headlong from a high Rock. *Faciladas* liv'd many Years poſſeſs'd of conſiderable Lands in the Kingdom of *Gojam*, and was at laſt kill'd fighting againſt the *Galas. Socinios* we now ſpeak of was Son to this *Faciladas*, and had ſpent his firſt Youthful Years in great Adverſity, yet always with a Reſolution above his Fortune.

Aſpires to the Throne. He had been ſome time up in Arms, without aſpiring to the Empire, to oblige thoſe in Command to give him his Fathers Lands, which they poſſeſs'd; but when he found the Throne Vacant by the Death of his Kinſman *Za Danguil*, and that *Jacob* before rejected, as being a Baſtard to *Malac Segued*, was very remote in the Kingdom of *Narea*, he began to entertain Thoughts of obtaining the Empire, which Fortune now offer'd him. Beſides, he was very well attended by many brave Men, who had follow'd him in all his Wars, and encouraged him to lay hold of this favourable Opportunity, ſince he had the beſt Title to the Crown, and they would Sacrifice their Lives to ſet it on his Head. *Socinios* approving of their Advice, and reſolving to loſe no Time, ſent immediately a Man of Quality call'd *Bella Chriſtos*, from the Kingdom of *Amara*, where he then was, to *Ras Athanateus*, the Viceroy of *Gojam*, deſiring he would aſſiſt him with his Forces. He ſtay'd not for an Anſwer, but paſſing the *Nile*, enter'd that Kingdom of *Gojam*, and ſent again to *Athanateus* to come and meet him. He not knowing which way to avoid it, or what Party to take, came and joyn'd him with all his Troops,

by

by whom, and thofe he had before *Socinios*, was faluted Emperor, by the Name of *Sultan Segued*.

He fent next to *Za Selaffe*, as the Prime Contriver of all the Rebellion, to come to meet him, fince he was admitted to the Throne of his Fore-fathers; who after confulting with his Affoci-ates, return'd for Anfwer, that they thought the Crown belong'd to *Jacob*, as having been once poffefs'd of it, yet if he came not by *June* they would admit him. *Socinios* not liking this Anfwer, fent again a Nobleman and a Monk, with a Letter, importing, That fince he had been once proclaim'd, he would never refign the Empire to *Jacob*, nor to his own Father, if he fhould come to Life again. *Za Selaffe* fecur'd the Meffengers, and march'd with his whole Army to *Gojam*, to deliver his Anfwer with Sword in Hand; but *Socinios* retir'd into the Kingdom of *Amara*, being then Sick, as alfo to gain Time, hoping many would come over to him, and he might end the Quarrel without Bloodfhed. The Summer of 1605 was now almoft fpent, and *Jacob* came not from *Narea*, nor any News of him, whereupon the Great Men per-fwaded *Za Selaffe* not to lofe Time, but rather to own *Socinios*. He, fearing to be forfaken by them, comply'd, and fent to invite *The Traitor* and acknowledge him as Emperor. *Socinios* fent a Monk to ad- *Za Selaffe* minifter to them the Oath of Fidelity, and excommunicate fuch *fubmits to* as fhould refufe to take it, which is the greateft Tye among *him.* them. They all fwore, and proclaim'd *Socinios*, Ten of them fetting out immediately, and meeting him in *Begameder*, whither he was already advanc'd, congratulating his Acceffion to the Crown, and protefting to ftand by him againft all Pretenders, and even *Jacob* himfelf by Name, fhould he then come from *Narea*. How well they kept their Promife we fhall fee in the next Chapter.

CHAP.

C H A P. XII.

Socinios forsaken by the Abyssines, and Jacob enthron'd; he moves to fight Socinios, and is deserted by the Traitor Za Selasse; Jacob is kill'd, Socirios Emperor, his Character; the end of Za Selasse, and Ras Athanateus; the Emperor's Affection to the Fathers.

Revolts again to Jacob.

WHILST those Great Men above mention'd were in the Kingdom of *Begameder*, doing Homage to *Socinios*, in the behalf of *Za Selasse*, News was brought him that *Jacob* was near *Dambea*, with Orders to go meet him. The Traitor believing there was more to be got by *Jacob* than by *Socinios*, without any Regard to the Oath he had just taken, went immediately to meet and own the former, being follow'd by all the Army, and others he had bred to his Beck. At the same time he writ privately to those he had sent to *Socinios*, bidding them get away as fast as they could, because his Mind was alter'd; which they did so slily, that *Socinios* could only take two of them, who paid for all the Rest. That Emperor finding himself too weak to call *Za Selasse*

Socinios withdraws.

to an Account for his Perjury, and *Jacob* for his Usurpation, retired again into the Kingdom of *Amara*, till a more favourable Conjuncture.

Jacob proclaim'd Emperor.

Great was the Joy with which the new Emperor *Jacob* was receiv'd by the Army, and all other People, as if they had only desir'd to see such Changes every Day. *Za Selasse* was made Governor General, and as it were the Emperor's General. *Ras Athanateus* hearing what had happen'd, came in with his Forces:

Jacob offers to compound with Socinios.

Jacob however considering the Instability of human Felicities, would have compounded with *Socinios*, offering him the Kingdoms of *Amara*, *Oleac* and *Xaoa*, with all the Lands his Father enjoy'd, provided he would quit his Claim to the Empire. *Socinios* answer'd, That God had plac'd him on the Throne, and therefore he would have all or none. *Jacob* hearing this resolute Answer, and finding himself very strong, march'd immediately towards *Socinios*, or *Sultan Segued*, for by this Name we must call him, and encamp'd close by him. He observing what a Multitude

tude

tude follow'd his Competitor, thought it beſt to draw back for the preſent, till a better Opportunity.

When *Jacob* march'd againſt *Sultan Segued*, the Traitor *Za Selaſſe* was not with him, for that tricking haughty Knave could not endure to ſee any Man above himſelf, and was willing to try which ſide was like to have the better, before he would eſpouſe either ; but all his wicked Policy avail'd him not, for he fell into a Snare he little imagin'd, which was thus : *Sultan Segued* being inform'd by his Spies, that *Za Selaſſe* was marching ſecurely at a diſtance from *Jacob*, lay in Ambuſh for him in a Bottom by which he was to paſs, call'd *Monta Deſer*, where he attack'd him ſo unexpectedly, and with ſuch Bravery, that he entirely routed his Forces, killing a great Number and taking many Priſoners ; ſo that *Za Selaſſe* himſelf narrowly eſcap'd with very few Attendants, and leaving behind all his Army and Treaſure. Thus he came much dejected to the Emperor *Jacob*'s Camp, who receiv'd him with an uneaſy Countenance, either becauſe he knew why he had ſtay'd behind, or that he was troubled for the loſs of ſo many Men, and look'd upon it as an ill Omen of his future Succeſs. *Za Selaſſe*, who could not brook being ſlighted by any Man, being a falſe Villain, preſently forgot to what a Pitch *Jacob* had rais'd him, and without further delay writ privately to *Sultan Segued*, that he would come over to him, and follow'd the Letter himſelf, meeting him in the Kingdom of *Gojam*, of which *Jacob* had made him Viceroy.

The Emperor *Jacob* was much troubled at the Loſs of ſo great a Man, and fearing that others might follow him, reſolv'd to give Battel, as ſoon as poſſible. To this end he March'd up and incamped in Sight of his Enemy, but the Ground being Marſhy, he decamp'd, and mov'd ſtill in Sight of him to *Debra Zeyte*, whence after halting awhile he advanc'd to a Valley near the Banks of *Lebert. Sultan Segued*, like another *Fabius Maximus*, kept along the Mountains, and high Grounds, watching all Opportunities. At length on Saturday Morning, being the 10th of March 1607 *Sultan Segued*'s Army moving from the Place, where they had lain that Night, the Enemy, who were reckoned Thirty to one, believing they had fled, purſu'd them with great Shouts. *Sultan Segued* had no Thoughts of fighting that Day, but obſerving how his Adverſaries came on, he encourag'd his Troops with Promiſe of Rewards, and of ſharing with them in the Danger, and then led them on. His Men were ſo animated with his Words, and Example, that coming down the Hills, like an Impetuous Torrent, they gave *Jacob*'s Army ſuch a Charge, that the *Ethiopian* Hiſtorian *Tino*, ſays the Enemies fell down before his Pace, as the

withered

Socinios routs Za Selaſſe.

Who revolts to him from Jacob.

Jacob routed and kill'd.

wither'd Leaves do in Autumn before the Wind. *Jacob* himself
was born down in the Hurly Burly, no Man being able to boast
that he had kill'd him. There also dy'd their *Abuna Peter*, who
had taken that Side, the Person that slew him, alledging for his
Excuse, that he thought he had kill'd a *Turk*. Thus ended the unfortunate *Jacob*, twice rais'd to the Throne, the first Time to be
sent to Banishment, and the 2d to quit it with his Life.

Many kill'd falling from Precipces. *Sultan Segued* being inform'd of his Death, immediatly
order'd the Pursuit to cease, to spare the Multitude; yet Fear had
so possess'd the routed Army, that there was no stopping their
Flight, which they continu'd in the Night, many of them in the
dark falling headlong from the Rocks. The next Day 600 Horse
were found dash'd in Pieces, at the Foot of a Rock an hundred
yards high, and more dy'd this Way, than by the Sword. *F.
Emanuel d' Almeyda* affirms, that one *Emanuel Gonzalves*, a *Portuguese*, who was living in his Days, told him, That he flying among
the Rest, his Horse took a leap off one of those Rocks, and he seeing
the desperate fall, let go his Bridle, and took fast hold of the
Branch of a Tree, by which he hung, whilst the Horse falling,
was dash'd in Pieces. He spent the Night on the Tree, and the
next Morning having view'd the Dangr he escap'd, came down
safe. *Ras Athanateus*, who as has been said, had joyn'd *Jacob*, got
off, and took Sanctuary in the Monastery of *Dima* , and was afterwards pardon'd, the Emperors Brother *Ras Sela Chriftos*, and
others interceding for him. All the rest that escap'd were forgi-
ven, and restor'd their Employments to them. Only one *Mahardin*,
of *Moorish* Race, pay'd for all, his Head being struck off, because
he was the first that wounded the late Emperor *Za Danguil* with
his Lance, in the Battle where he was kill'd. Of the Victors only
three were kill'd. Some *Portuguese*'s were also slain, who had
sided with *Jacob*, and gave him great Assurance of Success.

Socinios, or Sultan Segued restor'd. *Sultan Segued* gain'd more Reputation by his Clemency after the
Victory, than he had done by his Valour in the Battel; and that
purchas'd him the Affection of all his Enemies, who came in to
submit themselves to him. He was 33 Years of Age, very gen-
teel, and well shap'd, long visag'd but proportionable, his Head
spread, his Eyes of a Hazle Colour, sparkling, and very amiable,
so that he seem'd to oblige all Men with his Looks, his Nose
sharp, his Lips thin, his Beard black, and broad, his Stature a-
bove the Middle Size, well set, and brawny, and only his Tawny Complexion show'd him not to be an *European*. He was an
excellent Horse-Man, brave, resolute, sharp witted, well read in
the *Ethiopian* Books, descreet, Courteous, Bountifull, Martial,
enur'd to Hardship, as having been above ten Years continually
in

in Arms, without one Days Intermiffion. He refted three Days
after his Victory in the Field of Battel, rejoicing, dividing the
Booty with wonderfull Generofity, rewarding the Soldiers who
had fignaliz'd themfelves, and endeavouring to pleife all Men.
This done he fet forward for *Coga*, a Place betwixt *Dambea*, and
Begameder, where *Jacob* us'd to keep his Court.

The Mifchievous Traitor *Za Selaffe*, was meanly born, and had *Za Selaffe*
ferv'd fome Men of Quality, by whom for his ready Wit, and *his many Vil-*
Vivacity he was preferr'd to the Emperor *Malac Segud*. His Son *lanies.*
and Succeffor *Jacob* held him in great Efteem on Account of his
Readinefs in Difpatch of Bufinefs, giving him many Lands and
preferring him in the Army, till he came to be General. Yet
the ungrateful Wretch rebell'd againft his Benefactor, as has been
faid, and was by him therefore banifh'd to *Narea*. The Emperor *Za Danguil* recall'd, and rais'd him again, and he again rofe up
in Arms, and was the Death of that Prince, reftoring *Jacob*, who
in Requital made him Viceroy of *Gojam*, with the Title of *Behet
Oaded*, which is as much as the Emperors Vicar, or Lieutenant,
throughout all his Dominions, to requite all which Favours, he a-
gain betray'd *Jacob*, going over to *Sultan Segued*. This Monfter
had more Mifchief in his Head againft the laft mention'd Emperor,
but his Reward was now at Hand, for, contrary to his Natural
Sagacity, he let flip fome Words, which were his Ruin, faying,
Some wife Men had foretold, that he was to kill three Kings, and
he had deftroy'd two already. Thefe Words were prefently carry'd to *Sultan Segued*, who, tho' not credulous of Prophecies, was
unwilling that *Za Selaffe* fhould continue to verify them, being
fo likely a Man to carry on any wicked Defign. For this reafon
he kept Spies upon him continually, and he obferving it, contriv'd
to get away from the Court, which the Emperor hearing, he
caus'd him to be fecur'd, and fent to the ftrong Mountain call'd
Guzman in the Kingdom of *Gojam*. After a Years Imprifonment
he made his Efcape to the Province of *Oleca*, where gathering fome
Men, he became a famous Ringleader of Robbers, like the *Banditti*
in *Italy*. After fome Time, he made an Incurfion into the King- *His deferved*
dome of *Gojam*, where he had been Viceroy; there the People ly- *End.*
ing in Ambufh furpriz'd, and kill'd him, fending his Head, ftuck
upon a Spear, to the Emperor, who caus'd it to be fet up before
his Palace, for all Men to fee the End of that common Difturber.

Ras Athanateus, who had alfo been fufficiently embroil'd in Re- *And of A-*
bellion, went not unrewarded, for the Emperor *Sultan Segued*, re- *thanateus.*
membering his Ambitious Practices took a Diflike to him, and
gave away many of his Lands to others of the Royal Family. To
forward his Ruin, his Wife, the Daughter of the Emperor *Malac
Segued*

Segned, shook him off, as is usual in *Ethiopia,* and being thus for-saken by all People, and even his Wife, he ended his Life in a very mean Condition, tho' he had been the greatest Man in the Empire, next the Emperor.

Lands given the Jesuits for ever. The new Emperor *Socinios,* granted that the Lands given to the *Jesuits* should be settled upon them for ever, which in that Country, is done after this Manner. An *Azage,* or an *Umbar,* who is a sort of Judge, goes in the Emperor's Name, quite round the said Lands, upon the Borders of them, with the In-perial Waights playing, to call together the People from the Neigh-bouring Parts, who never fail upon this Signal, and these are to be Witnesses to the Landmarks then plac'd. For the more Surety there are Goats kill'd in several Places, and their Heads bury'd, which serve also as Landmarks, and they are severely punish'd, who presume to remove any of these Boundaries. The Lands thus given in *Ethiopia* enjoy great Immunities, and are perpetual; but in such Nature as may be expected in a Country so subject to Changes, and Revolutions, as may be seen in this Work.

C H A P. XIII.

The Fathers going to Court are treated by the Emperor at Dinner; the Description of his Table; he writes to the Pope, and King of Spain; an Impostor pre-tends himself to be the Emperor Jacob, *and raises a Rebellion; he is several Times routed; the Ceremony of the Emperor's Coronation.*

THE *Jesuits* had been gone from Court but little above a Month before the Emperor, missing their Company, sent to call them to Court, with Orders, because it was then Winter, and bad travel-ling by Land, that they should come by the Lake of *Dambea.* They imbark'd in *Tancoas,* which are very little Boats made of *Tabua* being very large Rushes, before spoken of, as well as the Boats themselves. In these they coasted along, not daring to venture out, because the least Motion of the Water oversets them,

as

as do the River Horses to devour those that are in them ; and in
striking over a small Creek they were in great Danger from one of *River Horses*
those Monsters making at them, but escap'd almost miraculously to
the other Shore, where that Creature left them for want of Water.
They arriv'd safe at *Coga*, where the Emperor came to receive
them at the Door of his Apartment and invited them to dine with
him the next Day.

We will here give an Account of the Meanness of that Princes,
Table, to compare it with the Grandeur of the Ancient *Romans*. *The Empe-*
Two Tables were plac'd in the Antichamber, a small one for the *ror's Enter-*
Emperor, and a larger for the Fathers, both of them without any *tainment.*
curious Damask Cloth, or Napkins, or gilt Plate. When Dinner Time came, a Curtin was drawn betwixt the Emperor's Table, and that for the Fathers, an inviolable Custom in *Ethiopia*,
where no Man sees the Emperor at Dinner, but only two or three
Servants that Wait. Then came in ten Women, bringing the
Dinner, they in the same Dress as those who serve great Ladies,
being a Sort of Gown of course Cotton Cloth, very long and
wide, girt about with a great Sash, over which the Gown being
drawn up hangs in large Folds. These Women bring two or three
Macobos, which are like large Table baskets, and very lofty, because cover'd with high Lids, like Caps, the whole made of Straw,
or Rushes of several Colours. In these *Macobos*, or Baskets, were
20, or 30 *Apas*, that is thin Cakes, like our frying Oat Cakes,
made of Wheat, Pease, and their Grain call'd *Tef*. These *Apas*
are very large, and thin, at least half a yard Diameter, and some
three Quarters. After these Women follow'd others, bringing several
Sorts of Pottage, or Broth, in black Earthen Porringers, cover'd
with Things like Hats, made of fine Straw, the Body of those
Hats being very tall, and slender, but the Brims broad, to
cover the Porringers, which are also very wide, but not deep.

The Table is a round Board, an Ell, or yard and half Diame- *Homely Ser-*
ter, plac'd on Carpets on the Ground, which they cover all over *vice.*
with the *Apas*, without any other Cloth, or Napkins, and on
those *Apas* they place the Porringers. And this is all the State of
the *Ethiopian* Tables, for they have neither Knife, Fork, nor
Spoon, Salt, Pepper Caster or any other Utensil. And it is to
be observ'd, that those very *Apas* which serve instead of Napkins,
and Dishes, are also part of the Food. When the *Barindo*, which
is the raw Beef, being the greatest Dainty at the Table, is brought
in, they lay it on the *Apas*, and the Emperor of *Ethiopia* himself
takes out a little Knife he carries about him, and cuts the Beef,
or has it cut by his Pages, who only wait at Table, without any
Steward, Controler, Carvers, Cupbearers, or any other Officers.

Great Men fed by others. The same Pages put the Morsels into his Mouth, which Custom is observ'd, not only by the Emperor, but by all the Great Men of *Ethiopia*, who look upon it as too much Trouble to feed themselves. Nor is this the worst, for these Morsels are generally of the soft of the Bread, or of the *Apas* crumbled in the Hand, wetted in several Liquors and so Moulded over, as if they were kneeding it, and sometimes these Morsels are so big, that they can scarce be put into the Mouth, and yet they thrust them in, much as we cram Chickens.

Drinking after the Meal. Thus much as to the Emperor's Table, and indeed those Emperors are much in the right, in not suffering any Body to use such a disagreable way of feeding. Nothing has been hitherto said of their Wine, because they never drink, whilst they are eating; but when all is taken away, they bring in the Pitchers, and then discourse, as long as the Liquor lasts; so as soon as the Liquor is out, they all slip away, without taking the least Notice of one another.

An Impostor represents the Emp. Jacob. All Countries can produce Instances of Impostors, who have taken upon them to represent others, in order to raise themselves, and *Ethiopia* at this Time afforded one very remarkable. The Emperor *Sultan Segued* repairing to his Court at *Coga* in the beginning of the Winter 1608, sent his Brother *Cella Christos*, Viceroy into *Tygre*, and *Asa Christos* his Brother by the Mother's Side into *Begameder*. At the same Time a poor rascally Youth durst presume to feign he was the Emperor *Jacob*, kill'd the Year before, as has been related. He being a crafty contriving Knave, chose the propereſt Place for his Purpose, which was the Monastery of *Bisan*, not far from the Port of *Mazua*, on the Mountains, which look upon the Red Sea, the Monks being of the Reform'd Order of Abba *Euſtateus*, and very numerous, as spreading all about the Country, and the only Curates, in those Parts. The pretended *Jacob* declar'd himself to these Men, and they, hoping to be favour'd by him, gave out that it had pleas'd God to send them the true Emperor *Jacob*, which the credulous People of *Tygre* believing, they flock'd thither to own and support him, without examining any farther.

His Diſguiſe and Arts. This Impostor being nothing like the true *Jacob* in Countenance, wore a Scarfe on his Head, which coming down under his Chin, he spread part of it over his Mouth covering the greatest Part of his Face, alledging, he did it, because in the Battel he had receiv'd a Stroke of a Spear, which beat out his Teeth, and had left a great Deformity. Many, without farther examining, pity'd his Misfortune, others brought him in Mules, and Horses, and others Arms, hoping to be generously rewarded, which he
was

was not short in promising, as venturing nothing of his own. And the best was, that whensoever he wanted any thing, he show'd that Piece of a Face, and immediately all that beheld it, rais'd a Dismal Cry of Lamentation out of Pity, and gave him all they had. Thus the *Ethiopians* being fond of Novelty flock'd to him daily in Throngs, and particularly all such as liv'd by robbing found in him Protection.

Being now follow'd by a great Multitude, he came down from the Mountains of *Bisan*, towards *Debaroa*, and having taken a little Gold from a Caravan of Natives, beat it out into Plates, which he put about his Hat, all the Crown of the Emperors of *Ethiopia*, being only a Hat lin'd with Silk, and plated with Gold, *Is twice de-* and Silver. The Viceroy of *Tygre Cella Christos* hearing of the *feated, and* Impostor's progress, march'd against him, with what Forces he *flyes to the* could gather, and tho' much inferior in Number, his Men being *Mountains.* disciplin'd, routed him, and he fled to the high Mountains, which were close by. All the Kingdom of *Tygre* was now in Confusion, and many Bands of Robbers rang'd about; one of which containing 800 Men, and commanded by the Governor of *Auxum* whom they call *Nebret*, designing to fall upon *Fremona*, the Viceroy hasted to save that Place, whereupon the Robber return'd. The Impostor hearing, that the Viceroy was gone, came down again from the Mountains, gathering in a few Days 25000 arm'd Men, and march'd to plunder *Fremona*, whence he was inform'd the Viceroy had withdrawn. The People of the Town fled, and he drew near, but understanding that the Viceroy was at Hand, retir'd again into the Mountains. His Men seeing how small a Number follow'd the Viceroy came down, and he falling on vigorously drove them back again with a mighty Slaughter, which so discourag'd the Rebel, that he fled again to the Mountains of the *A-macens*, beyond *Debaroa*, upon the Sea Coast.

The Viceroy perceiving he could not take the Rebel, who as fast as he lost any Men, gather'd more, and that all the Kingdom of *Tygre*, the best in *Ethiopia*, was in Confusion, he writ to his Brother the Emperor, acquainting him, that his Presence was necessary, for the rectifying of these Disorders. *Sultan Segued* being upon his March, receiv'd Advice, that the *Gallas*, had broke into the Kingdom of *Begameder*, against whom he return'd, overthrew them, and came back to *Coga*, where he continu'd eight Days. In the mean while a Report was spread abroad throughout *Tygre* that the Emperor had been routed and kill'd by the *Gal-* *Routed a 3d* *las*, which put all that Kingdom into an Uproar. The Impostor *Time.* receiv'd the same News, with the Addition that the Viceroy was fled, and had left all his Tents behind him. This incourag'd the Rebel to come down into the Plain, where he was soon undeceived, for the Viceroy met, and after a sharp Dispute routed him, with greater Slaughter than before; yet the Counterfeit Emperor got off again to his Mountains.

As soon as the Emperor had settled his Affairs at *Coga*, he set forwards for *Tygre*, and pass'd the Mountain *Lamalmon*, which parts that Kingdom from the Inland of *Ethiopia*, incamping near *Axzum*, where he resolv'd to be crown'd, as we have said is the *The Emperor* Custom of those Princes, being met by the Viceroy, his Brother, *crown'd.* and *F. Peter Pays*, whom he receiv'd very graciously. On Sunday the 23th of March 1609, the Day appointed for the Coronation, the Masters of the Ceremonies came, bringing the *Ritual*, which they read, and expounded to him. Then the Foot drew up being about 25000 Men, who march'd before, and after them the Horse, in Number 1500, all in their best Accoutrements, and lastly came the Emperor, with all the Prime Persons, richly clad, and well mounted with Costly Furniture. He had on a fine Vest of Crimson Damask, and over it a *Turkish* Robe of Brocade, like the ancient *Roman* Gowns, the Sleeves streight, but so long that they hung down to the Ground, as would the Vest, and upper Garment, if let loose, the first of which was girt with a broad Girdle, all of Pieces of Gold curiously wrought, and on his Neck a thick Chain of Gold which went several Times about, hanging down on his Breast, and the Ends of it falling deep behind, all which, he being a handsome Man, became him very well.

About two Musket-shots from the Church of *Axzum*, is a large Stone all over carv'd with unknown Characters, near to which they usually perform the Ceremony of cutting the Line or Cord, mention'd in the first Book, which is stretch'd across the way *Ridiculous* by the Maidens of *Sion*. There the Emperor alighted, with all *Ceremonies.* his Court, the Ground was cover'd with large and rich Carpets, the Great Men drew up on both sides, the Maidens stopp'd the way, crossing it with the Silk Line, up to which the Emperor went three times, and being ask'd by the Maidens, Who he was, the first and second time answer'd, *I am King of* Israel. The Maids reply'd, *Then you are not our King.* Then he drew back smiling, as among others was testify'd by the Captain of the *Portuguese*, who was present, and to whom the Emperor the Night before had said, He thought that Ceremony impertinent and ridiculous. Being ask'd the third Time, Who he was? He answer'd, *I am King of* Sion, and drawing the Sword he wore cut the Line, the Maids then saying, *You are truly our King of* Sion; and then the Air resounded with Acclamations of Joy, Vollies of small Shot, and the Noise of Trumpets, Kettle Drums, Waights, and all other Musical Instruments. Near to the Silk Line waited the

Abuna

Abuna Simon, who came with him for this purpose from *Dambea,* with all the Clergy, Monks and *Debteras,* all of them singing Pſalms, and other Songs in their Language. Thence they conducted him to the firſt Court before the Church, where the Coronation was perform'd with the uſual Ceremonies. Then the Emperor went into the Church, where he heard Maſs, and communicated, and thence return'd to the Camp with the Crown on his Head. They uſe no Scepter in *Ethiopia,* nor is the Crown *The Crown.* any other than a Hat with broad Brims, lin'd with blue Velvet, and cover'd with Gold and Silver Plates, ſhap'd like Flower de Luces, and ſome falſe Jewels; for they have no true Stones, nor can they be perſwaded they ſhould be of ſuch value among us.

CHAP. XIV.

The Emperor returns out of Tigre; *the Viceroy Defeats the Impoſtor's Forces; he is taken and beheaded;* F. *Peter Pays obtains the Emperor's Pardon for ſeveral Rebels.*

THE Fame of the Solemnity of the Emperor's Coronation being ſpread Abroad, could not but mortify the Impoſtor and his Followers, who had thought him Dead; yet the Emperor *Two other* was not willing to leave him ſo, for hearing he skulk'd on the *Rebels cut off.* Mountains about *Debaroa,* he march'd thither after him. Before he mov'd he ſent his Brother *Ras Cella Chriſtos* to *Dambea,* againſt two other Rebels that were raiſing Troubles there, one of whom he kill'd in the Field, and ſent the other Priſoner to the Emperor, who cauſ'd his Head to be ſtruck off. In his way he viſited the Fathers Houſe at *Fremona,* and gave them the value of 300 Pieces of Eight, leaving the *Abuna Simon* there to be inſtructed in the Catholick Faith. As ſoon as the Rebel was inform'd of the Emperor's Approach, not being able to withſtand him, he diſmiſs'd *The Impoſtor* what Forces he had, and hid himſelf in the Mountains of *Baroa, in a Cave.* and being perfectly acquainted with them, found there a very private Cave, in which he lay concealed with only 4 Servants,

and

and such was his Precipitation, that he had not leisure to lay in any other Store besides a few Goats, to live upon their Milk. This Contrivance so far avail'd him, that tho' the Emperor ascended the Mountains, and employ'd all his Army in searching every Hole and Corner, he could never find him out. Hereupon, the Winter drawing near, the Emperor set forward for *Dambea*, taking with him his Brother *Ras Cella Christos*, who was return'd to him after subduing the Rebels above mention'd, and leaving in his Place as Viceroy of *Tigre*, a Nobleman of singular Wisdom and Valour, call'd *Ansala Christos*, with particular Charge to pursue the Impostor to Death; and this done came himself to *Coga* on the 7th of *July* 1609.

Defeat of another Rebel. The new Viceroy *Ansala Christos*, left no Stone unturn'd for finding out of the pretended *Jacob*, but he kept so close that all prov'd in vain. In the mean while he happen'd to fall Sick, and lay encamp'd near *Fremona*, with a very small number of Men, which a Man of Quality of the House of *Sire*, whose Name was *Sabat Ab*, who liv'd like an Outlaw, and sided with the false *Jacob*, understanding, be gather'd 1500 Robbers, thinking to surprize and murther the Viceroy at *Guelguel* where he lay. He march'd in order to it all Night, and had certainly succeeded, but that one of his Men stole away, and taking the shorter Cut, gave the Viceroy timely Intelligence. Those few Men the Viceroy had were drawn out under the Shelter of the Houses, that they might not be seen by the Enemy, who entring the Place without the least Apprehension, were receiv'd with a Volley of Shot, which so terrify'd and daunted them, being altogether unprepar'd for Fight, that most of them fell flat on their Faces at the first Fire, and then starting up fled without fighting one stroke, the Viceroys Men pursuing them with great Slaughter, and returning with 17 Prisoners.

He is taken and executed This Success seem'd to Cure the Viceroy, who presently drew near the Mountains where the Impostor skulk'd, who knowing him to be an active Discreet Man, durst not trust to those Fastnesses, and therefore went away to *Bora*, another Mountainous Part of the Country, where there were two Great Men related to the late Emperor *Jacob*, who whilst they thought him to be the Man he gave out, promis'd to stand by him with their Lives and Fortunes. He repair'd to them with only 600 Men, and was affectionately receiv'd, believing him to be what he profess'd; but they being perfectly well acquainted with the true *Jacob*, could not be impos'd upon by this Cheat, tho' he show'd them but a small part of his Face. They presently agreed to secure him, and discover his Face; but he suspecting it, fled with his 600 Men,

and

and they furrounded the Mountain fearching every lurking Place, where many of his Followers were kill'd, and at length the Impoftor himfelf was taken, his Muffler pull'd off, and it appear'd that he had not the leaft Scar or Hurt in his Face. Thus was he expos'd to all Perfons thereabouts, and then his Head cut off, which thofe two Noblemen fent to the Emperor, and he order'd it to be carry'd throughout the Kingdom of *Tygre*, that all Men might fee by whom they had been deluded.

Thofe that deliver'd him fue for Pardon.

This Sight foon pacify'd all that Kingdom, the People readily fubmitting to the true Emperor, who punifh'd fome few, but pardon'd many more. *Amada Guerguis,* one of thofe two Brothers who had kill'd the Impoftor, came to the Viceroy, intreating him to intercede with the Emperor to Pardon them, for having at firft fided with the counterfeit *Jacob,* alledging the Merit of taking him off; fo. ftill they were guilty of high Treafon, becaufe they took Part with him, as long as they thought he was the true *Jacob,* tho' they fell off when they found him to be a Cheat.

The end of the fecond Book.

THE

THE
TRAVELS
OF THE
JESUITS
IN
ETHIOPIA.

BOOK III.

CHAP. I.

The Emperor's Brother Ras Cella Chriſtos *converted;
the Emperor contrives to ſend an Embaſſador to Portugal and* Rome; *he ſets out with one of the Fathers
for* Narea, *their Journey thither; an Account of that
Kingdom, and their Reception there.*

*The Court
removes.*

WE begin this Third Book with the Year 1610. It is uſual
in *Ethiopia* for the Emperors to remove their Court, leaving nothing behind them but the bare Fields, or Mountains, on which they encamp'd, becauſe, as h:s been ſaid, all the
Houſes, Churches and Palaces there are built with Poles, *Bamboo*
Canes and Straw, or at beſt with Stone, Clay or Mud. When
they remove, they carry away the Timber and *Bamboes,* which
ſerve

ferve for Windows, Doors, and Beams, leaving the Straw, which foon rots, the Clay, which returns to the Earth it came from, and the Stones. So it was done this Year 1610, when the Emperor left *Coefa*, and remov'd to *Deghana*, a Place near the Lake of *Dambea*, on the North Side, and clofe by *Gorgorra*, where the Fathers were fettled. There the Court continu'd a Year, and mov'd on Account of Sicknefs to a Peninfula call'd *New Gorgorra*, near the Old, where the Fathers dwelt. Here the Fathers had frequent Conferences with the Emperor and his Brother *Ras Cella Chriftos*. The Emperor was a judicious Man, and faw into the Truth of the Catholick Doctrine, and therefore contriv'd that his Nobility fhould be prefent, when there were any Difputes about Religion, and they were amaz'd to fee their *Haymanot Abben*, which is their *Bibliotheca Patrum*, teach the very fame the Fathers defended, concerning the two diftinct Natures in our Saviour, finding the contrary only in the Writings of fome Patriarchs of *Alexandria*, who liv'd after the Heretick *Diofcorus*.

In the Year 1612, the Emperor going to *Gojam*, made his Brother *Rae Cella Chriftos* Viceroy of that Kingdom, which was almoft the fame as making him King, becaufe he enjoy'd all the Revenues of that Country, and was obey'd like the Emperor himfelf. The new Viceroy was affable, and generous, and a great Favourer of the Fathers, and the *Portuguefes*, well read in all the *Ethiopian* Books, and therefore lov'd to hear the Difputes between the Fathers, and the Native learned Men. At length, they being fully convinc'd, he not only embrac'd the Catholick Faith, but publickly own'd it, and conftantly perfifted in it till his Death. His Reputation, and Intereft being fo great, the Example he gave was foon follow'd by moft of his Officers, who were all reconcil'd to the Church. Next the Viceroy order'd a Church, and a Refidence for the Fathers to be built, being that of *Collela*, the firft in the Kingdom of *Gojam*, and the third the *Jefuits* had in *Ethiopia*, whereof the firft was at *Fremona*, in the Kingdom of *Tygre*, and the 2d at *Gorgorra*, in that of *Dambea*. To this purpofe he beftow'd good Lands on the faid Church, and for the Maintenance of the Widows, and Orphans of many Sons of the *Portuguefes*, who were difpers'd about the Empire, and in great Want.

In the Year 1607, when the Emperor *Sultan Segued* began his Reign, *F. Pays* perceiving the good Difpofition there was in him towards the Catholick Faith, and how kind he was to the *Portuguefes*, fent an Account to his Catholick Majefty, King *Philip* the 2d. That Prince upon the Receipt of this Intelligence writ to the faid Emperor, congratulating his Acceffion to the Throne, and exhorting him to proceed in what he had fo well begun. *Sultan Segued Difpofition.*

The Emperor's Brother converted.

Churches built.

The Emperor's good

gued was highly pleas'd with that Letter, and immediately contriv'd not only to anfwer it, but how to fend an Embaffador to *India*, and *Portugal*. Many Letters pafs'd between this Emperor, the King of *Spain*, and the Pope, which are here for Brevity Sake omitted, tho' we could infert them all, the Originals being ftill preferv'd at *Lisbon*, among the Records, which will verify the Truth of what is here deliver'd, but that the inferting of them would too much enlarge this Volume, and therefore they are pafs'd by in this Tranflation, tho' feveral of them are in the *Portuguefe* Original ; and no Queftion to be made of their being true Copies, fince the Author refers to the Place where they may be feen.

In all his Letters, the Emperor prefs'd for a Supply of 1000 Men to enable him to declare for the See of *Rome*, as forefeeing the Difficulties that would arife in that Undertaking. Therefore not

Sends an Embaffador to Portugal. satisfyed with the Letters that went by the way of *Mazua*, he contriv'd to fend an Embaffador of his own, through his Kingdom of *Narea*, to the Coaft of *Melinde*, that he might there imbark for *India*, and thence fail in the Fleet to *Portugal*. This he thought the fafeft Method for his Embaffador to efcape falling into the Hands of the *Turks*, at *Mazua*, and believing the way from *Narea* to *Melinde* to be fhort, and eafy. He acquainted the Fathers with his Defign, and the Reafons of it, defiring, for his better Reception, that one of them would go with him. They all offer'd their Service, but the Lot fell upon *F. Antony Fernandez*, and the Emperor appointed for his Embaffador *Tacur Egzy*, a Perfon of great Prudence, and Refolution, and very Zealous for the Catholick Religion, which he had already embrac'd; his Name of *Tecur Egzy* fignifying, beloved of the Lord. Both he, and the Father forefaw the Difficulties, and Impracticablnefs of this Journey, by reafon of the length of the unknown Way, among *Moors*, *Turks*, *Cafres*, and other Barbarous Nations; however they prepar'd for it, and the Emperor having deliver'd his Letters, and furnifh'd all Neceffaries, they fet out at the Beginning of *March* 1613 from *Dambea*, to *Gojam*, with 10 *Portuguefes*, 4 of whom offer'd to attend them to *India*, and the other 6 to return from the Kingdom of *Narea*.

His Way to Narea. The Viceroy entertain'd them with fingular Affection, till fome *Gallas*, and *Xates* came to him, whom he had fent for, to convoy them fafe to *Narea*, becaufe much of the Way is inhabited by thofe two Nations. Thefe being well rewarded, and promis'd a greater Recompence upon their bringing News of the Fathers being fafe in *Narea*, they fet out from *Ombrama*, where the Viceroy was incampt'd, on the 15*th* of *April* 1613, taking about 40 Men

arm'd

arm'd with Darts, and Targets, along with them. They were
foon fenfible of the great Difficulties they fhould meet with in
fuch a tedious, and unfrequentted Journey ; for having travell'd
two, or three Days Weftward, through the Lands of the *Gongas,*
they came to *Sinaffa,* the Principal Town of the Heathen *Gongas,*
and asking there in the Viceroys Name for a Guard to conduct
them the reft of the Way, as for as the *Nile,* they were flatly
deny'd, which was as good as declaring they would fall upon,
rob, and kill them by the Way, and if they found fuch ill Entertainment in the Emperor's Dominions, what muft they expect from the *Moors, Turks,* and *Cafres,* through whofe Lands they
were to pafs. They were oblig'd to fend back one of the *Portuguefes* that attended the Father, who offer'd to go alone, and acquaint the Viceroy with what had happened, as he did, which much
troubled the Viceroy, and he fent 3 Commanders with Men to guard
the Fathers, and punifh the *Gongars.* Thefe *Gongars* underftanding,
that a Meffenger was gone to the Viceroy, prefently gave the
Guard demanded of them, which in three Days conducted
them to the Place where they were to pafs the *Nile,* call'd *Mina,* **Dangerous**
and lies upon the Place where it turns towards the North, almoft **croffing the**
Weft from its Source ; but is there ground very confiderable, and **Nile.**
carryes much Water, and was then very boifterous, and difficult
to pafs over, there being no Bridges, nor Ferries. Every Man
muft fhift the beft he can, and they were fain to make a Float of
Sticks ty'd together with fome *Gourds* or *Calabafhes* they had provided to fupport it ; fome young Men fwam before and drew this
Float, and others fwimming behind thruft it forward, and
this being a very tedious Way, they fpent a whole Day in going
forward, and backward.

Hence they travel'd continually due South, till they came to *Na-*
rea, about 50 Leagues, efcaping many Dangers from the *Galas,* and **Barbarous**
other Robbers. The next Day they came into a Country of *Cafres,*
who are fubject to the Emperor, but much more to their Avarice.
Thefe iffuing out of their Dens, like wild Beafts, came with their
Weapons in their Hands to rob them ; but finding fome Oppofi-
tions and being charg'd in the Emperor's Name to defift, were
fatisfy'd with a few Stones of Salt, and fome little Muzlin ; but
the Rain falling made them hafte back to their Dens, without
calling more of their Neighbours, and the Travellers improving
that favourable Opportunity hafted away. The fame Day their
Guide, who was to lead them through By-ways, to advoid the
Cafres, carry'd them through a clofe Wood, very difficult to pafs,
and then down a fteep Defcent, to a great River call'd *Maleg,* to
which they came about Night, and feeking a Place to ford it the
next Day, could find none, which made them fufpect leaft the

Guide

Guid defign'd to betray them, as he had done a great Man before, and therefore the Father order'd him to be ftrictly guarded but well us'd. However they found a Ford, and travell'd more peaceably on the other fide, being remov'd farther from the *Cafres*. Then they foon enter'd *Narea*, and went up a ftrong Mountain, where the chief Commander of the Kingdom refided, who receiv'd the Father, and the Embaffador very honourably, becaufe they had fprecial Recommendations from the Viceroy *Ras Cella Chriftos*, and better ftill from a good Prefent they made him.

Narea *Kingdom defcrib'd*   This Kingdom of *Narea*, is the moft Southern of all the Empire of *Ethiopia*. From *Maxna* to *Narea* they reckon 200 Leagues, moft of the Way South Weft, that is to *Mine*, a Town of *Gojam*, where the *Nile* is crofs'd the 2d Time to go to *Narea*, and thence they go due South, and thus the middle of *Dambea* is in 13 Degrees and a half of North Latitude, *Mine* in 12, and *Narea* in 8. This Kingdom is not fo large as fome make it, including in it the Lands of the *Cafres*, which lye round about, and run from thence towards the Coaft of *Melinde*, which is to the South Eaft, and thofe that run towards *Angola* lying Weft from it. The Trade *Narea* has with thefe *Cafres*, makes it abound in Gold, which it receives of them in exchange for Cloth, Cows, Salt, and other Commodities. That which is properly call'd *Narea*, and fubject to the Emperor, is not above 30, or 40 Leagues in Extent. The Natives feem to be the beft People in *Ethiopia*, as is own'd by the *Abyffines* themfelves. They are well fhap'd, their Countenances nothing like *Cafres*, their Lips thin, their Nofes fharp, their Colour not very black ; they keep their Word, and are fincere, without any of the Falfhood, Lyes, and Inventions of the *Amaras*. The Land yeilds Plenty of Grain, and feeds Abundance of Cattle. Gold is dealt for by Weight, as is us'd throughout all *Ethiopia*; befides they have light Bits of Iron, beat out flat, two Fingers broad, and 3 in Length, which pafs for Mony. They were all formerly Heathens; but in the Days of the Emperor *Malac Segued*, about 60 Years before this Time we now fpeak of, they had embrac'd Chriftianity, with all the Errors of the *Abyffines*, and till then no Father of the Society had been there. The Men are brave, and defend their own Country very well, for tho' the *Gallas* have poffefs'd themfelves of the greateft Part of *Ethiopia*, and are continually making Incurfions upon them, they have never been able to prevail againft the bold *Nareas*, and this without any Affiftance from the Emperor, to whom neverthelefs they pay Tribute, rather out of their own innate Loyalty, than that he can compell them to it ; becaufe the Emperors Forces can not come at them, without marching through the Country of the *Gallas* ;

befides

besides that there being always some in Rebellion nearer the Court, he his oblig'd to observe them.

From *Gonea* the Embassador and Father went to the Court of the *Benero*, so they call the *Xumo*, or Governour of *Narea*. They came to it in 6 Days, the first of them through Lands almost Desert, the *Gallas* having made an Incursion there sometime before. *The Viceroys Behaviour.*
The following Days through a Country well cultivated and peopled The *Benero* receiv'd the Father courteously enough, tho' without any particular Marks of Honour, and Esteem ; the reason whereof he soon understood was, because there was a Schismatick Monk, who was the *Abunas* Vicar, and suspected that the Father came to deprive him of his Dignity, and the Profits of it, which were considerable. The Father understanding it, visited the said. Monk, undeceiv'd him, begg'd he would favour him with his Interest in the Viceroy, and with a small Present, wholly appeas'd him.

The *Benero* was not so easily reconcil'd, for he endeavour'd to dive deeper into the Occasion of the Embassador's going for *India*, and us'd all means to discover it ; and tho' none but the Father, and the Embassador were entrusted with the Secret, yet he suspected it was to bring *Portuguese*, who might came through that Kingdom, and in their Way subdue it, and force them to embrace the Catholick Religion. Hereupon he advis'd with the great Men of his Court, by whom it was agreed that the Father, and Embassador, must not be permitted to go the Way they had design'd which was the best, lest the *Portuguese* should become acquainted with it, and therefore they should put them into another, which was farther about, and very troublesome, through a Country call'd *Balij*. This being determin'd, after much contesting with the Father, he flatly told him, it was in vain to contend, for he should not go that Way. The Father finding no other Remedy, and being earnest to proceed, was fain to submit, and say he would go by *Balij*. *He puts the Embassador out of his Way*

Balij is a Kingdom, that formerly was subject to the Emperor, but now possess'd by the *Galas*, and *Moors*, bordering on that of *Adel*, being East of *Narea*, so that is was going backward, and taking a great Compass to come at the Sea, near Cape *Guardasuy*, and about the midst between it, and Cape *Magadoxa*, which was almost impracticable. Now to deal plainly, the Way the Father propos'd through *Cafa*, was no better than this, because proceeding South from *Narea* there is no coming at the Sea, without travelling many hundred Leagues, to the Cape of Good Hope, as may appear by all Modern Maps, so that the whole Project had nothing of likelihood. So soon as the *Benero* perceiv'd the Father condescended to go by *Balij*, being satisfy'd no Harm could come to him that Way, as being very remote, he gave him free Leave to depart, and with it about 30 Crowns in Gold, to *Balij Kingdom.*

help

help bear his Charges, making many Excuses for the smalness of the Gift. Then he sent Orders to one of his Officers to conduct the Father safe, through all his Country; and this Way being through the Kingdom of *Gingiro*, and one Embassador from that King being then at his Court, he dispatch'd him speedily, recommending to him the Father, and the Embassador, and desiring he would take them along with him, and secure them on the Road, which he readily agreed to.

C H A P. II.

The Embassador, and the Father depart from Narea, *for the Kingdom of* Gingiro, *and pass the River* Zebee ; *their Reception by that King ; Description of that Kingdom, and the Barbarous Customs of the People, Manner of their Electing a King ; and the Fathers repassing the* Zebee.

THE Embassador, and Father, leaving the Court of *Narea*, travell'd thence to the Eastward, and the first Day came to the Place where the Commander resided, who was to convoy them. He receiv'd them well at first, in hopes of some mighty Present ; but finding that did not answer the Expectation of his Avarice, detain'd them 8 Days, and then appointed 80 Soldiers to conduct them to the Frontiers of *Narea*. They travell'd with this Guard 4 Days, through a Desert Country, taking long Journies for fear of the *Gallas*, who make great Inroads that Way, and the 4th Day the *Nareas* departed, leaving the Travellers in much Danger, who sent some still before to discover, with Directions, if they spy'd any *Galas*, to make a Signal, that they might hide themselves in the Woods. Going down a high Mountain at Noon, the *Gingiro* Embassador advis'd them, before they came to the Bottom to sculk in the Wood, till the Evening, and cross the Plain by Night, because the *Gallas* graze their Cattel on it by Day. About four in the Afternoon, they slunck into the Thicket, a Shore of Rain that fell favouring them, for it oblig'd the *Gallas* to retire to their Huts tho' it wetted the weary Travellers, who were doubly fatigu'd at Night, the Wood they were in being intricate by

Progress of the Embassador and Father.

Day

Day, and much more difficult to penetrate in the Dark. At Midnight they halted to reft under fome tall Trees, refrefhing themfelves with a Fire, the Wood affording Fuel; but as for their Supper it confifted of only a little parch'd Barley, fparingly dealt about, which is the chief Provifion Travellers take with them in *Ethiopia.* The next Day after Noon they went down a fteep craggy Mountain, and came to the River *Zebee.*

This River rouls more Water than the *Nile,* and in this Place, to which they were brought by the *Gingiro* Embaffador, it tumbles down fuch dreadful Precipices of upright Rocks, that the dafhing of the Waters makes a moft hideous Noife. But that which moft terrify'd the Travellers was the Bridge they were to pafs, which was nothing but a fingle Piece of Wood, fo long that it reach'd acrofs the River, from one Rock to another, the Breadth whereof was not fmall, and the Depth fo great, that it was frightful to behold; befides that, in going upon it the Plank bow'd and gave way, as if it had been a Green Twig. Yet thus they pafs'd over one by one, ftriving who fhould go foremoft, thinking themfelves fafe from the *Gallas* on the other fide, and the dread of them was more prevalent than the Terror of the Bridge. After all they had not got over the Mules, but left it 10 Men to look to them, believing they might fave themfelves if the *Gallas* fhould come, and the next Day Providence brought two Men of the Country that way, who conducted them to a Ford.

Zebee River.

Dangerous Bridge.

Being pafs'd the River, they proceeded a little farther to a Town, whence they fent to acquaint the King of *Gingiro* with their coming, and defire leave to repair to his Court, and deliver the Emperor of *Ethiopia's* Letters. He being then very bufy about fome Superftitious Charms, they were feign to ftay there a Week, when having obtain'd leave, they fet out and came to Court the fame Day. Going in to fpeak with him, they found him prepar'd for their Reception. He was according to Cuftom in a fort of rail'd Tower, about fix Yards high, little more or lefs, 7 Yards and a half over, as we fhall fee anon, and the Stairs up to it in the back Part. All the Courtiers ftood below, and he on the top of the Elevation, which was not unlike a Cart Wheel, fitting on a Carpet, and there it is he gives Audiehce, decides Controverfes, and difpatches all Bufinefs. He was clad in a white Silk *Indian* Garment, and was himfelf as black as a Cole, but had not the Features of a *Cafre.*

The King of Gingiro's Audience.

The Emperor's Letter being fent to him, he, to fhow his Breeding, came down from his Throne, or Balcony, receiv'd it ftanding, enquir'd after the Emperor's Health, and being anfwer'd, went up again to his Seat. This Refpect he pays the Emperor of
Courtefy,

Ceremonies of it.

Courtesy, for he is none of his Subject. Being seated, he read the Letter, and continu'd a while, discoursing with the Embassador and the Father, by means of an Interpreter, who every time the King said any thing to him to tell the Father, kiss'd the Tips of his Fingers of both Hands; then falling down, kiss'd the Ground, and went to the Father, who stood at a little distance, to tell him what the King said. Returning with the Answer, he again kiss'd the Tips of his Fingers, before he deliver'd it, and bowing went to the King, with which Ceremonies the Discourse held for a considerable space. At length, the King bid the Father go and repose himself, and as to what the Emperor desir'd of him in his Letter, which was to use them well, and allow them a good Guard thro' his Dominions, he would perform it very readily.

The next Day the Father thought fit to present the King, because those Infidels are altogether bent upon their Interest, and *Presents of* accordingly he carried him some *India* black Stuffs, which he *the King and* seem'd to make great Account of, as being a Thing seldom seen *the Father.* in his Country. The King to requite him, when he took his leave, sent him a Female Slave, the Daughter of one of the principal Men of that Country. The Father return'd Thanks for the Favour, but said, he did not use to take Women along with him, and the King excusing his mistake, gave him a Man Slave, and a good Mule, which he accepted of, and sent Men to help them cross the River *Zebee* again, to go into the Kingdom of *Cambate.*

The first Days Journey brought them to the River, where they were in an Agony about passing it; for the King's Guides being well acquainted with the manner of it, contriv'd such a Method, as, tho' altogether new to them, seem'd no less dangerous, than *Strange way* the Plank instead of a Bridge, and was thus. They kill'd a Cow, *of crossing* and of the Hide made a great Sack, into which they put the Bag- *a River.* gage, and blowing strongly fill'd it full of Wind like a Bladder; and this was to carry the Luggage, and serve for a Boat. Then they took two Poles, like those our Chairs are carry'd on, and ty'd them very fast to the blown Hide, and to these Poles two Men hung on the one side and two on the other, who were to hold very steady, and be of equal weight to Ballance, for the Thing was like a Scale, and therefore, if the weight was not a like, or any one happen'd to move all must plunge, and the Stream being very rapid, they were in imminent Danger of their Lives. This new Machine was guided before by a good Swimmer, pulling a Rope made fast to the Hide, or the ends of the Poles. Two others swam behind, thrusting the Invention forward. Thus they cross'd the River, and landed much lower on

the

the oppofite fide, than where they took the Water, both becaufe of the violent Current, and in regard there was no landing Place higher. A wholeDay was fpent in paffing over after this manner,for it coft much time to poife the weight right, and then to crofs the Stream. There let us leave them, to give fome Account of the Kingdom of *Gingiro,* as deliver'd by *F. Antony Fernandez,* and other credible Eye-witneffes.

The River *Zebee* above mention'd, almoft encompaffes this Kingdom, making it a fort of Peninfula, and then runs to empty itfelf towards the Coaft of *Melinde.* The Kingdom is fmall, the Natives of the Colour of *Cafres,* but not like them in Features. They are all Heathens, and much addicted to Sorcery, having fome abominable Cuftoms among them, worthy to be known for their Strangenefs. *Gingiro* fignifies, an Ape, or Monkey, and is the propereft name for that King; becaufe in the firft Place he is very black, as has been faid, and fitting alone on that fort of Turret, where he difpatches Bufinefs, looks like a Monkey on a Block; befides his ftrange Motions, and Geftures, which much refemble an Ape. The Name futis with him upon another Account, for if he happens to be wounded in War, his Fellows prefently kill him, or if they happen to fail, his Kindred do it, without Remiffion, tho' he never fo much intreats for Mercy; and this they fay they do, that he may not die by his Enemies Hands. The fame is practis'd among Monkeys, who being once wounded either deftroy themfelves, or are kill'd by the reft, for they never give over licking, fcratching, and clawing the Hurt, till they tear out their Bowels, or otherwife occafion their own Death.

Gingiro Kingdom defcrib'd.

Its King.

Tho' in thefe particulars they all refemble Monkeys, yet they take much State upon them. When the King is to go abroad, he muft do it before the Sun rifes; and if the Sun happens to be up firft, the King is fhut up all the Day, and difpatches no Bufinefs; and the Reafon they give for it is,becaufe, fay they, two Suns can not fhine equal in the World, and fince the King does not gain the Preference of the other, he does not think fit to follow him; therefore the next Day after he has mifs'd he takes Care to be abroad much the foonett.

His foolifh State.

The Ceremonies us'd at the Election of this King are fingular. They wrap up the Dead King's Body in coftly Garments, and killing a Cow, put it into the Hide; then all thofe who hope to fucceed him,being his Sons,or others of the Royal Blood,flying from the Honour they covet,abfcond, and hide themfelves in the Woods. This done the Electors, who are all great Sorcerers, agree among themfelves who fhall be King, and go out to feek him, when en-

Cere, his E.

tring

tring the Woods by means of their Enchantments, they fay, a
large Bird they call *Liber* as big as an Eagle, comes down with
mighty Cries over the Place where he is hid, and they find him
encompafs'd by Lyons, Tygers, Snakes, and other Creatures gather'd about him by Witchcraft. The Elect, as fierce as thofe
Beafts, rufhes out upon thofe who feek him, wounding, and fometimes killing fome of them, to prevent being feiz'd. They take
all in good part, defending themfelves the beft they can, till they
have feiz'd him. Thus they carry him away by force, he ftill
ftruggling, and feeming to refufe taking upon him the Burthen of
Government, all which is meer Cheat and Hypocrify.

His Enthron-ing.   When the King Elect is conducted home, there is always a Battel by the way, becaufe there is a certain Family, which of Old
Cuftom, Time out of Mind, may force the King from the Electors
and enthrone him, by which means they will become the great
Favourites: For this reafon, they with all their Adherents wait
the coming of the Electors and their Party, whom they Charge;
the Victors carry off the King, and with great Rejoycing place
him on the Throne above-mention'd, and then that Party has all
the greateft Places and Honours; but they have enough to Coun-
terbalance, as we fhall foon fee. The King being brought to the
Court, they conduct him into a Tent, and on the 7th Day after
the Death of the former King, the Sorcerers bring a Worm, they
fay comes out of the Dead Man's Nofe, which being wrapp'd up
in a Piece of Silk, they caufe the new King to kill, by fqueezing
its Head between his Teeth. Next follows the Funeral of the
Dead King, whom they carry to his Grave, dragging him along
the Ground, and defiring he will give his Bleffing to thofe Lands
they draw him over. Being come to the Place of Burial, which
Burial of the dead King. is a Thicket or Wood, the ancient Repofitory of thofe Kings, they
dig a Hole and throw him into it, without covering the Carcafs
with Earth, but leaving it expos'd to the Air, as if the Earth were
unworthy to cover the Body of a King, who vy'd with the Sun,
and therefore the Heaven alone muft be his *Maufoleum.* On the
Funeral Day they kill many Cows clofe to the Grave, fo that
their Blood may run in and touch the Dead Body; and from
that time forward, till the next King Dies, they kill a Cow there
every Day, and make the Blood run in, the Profit whereof belongs to their Priefts, or Sorcerers, for they fhed the Blood, but
eat the Flefh.

Let us return to the new King, whom we left killing the
Worm, which when he has done, they give great Shouts of Joy,
proclaim, and enthrone him, on that Loft before defcrib'd, and
thus ends the Solemnity, which is follow'd by Sorrow; for then
the

the new King calls all the dead one's Favourites, and tells them, *That since they were so much his Friends, whilst living, that His Favourite they never stirr'd from him, it is but Reason they should bear him kill'd, and Company in Death, and continue his Favourites in the other House burnt. World.* This said, he orders them all to be kill'd, and then chuses others to fill their Places; and so acceptable is the Favour of Kings, that there never want Pretenders to those Employments, who value not hazarding their Lives, so they may obtain their ambitious Ends. This barbarous Custom is palliated with the Love, and Care they ought to take of the Kings Person; to show them who are about him, how sollicitious they are to be for his Safety, since their own depends on it. Then they burn the House the old King liv'd in, with all his Moveables, Goods, and Furniture, not sparing any thing, tho' never so valuable; and even when any private Man dies, they burn, not only his House, but the very Trees and Plants that are about it, and being ask'd, why they do so, They answer, to the End, that the Dead Man, who was us'd to those Places, do not return to them, invited by his former Habitation, and delight in walking among those Trees.

Since the old Kings Palace is burnt, let us view the Grandeur of the New ones. Under the Loft which serves him for a Throne stands his House, and by the Outside may be guess'd what is within. The House is round, about 6 Yards, or little better Diameter, the walls are either Wood, or Stone, and Clay, the Roof, and Rafters, which ascend towards the Top, are ill shap'd Poles, the Ends whereof meet and rest on a Thing like a Cart wheel, which is in the Middle, and serves for a Center, and on this Wheel on the Top, the Kings sits, as it were on a Throne, the other Ends of the Rafters about resting on the Wall; so that the stately structure lookes like a Parrot's Cage. To provide a Column for this Palace, they go into the Wood, and find out a strait, but not very thick Tree, and before they fell it, cut a Man's Throat at the Foot of it, who is the first they meet with of a Certain Family they have in the Kingdom, which on this Account is exempt from all other Duties, whereof we shall soon speak. Nor does their barbarous Cruelty end here, for when the House is built, and the King conducted to it, before he sets in his foot, they kill another Man of that same Family, if the House has but one Door, or two Men if there are two Doors, and with the Blood of these Victimes they daub and paint the Threshold, and Posts.

The King's Palace.

This

He sells and
gives his
Subjects as
Slaves.

This is a costly Duty incumbent on this Family, which exempts it from all others, yet are those so heavy, that they are not inferior to the Murder of two, or three of them; for whensoever the King of *Gingiro* buys any rare Goods, brought him by foreign Merchants, he agrees to give them in Exchange, ten, twenty, or more Slaves, to which Purpose he only sends his Servants, who going into any Houses indifferently take away the Sons, or Daughters of the Inhabitants, and deliver them to the Merchants. The same he does, whensoever he presents a Slave, or Slaves to any Person of Note, ordering then the best and handsomest to be taken, alledging, that what is given must be of the best. Such was the Woman Slave he would have given the Father. From this Duty that Family is exempt, of which we said some are kill'd at the Palace Doors, and so great is the Veneration they pay their King, and this Custom has so far prevail'd, that no Man offers to mutter at it, and unhappy he that should seem to disapprove of these barbarous Actions, for he would suffer Death, without Remission.

Cruel
Custom.

There is another Ceremony, before we conclude with this King of *Gingiro*. On the Day he enters upon the Government, the first Thing he does, is to send about his Kingdom, to find out all the Men, and Women, that have scald Heads, who being brought together, and sent over the River *Zebee*, are there slaughter'd. The Reason they give for it is, that other People may not be infected by them, and so the Distemper come to the King, whom we will now leave to follow *F. Antony Fernandez*.

CHAP.

C H A P. III.

The Father and Embassador enter the Kingdom of Cambate ; *the Crosses they met with there ; they proceed to* Alaba ; *are there imprison'd, and at last oblig'd to return back into* Ethiopia.

THE Father departing the Kingdom of *Gingiro*, and travelling Eastward, came to *Sangara*, a Village in that of *Cambate*, then govern'd by *Amelmal*, who still acknowledg'd the Emperor of *Ethiopia* for his Sovereign ; and on the left Hand, are a People call'd *Gura Gues*, who are also subject to the Emperor. The Father stay'd two Days at *Sangara*, being told, they should then meet Company, who came to a Fair, but the Truth was, they had no Fair but robbing, for they did it only to give notice to their Neighbours, that they might all together fall upon his Company, and plunder them ; for when they set out, there met them 5 *Gentiles* of the *Gura Gues* a horse back, with many others afoot, all arm'd, who all together attack'd the Fathers Retinue, being but 17 that had Weapons, but they fighting for their Lives made the Robbers give Way. Yet a Kinsman of the Embassadors, being wounded with a poison'd Arrow dy'd a few Days after. The Embassador's Family would have reveng'd his Death, but that the Father disswaded them, and the *Gura Gues* seeing they could get nothing by Force, were glad to take what they would give them.

The Embassador set up on.

Having escap'd this, and other Dangers, they came to the Place where the Governour *Amelmal* was, and gave them a good Reception at first, on Account of the Letters of Recommendation they brought from the Emperor. But at the same Time, there came thither, one *Manquer*, an *Ethiopian*, on Pretence of receiving the Tribute that Governour paid the Emperor ; but in reality, sent by several great Men at Court, who were Enemies to the Catholick Religion, to perswade the Governour, not to suffer the *Portuguese* and Embassador to proceed any farther, because they were going without the Emperor's Leave, to bring *Portuguese* arm'd with Guns, and fire Arms, which kill at a great Distance, to oblige them to depart from the Faith of their Forefathers,

A Perfidious Ethiopian.

and

and to embrace that of *Rome*. Nor did the base *Abyssine* think it enough, to inculcate this to *Amelmal*, but us'd means to stir up all the People of the Country to mutiny, and the Neighbouring *Gallas*, and *Moors* with these Jealousies, they being very susceptible of them.

This mov'd *Amelmal* to cause the Father, and his Companions to be examin'd, and finding all that *Manquer* had urg'd to be groundless, he would have dismiss'd them ; but that *Manquer* *The Embassa-* protested so earnestly to the contrary, that he was feign to send to *dor stopp'd.* the Emperor to know, whether it was his will that those Men should pass, and the Letters they brought true or false. Three Months after, when they expected an Answer, the Messengers, being one from *Amelmal*, one from *Manquer*, and one from the Father, return'd, saying, they had been taken, and kept Prisoners all that while, in a Town, but three Days Journey from thence. They were feign to send others again, and arm themselves with Patience, against the wicked *Manquer*, who, besides endeavouring to cause their Baggage to be seiz'd, us'd all his Means to have his Servants pick Quarrels with the Embassador's, that so they might be sent back ; and one of his Men being highly provok'd by one of *Manquer*'s kill'd him, for which he was imprison'd, but made his Escape.

Sends to the At length, those who had been sent, with an Account of the *Emperor.* Embassador's being detain'd came to Court, and the Emperor hearing them was highly incens'd against *Amelmal* and *Manquer*, both whom he would certainly have punish'd severely, had not they been so remote, and where he could not reach them, *Cambate* at this time being quite fallen off from him, and belonging to several *Moorish* and *Galla* Lords: The Emperor did what lay in his Power, which was to send one *Baharo*, a Man well known in those Parts Express, with a Letter to *Amelmal*, ordering the Father, and the Embassador to be furnish'd with all they wanted, out of his Revenues, and earnestly pressing him to recommend them by all means to the Neighbouring Kings, and Sovereigns ; and at the same time he sent *Amelmal*, some rich Vests, and the like to the *Moor Alico*, who govern'd the next Country they were to go into, after they were out of *Amelmal*'s Jurisdiction.

Proceeds to This Order of the Emperor's came to *Cambate* in June 1614 *Alaba.* which was punctually obey'd by the Governor, who gave the' Embassador seven Horses, believing them to be the best Present he could bestow on the petty Kings, through whose Dominions he was to pass. The Father, and the Embassador prepar'd to depart, having now spent 14 Months since they came from the Emperor's Court, and some of their Followers considering the many

Dangers

Dangers they had run, took Leave, and return'd. As soon as *Manquer* perceiv'd that *Amelmal* difmifs'd the Father and Embaffador, who of Neceffity muft pafs through the Country of the *Moor Alico*, he prefently fent Letters thither, which fet all againft them, fo that when he came to *Alaba*, the Refidence of that Infidel, he foon fhow'd himfelf ill affected; and tho' he receiv'd the Emperor's Letter, and the Vefts brought by *Baharo*, and on that Account diffembled with them for two Days, yet the third Day the wicked *Manquer* came thither, havingmade his efcape from *Amelmal*, who intended to have fecur'd him till the Father was pafs'd beyond *Alaba*.

As foon as that bafe Man came, *Alico* fecur'd *Baharo* that *Is ſtopp'd brought* him the Letter, and Vefts, and then the Father, and *there*. Embaffador, keeping them apart, and feizing all their Goods, their Mules, and the Horfes they brought to prefent, fearching them rigoroufly, and yet it pleas'd God, they did not find the Letters, which the Father had ty'd about the Brawn of his Arm, for had they met with them, the Emperor asking for a Supply of *Portuguefes*, would have confirm'd what *Manquer* fpoke only by guefs. *Alico* being perfwaded, that if any *Portuguefes* came, they would pafs that way, and poffefs themfelves of his Country, he would certainly have murder'd them, which was what *Manquer* advis'd. The Father confidering the Danger of another Search, when he was alone, ask'd for Fire, on Pretence of taking Tabacco, which he had never us'd, tho' it was then much practis'd in that Country; when he had Fire, being left alone, he burnt all the Letters.

Their Inprifonment lafted ten Days, during which time feveral Councils were held, to debate, whether they fhould live or die; *Manquer* ftill preffing for the latter; but feveral great Men reprefented it as a heinous thing to *Alico*, and contrary to the Law of Nations, that he fhould Imprifon a Meffenger, by whom he had receiv'd Letters, and Vefts, fent him by an Emperor, and therefore he order'd him to be immediately fet at Liberty, and for the reft, he took the Advice of a Man in great Authority among them, which was not to kill, but oblige them to return back. *Alico* did fo, but would not let them go through *Amelmal*'s Province, for Fear he fhould fuffer them to proceed fome other way, or make War on him upon the Embaffador's Complaint. *Manquer* inrag'd that he could not have their Blood, perfwaded *Alico* to keep three of the *Portuguefes*, who were with the Father, alledging, they might ferve him in his Wars. This was accordingly done, and the Father departed much griev'd, both for the Lofs of his Companions, and the Difappointment of his Journey.

Forc'd back to Ethiopia.

The

Narrowly e-
scapes being
robb'd.

The same Day the Father set out from *Alaba*, some *Moors* who had Notice of their departure, met to gether, to Way-lay, and murder them, so to take the little they had left; but a mighty Rain falling, and those Infidels believing they would not travel through it, as they did with all possible Speed, they escap'd that Danger. Being come to a Town, they soon perceiv'd by the Assemblies of the *Moors*, that they should not be safe that Night. *Baharo* the Emperor's Express meeting a *Galla* there, ask'd him, whether he knew one *Amuma*, a powerfull Man of his own Nation. He answer'd, He not only knew him, but was his Servant, and told him he was not far off. They promis'd him a good Reward, if he would go call him, and to give *Amuma* a stately Horse, if he would come. The Servant went, and brought his Master, who taking the Father and his Companions under his protection, all the Designs of the *Moors* were disappointment.

Conducted by
a Galla.

This *Galla* conducted them two Days Journey from thence, to the Place of his Residence, where he treated them with Plenty of Milk, and Beef, and then bore them Company three Days farther. A Parcel of *Gallas* lay in the way to cut them off, but perceiving by whom they were defended, forbore. The same *Amuma* deliver'd them from another Parcel of his Nation, who were celebrating some Festival of their Idols, and would have sacrific'd them. In fine it pleas'd God to deliver them from many more Dangers, till they came to an *Amba*, or strong Mountain inhabited by Christians, who were subject to the Emperor, whence the Father sent that Monarch an Account of all that had befallen him, offering to try any other way, if his Majesty should think fit. But the Emperor sent them Orders to repair to his Court, whence they had set out in *February* 1613, and return'd in *September* 1614, having spent a Year and 7 Months in their Journey, and they were receiv'd very honourably. Two of the *Portuguese* left at *Alaba* found means to escape, the third dying a natural Death.

Marquer the
Villains
death.

The Villain *Manquer* presuming to return to Court, relying on his Friends there, and denying all he had done, was therefore upon full Conviction condemn'd to Death, but Father *Antony Fernandez* begg'd his Life of the Emperor. Yet he could not escape divine Vengeance, for being conducted to a Mountain, whither he was banish'd, he made his Escape to the *Gallas*, and returning with them to make an Incursion, in which they were repuls'd, in the Flight he had his Leg broke, and the *Gallas* to put him out of Pain, kill'd him.

CHAP.

C H A P. IV.

Controversies about Religion. F. Pays *builds the Emperor a Palace, after the* European *Manner, A Conspiracy to murder that Prince. The Rebels routed.*

WE left the Emperor's Court, to conduct *F. Anthony Fernandez* on his Journey, and having now brought him back, it is Time for us alio return to it. The Emperor, and many more being now convinc'd of the Truth of the Catholick Faith, and many great Men publickly professing it.

Proclamation made for Catholick Faith.

Proclamation was made, that for the future, none should presume to maintain there was but one Nature in *Christ*; but that all should own two distinct Natures the Human, and Divine, both united in the divine Person. *Simon,* the *Abuna* was then absent, but hearing what had hapned, hasted to Court, threatning to thunder out Excommunications, and Anathemas, and being favour'd by the Emperors Brother *Ras Emana Christos,* and other great Persons, had the boldness to affix an Excommunication on the Gats of one of the Churches of the Camp, against all those who should embrace the Faith of the *Portuguefes.* The Emperor was, much offended at the *Abuna*'s Presumption, and immediately gave order, that Proclamation should be made, to give Leave to all Persons to embrace the Faith the Fathers preach'd, and had been justify'd in the publick Disputations, which was accordingly done.

The Abuna *Excommunicates those that embrace it.*

At this Time, the Emperor was oblig'd to go chastise the *Agaus* in the Kingdom of *Gojam,* who refus'd to pay their Taxes, and had affronted some of his Officers, and being forc'd to winter there, the *Abuna* laid hold of that Opportunity, of his Absence, to persecute the Catholicks; writting circular Letters to stir up all his Followers to take up Arms, in Defence of the Faith of their Ancestors; and affixing another Excommunication against such as should say, there were two distinct natures in *Christ.* Elos, or *Elios,* so they pronounce *Julius,* the Emperor's Son-in-Law, a bold, but haughty ignorant Man, was then Viceroy of *Tygre*; who being very obstinate in his Errors, and an Enemy to *Ras Cella Christos,* as soon as he receiv'd the *Abuna*'s Letter, began to persecute the Fathers, and other Catholicks at *Fremona,* seizing all the Estates of the *Abyssines,* both Men and Women, who had embrac'd that Faith. As soon as the Emperor had notice of these

Catholicks Persecuted.

Pro-

Proceedings, he writ to the *Abuna* to repair to him, to *Achafe*, where he then was, that all his Scruples might be remov'd. He also order'd F. *Pays* to come to him, which he did, and gave him an Account of what had been done in *Tygre*, whereupon the Emperor sent Expref Commands to that Viceroy to restore all the Catholicks.

Obstinacy of Schismaticks. Many great Men, and the Emperor's own Mother now desir'd the Emperor to desist, because they were inform'd, that there was Danger of a mighty Rebellion, the very Monks being in Arms to defend their Opinions; but both he, and his Brother *Ras Cella Christos* continu'd firm in their Resolution. The *Abuna* came now to the Camp, follow'd by so many of their Monks, and Nuns, that they far outnumber'd the Army, protesting they would all dye for the Faith of their Ancestors, stand by their Master *Dioscorus*, and begging of the Emperor, that he would make no Innovation, He rejected them, and they grew so inrag'd, that many of them conspir'd to murder him, and his Brother *Ras Cella Christos.*

F. Pays builds a Palace. The Emperor having subdu'd the *Agaus*, return'd in *May* 1614 to *Gorgorra*, where he had kept his Winter Camp, which is his Court, for two Years. This Camp was curiously seated, being in a Peninsula almost enclos'd by the Waters of the great Lake, which they call the Sea of *Dambea.* There F. *Pays* resolv'd to build him a Palace after the *European* Manner, to oblige him, and show the *Ethiopians* that what they reported of the Palaces, and Monasteries in *Europe*, was not impoffible, as they believ'd. He was encourag'd to it by finding in that Place a Quarry of very good white Stone, and therefore presently gave Directions for making Hammers, Mallets, Chizzels and all other Necessary Tools, handling them himself, and teaching the new Workmen, to dig, hew, and square the Stones for the Fabrick; and the same he did as to all the Joyners, and Carpenters Part. Still he wanted Lime, and found no Stone proper to make it, and therefore made use of a binding Sort of Clay. He rais'd large, and strong Walls, fac'd both within, and without with square Stones, well wrought, and joyn'd, so that the building being finish'd, might have serv'd any Prince in *Europe* for a Country House. Among the Rest, there was one fair Room about 50 Foot long, and 15 in Breath, and on the same Floor, a square Bedchamber, with a spacious Stair Case in the Middle, from the lower to the upper Floor, and from that another which ascended to the flat Roof of the House, about which was a handsome Parapet. At the Top of the Stairs was a little Room, like a Closet, which the Emperor was much pleas'd with, because from it he had the distant View of all

that

that great Lake, and the adjacent Country, and saw at hand all that came in, and out, without being himself discover'd by any Body. The Father put a sort of Spring Lock upon the Door, of the Stairs that went out upon the Top of the House, which the Emperor said, would be better alter'd, that he might not always stand in need of the Key to open it, but Father *Pays* answer'd, *Your Majesty may have occasion for it as it is*, and how true this prov'd we shall see hereafter. This Building amaz'd all the *Abyssines*, who came from the remotest Parts to behold it, and what most surpriz'd them was to see an upper Floor, and having no Name to express it by, they call'd it *Babet Laybet*, that is, *a House upon a House*. This Work gain'd the Fathers much Reputation, convincing the People, that what they told them of the mighty Structures in *Europe* was true.

Elios Viceroy of *Tygre*, and the Emperor's Son in Law, *Amana Chriftos* the Emperor's Brother, and the Eunuch *Caflo*, who was High Steward, being enrag'd because many were converted, conspir'd together to deftroy the Emperor, and his Brother *Ras Cella Chriftos*. To this Purpofe they contriv'd that the *Abuna* should raise a Mutiny, by fixing an Excommunication against all that maintain'd two diftinct Natures in *Chrift*, and forbidding all to converse with them, even Children with their Parents, and Servants with their Masters. The Emperor perceiving what the wicked *Abuna* drove at, sent to let him know, that if he did not immediately take off his Excommunication, his Head should answer for it; and he fearing his Life, as readily obey'd. This Project failing, the three Traitors agreed to murder the Emperor themselves, the Eunuch *Caflo* having the Liberty to go in at all Times, on Account of his Employment. Accordingly knowing the Emperor was above alone, the said *Caflo* and *Elios* left the other Servants below, and went up to murder him. *Ite Amata*, the Emperor's Kinswoman, knowing their Defign, sent the Emperor notice of it, at the very Time they were going to put it in Execution; and tho' they came immediately, his Courage was so great that he appear'd not at all difturb'd, but receiv'd them very gracioufly. They came with their Swords in the Scabbards in their Hands, as is the Cuftom, and after some few Words spoken, the Emperor rifing, as if it were to walk, laid his Hand on *Elios*'s Sword, by way of Familiarity, and went to the Stairs that led up to the Top of the House, the others follow'd, thinking they might better do what they came about in that Place, but when they were at the Door, which as was faid before shut with a Spring Lock, the Emperor clapt it to, leaving them on the Stairs, and going up himfelf, fo that they were difappoint'd,

Conspiracy against the Emperor.

with-

without any Noise or Disturbance, and the Emperor remember'd what *F. Pays* had said, That he might have Occasion for that Spring Lock.

Julios the Emperor's Son-in-Law, was much concern'd at this Disappointment of murdering of him in private, and therefore resolv'd to break out into open Rebellion, which was no difficult matter to do, *Ethiopia* being, as has been said, and we shall have Occasion to see a Continual Scene of Insurrections, Mutinies, and Treasons. The motive he pretended, according to the *Ethiopian* Historian *Azage Tino*, and the two Fathers who were there, was the Emperor's taking the Dignity of *Raz*, which is the Highest in the Empire, and the Viceroyship, from his own Brother *Emana Christos*, and confering it on his other Brother *Cella Christos*, who was a great Favourer of the Catholicks. The *Moors* having made an Irruption into *Ethiopia*, next the Frontiers of the *Funchos*, and the Emperor marching with his Forces to repel them, *Julios* laid hold jofthat Opportunity, of his Absence, to make Proclamation, enoyning all those, who acknowledg'd two distinct Natures in *Christ* to depart the Province of *Ogara*, where he was Governour, and the others to joyn him, in Defence of their Religion; by which means he gather'd a numerous Army, and drew towards the *Nile*, to go over into the Province of *Gojam*, where *Cella Christos* resided. The Emperor was now return'd into the Province of *Dambea*, where being inform'd of the Rebellion of *Julios*, and the Danger of his Brother *Cella Christos*, he sent some Troops with all Expedition to his Relief.

In an Island of the Lake the *Nile* falls into, *Julios* found *Simon*, the *Abuna*, who advis'd him, to turn his Forces directly against the Emperor himself, whom he might easily destroy, most of his Commanders being corupted. The Council being approv'd of they both march'd together, the *Abuna* encouraging the Soldiers, and assuring them of Heaven if they dy'd in that Service. The Emperor, who thought of nothing less, was much surpriz'd when his Scouts brought him Advice of the Enemies Approach, to whom he was very much inferior in Strength; but being a Man of extraordinary Bravery, and Conduct, after sending to his Brother *Cella Christos*, to come to his Assistance, he mov'd undauntedly towards the Rebels, and the two Armies came in Sight of one another on the 5th of *May* 1613, the Emperor posting himself advantageously, to shun the Shock of the Enemies Horse, which were much supeiror to his.

The next Morning *Julios* being impatient to put an End to the War, and concluding the Conspirators on the other Side would not fail to joyn him, after drawing out his Army, rode himself up to the Emperors Troops, with only six, or seven Volunriers.

His

His Patrisans, not daring to betray their Monarch so barefac'd, suffer'd him to ride through, and he made on, crying out, *Where is the Emperor.* In this Manner he came to a Battalion of *Tygres*, that stood near the Emperor's Tent, and were not privy to the Treason, one of whom knock'd him down with a Stone, and another coming up first run him through, and then cut off his Head. His Followers were soon hew'd down, and his Army took to their Heels, the Imperialists pursuing them with much Slaughter, till the Emperor founded a Retreat. The *Abuna* a-maz'd at this wonderfull overthrow had not Power to fly, but was kill'd, and his Head chopp'd off; which they presented to the Emperor, who was thus secur'd on the Throne and the Rebellion suppress'd.

C H A P. V.

Description of the Nation of the Agaus. *Two Rebellions suppress'd.* F. Pays *builds a Church. The Emperor professes the Faith of the* Latin *Church. Two new Fathers come into* Ethiopia, *and two others die.*

MANY Gentiles of the Nation call'd *Agaus*, being about this Time converted, it gives us Occasion to speak of those People. There are two Provinces of them in *Ethiopia*, the one in the Kingdom of *Begameder*, call'd *Lasta*, being a Hilly Country, full of such steep, and lofty Mountains, that they are almost impregnable, which was the Reason that several Rebels had maintain'd themselves there above ten Years, against all the Power of the Emperor. There is another Province of *Agaus*, in the Kingdom of *Gojam*, consisting also of high Mountains, tho' not altogether so lofty as those of *Begameder*. This Province, being about 20 Leagues in Length, and between 6, and 7 in Breadth, is divided into about 20 Districts, all the Inhabitants living near the *Nile*. These Mountains abound in Provisions, and are full of Woods, and thick of Bamboes, so very close, that they serve them instead of Walls, and Trenches against their Enemies; for through them they cut close narrow Ways, with so many Turning,s and Windings, that they look like Labyrinths, and in.

Agaus in 2 Kingdoms.

Time

Time of War, they shut themselves up among those Bamboes, about a mile from the Entrance, stopping up the Ways with Trees laid across. Besides, the Natives, like wild Beasts, bred among those Thickets, and acquainted with all the Avenues destroy such as attack them, with their Bows, and Arrows. These their close Thickets they call *Secutes.*

Their Customes, Habit &c.
Nor are these Wooden Fortifications their only Security, for they have mighty Dens and Caves under Ground made by Nature in the solid Rocks, the Entrance into them narrow, but opening within, so that they can receive, and entertain a great Number of People, and some of them have Water within. These they call *Furiatas*, and there they hide themselves till their Enemy is pass'd by. The *Agaus* of *Gojam* are much addicted to Sorcery. Besides their common Provision, which is chiefly Millet, they have much Honey, a good Commodity in *Ethiopia*, because they make their Liquor of it, Abundance of fine Cattel, and like a wild Mountain People, they wear no Cloth, but only Cows Hides, whose Flesh they eat Raw, like the *Abyssines.* These Hides they beat very much, with an unweldy Sort of Instruments, till they become as soft, and limber, as *Spanish* Leather, and then dye them red, which is the Colour they are most fond of. Every Man and Woman covers himself with one of these Hides, throwing them over their shoulders and girding them about their Wastes, without any other Garment. They are generally of a dark Sooty Colour, not so black as the *Abyssines*, well featur'd, and good Soldiers, tho' they use not to go meet their Enemies out of their own Country, but are satisfy'd with defending it, and it were to be wish'd that those who value themselves upon being more civiliz'd were of the same Mind. Thus the *Agaus* maintain'd their Ground for many Ages, not only against the *Cafres* their next Neighbours to the West-ward, but even against all the Power of the *Ethiopian* Emperors, to whom they scarce ever paid any Acknowledgment.

It is true the Imperial Troops did sometimes make Incursions into their Lands, as did other Plunderers, driving away considerable Booties of all Sorts of Cattel, but it is no less certain that they often paid dear for it, and many who came off well the first Time did not care for returning. The *Agaus* look'd upon War with the *Abyssines*, as a less Evil than Peace, because they did them little Damage in War, and their opression was great in Time of Peace. However the Emperor *Sultan Segued*, being a brave, and fortunate Commander, press'd them so hard in the Years 1613, and 1614, piercing into their Lands, and wintering there, that they were oblig'd to submit, and apply'd themselves

Their Conversion.

felves to *F. Pays*, then at *Gorgorra*, to interceed for them with the Emperor, that they might have a favourable Reception, offering him a confiderable Prefent, which he refus'd, defiring no other Reward, but that they would take him into their Country, to teach them the way of Salvation. They accepted the Condition, and the Emperor fhowing them much Kindnefs on the Father's Account, *F. Francis Antony de Angelis*, was fent with them inftead of *F. Pays*, who converted many, and erected feveral Churches.

The Emperor had prevail'd with the *Baffa* of *Suaqhem* to give free Paffage to fome Fathers he would fend for out of *India*, who came thither from *Goa* in the Year 1620, were well receiv'd by that *Turk*, and fafely conducted to *Fremona*, where, it being then the rainy Seafon they were order'd to Winter. Their Names were *F. James de Mattos*, a *Portuguefe*, and *F. Antony Bruno*, *Sicilian*. *F. James Mattos* went the following Summer to the Emperor's Court, and had an honourable Reception, but *F. Lawrence*, who refided at *Fremona* dying, he return'd thither, to attend the Converts in that Kingdom, and receive the Supplies the King of *Portugal* fent the *Portuguefes* yearly out of the Cuftoms of *Diu*.

Two Jefuits *come into* E*thiopia.*

The Emperor growing daily more zealous in eftablifhing the true Doctrine, in his Dominions, and being fully convinc'd of the Certainty of there being two diftinct Natures in *Chrift*, refolv'd now to abolifh another Error the *Ethiopians* had taken from the *Jews*, and accordingly fet out a Proclamation, forbidding all Perfons for the Future to keep Saturday holy, but only Sunday, as the true Chriftian Sabbath. That Abufe was fo ftrongly rooted in the Hearts of the People, that it caus'd a general Uneafinefs, and fome Perfons durft prefume to fend the Emperor a Letter, without any Name, full of bafe, threatning, and reviling Expreffions. That Monarch not being able to difcover the Offenders; iffu'd out a Second Proclamation, enjoyning all Perfons to work upon Saturdays, and in Cafe they did not, for the firft Offence they fhould forfeit a Piece of Cloth, worth about a Crown, and for the fecond all their Goods. This Penalty was firft inflicted on one *Buco*, a brave Commander, who was afterwards converted.

Saturday for true Doctrine, bid to be kept holy.

Jonael, one of the greateft Men in *Ethiopia*, was at this Time Viceroy of *Begameder*, whom the Emperor order'd to publifh the aforefaid Proclamation in that Country. He did fo, tho' not with a Defign to fee it obey'd, but rather to ftir up the People to Rebellion, being himfelf refolv'd to head them, as he actually did in *October* 1620, withdrawing with fuch as would follow him to the Mountains on the Frontiers of the Kingdom, next the *Gallas*, whom he had before engag'd to come to his Affiftance. This News being brought to Court much perplex'd the Emperor, who

Rebellion upon it.

knowing

knowing he had many Traitors about him, beheaded some of those he could convict, and banish'd others; but all to little Effect, for the Remedies seem'd to heighten the Distemper. Next he

The Traitor kill'd. march'd against the Rebels, but perceiving the Mountains they lurk'd in, were impregnable, he sat down at the Foot of them, not questioning but many of those Outlaws would come over to him, as they soon did, and *Jonael* finding himself almost abandon'd fled to the *Gallas,* his Confederates, who being corrupted by the Emperor kill'd him.

Another Rebellion suppress'd. In 1621, the *Damotes,* a People in the Southern Parts of the Kingdom of *Gojam* rose in Arms, on the same Account of keeping the Saturday, at the Instigation of their Monks, and *Batavis,* who are a Sort of Anchorites; but the Viceroy *Ras Cella Christos* defeated them, killing above 3000, and among them many of those Religious Hermits. This same Year *F. Pays* built a Stately Church of whole Square Stones, very bewtifull, and Masterly. Over the high Altar was a curious Arch, with several Compleat Columns,

A Church built. and six others of the *Jonick* Order in the Frontispiece; and a Steeple for the Bells with a winding Stair Case, and a flat Roof enclos'd with a Parapet about it, whence there was a delightful Prospect of the Lake and Plains of *Dambea.* The Emperor came two Days Journey to see this Structure, the like whereof had not been known in *Ethiopia,* and went into it barefoot, leaving a considerable Present to it, at his Departure.

The Emperor embraces the Latin Faith. The following Year 1622, he publickly profess'd the *Latin* Faith putting away all his Wives, except the first, at *Focara,* near the great Lake of *Dambea,* next *Begameder,* betwixt *Anfras,* and *Dara.* Soon after *F. Pays,* who had converted, and receiv'd him into the Church dy'd at *Gorgorra,* having spent 19 Years in this Mission, besides the 7 he was a Captive in *Arabia.* He left an ample Relation of all the Affairs of *Ethiopia* till his Death, whence

These Accounts by whom writ. much of what is here said has been taken, and the Original is still preserv'd at *Rome,* in the Secretaries Office of the Crown of *Portugal.* This same Year also dy'd *F. Francis Antony de Angelis* an *Italian,* who came into *Ethiopia* in the Year 1604, and was a great Master of the *Amara* Language, which is that they speak at Court. These Persons Deaths are particularly here mention'd, as being those who travell'd these Countries, and to whose Accounts we are beholding for all the knowledge we have of them.

CHAP.

CHAP. VI.

The Travels of F. Emanuel d' Almeyda, *and 3 others from* Bazaim, *in* India, *to the Emperor of* Ethiopia's *Court.*

AT this same Time *F. Emanuel d' Almeyda,* residing at *Baza-* 4 Jesuits *sent* im was sent into *Ethiopia* with three Companions, which *into* Ethio- were *F. Emanuel Barradas, F. Lewis Cardeyra,* and *F. Francis Car-* pia. *valho,* an Account of whose Voyage, and Journey by Land we will here give, as deliver'd by the first of the four.

We made ready with all possible Speed, and on the 28*th* of *November* 1622, imbark'd on a *Paguel,* being a small *Indian* Ves- sel, and set Sale with the Northern Squadron, which convoy'd the trading Ships, *James de Mello de Castro,* being Commodore. We put into *Damam,* and that very afternoon sail'd again; but were forc'd back to the same Port the next Day, our Squadron of Men of War, being in Pursuit of six *Dutch* Ships, we descry'd that Day, making from *Suratte* towards *Goa.* Having waited there 15 Days for the *Dieu* Squadron, and being impatient of Delay, we hir'd an *Almadie,* as far as *Goga,* designing to travel thence by Land to *Diu.* At *Goga* we staid a whole Month, by Reason the Road by Land was infested with *Resbuto* Robbers, which oblig'd us to wait for the Fleet, and in it arriv'd at *Diu,* two Months af- ter we left *Bazaim,* At *Diu,* the Commander, and Factor, in- stead of forwarding, put us to much Trouble : but having di- spatch'd our Affairs the best we could we imbark'd for *Suaquem,* on the 24*th* of *March* 1623.

The Vessel we were in, was a Pink belonging to *Luke de Sousa,* freighted by *Lanlegt Dossi,* and commanded by *Rapogi Sangovi,* and tow'd a large Vessel as big as a Ship, and so heavy loaded, that it could scarce move, and the worse because so ill stow'd, that as soon as she anchor'd she heel'd to one Side, and had like to sink, This, and the slackness of the *Monson,* made it late before we had Sight of *Socotora,* and it was no small Vexation to us to see the *Superstitions.* continual Superstitions of the *Gentiles,* and *Mahometans,* the *Bani- ans* offering several sweet Gums, and perfumes to their *Pagods,* or Idols, in the Poop, and the *Mahometans* in the Fore-Castle calling

E e upon

upon their false Prophet for a fair Wind, and dedicating to him a Figure, like a Horse made of *Bamboes*, with several little Flags about it, and pretending that their holy one enter'd into an old *Moor*, which he represented, acting the Mad-Man, and striking all that stood in his Way, with a Ropes End ; at the same Time answering those who ask'd him, when they should see Cape *Guardafuy*, enter the Red Sea, and come to *Suaquem* ; and all his answers prov'd as false as the Prophet they came from, but they were all well pleas'd, and credulous not the least out of Countenance, tho' every thing afterwards fell out quite contrary to what their Prophet had foretold.

In short, the Wind being scant we could neither come to anchor at *Socotora* tho' we had Sight of it, nor at *Caixem*, which we stood for several Days, but went to winter at *Dofar*. There the Vessel lay at Anchor, from the 18th of *May* till the 16th of *October*, and we all that while aboard, without ever going ashore, but in continual Frights, few Days passing without News being brought, once that they had Intelligence of us at Land, another Time that the Petty King was coming, or sending to fetch us ; sometimes that there were *Dutch* Ships on the Coast, and could not miss seeing us ; then that there were *Turkish* Ships, and Gallyes come from *Moca*, which would probably touch at *Dofar*, or else we should meet them in our Way. This put us to the Trouble of hiding ourselves frequently in several Holes about the Ship, as often as any People came aboard from Land, besides the want of Provisions, which oblig'd us to shift with Rice, and some Fish, when it was to be had. The Water was a greater suffering being very brackish, or almost salt, which fill'd us full of the Itch, and that, tho' we let blood for it, held us to *Suaquem*, and some even into *Ethiopia*. The Sailers suffer'd much, tho' they were most of the Time ashore, many of them falling sick of Fevers; and others of the Itch, but what griev'd them most was the Money they exacted from them for anchoring, being above 2000 Pieces of Eight, besides the Loss sustain'd in their Goods, which taking wet, were spoil'd.

Jesuits winter al Dofar.

I shall say little of *Dofar*, because I was not in the Place; but it is well known to be on the Coast of *Arabia* in about 15, or 16 Degrees Latitude, betwixt *Cayxem*, and *Curiamuria*. The City is small, the Inhabitants poor, the petty King was Brother, and Subject to him of *Xaer*, who is Lord of many Lands in this Part of *Arabia*, which hereabouts is neither populous, nor wealthy. On the same Coast, between *Xaer* and *Dofar*, is the City, and Kingdom of *Cayxem*. This King of *Xaer* and *Dofar* is Master of most of the Frankincense in the World, growing on very high
naked

naked Mountains, which run about 40, or 50 Leagues from *Do-* *far* to *Cayxem*, on small Trees, or Shrubs, bearing few Leaves, *Frankincense.* and no Fruit, but the Frankincense, which is its Rosin. Along the pleasant Coast of *Dofar* there are Abundance of Palm Trees, *Indian* Fig-Trees, much *Betele*, and Plenty of Grapes ; and this Verdure it has by pertaking of two Winters, that of *India*, which brings many Clouds, tho' they discharge no heavy, but only small Rain, yet lasting for above 3 Months and a half ; and that of the *Arabian* Gulph, which is at the same time as ours. Here are great Numbers of Wells, and the Country is so moist, that, as I was told it occasions both Men, and Women to have one Leg and Foot of a monstrous Thickness.

On the 16*th* of *October* we weigh'd Anchor, and arriv'd at *Suaquem* on the 4*th* of *December.* Our Voyage was tedious be- *Red Sea.* cause the *Monson* began weak, which made us many Days in reaching of *Adem* ; but it prov'd so favorable afterwards in the most dangerous Places, that we enter'd the Red Sea with a fresh Gale by Night, that we might not be seen by some *Turkish* Vessels that use to lye there, to carry the Ships to *Moca*, and we enter'd on the Side of *Ethiopia*, that is, between it, and the smal Island that lyes in the Mouth of the Streight betwixt it, and *Arabia*;because, tho' the *Arabian* Channel be deeper, and safer, yet the *Turkish* Vessels that guard the entrance use to lie at Anchor, behind certain Headlands of *Arabia.* The next Morning we discover'd the Mountains above *Moca*, and those in *Ethiopia*, opposite to them, and at Noon pass'd by the Island *Jabel Jaquer*, lying almost in the midst of this Sea, between the two Coasts. The *Banians*, and *Moors* saluted it, as they use to do, with sundry superstitious Ceremonies, offering it some Eatables, and talking to it, asking Questions and answering as they thought fit.

A little beyond it begins a Chain of small Islands, so close together that we sometimes saw 6 or 7 in a Row, and some of those that lie farther off are so visible, that they take away the *Chian of I-* Sight of the others behind them. This Chain of little Isles, is like *slands.* a Ridge in the Red-Sea, dividing all the Length of it, as the *Apenine* does *Italy.* The common Course they run for *Suaquem* is for the length of the three or four first Channels, between these Islands, and the Coast of *Arabia*, then they cross the Gulph in three or four Days to the Coast of *Africk*, steering Norwest, and indeavouring to come up with the Land opposite to a Parcel of Islands call'd *Arquico*, where they take Pilots of the Country, there being no sailing along the Coast from,thence to *Suaquem* without them, by reason it is all full of Isles and Banks of Sand,some of them above, and others under Water. We fell in with the Land too low, and had much Trouble about that time with contrary

E 2 Winds

winds, blowing hard; yet having taken a Pilot, we held on our Course, through that Labyrinth of Islands, and Sands, till we came almost in Sight of *Suaquem*, where the Wind failing us, we were 10, or 12 Days gaining less than 8 Leagues, and then dropt Anchor, on the *4th* of *December*, 50 Days after we had left *Dofar*.

Bassa *honours the* Jesuits.

The next Day we landed, 8 Months, and 12 Days after our imbarking at *Diu*, going immediately with the Captain, the Pilot, and chief Merchants, to wait upon the *Bassa*, who receiv'd us in honourable, and affable Manner, saying, he would permit us to go peaceably into *Ethiopia*, because he was a Friend to the Emperor, and desir'd to keep a good Correspondence with him, and the Emperor had sent to desire of him, that he would be kind to, and send the Fathers that should happen to come thither, safe to him. He order'd us all to put on *Cabayas*, that is Vests, which is the greatest Honour he bestows on those he favours; but we knowing how little it is worth, and how dear it commonly costs, excus'd ourselves, and only I put on one, that we might not seem to slight his kindness. The Captain, the Pilot, and I went away with our Vests, a Horseback, to our Lodgings, where we took them off, as is the Custome, and with them to lighten the Purse of 50, or 60 Pieces of eight, for the *Bassa's* Servants, who invented this Custome for their own Profit. So much they cost the Captain, and the Pilot; for I having declar'd, that I was a poor religious Man, and not ambitious of so expensive an Honour, the *Bassa* had order'd they should not demand any Fees of me; however the show cost me 6, or 7 Pieces of eight.

Their Present to him, and others.

The next Day we carry'd the *Bassa* the Present brought for him, which purchases Leave to pass through his Liberties. The principal Things it consisted of were, a *China* Counterpane, a Dimity Quilt curiously wrought with Silk, a Velvet Carpet, an inlaid Escritoire made at *Diu*, some *China* Dishes, and Salvers, and some other Curiosities. After the *Bassa's*, we carry'd another Present to his *Quequea*, who is the Person that governs all things next to him, and a third to the *Amin*, being the Chief Officer of the Custom-house. Nor is this all, for there are many more that crave, and must be serv'd, as Clerks, Commanders upon Passes, Guards, Door Keepers, in short they all suck and draw as much as they can. Above all the Duties on Goods were exhorbitant, for they valu'd Commodities at one half more than they were worth, and according to that Rate took 16 per Cent. besides five Pieces of every Sort in the Hundred. When we were thus well shorn, he dismiss'd us for *Massua*, in honourable Manner, with Letters of Recommendation, ordering the *Quequea*, and *Amin*

to

to permit us to go on our Way, without touching our Eqnipage, or opening our Parcels, or exacting any more Duties, and to allow us a good Guard, for some Days Journey.

We stay'd 16 Days at *Suaquem*, unpacking the Cloathing, sent in Charity to the Christians of *Ethiopia*, and resting ourselves; during which Time we were partly cur'd of the Itch, and recover'd the Fatigues of the Sea, the Air being good, because it was then Winter, and very mild, and there were good Provisions, of Beef, Mutton, Fish, and some Fruit, as Melons &c. All very good, and cheap. All this comes from the Continent, which is inhabited by *Moors* call'd *Funchos*. They are generally tall, and slender, their Eyes very small, their King has a Share in the Profits of the Custom-House, which the *Turks* allow him, that he may supply them with Provisions, and let the Caravans pass. *Suaquem* is a very small Island, about two Musket Shot in Length, and one and a half in Breadth, the Channel that parts it from the Continent being about the same Distance over. Some of the Houses are built with Stone, and Mud, others with Timber, and all cover'd with Mats. Sua-quem.

We departed *Suaquem* on the 21*st* of *December*, in a *Gelva*, or small Vessel; and got to *Mazua* in six Days, coasting along by Day, and lying at Anchor in the Night. *Mazua* is like *Suaquem*, an Island, little larger, and close to the Coast of *Africk*, some of the Houses of Stone, and Mud, but plaister'd, and white-wash'd, and others of Wood, and Mats. There are some Cisterns, and a Bastion at the Entrance over the Bar, with few Guns on it. The River is shallow, and can bear only the little Ships of *Diu*, which ride before it, between *Mazua*, and *Arquico*, or *Deghano*, for so the Natives call it. *Deghano*, or *Arquico* is a Town lying along the Coast, having many Wels, dug in the Sand, whence they have all the Water us'd there, and carry'd over daily in three, or four Barks to *Mazua*, and with it they water some small Gardens of several Sorts of Herbs, as also Lemon, and Pomgranate Trees, which thrive well there. When I came thither this first Time, it had no other Fortification, but only an Enclosure of Stone, and mud two Yards and a half high, and at the End a poor House, one Story high, where the *Quequea* liv'd, but when I return'd in *July* 1633, the wall was built with Lime and Stone; some say the square Fort adjoyning to the *Quequea's* House is of Stone, and Earth, it has four Bastions, at the Angles, they and the Wall five, or six Yards high, it stands near the Wels, to guard the Water. Mazua. Arquico.

Having presented the *Quequela*, *Amin*, and other Officers, and shown them the *Baffa's* Pass, notwithstanding the which they

they exacted upon us, we departed thence on the 16 of *January*, attended by almost all the Garrison of *Arquico*, being then about 20 Musketiers, tho at present they amount to above 200. They bore us company a Day and halfs Journey, till we met with People belonging to *Zabot*, a Village the Emperor had given the Fathers, chiefly that the Men of it, being above 300, arm'd with Javelins, and Targets, should go receive them at their coming, and the Goods they brought for Charity, and conduct them to *Debaroa*; because there are generally great Bands of Robbers all along that Road, being most of them Inhabitants of the neighbouring Towns, who by reason the Country is very Mountainous, Desert in many Places, and so remote from the, Court, have little Regard for the Emperor, retaining nothing but the Name of Subjects. Besides those already mention'd, the Viceroy *Keba Christos*, a Zealous Catholick, being then in his Camp near *Debaroa*, sent his Brother *Asma Guergnis*, and the *Bahar Nagais Acaba Christos*, to guard us, with a good number of Men. All this was little enough, for the Fame of our coming, and bringing a considerable Caravan, had mov'd the Robbers to summon one another from all Parts, so that there were great Numbers of them ready to fall upon us.

Zabot *Village.*

We spent four or five Days in getting through the dangerous Passes, for the most Part climbing excessive high Mountains, among which there were some Lands till'd, and spacious Meadows, where great numbers of stately fat Cows and Oxen graz'd, which continue so all the Year, for in *December*, *January*, and *February* they feed in these Grounds towards the Sea, where it is then Winter, and in *June*, *July*, *August* and *September*, they go farther up the Country, to take the Winter there.

Good Cattel.

Asmara is a high Country, but not so Mountainous, 8 or 9 Leagues short of *Dabaroa*, where the Inland Winter of *Ethiopia* ends. From that Place towards the Sea, we could see the thick Clouds, and mighty Showers attending the Winter on the Coast, hang over the Mountains, and high Vales, without fearing to be wet, the Natives assuring us they never came thither. A little beyond *Asmara* we met with a Regiment of *Portugueses*, belonging to *Maegoga*, and among them *John Gabriel*, a Man in Esteem, who for several Years had commanded all of that Nation in *Ethiopia*. With them came 5 Servants of the Viceroys and brought 5 Mules he sent us, one for each of the Fathers, and the 5th for *Emanuel Magro*, who bore us Company from *India*; they were good Beasts and serv'd us several Years. That same Prince gave four Mules more to other 4 Fathers that came in *July*, and the next Year sent 7 to the Patriarch and Fathers, he

Asmara Country.

brought

brought with him, which are no small Gifts for a Country that is not wealthy.

The next Day we came to the Viceroy's Camp, who order'd all his Men to receive us in a spacious Plain, being about 1500 Soldiers, 300 of them mounted on Mules, many of whom led very fine Horses. The Viceroy himself embrac'd us with singular joy, and after a splendid Entertainment, we went to lie half a League further, at a Village of our own call'd *Adegada* , where we were visited by him the next morning, and continu'd four Days, during which Time above 200 new Converts receiv'd the Blessed Sacrament, besides the old Catholicks. *Reception of the Jesuits.*

Here many *Portuguefes* of *Maegoga* and the Viceroy appointed us a good Guard, so that we pass'd the Desert of *Serae,* lying between *Debaroa* and *Maegoga,* being 10 or 12 Leagues in Length, attended by above 600 arm'd Men. In this Place, besides Tigers, Lions, Ounces, and Elephants, there are Abundance of Robbers, resorting to it from all Parts of *Tigre,* and particularly from some neighbouring Mountains, which are so uncouth, that they seldom own any Subjection to the Viceroy, and at that Time, they were in Rebellion. Towards the End of this Desert we cross'd the River *Marebo,* and at a small Distance from it met *F. James de Mattos,* who was come a Days Journey from *Maegoga* to expect us, having liv'd there above a year without the Company of any other Father. *Seraoe Defert.*

The next Day we arriv'd at *Fremona,* a Town in the small Territory call'd *Maegoga,* and suppos'd by some to have taken its name from *Fremonatios,* the first Bishops of *Aczum,* whom our Books call *Frumentus.* The name of *Maegoga* was taken from the Water-running close by, it being usual in *Tigre* to give Denominations to Territories from the Waters. *Mae* signifies water, in their ancient Language, which is that of their Books, and *Goga,* or *Guagua,* for so they write and pronounce it, is the Noise made by the said Water of two Streams there are, one coming from the North, the other from the North East, washing the Foot of certain high Mountains, lying to the Eastward. At the Conflux of these two Streams, a small Hill rises above the Plain, on which stands the Town of *Fremona,* above which it still rises gently to the Westward, where it forms another Head. From the mid way is another still greater Ascent, turning towards the South, or South West. The Fathers had for Fear of the many Robbers thereabouts, built a House of Stone, and Clay, on the second Head above mention'd, to which several others being afterwards added, the Place became strong, for that Country being enclos'd by 7 or 8 Bastions, with lofty Curtins between them. *Fremona Town. Maegoga Territory.*

This

This Place defended by 20, or 30 Muskets, and one Drake, manag'd by the Sons of the *Portuguefes* was look'd upon as impregnable.   The Town lies scatter'd all about the Hill, having now
many Houfes of Stone and Clay, with Enclofures of the fame,
there being great Plenty of Stone, and very fit for any Work;
which they dig in Pieces 3, or 4 Inches thick, of what Length,
and Breadth they pleafe, and is, taken out of the Quarry without the Help of Pick-axes, or Wedges, only digging, and parting
them with flight Iron Crows.   The Clay is all red, and fo glu-
tinous, that it faves Lime.   In this Place we refted fome Days,
waiting for the Emperor's Orders to go on to *Dambea,* which
foon came, with Directions to the Viceroy to affign us a good
Guard, as he did, commanding the *Nebtet* of *Aczum* to conduct
us with his Men, as far as *Sire,* and the *Xumo* of *Sire* to fee us fafe
beyond the Defert, which both punctually obey'd.

We came to *Fremona* about the Beginning of *February* 1624,
and departed thence on the laft Day of the fame Month, three of
us, leaving *F. Emanuel Barradas,* with *F. James de Mattos,* to
Ganeta Jefus affift him in ferving the many Converts of the Kingdom of *Tigre,*
Our Journey to *Ganeta Jefus* took us up 20 Days, and there we
had a Refidence, where *F. Lewis de Azevedo* then was, and the
Emperor fent to order us, not to make any Stay.   At break of
Day we fet out and came at Noon to the Top of a very high and
fteep Afcent, for the Territory of *Daucaz* is a Spot of Ground, a-
bout a League in Length, and little lefs in Breadth.   All this
is very high Land, no way acceffible without climbing Moun-
Dancaz. tains of a vaft Heigth, for 3, or 4 Hours, and thefe are almoft upright.   This is an excellent Situation for a City, were it in *Europe,*
being full of Srrings, and Rivulets, Meddows, and Corn Fields;
tho' there are few Trees, but that is not the Fault of the Soil, but
of the Inhabitants, who are continually cutting them down, and
never plant any.   Near the middle of this Territory, on a fmall
Ridge was the Emperor's Camp, or Town, containing about 8,
or 9000 Houfes, all of them of Timber, or Stone, and Clay,
thatch'd, and being for the moft Part round, they look'd more
like a Parcel of Hay Reeks than a City.   The Patriarch coming
over 4, or 5 Years after, brought with him fome Mafons, who
built the Emperor a Palace of Lime, and Stone, which in that
Country was wonderfull, the like having never been there feen
before, and would have been reckned a noble Structure in any other
Parts.

Jefuits Re-   Half a League from the Camp we were met by all the Prime
ceptions at Men of Quality, attended by feveral Bodies of Horfe, and Foot,
Court.   who conducted us to the Camp, where the Emperor receiv'd us
in

in a ground Room, fitting on his Couch, which is his Throne, on curious filk Quilts, leaning on Brocade Cufhions. The Room was richly hung, the Viceroys ftanding along the Walls, the great Men clad in Vefts of Velvet, Cloth of Gold, Brocade, or Satin, with their broad rich Swords in their Hands, as is us'd at Court. The Emperor had a noble Prefence, being tall, well favour'd, large beautifull Eyes, a fharp Nofe, a broad hanfome Beard, cloath'd in Crimfon Velvet to the Knees, with *Moorifh* Breeches of the fame, a Girdle of feveral thick Gold Plates, and a loofe upper Damask Garment of the fame Colour. He fcarce fuffer'd us to kifs his Hand, but order'd we fhould fit down near his Couch, the Nobility afterwards feating themfelves by Degrees. After the ufual Ceremonies, and delivering him a Letter from *F. Mutius Vitellefchi*, the General of our Order, he difmifs'd us, fent a plentiful Entertainment after us, of feveral Cows, Pots of Wine, and Honey, *Apas*, or Cakes of Bread, &c. Some Days after we retir'd to reft us at our Refidence of *Gorgorra.* Thus far *F. Emanuel d' Almeyda*'s Relation.

C H A P. VII.

Several Fathers fent into Ethiopia. Ras Cella Chri- ftos *the Emperor's Brother fuppreffes a Rebellion.* Don Alfonfo Mendez *appointed Patriarch fails from* Lisbon *to* Goa.

F. *Mutius Vitellefchi*, the General of the *Jefuits* had order'd the Vifitor in *India*, to fend 12 more into *Ethiopia*, upon the News of the great Progref made in that Country. Four being already as far as *Dofar* on their Way, the Vifitor appointed 8 more, and in regard it was fear'd, the *Turks* would not per- mit fo many to pafs the fame way, four were order'd to go by *Mazua*, 2 by *Melinde*, and 2 by *Zeia.*

The firft 4 had a good Voyage from *Diu* to *Mazua*, where they arriv'd on the 2d of *May*, having fet out about the latter end of 4 Jefuits *March*. Here they were detain'd by the *Baffa* of *Suaquem*, till he *more pafs by* had receiv'd a Prefent he expected from the Emperor of *Ethiopia, the way of* being a *Zecora*, or that curious Creature before defcrib'd, which the Mazua.

Por-

Portugueses call *Burro do Matto*, that is a wild Ass. The Heat was so violent during their Stay in that small Island, that all their Skin being parch'd came off in Fleaks, and Scurf, but being satisfy'd to escape with their Lives, as soon as dismiss'd, they proceeded on their Journey and came safe to *Fremona*.

2 from Me-linde return to India.
Those two appointed to go by the Way of *Melinde*, after visiting all the Ports on that Coast, and inquiring in all Places how they might proceed on their intended Journey, finding no Directions, nor any Person that could pretend to guide them, return'd at last into *India*. It is not to be wonder'd they should find no way, the nearest Port on that Coast being at least 150 Leagues in a streight Line from any Part of the *Abissines* Dominions, and all among the most Brutal, Barbarous, and Inhuman Nations that *Africk* affords.

The two that were to attempt passing through *Zeyla*, tho' well recommended by the *Moorish* King of *Caixem*, were immediately seiz'd by that Barbarous Prince of *Zeyla*, or *Adel*, and after some Days imprisonment put to Death in their dark Confinement.

2 put to Death at Zeyla.

This same Year 1624, the Emperor put out a Declaration, in Favour of the Catholick Religion, which much provok'd the adverse Party, who knowing they could never prevail as long as the Emperor and his Brother *Ras Cella Christos* were throughly united, they work'd so far by false Insinuations, that the Sovereign growing Jealous remov'd his said Brother from the Viceroyship of *Gojam*, and tho' he was soon restor'd, yet this Jealousy was never quite extinguish'd, but produc'd many Mischiefs, which afterwards ensu'd.

Practises about Religion.

Ras Gella Christos at this Time dedicate l the Church of Lime and Stone the Fathers had built for him, at *Cerca*, in the Kingdom of *Gojam* ; and having receiv'd Orders from the Emperor to march against the Rebels in the Kingdom of *Amahara*, under the Son of *Cabrael*, he set forward, notwithstanding all the Difficulties, that might have obstructed, it being then the Depth of Winter. The Rebels fled at the Sight of his Advanc'd Parties, which slew many, and took all their Baggage, their Ringleader retiring to an inaccessible Mountain, with the Remains of his broken Forces, one of the *Gallas* who was in the Imperial Camp, undertook for a considerable Reward to betray him to *Cella Christos*. To this purpose he pretended to desert, and coming to the General of the Rebels, perswaded him to go over to his Country, where he would prevail with those People to espouse his Quarrel. His advice was follow'd, and the Traitor being conducted to a Town of that Nation, his deceitfull Guide perswaded his Countrymen rather to deliver him up to the Emperor's Brother, for a good Reward,
than

Ras Cella Christos defeats Rebels.

than pretend to support his broken Fortune. Accordingly they
dash'd out his Brains, with their Clubs, and sent his Jaws and
Beard which was all that remain'd unbroken to *Ras Cella Christos.*
He in the mean while 'had gain'd-the Mountain, where he found
all the Treasure belonging to those Outlaws, which he diſtributed
among his Men, only reſerving for himſelf ſome Things to be reſtor'd
to an ancient Church, whence they had been taken by the Rebels.
F. Emanuel de Almeyda ſaw them, and ſays they were a
gold Chalice, that would hold about three Pints, and weigh'd
two Pounds, a Paten above three Spans in Compaſs, three Spoons
wherewith they gave the conſecrated Wine, two of them Gold,
and one Silver, a great Bible, bound in Crimſon Velvet, all
pleated with Gold.

The News of this Succeſs was brought to the Emperor; at the
Time when our Patriarch *Don Alfonſo. Mendez* was at *Gorgorra,*
ordaining the firſt Prieſts in *Ethiopia*; yet this could not ſtop the
Progreſs of Envy, which never ceas'd to Miſreprefent him to the
Emperor. But we muſt leave that Affair to give an Account of
the aforeſaid Patriarchs coming into that Country.

The Emperor of *Ethiopia* having made preſſing Inſtances to the F. Alfonſo
Pope and King of *Portugal* to ſend him a Patriarch, notwithſtand- M ndez *Pa-*
ing the two former Prelates ſent thither had been ſo ill treated *triarch.*
by that Princes Predeceſſors, King *Philip* the 4th of *Spain,* nam'd
to that Dignity *F. Alfonſo Mendez,* of the Society of *Jeſus,*
Doctor of Divinity, and a Perſon excellently qualify'd for that
Function. Life being very uncertain in ſuch a tedious Voyage,
it was thought fit to appoint others to ſucced him, the firſt of
which was *F. James Seco,* with the Title of Biſhop of *Nice,* the
2d *F. John de Rocha,* ſtil'd Biſhop of *Hierapolis,* who were all
three conſecrated at *Lisbon,*in the Year 1623. Theſe three, with
ſeventeen more of the Society, imbark'd in *March,* that ſame Year,
and arriv'd in *September* at *Mozambique,* where they were forc'd
to Winter, which being paſs'd they reach'd *Goa* on the 28th of
May 1624, the Biſhop of *Nice,* above mention'd, dying by the
Way. The Patriarch's Voyage from that City to the Port of
Baylur, and his Journey thence by Land to *Fremona* we will deliver out of a Letter of his own, in the following Chapter.

C H A P. VIII.

The Patriarch Don Alfonso Mendez *his Letter,
giving an Account of his Voyage from* Goa *to* Baylur,
and his Journey by Land thence to Fremona.

The Patriarch to go by Dancali.

I Departed *Goa,* says the Patriarch, on the 17th of *November,* 1624, for *Diu,* intending to imbark there for *Suaquem,* or *Mazua;* but receiv'd Letters at Sea from the Father Rector at *Diu,* giving me to understand, there was no Ship there to carry me to either of those Ports, the *Banians* positively refusing to go thither, because they had the foregoing Year been unreasonably exacted upon by the *Baffa,* and other Officers of the Custom-House: Besides there were Letters newly come from the Emperor, and Fathers in *Ethiopia,* advising, that I should not go by the Way of *Suaquem,* or *Mazua;* but repair to a Port of the King of *Dancali,* who is a very good Neighbour, and almost subject to the Emperor, which Port is call'd *Baylur,* and is 12 Leagues within the Mouth of the Streights, for that Way I might take with me what Men, Church Stuff, Books, or other Goods I pleas'd, and be as safe as in the Emperor's own Dominions. At the same Time they advis'd that no Merchant Ships must venture to that Port, but only Men of War, Galliots that could row, or other such light Vessels, that might be out of Danger of the *Turks* of *Moca,* which lies just opposite. Adding that notice should be given of the Time I was to set out, that all things might be in Readiness, and a number of Men to conduct me. Besides these I receiv'd Letters from the Emperor of *Ethiopia,* and his Brother *Ras Cella Chriflos,* the great Promoter of Christianity, which are here omitted as too tedious.

His Company.

I touch'd at *Bazaim Damam,* and *Goga,* and arriv'd at *Diu* on the 2d of *February.* Four Galliots fitted out for this Purpose at *Bazaim* coming to this Port on the 23d of *March,* I imbark'd on the 2d of *April,* and set sail the next Morning, with four Fathers of the Society, which were *F. Jerome Lobo, F. Bruno d Santa Cruz, F. John Velafco,* and *F. Francis Marquez,* two Lay-Brothers being *Emanuel Luis,* and *John Martins,* and 13 Lay-Men, one of them a Servant I brought from *Portugal,* 5 good Musitians, a *Abyffine,* two Masons, and two other Servants.

The

The Wind being flack, and fteady, we had Sight of the I- *Escapes great* fland *Zocotora* on the 18*th*, and ftanding for it all Night had like *Danger at* to be caft away about break of Day, being juft ready to run up- *Sea.* on a Shoal that buts out from the Ifland to the Eaftward; but that the Captain, who at other Times us'd to rely upon the Sail. ors, ftepp'd to the Head, and looking out, faw the Sea ripple under the Cutwater, which made him cry to the Steerfman to put the Helm up hard a Lee, and the Galiot, which at other Times did not readily anfwer the Helm, and muft now upon the leaft fticking have fplit upon a Rock, came about as fwift as the ableft Horfeman could have done, to the Admiration of all the Men, and particularly of the Captain, who, tho' well ac-quainted with the Sea, and having run many Dangers, de-clar'd he never was in any like this, and look'd all the Day af-ter as pale as a Ghoft, protefting the Deliverance was mira-culous.

Running along the North Side of the Ifland, we came to the *Refrefh'd* watering Place, where the King of *Caixem* has a Town, and in *from Shore.* it a very hanfome Houfe, with a Gallery, after the Manner of *India*, and *Portugal*. The King's Factor, being the Prime Man there, was frighted, and drew out all the Men in Arms, to be in a Readinefs, but underftanding they were *Portuguefe* Veffels, prefently fent out an *Almadie* to compliment the Commodore, and offer fuch frefh Provifions as the Country afforded, which we ftood in need of, and accordingly, the next Day fent us a con-fiderable Prefent of Flefh, and Tamarinds ; not only for the Captain, but for the Fathers.

That night we ftood off from the Ifland, and pafs'd between *Abdaluria*, and the 2 Sifters, and on the 21*ft* in the Morning difcover'd Cape *Guardafuy*. On the 29*th* we enter'd the Mouth of *Arrive at* the Red Sea, and the next morning by break of Day were fix or fe- *Baylur.* ven Leagues within it, ftill inclining towards the Coaft of *Ethiopia* ; without having Sight of *Moca*, or fo much as of the Iflands, where generally the *Turkifh* Galleys, or other Veffels ufe to cruize. On the 2d of *May* we found our defir'd Port of *Baylur*, which we might have got into the next Day after our entering the Mouth of the Red Sea, being the 30*th* of *April*, had our Pilots known how to hit it. In the Port were three or four fmall Veffels of *Moca*, which feeing ours that row'd, and had fharp Beaks, fell very haftily to landing all they had aboard. An *Almadie* of ours went before, and the *Xeque*, or Governour plac'd there by the King, who refides about fix or feven Leagues from thence, coming out to her, the Interpeter told him, There were three Ships come from *India*, which intended to water ; giving him his

Prefent

Present, and so to prosecute their Voyage. He in a great Fright, answer'd. He would give them all the Water they had Occasion for, but they must be gone immediatly, and would have sent Hostages presently ; but the Interpreter reply'd. They would go ashore the next Morning.

Is well received.

Being assur'd that was *Baylur*, we drew as near to Land, as the Sea would permit, which is there very shoal, and full of Flats. As soon as the least of our Ships came up with the *Turkish* Vessels, and made it self Master of them, the Interpreter went ashore, and told the *Xeque* the Truth of the Matter, That the Emperor of *Ethiopia* had sent for Fathers to *India*, and directed them to come to that Port, because the King was his Friend, and had engag'd to give them a good Reception; that they were aboard, but that no arm'd Men should land, or do any Harm. This satisfy'd the *Xeque*, who said, They had receiv'd such orders from their King three Years before, and he the Emperor's Presents to that Effect. An old Man, who is a Sort of Judge there, whom they call *Furto*, added, that he came about a Month since from the King's Camp, and whilst he was there, Letters were brought from the Emperor of the same Purport both of them then came aboard, in very friendly Manner, which was a great Satisfaction to us.

Troublesome travelling.

We departed *Baylur* on the 5th of *May*, afternoon, not so well furnish'd as we expected, for tho' they had premis'd us, and there was need of many more Camels, yet we being very hasty to be gone, as apprehending the Neighbourhood of *Moca*, they found us but 14, which oblig'd us to leave behind much of our Goods, taking only the most valuable, we being now 22 Persons, with two that joyn'd us from the Ships. Only six Asses could be got, so that we rode by Turns, and went a foot most Part of the Way, which when it was not loose Sand, was over Mountains of Iron Mines, the Stones whereof are like the Dross that comes from the Furnaces, and so sharp pointed, that they spoilt a Pair of Shooes in a Day, and there being no great Stock of them, most of my Companions were forc'd to make use of the Pack-thread Buskins we carry'd for the Servants, and not being us'd to them, their Feet were much gall'd, and Bloody, following the Camels eleven Days our Journey lasted. Some of them to partake of the Blessing the Prophet *Isaiah* gives the Feet of, Ministers of the Gospel, would not ride at all, eating very little besides Rice we had with us, meeting no Town to furnish us with Provisions; and the Heat so violent that it melted the Wax in our Boxes, without any Shade, but that of Briers, which did us more Harm than good, lying on the hard Ground, and drinking brackish

Water

Water, of a very ill Scent, and sometimes but little of that. Yet the greatest Vexation we had was the Company of the Camel Divers, who dealt with us most barbarously, and could never be corrected by the old *Furto* above mention'd, who went along with us, continually craving something, and with a Design to inform his King, what he might demand of us. This Man, the Kinder we were to him, the worse he treated us, obliging us to maintain, and cook for him, and he would always be the first serv'd, and if at any Time his Meat was not so soon-ready as he expected, he reveng'd himself by not travelling that Day, and playing us a thousand Dog Tricks, striking our Men, all which we were fain to bear, for Fear our Goods should be left in that Desert, which he would be very apt to do, because he was paid before hand, for the Hire of the Camels, without which he would not have stir'd a Foot with us.

The King of *Dancali* being inform'd of our Arrival, came six *Reception by* Days Journey, from remoter Parts, to a better Country, where *the King of* there was good Water, and sent his Brother before to receive, or *Dancali.* rather to pillage us, for soon after we met; he sent to put us in mind, we should give him his Present, which we could not avoid delivering in that very Place, tho' we pleaded the Things were all disperf'd in the several Packs, that were to be open'd when we came to the King, his Brother's Camp. To show what Difference there is in Men's Fancies, he willingly accepted of all that was Clothing, and only rejected, and desir'd us to change him a little Cabinet of *Diu*, curiously inlay'd, which is worth there five *Cruzados*, that is about 13 or 14 Shillings, for a Bit of Cloth, worth about eight Pence. The King made the same Account of some Curiosities of *China* we offer'd him, parting with them immediately, and being extremely, fond of the Cloathing, tho' of very small Value; The Reason his People gave for this was, that, he always living in Tents, Curiosities were of no use there, nor had he any thing worth keeping in them.

The next Day, the King sent us four Mules for the four Principal Fathers to come into his Camp in more state, among which *Lobo 49* one fell to my Share, because I was reckoned the Great Father, for so they call they Superior. This Name sunk that of Patriarch, or *Abuna*, of which the King had receiv'd some Intelligence, brought him out of *Ethiopia*, by the *Moorish* Commander, and the *Portuguese*, that came from thence. Seeing us all in the same Habit, which was always that the Society wear in *India*, they ask'd for the *Abuna*, that came from *Rome*, and we answer'd, He dy'd at Sea, meaning the Bishop of *Nice*, at which the King was as much concern'd as we, thinking he had lost a considera-

ble

ble Prize in him. He prepar'd to receive us in a Hall, like that the Poets defcribe the firft King of *Rome* had, round, enclos'd and cover'd with Hay, and fo low, that it oblig'd me to bow lower than I had intended. Nor could the Wind be confin'd in it,

His poor Equipage.

being open on all Sides. On one of them the Floor, was rais'd about four Fingers above the reft, and on it a fmall Carpet of *Lar* in *Perfia*, worn fo thread bare, that it look'd as if it had ferv'd all his Predeceffors, with a fmall Cufhion of the fame Antiquity, which when he was better provided with what we gave him, he order'd to be laid for us to fit down before him, inftead of a Leather we had at the firft Vifits, and we afterwards faw it on his Horfe. His Canopy was a Piece of courfe Cloth, on the right Hand a Chair, which was once good, with Silver Plates, and on the left two very large Calabafhes, full of a Liquor, he us'd inftead of Wine, and took of it often, before his Vifiters, and thefe were the Kittledrums that went before him, when he came thither from his Tent, which was a fmall Diftance, and might for Antiquity have ferv'd *Ifmael*, from whom they boaft they are defcended.

His Gravity, and Sedatenefs was well becoming a King, and he

His Behaviour.

fhow'd it in defpifing a fmall Prefent we carry'd him for Admittance as his Servants told us was ufual, referving the reft for another Time, which he did that we might not think that fufficient; nor did he fhow much liking of the great Prefent, tho' it was of confiderable Value, nor that he could find Fault with it, but that there might be Room for us to give more, and him to crave on, as he did during all the 17 Days we ftay'd there, which very much vex'd us, and yet we were much oblig'd to him, for tho' he fancy'd we brought much more than in Reality we had, and both himfelf and his People were very greedy, which is occafion'd by the Country being fo poor, that for above 50 Leagues I travell'd through, there is not one Foot fit to be fow'd, and they live upon Flefh, and Milk, and fome Corn brought them out of *Ethiopia*; yet he never order'd our Goods to be fearch'd, nor faw any of them, nor exacted any Duties. The Fathers that went by the Way of *Mazua*, and *Suaquem* faid we fhould not have come off there for 190 Pieces of Eight.

Here we began to be pinch'd with Hunger, for tho' the Rectors of *Bazaim*, and *Tana* had furnifh'd us with Provifion enough to

Hard Fare.

ferve us both by Sea and Land, it was left at *Baylur*, both for want of Carriage, and becaufe they told us there was Plenty enough at the King's Camp; but we found fo little, that it was a great happirefs to meet with half a Peck of Millet, which we eat by Meafure, either boil'd, or roafted, there being no conveniency for

grinding

grinding, and very often we fed upon nothing but Flesh, which they sold us very dear, knowing we must eat, and they had then a good Opportunity to furnish themselves with Cloathing, which at length began to fail, and none having Faith enough to trust us, we were oblig'd to shorten our Allowance. At our taking Leave, the King would have me, as being the great Father, to ride his own Horse, from his Tent to ours, magnifying the Honour he did us therein, and telling us, that even his own Brother did not mount his Horse. There was no diswading him from it, tho we urg'd that the Fathers did not use to ride a Horseback, for he was resolv'd the Emperor should know he did his Masters that Honour, so that I was oblig'd to mount, and went back with great noise of Horse-bells, and well attended. *Honour done the Patriarch.*

The next Day, being the 5th of *June*, we were dismiss'd, with more Honour than Conveniency, having but one He Mule, besides the Beasts we brought from *Baylur*, so that we were little mended, except my self, who had a good Mule given me by *Paul Nogueyra*, who would never ride in all the Way, alledging he could not do it, when the Fathers went a foot. Thus we travell'd through uncooth Lands, but with Plenty of good Water, the *Moorish* Commander, and his Men going along with us, as also a Renegado *Abyssine*, who was his Father in Law.

The Boundary between the Kingdoms of *Dancali* and *Tygre*, is a Plain four Days Journey in Length, and one in Breadth, which they call the Country of Salt, for there is found all that they use in *Ethiopia* instead of Mony; being Bricks, almost a Span long, and four fingers thick and broad, wonderful white, fine, and hard, and there is never any miss of it, tho they carry away never so much; and this Quantity is so great, that we met a Caravan of it, wherein we believ'd there could be no less than 600 Beast of Burden, Camels, Mules, and Asses, of which the Camels carry 600 of those Bricks, and the Asses 140, or 150, and these continually going, and coming. They tell many Stories concerning this Salt Field; and among the rest, that in some Part of it, there are Houses that look like Stone, in which they hear human Voices, and of several other Creatures, and that they call such as pass that Way, by their Names, and yet nothing can be seen. The *Moorish* Commander told me, that as he went by there, with a Lion *Ras Cella Christos* sent to *Moca*, three or four of his Servants vanish'd on a sudden, and he could never hear of them after. In one Place there is a Mount of Red Salt, which is much us'd in Phisick. This is to be pass'd over by Night, because the Heat is so violent in the Day, that Travellers, and Beasts are stifled, and the very Shoes parch up, as if they were laid on burning Coals. We enter'd upon it at three in the Afternoon, *Rock Salt grows.* *Red Salt.*

G g   and

and it pleas'd God that the Sun clouded, which the Renegado *Moor* attributed to his Prayers. We travell'd all the Night to get over the Salt Hill, only resting three times, whilst the Camels Burdens were set down, and loaded again; and on the 11th of *June* in the Morning came to a parcel of Stones, where they told us, the Salt was at an End. Here we all saw towards our Right, a Star in the Sky larger than the Planet call'd the Morning Star, very beautifull and bright, continuing fix'd in the same Place, whilst a Man might say the Lords Prayer, and an *Ave Mary*. On a sudden it enlightened all the Horizon, and rejoyc'd our Hearts.

Dangerous Ways.

We were oblig'd to travel all Day, that we might come to Water in the Evening, and had another Iron Mountain to pass, like that of *Dancali*, where our *Portuguese* Companion bid us strike off a shorter Way than the Caravan could go, along which we travell'd afoot at least six Hours, almost perish'd for want of Drink, till a *Moor* we met accidentally conducted us to the Water, and there the Caravan join'd us at Night. We made but a short stay here, being told that the *Gallas* us'd to resort to that Water, and therefore travell'd on all Night to get over a great Plain they continually haunt, which we found strew'd with the Bones of 160 Persons those Barbarians had butcher'd, and frighted us, seeing the Track of their passing that way the same Night, and yet we could not get over it, till Eight or Nine the next Morning, when we took to the Mountains, where those People seldom go, and rested there all the remaining Part of the Day.

Pleasant River.

The next Night we travers'd another Plain of the *Gallas* shorter than the other, and then came upon the Bank of a River, along which we travell'd two Days, and I think it may be reckn'd one of the pleasantest in the World, for the Water is clear and cool, and the Herbs growing along it sweet, as Penny Royal, Basil, and many more we know not. The Banks are cover'd with Tamarind, and those Trees they call of the *Pagod* in *India*, besides many others, on which there were abundance of Monkeys, skipping about and making Faces at us. Here we met a Man, who brought us Letters from the Fathers, and said *F. Emanuel Barradas* would be with us the next Day at Noon. The Renegado told us, the Camels should go no farther, unless we gave something more for them; and at Night, that we must lie still all the next Day, because their House was hard by, and they would go kill a Cow, in Honour of *S. Michael*, whose Festival is kept in *Ethiopia* on the 16th of *June*, and the *Moors* observe it. That Night four or five Men came up to us, sent by *F. Emanuel Barradas*, with Provisions.

The

The next Day, at 9 of the Clock, we came to the Foot of the Mountain *Sanafe* where began the Command of the *Moorish* Captain that went for us, and so far we had hir'd the Camels, who could not go up it, because very high, and steep. Soon after we had set up our Tent, came F. *Barradas*, with several *Ethiopians* of Quality, many *Porteguefes*, Mules for all the Fathers, a very fine one for the Patriarch and abundance of Provisions. Here F. *Barradas* advis'd me to put on the Episcopal Robes, which when the *Moorish* Commander saw, he was much surpris'd, and begg'd my Pardon for not having known me sooner, to pay that Honour that was due to my Dignity, and the Renegado hearing of it was so confoounded, that he durst not show his Face. On the 17*th* we ascended the Mountain, which is higher than the *Alps*, as one of our Companions said, who had pass'd them, and thicker of Cedars, Cypress, and other Trees, and sweet Herbs, the common Weed on it being extraordinary high Tufts of Sage, and white Roses. Going down again, we came into Till'd Grounds, full of Barley, and Millet, which we had not seen before. The *Xumo* of *Agamea* met us at the Place where we lay that Night, he and the others with him bringing Presents of 2 or 300 *Apas*, or Cakes of Bread each, and 2, or 3, Cows, as also four, five or six Camels loaden with Meltheglin, all which was divided among the Company, and tho' perhaps the Presents might be the more considerable, because they were for Guests, who came from such remote Parts, it is a settled Custom in *Ethiopia* to entertain, and give a Days Provision to all Passengers, according to their Quality, and if it be not done the Traveller may the next Day complain of the Governour of the Town. The *Xumo* of *Amba Senete*, to whose House we came the 3*d* Night, gave us there 8 Cows, and we were entertain'd after the *Ethiopian* Manner, a Round Table being spread on the Ground, and on it many *Apas*, as broad as Peck Loaves, made of Wheat, and a sort of Pease much valu'd in that Country, on which they lay the Meat, so they are both eaten together, both Flesh and Dish.

Being thus attended by a great number of Horse Men, richly clad, who went before Skrimishing with their Jrvealins, and Targets, we came to *Fremona*, which is a large and famous Town in these Parts, on the 21*st* of *June*. Thus far the Patriarch's Letter.

Gg 2　　　　　　CHAP

Sanafe Mountain.

C H A P.   IX.

The Patriarch's Journey to the Court. His Reception
there. The Progress of Religion. Several Rebellions,
and Contrivances of the Schismaticks for subverting
the Roman *Religion.*

Dangerous
Season to
Travel.

THe Patriarch coming to *Fremona* when the Winter began,
which is there on the 21*st* of *June*, and ends in *September*, he
was forc'd to stay all *October*, and a great part of *November*, because
it is extraordinary dangerous travelling from *Tygre* to *Dambea*,
during those Months, being very subject to Fevers, and other
malignant Distempers, occasion'd by the Corruption of the Air
in those Deserts, the Sun Beams perfectly burning in those low
boggy Grounds, which so scorches up the Grafs, and Shrubs that
they exhale such noxious Vapours, as seldom fail to prove
mortal to any that pass.

Reception of
the Patriarch

At *Gorgorra*, the Patriarch gave Ordination conditionally to
20 Clergy Men, and Monks, who had receiv'd it before from the
Abuna, and some of them that had Wives were permitted to keep
them, as is us'd in the *Greek* Church, that the Parishes might not
be destitute of Curates. Half a League from the Emperors Camp
he was met by the best of the Court and 15, or 16000 Arm'd Men,
both Horse and Foot, all in their best Apparel, which in the People of Quality consists of Vests of several sorts of Silk, as Velvet, Satin, Brocade of *Mecca* all after the *Turkish* Fashion. The
Apparel of the common Sort consists of Callicoes, Buckrams,
and other *Indian* Stuffs. The richest, over their Silks have large

Habit of E-
thiopia.

Gold Chains, rich Sashes, wear curious Gold Bracelets, broad
Swords, or Hangers plated with Gold, and Silver. The Gentle-
men were well mounted and accouter'd, the rising parts of their
Saddles higher than ours, and plated with Silver on Silk of several Colours. All these Horsemen coming up with the Patri-
arch made him a low Bow, and then opening to the Right and Left,
took him in the Midst of them, the Air resounding with the
Noise of Kettle Drums, Pipes, and Shouts. Thus was he con-
ducted to a Tent, at a small distance from the Camp, where he
alighted to put on his Bishops Rocket, and Hat, all the great
Men kissing his Hand. Then he proceeded to another Tent, at the
Entrance into the Camp, where having put on a Cope and white
Mighter, he mounted a Py'd Horse, with a Horse-Cloth of white
Damask,

Damask, which the Emperor had sent very richly trapp'd, and thus under a Canopy, carry'd by 6 Viceroys, and Prime Noblemen, he proceeded to the Church of *Gan Jabet, Serca Chriftos*, the Lord High Steward leading his Horfe, the Mufick founding all the Way. At the Church he was receiv'd with a Difcharge of fome Cannon the Emperor has, and all the fmall Shot, the *Benedictus* being fung by excellent Voices. The Emperor was in the Chancel richly clad, with his Gold Crown on his Head, fitting on his Imperial Seat, with a Cufhion of Cloth of Gold, and Brocade at his Feet, where he receiv'd, and imbrac'd the Patriarch, who then went up to the Altar, and made a fhort Speech, which was much applauded.

When the Ceremony was over, they all withdrew, and after a fmall Repofe the Patriarch went to Court, where the Emperor feated him in a Chair equal with himfelf, and this he practis'd as often as he afterwards came to fee him. They then appointed a Day on which the Emperor and all the great Men, both Clergy, and Laity, where in folemn Manner publickly to fwear Obedience to the Church of *Rome*, which was on the 11th of *February* 1626. The Palace being then richly adorn'd, and all the Men of Note affembled, the Emperor, and the Patriarch fate down on two Chairs, and the latter made a long Speech, or Sermon to the Audience, to prove the Supremacy of the Church of *Rome*. Then *Mecha Chriftos*, the Emperor's Coufin, Lord High Steward, and Viceroy of *Cenwen*, fpoke by his Order, the Emperor himfelf prompting, where he mifs'd in any thing he had been directed to fay. Then the Emperor taking the New Teftament in his Hands open, knelt down before the Patriarch, and took the Oath of Supremacy to the Pope, which was afterwards perform'd by all the Nobility, and Clergy. Next they all took an Oath to Prince *Faciladas* as Heir to the Crown. Proclamation was then made, that no Clergy Men, or Monks, fhould for the future fay Mafs, or perform other Ecclefiaftical Functions, till they had been with the Patriarch; in regard it was much doubted, whether they were legally ordain'd; for befides that they did not confer any leffer Orders, the Ordination of the Deacons confifted in anointing their Heads, and cutting off fome Hair, and that of the Priefts in taking a Loaf off the Church Window with their own Hands. And it once hapened, that almoft 3000 reforting to the *Alexandrian Abuna*, to be ordain'd, he being then bufy, bid them all take what Orders they would, and go about their Bufinefs. It was alfo order'd that all Perfons whatfoever fhould embrace the *Roman* Faith, upon Pain of Death, to fuch as fhould refufe it, and that none fhould prefume to conceal them.

Honour done he Patriarch.

Oath of Supremacy taken to the Pope.

Ethiopian Ordination.

Next.

Next the Emperor gave the Patriarch Lands, on the Borders of
Dambea, adjoyning to *Begameder*, where he order'd him a House
to be built, and furnish'd with all Conveniencies for himself, and
Family, and a Seminary for 60 Young *Abyssines*, and Sons of
Lands, and *Portuguese*, to learn to write, and read both Languages and be
House given instruct'd in matters of Faith. Another House was built for
the Patriarch the Patriarch in the Camp at *Dancaz*, where the Emperor us'd to
reside in Winter, and that Prelate preach'd there on most Sundays, the *Ethiopians* delighting in hearing many Texts of Scripture quoted. Many of them mislik'd the Custom introduc'd by
the *Portuguese* of praying on their Knees, and some contended that
the Altars ought to be portable, without any Stone. The Patriarch employ'd himself in collecting, and expounding the Synods,
till the 6*th* General Council, because the main Errors of the *Aby-*
ssines were relating to the Incarnation, whereof little is said in the other Synods because those Heresies had been sufficiently confuted before. He also compos'd a Catechism, in showing all the Errors
not only of the *Abyssines*, but of all other Oriental Nations, in
putting which Books into the *Ethiopian* Tongue he was much af-
sisted by a Noble Man call'd *Oda Christos*, who had an excellent
Talent that way.

A mighty Progress was made in Converting of the People, the
A Church Patriarch sending abroad several Priests, and Monks he had Or-
built dain'd, to instruct and administer the Sacraments. Two of these
were murder'd in the Province of *Ceguade*, which is the most
Eastern Part of the Kingdom of *Tygre*. At this time was the
Solemnity of the Dedication of the new Church built at *Gorgorra*,
with Lime and Stone, where the Vestry, and Choir being vault-
ed, and many Roses curiously cut in white Stone, the *Abyssines*,
who had never before seen a Stone Roof came from very far to admire this strange Work. This same Year 1626, the Kingdom of
Tygre suffer'd by a dreadful Plague of Locusts, which are frequent
Locusts. in *Ethiopia*, by reason of its being a Mountainous Country, and
full of Deserts, where such Vermin generally breed, and there are
such Multitudes of these Locusts, that they look like vast thick
Clouds, and their Teeth are so sharp, that they destroy all the
Grass, and the Leaves on the Trees, leaving all the Provinces
they pass through desolate. This Plague was so dreadful in
Tygre that whole Provinces were utterly unpeopled, particularly
that of *Bur*, near the Red Sea, next to *Dafalo*, and so great a
Famine ensu'd, there being nothing for Men, or Beasts to eat, that
very few escap'd, who all went a way to other Countries 5000
of whom came th *Gane a Jesu*, in *Dambea*, where the Emperor
then was; looking more like Ghosts than Men, as having nothing
                                                                    left

left but the bare Skin upon their Bones, who were all reliev'd by the Emperor.

As soon as poffible the Patriarch went upon his Vifitation, beginning at the Province of *Ogar*, which is 15 Leagues long, and 10 in Breadth, being high Land, and confequently very cold, but fruitfull in Wheat, and Barley. On the North it is bounded by Mount *Lamal*, on the South it joyns to *Dancaz*, and contain'd above 60 Churches, befides fome Monafteries. This fame Year 1627, the barbarous *Gallas* broke into the Kingdom of *Gojam*, where furprizing the Viceroy *Buco*, with a very fmall Number of Men, they kill'd him ; but *Ras Cella Chriftos* offering them Battle, tho' with much inferior Force to theirs, they fled by Night over the River, and thus the Country was deliver'd of them.

Ogar Pro-vince.

Five Fathers arriv'd in *May* 1628, at *Mazua*, from *Din*, for the Miffion of *Ethiopia*, and were detain'd there four Months by the *Turks*, but at length, after much Trouble, and Charge they got away, and arriv'd fafe at *Fremona.* Soon after *Tecla Guerguis*, Viceroy of *Tygre* broke out into open Rebellion againft the Emperor, declaring for the Faith of *Alexandria.* The Emperor having receiv'd the News, order'd *Keba Chriftos*, who had been before Viceroy of that Kingdom to march againft the Rebel. He drew 500 Targetiers, and 100 Horfe out of the Kingdom of *Gojam*, to which he joyn'd another Body of 1000 Men, call'd *Coapaet*, which fignifies Stars, being the ancienteft, and beft Troops in *Ethiopia*, with thefe he March'd fo indefatigably, that tho' the Rebels were 100 Leagues from him, he came up with them, and put an End to the War in a Month, making a great Slaughter, and taking their Ring-leader the Viceroy, whom the Emperor caus'd to be hang'd in his Camp.

5 other Jefu-its came into Ethiopia.

Rebellion for Religion fup-preff'd.

This Year the Catholick Religion feem'd to be at its higheft Pitch, for there were then in *Ethiopia* 19 Priefts of the Society, befides very many of Natives that had receiv'd Ordination from the Patriarch, and the Number of Converts was incredible. The Foundation of a New Cathedral was now laid, and many other Churches much improv'd ; but amidft this Profperity the Seeds of all following Mifchiefs were fown, *Melcha Chriftos*, a Rank Scifmatick, underhand incenfing the Emperor againft his Brother *Ras Cella Chriftos*, and laying the Foundation of the many Rebellions that afterwards enfu'd.

Converfions, and Plots.

The firft of them was in the Year 1629, by the *Agaus* of *Begameder*, who live among Mountains of a prodigious Height, and abounding in Provifions, againft whom the Emperor march'd in Perfon, with 15000 Foot and 2000 Horfe; but attacking them indifcreetly in

Rebellion and Invafion.

in their Faftneffes, was repuls'd with confiderable Lofs, and fo return'd to *Dancaz*. Thence he fent to call his Brother *Ras
Cella Chriftos*, who was then in Difgrace, yet c me immediately,
and advancing towards the Rebels, defeated fuch as were come
down from the Mountains. This done another Rebellion breaking out at *Amahara*, under one *Laca Mariam*, *Ras* came upon him
fo unexpected, that he and moft of his Men perifh'd by the
Sword, or in the Flight falling off the Precipices. This broke not
the others that were further on the Mountains of *Lafta*, againft
whom the Emperor fent the Viceroy of *Tygre*, *Keba Chriftos*, who
venturing too far, with an inferior Force, was there kil'd by
thofe Peafants, and his fmall Troops utterly routed. Misfortunes
feldom come alone, and fo it hapened now, for much about this
fame Time, the *Gallas* made an Iruption into the Kingdom of
Gojam, where *Tecur Egzi*, Lieutenant to *Ras Cella Chriftos* oppo-
fing them with too fmall a Power, was himfelf fl in, and his
Troops defeated. Thefe two Commanders *Keba Chriftos*, and
Tecur Egzi, were the two Main Pillars of the Catholick Religion,
next to the Emperor, and his Brother *Ras Cella Chriftos*, and they
failing there foon enfu'd an extraordinary Change, fuch as were
of the contrary Opinion about the Emperor, laying hold of al
Opportunities to alienate him from the Religion he had em.
brac'd.

*Accidents
that over
threw Reli-
gion.*
Two Accidents now happned, which contributed very much
to the Revolution that was at hand. The firft that a famous
Monk, who had been for many Years *Ichege*, that is General of
the Religious Order of *Tecla Haymanot*, dy'd obftinate in his
Schifm, and was neverthelefs bury'd before the High-Altar in a
Church; which the Patriarch hearing of, he fent a Reprimand
to the Prieft that Church belong'd to, telling him, The Church
was defil'd by that Body, and unfit for divine Service. Hereupon
the faid Prieft took up the Body, and caft it out, which gave
great Scandal. the People complaining, that the *Portuguefes*, under Colour of propagating the *Roman* Faith, infulted the very
dead, and would not fuffer them to lie in their Graves. The
other Cafe was, that the Patriarch caus'd a Woman convicted
of Witchcraft, and who had confefs'd it herfelf, to be imprifon'd for a few Days; but perceiving it gave a Difguft, he difmifs'd her again, without any farther Punifhment. The Reafon
why this was fo heinoufly refented is becaufe it is a pofitive receiv'd Opinion in *Ethiopia*, that there can be no Contract, or
Familiarity with the Devil, fo as to do Harm to any Perfon by
way of Witchcraft. The original of this Notion proceeded from
very many having been formerly deftroy'd by Poifon, whofe
                                                    Death

Deaths they then attributed to Sorcery, and to obviate that, it was decreed, that no Person should say, there was any *Buda*, that is Witch, or Wizard. To confirm their Opinon they say, that whosoever believes there are any such Sorcerers, must of necessity grant there are two Gods, for none but God has Power to give or take away Life. If we urge Scripture, as *Pharaoh's* Magicians, *Simon Magus*, and the like, they at best grant there were formerly Sorcerers in other Countries, but not in *Ethiopia*.

These were not all the Occasions of Offence. The Emperor *A lewd Prin-*had a lewd Daughter, call'd *Oenguelavit*, who had two Husbands *cess.* living, and yet liv'd in open Adultery with a third Person, which was *Za Christos*, who had been marry'd to another of the Emperor's Daughters. This infamous Woman would have prevail'd with the Patriarch to grant a Dispensation, for her to Marry her Adulterer, which that Prelate refusing, she meditated Revenge, and set all the great Men she had any Influence over against him. Many more Accidents concurr'd, which being improv'd by the Adverse Party occasion'd mighty Troubles, and these at length wrought upon the Emperor, as we shall soon see.

In the Year 1630, the Rebels of *Amara*, sent one with the Title of Viceroy, and a strong Body of Men to possess himself of *Rebels routed.* the Kingdom of *Tygre*. He being wholly intent upon feasting on a Saturday, which those People keep as religiously as Sunday, was surpriz'd, and set upon by the Emperor's Viceroy, and three *Xumos*, or great Men of that Kingdom, who slew 4000 of his Men, and took 32 Pair of Kettle-drums, which show'd how considerable their Victory was, because none are allow'd to use them but Commanders who have at least 400 Men. Another considerable Party of these People was entirely cut off by *Ras Cella Christos* on the Mountains: Notwithstanding this good Service, the Emperor upon the Insinuations of his Adversaries took from his Brother *Ras Cella Christos* the Viceroy-ship of *Gojam*, most of his Lands, and the best Troops he had, leaving him in such a Condition, that he was wholly unable to support his Dignity.

C H A P. X.

A New Bishop comes into Ethiopia ; *Troubles, and
Rebellions ; a great Victory obtain'd by the Emperor ;
he gives Liberty of Conscience, and dies ; the manner of his Funeral ; Cruelty of his Son, and Successor*
Faciladas.

THUS stood the Affairs in *Ethiopia* at the Arrival of *Don
Apollinaris d' Almeyda,* the new Bishop of *Nice,* chosen in
the Place of *Don James Seco,* who, as has been said, dy'd at
Sea. He landed at *Goa* on the 21st of *October* 1629, sail'd thence
again on the 18th of *November,* and reach'd not *Diu* till the
25th of *March.* From *Diu* he set out for *Suaquem,* but was
Turks worst- forc'd into the Island *Camaran,* on the Coast of *Arabia,*
ed in Arabia. whence he sent a good Present to the *Baffa,* to gain his Favour.
That Commander was then far off carrying on the War against
Inam, a powerful King of *Arabia,* who had newly defeated
him with the Slaughter of 12000 *Turks.* That King had not long
before taken the City of *Adem* from the *Turks,* and 3 Years after
this, in 1635 made himself Master of *Moca,* so that those In-
fidels lost all the Kingdom of *Yemen,* which is the best of *Arabia
Felix,* when they had been possess'd of it above 60 Years, and
by that Means enjoy'd a most considerable Trade in the Eastern
Parts, the Commodities of those Countries being brought to
Adem, Moca, Odida, Camarane and *Guida* by Merchants of
Nagana, Por, Mangalor, Diu, Goga, Surtate, Dabul, the *Malabar*
Coast, and *Achem.*

A Bishop gets The *Baffa* was well pleas'd to hear of the Arrival of the
into Ethiopia Bishop, remembering that a few Years before four *Italian* Religious Men of our Order landing at *Alexandria,* had been ransom'd for 6000 Pieces of Eight, notwithstanding they had the
Turks Pass, to go that Way into *Ethiopia.* However being told
by some *Turks,* that these were poor, had a Pass from the *Baffa*
of *'Suaquem,* and their Order very kind to the Merchants trading
to *Diu,* he dismiss'd them, and they sail'd in a small Vessel, on
the 12th of *July* for *Mazua.* In that passage, which is generally
perform'd in three or four Days, they spent 14, were suffer'd to

go

go from *Mazua*, without any Obstruction, and arriv'd at *Fremona*, on the 20*th* of *August*. There they continu'd 3 Months, because it was Winter, and came into the Emperor's Camp on the 16*th* of *December* 1630, had a very honourable Reception, and after a Fortnight's Stay, retir'd to the Patriarch's House at *Depsan*, in the Territory of *Anfras*, four Leagues from *Dancaz*.

The Emperor had lately depriv'd his Brother *Ras Cella Christos* of the Viceroy-ship of *Gojam*, and bestow'd it on his Nephew *Cerca Christos*. This was done through the sinister Insinuations of the Unkles Enemies, and particularly of Prince *Faciladas*, who envy'd *Ras*, and thought he should have a fitter Instrument for his Designs, in his Cousin. This new Viceroy of *Gojam* was now order'd, by the Emperor to go with all his Forces to convoy a Carravan, that was coming out of the Kingdom of *Narea*, and brought him the Gold that Country yearly pays, being in all 1000 *Oqueas*, which amount to 10000 Peices of Eight, and so poor is *Ethiopia*, that they look upon this as a mighty Treasure. *Cerca Christos* in his Way came to a Territory of the *Gafates*, near the *Nile*, which abounding in Grass, was full of those Peoples Cows, there very numerous, and stately, as also those of the Neighbouring *Demotes*. The Viceroy concluded that these Cows would yield him more Gold, than all that amounted to, which came from *Narea*, and which he was not like to be the better for, and therefore drove away so many, that at *Dancaz* it was said they were above 100000. The Emperor was much concern'd at this Insult, and sent him Orders to restore the Cows and deliver himself up Prisoner ; but he had other Thoughts, and accordingly made Proclamation in his Camp, declaring Prince *Faciladas* Emperor, and commanding all Persons to forsake the *Roman* Faith, and embrace that of *Alexandria*. The Prince nevertheless was so far from consenting to this Practice, that he march'd against him with his Army, which the Rebel perceiving he set up an Infant descended from the Royal Family, and at the Perswasion of the Schismatick Monks, murder'd two Persons for Professing the *Roman* Religion. The Emperor was much concern'd at the News of this fresh Rebellion, whilst the other of *Lasta* was still on foot, and therefore being sensible how he had been misled, sent again for his Brother *Ras Cella Christos*, to whom he was reconcil'd, and by his Advice sent more Forces to Prince *Faciladas*, with Orders to march immediately against the Rebel. The Prince did so, taking F. *Francis Marquez* along with him. The Viceroy fled hastily over the *Nile*, but was so closely pursu'd, that coming to a Battel, and being much inferior in Numbers, his Forces were routed, and he flying to a Mountain oblig'd

Rebellion of Cerca Christos.

He is taken and executed.

H h 2   three

three Days after to furrender himfelf to the Prince, by whom he was conducted to the Emperor's Camp, and there executed with feven of his Prime Commanders.

Actions with the Rebels of Lafta.

After this Succefs the Emperor foon flighted his Brother *Ras*, who retir'd to his own Houfe, whilft that Monarch march'd againft the Rebels of *Lafta*. He divided his Army into three Parts, to enter thefe Mountains fo many feveral Ways, which was done fuccefsfully enough, killing many of thofe Peafants, and gaining three of the moft difficult Paffes; yet after all this good Fortune a Party of the Imperialifts being worfted, that Prince was fo much difcourag'd, that fearing lelt his Provifions fhould be cut off, he flunk back to his Court at *Dancaz*, leaving that Kingdom of *Begameder* expos'd to the Fury of thofe Rebels.

Converfions,

Whilft thefe Things were in Agitation, the Patriarch made his Vifitation in the Kingdom of *Dambea*, and the Bifhop continu'd it where he could not come. F. *John Pereyra* was very fuccefsful among the *Damotes*, in his Refidence at *Ligenugus*, and no lefs among the *Zeytes*. Thefe laft formerly dwelt beyond the *Nile*, near the Kingdom of *Narea*; but their Country being conquer'd by the *Gallas*, they with the Emperor's Leave, retir'd over the *Nile*, and fettled in the Territory near *Lamogne*, and *Gombolim*, towards the *Agans*. After their coming thither they were baptiz'd, which was all they had of Chriftians, ftill following their former Barbarous Cuftoms. A *Xume*, or Governour of this Nation coming to the Viceroy's Camp, happen'd to hear the Fathers Doctrine, was much taken with it, and prevail'd with the faid Father to go preach among his People, who approv'd of all he taught them, and only thought it a difficult Matter to quit their many Wives; for among them, he who had 200 Cows might keep two Wives, and fo on one more for every hundred Cows; yet at length they renounc'd that, as well as their other Errors.

Liberty of Confcience.

Still the *Alexandrian* Party was powerful at Court, and never ceas'd to infinuate to the Emperor, that all the Troubles in the State were occafion'd by the Change in Religion, and that he could never be fafe till he allow'd the People more Liberty in that Point. He at length overcome by their Importunity, caus'd Proclamation to be made, that all Men might follow their ancient Cuftoms, provided they were not repugnant to Faith. The Patriarch complain'd, that this Proclamation had either been made otherwife than the Emperor order'd, or mifinterpreted by thofe who heard it, and alledg'd it gave full Liberty to return to the Faith of *Alexandria*, whereupon his Majefty comply'd, to have it publifh'd over again, and explain'd, in the Prefence of one of the

Fa-

Fathers, as the Prelate requir'd. It would be too tedious to mention all the Differences that arose, and Controversies between the Emperor, and the Patriarch, and therefore we must pass most of them by, as not Material, nor Pertinent to our Purpose, that we may entertain the Reader with what is more proper for this Work, those Points, being the Subject of an Ecclesiastical History; tho' at the same Time, we have thought fit to insert so much as may give him a true Idea of the Religion of the *Ethiopians*, and the Motives made Use of for banishing those Fathers, to whom we are at least oblig'd for as much as we know of that Country. Let us now return to the Wars.

The War of *Lasta* grew so troublesom, that the Empero was again forc'd to send for his Brother *Ras Cella Christos* to command; yet notwithstanding all he could alledge oblig'd him to march with only 3000 Men. The Mountaniers beset him with 20000, against whom he defended himself bravely all the Day; as did the Viceroy of *Begameder Kebra Christos*, who lay at a small Distance with his Forces; but their Men forsaking them in the Night, they were both necessitated to save themselves the best they could. This Misfortune so daunted the Emperor, that he retir'd to the Kingdom of *Gojam*; the Rebels, on the other Hand, propos'd to possess themselves of *Dancaz*, his usual Residence, and agreat Part of his Army was ready to forsake him. He being inform'd of the Enemies Resolution, and fearing if they were once Masters of his Court, that all the Empire would declare for them, left his Baggage behind, and march'd directly towards them all Night, with about 20000 Men. On the 27th of *June* 1632, his Scouts brought him Word, that the Rebels were advancing towards him with about 25000 Men, but ill arm'd. At noon the two Armies came in Sight of one another, the Imperial Horse in the Van, being about 2000, Then the Emperor himselfe clapp'd Spurs to his Horse, and being follow'd by the Cavalry obtain'd a compleat Victory the first Charge, the Peasants flying like so many Sheep before the Wolves. The Night coming on fav'd many of those Wretches, tho' others were beaten to Pieces, casting themselves down Precipices, the Pursuit being continu'd till late, when the Imperialists made themselves Masters of their Camp. The next Day the Slain appear'd to be about 8000.

Rebels of Lasta worst the Emperialists

Are themselves routed.

This Slaughter the *Alexandrian* Party took care to represent to the Emperor as caus'd by the Change of Religion, telling him whether he beat, or was beaten, still the loss was his own, since all those were his Subjects, and so tenacious in their Opinions, that he could never hope to enjoy Peace, till the Faith of their Ancestors was restor'd. In fine, the Prince his Son, his Empress,

Alexandian Faith restor'd

and most of the great ones giving him no Respite, he was so perplex'd that he took his Bed, and they having consulted together, gave publick Notice that all Men might return to their former Religion. The Patriarch hereupon made a Speech to the Emperor, blaming his Conduct after so glorious a Victory, and exhorting him not to fall off from what he had so well begun. To which he answer'd, He had done all that was in his Power, till all Men were ready to forsake him; but that still his Design was not to make any Alteration in Matters of Faith but only to allow of Customs, and would do nothing without acquainting his Lordship. Notwithstanding all the Endeavours of the Patriarch, Bishop, and Fathers, at length Proclamation was made in these Words, *Hear, Hear, we first gave you this Faith, believing it was good, but innumerable People have been kill'd about it, with* Elos, Cabrael, Tecla, Guerguis, Cerica Christos, *and now lately with these Peasants; for which Reason we restore you the Faith of your Fore-Fathers. The former Clergy-Men may return to their Churches, put in their Tabotes, and say Masses; and do you rejoice.* This Liberty threw them into many Errors, for being uncertain what to believe, some of their Monks affirm'd, that *Christ* was the Son of God, only by Grace; others that the Divinity dy'd with him on the Cross, but that he had two Divinities, one of which dy'd and the other surviv'd; others said, one Person was compos'd of the two; others confounded the Divine Nature with the Human; and others being quite puzzeled cry'd, *Christ* is true God, and true Man, and it is enough to know that. Nor was there less Division about Consecrating the Cup, some contending it could not be done with any Liquor but Wine, others that it should be with Water discolour'd with six or seven Raisins. At length they agreed it should be done as was us'd at *Alexandria*, and finding no abler Person to enquire of, they put the Question to an *Egyptian* Carpenter, who told them it was always done there in Wine, yet they resolv'd it should be with Water and Raisins. Because the Catholicks us'd to call upon the Name of *Jesus*, it was forbid so to do, under severe Penalties, and some Persons were run through with Javelins for not forbearing.

Errors.

A few Days after, there was a general Circumcision, and then follow'd an universal Baptism, after their former Manner, which being done they concluded themselves free from the Obligation of being ty'd to one Wife, that being one of their Grievances, and publickly declar'd, That for the future they would marry, and unmarry as they pleas'd. Accordingly, *Oengualavit*, the Emperor's eldest Daughter, marry'd her own Brother in Law *Za Christos*, he forsaking his other Wife, and she

he

her first Husband *Bella Christos*, both of them still living. However the Proclamation which allow'd of the *Alexandrian* Religion did not forbid the *Roman*, but gave Liberty of Conscience, so that the Fathers continu'd to say Mass, and Preach in their Churches; but soon after they were expell'd, and another Order publish'd, that all Persons should return to the *Alexandrian* Faith, and that none should for the future dispute with the Patriarch, or Fathers. The Emperor did not long survive this Change. Some would have it that he was poison'd, but it visibly appear'd that he broke his Heart with Grief, and Trouble; being in perpetual Anguish, till he dy'd in *September* 1632, at the Age of 61 Years, whereof he reign'd 24. At his Death, he declar'd he dy'd in the *Roman* Faith, having always kept F. *James de Matos*, and the Patriarch's Chaplain *Emanuel Magro*, about him. His Body was bury'd in the Church of *Ganeta Jesu*, 4 Leagues from *Dancaz*, where he dy'd. The Manner of his Funeral is thus related by F. *Manuel d' Almeyda*, who was present at it.

The Emperor Socinios, or Sultan Segued, dyes.

An *Egyptian* had made him a Bier, with small steps, almost Square, into which they put the Body, wrapp'd up in Buckram, covering it with a large Piece of Tafety, of Several colours. Before this Bier, or Coffin, were carry'd, first the Imperial Colours, being of two Sorts, the one they call *Sandecas*, and are Colour'd, Staves, for Poles, with Bals of Metal gilt on the Top, under which hang their little Banners, about a Span, and a half Square. The others are like Standards, of white Cloth, with some Red Stripes in the middle, neither of them bearing any Arms, or Device. There were five or six of each Sort, all advanc'd, without dragging, or striking them. By them went the Kettle-drums, beating at Times a melancholy Tone; then two or three of the best Horses he us'd to ride, with their richest Furniture; next several Pages, and other Servants, carry'd Parts of his Imperial Robes, and Ornaments, one his Vest, another his Sword, a third his Crown, and so others his Sash, his Beads, his Javelin, his Target, &c. These Things divers Persons took by Turns, showing them to excite Tears, and Sighs, and to this end the Queen herself carry'd his Crown on her Head a considerable Space. This was the Funeral Pomp of the Emperor *Socinios*, otherwise call'd *Sultan Segued*, all the Court, from the highest to the Lowest attending a foot, or a Horseback. The Queen, his Daughters, and all the Ladies then at Court, rode on Mules, their Hair cut off, and a Slip of fine white Cloth two Inches broad ty'd about their Heads, the Ends hanging behind. All the Company was in their Mourning, which is any old Rag, and those who would express

His Funeral.

is

it molt, put on a black Leather, or Cloth, and clip their Heads. There was no Sort of Light carry'd, nor any in the Church, but much weeping, till he was bury'd, and six or seven Monks stood at the Door reading the Psalms. The next Day they all return'd to *Dancax*, and when in Sight of it, drew up again as the Day before, carrying the empty Bier, or Coffin, and by it a Man clad in the Emperors Robes, and the Crown on his Head, riding on a Mule, with a Silk Umbrella over him, in all respects representing the Emperor. Before him w ent another with that Princes Head-piece, and Javelin, on his best Horse, with the richest Accoutrements. Near *Dancax* stood four or five Bodies of Troops, and other Persons belonging to the Court, who all came out to meet the Company, crying as loud as they could.

Facilladas the new Emperor. In this Manner they went all together, and with them F. *James de Mattos*, and *F. Emanuel de Almeyda*, who gives this Relation, to the Palace Gate, where they alighted, and the chief of them went into a large Tent, where the new King was, with some Noblemen, and then began a new Lamentation, which lasted near two Hours. The Fathers went home, and when the weeping was over, return'd to kiss the Kings Hand, condoling with him for his Fathers Death, and then congratulating his Succession to the Crown.

Murders 24 of his Brothers. The new Emperor *Facilladas* had 24 Brothers, all whom he afterwards inhumanly put to Death, only out of *Turkish* Policy, to secure the Crown upon his own Head, a Barbarity scarce to be paralell'd in History ; and then fell to persecuting all those that profess'd the Catholick Faith, like another *Dioclesian*.

CHAP.

C H A P.   XI.

Persecution of the Catholicks. The Patriarch, and Fathers banish'd to Fremona. *Four of the Latter sent away to* Goa. *Their Journey, and Voyage, and a particular Descripion of the City of* Adem.

FACILADAS being rais'd to the Throne, as has been seen in the last Chapter, took the Name of *Sultan Segued*, as his Father had done before him, and began to exercise much Cruelty towards the Catholiks, beginning with his own Unkle *Ras Cella Christos*, whom he depriv'd of all his Lands and Dignities, and sent him banish'd in Chains to *Cemen*, where he liv'd like a common Criminal, under a Guard. Next he order'd F. *James d' Mattos*, and F. *Joseph Giroco* to depart *Dancaz*, and to repair to *Ganeta Jesu*, where they had not been long, before they were with four others turn'd out, and sent to *Gorgorra*, and four of these again remov'd to *Colléla*, in which twelve of them liv'd some Time very hardly. The Patriarch, and Bishop had their Lands taken away, and scarce as much allow'd to Maintain them, and three Fathers, as was requisite for a Poor Vicar. The Fathers at *Fremona* were as hardly us'd by the Viceroy, and had been all murder'd by the Soldiers, but that the *Portuguefes* assembled, and defended themselves in that Sort of fortify'd Place. All others who profess'd the Catholick Faith, from the Emperor's own Cousin Germains so the Meanest, were stripp'd of what they had, and left to beg their Bread; and then the Emperor sent Orders to the Patriarch, and Bishop to deliver up all the Arms they had, and depart immediately to *Fremona*, a new *Abuna* being come into the Camp from the Kingdom of *Narea*, who said he would not give Ordination, till the Patriarch, and Fathers were either kill'd, or banish'd. After several Messages to and fro, the Arms were deliver'd, and the Fathers all turn'd out of their Residences, with Orders to repair to *Fremona*.

They set out accordingly, with one *Paul*, the Emperor's own Nephew, whom he had sent to guard them through the Deserts, which are full of Robbers; but he and his Men did what they were sent to prevent, plundering a great Part of the Baggage, and would have taken all, had not the *Portuguefes*, who

Faciladas call'd Sultan Segued.

Perfecution.

Jefuits banish'd and robb'd.

follow'd

follow'd the Patriarch defended it, and kill'd some of his Men. Yet would not this have sav'd the small remainder of their Goods, or even their Lives, had they not been afterwards faithfully affisted by *Tecla Salus*, and *Asma Guerguis*, two Commanders appointed to conduct them, after they were out of *Paul's* Liberties. In their way they pass'd one Brook twelve Time, every one of them in great Danger of their Lives, from those who were to guard them, who finally resolv'd to murder them all, and divide their Spoil, after the last Passage, in a small Plain, where they were to rest that Night. When they had pass'd the 11*th* Time, *Tecla Salus*, who had Intelligence of the wicked Design by his Spies, struck out of the Way, and led all the Company up a high Mountain, before they were discover'd by their Robbers, who bit their Fingers to be thus disappointed of their Prey. However they enclos'd the Mountain hoping to pick up some of the Mules, or Oxen, one of which last fell into their Hands loaded with Church-stuff, and *Paul* being charg'd with consenting to the Robbery then plainly told them, That what had hapned was nothing to what they were to expect.

The way lay'd.

The Mountain they were on had two Ways up to it, one to the North, and the other to the South. *Asma Guerguis* pitch'd his Tent on that to the Northward, which is the easiest, and next to *Ambo*, where the Robbers, expected us, our Men pitching theirs next him. On the South Pass, being at some Distance *Tecla Salus* lay, and the Fathers on the Top. The next Morning, both the Robbers, and *Paul's* Men began to ascend the Mountain, but retir'd several Times, upon only presenting one Musket we had, and fled in great Disorder, when it was fir'd. Nevertheless they ventur'd to return again, and found such a hot Reception, the very Women among us fighting like good Soldiers, that they immediately turn'd their Backs, and

Arrive safe at Fremona.

were pursu'd down to the very brook, whence they did not offer to return any more. A sufficient Number of the Troops of *Tecla Salus*, and *Asma Guerguis* joyning the Fathers the Day after, they proceeded on their Journey in Safety, and came to *Fremona* on the 24*th* of *April* 1633.

4 Sent away before.

Here they suffer'd much Want, most of their Lands being taken from them, besides that they hourly expected to be sent away, and deliver'd up to the *Turks* upon the Sea Coast, for which Reason it was resolv'd to send four Fathers before, to lessen the Expence, and procure some Relief. One of these four was F. *Emanuel d'Almeyda*, who gives an Account of their Journey, and Voyage as follows. At the End of *April* 1633 there were of us, at *Fremona*, 18 Fathers, one lay Brother, and two Prelates, being the Patriarch, and the Bishop, where it was agreed that some of

us

us fhould go over to *India*, for Relief in our Diftrefs, and accordingly my felf and three others were pitch'd upon. The Undertaking was Difficult, becaufe if we offer'd to go the direct Road, we fhould certainly be ftopp'd by the Emperor's Officers, as not having his Pafs. We therefore agreed, by the Interpofition of a Lady, call'd *Oziero*, who ftill preferv'd her Affection towards us, that a *Xumo*, or Lord of *Bur*, whofe Name was *Xiay*, fhould fecure our Paffage through his Lands, and guard us to *Arquico.* It was a great Compafs about, and the *They come to* Woods and Mountains full of Lions, Tigers, and more fierce, *the Coaft.* and cruel *Moors*, from whom God protected us, gaining the Favour of the *Xumo*, who guarded us, with Gifts, and Prefents, out of that little we had. We came to the Coaft near *Defalo,* ten Leagues from *Mazua*, which was the worft of all our Way, for the Sun fcorch'd on thofe Sands, like Fire, fo that the Ground we lay on was as hot, as a Hearth, or Oven, and the Heat was no lefs violent at *Mazua*, when we came thither, which was about the middle of *July.* Before our Departure from *Fremona*, we had by Means of fome *Baneans* procur'd a Pafs from the *Baffa* of *Suaqnem*, for 400 Pieces of Eight. That *Baffa* dying in this Interval of Time, his Succeffor exacted as much more for confirming of our Pafs, and his Deputy he newly fent to govern at *Mazua*, and *Arquico* oblig'd us to pay 600 more to allow us to depart, which Sum we were oblig'd to borrow of the *Baneans* to repay them at *Diu.* At length we imbark'd on a fmall Veffel for *Adem*, not being permitted to go to *Cayxem*, four Fathers of the Society, two Priefts born in *India*, and *Sail for In-* fourteen *Abyffine* Servants, who would go with us. We fet *dia.* fail on the 19*th* of *Auguft*, and the next Day came upon the Ifland *Dalec*, a low Land, poor, and deftitute of all Neceffaries; but clofe by it there is a Pearl Fifhery, tho' not confiderable, all which the *Baffa* of *Suaquem* takes to himfelf, having Officers there on the fifhing Days. Having water'd there, we held on our Courfe along the Coaft of *Dancali*, fail'd through the Mouth of the *Red Sea* on the 29*th* of *Auguft*, and holding on our Courfe all Night, mifs'd the Flats, lying in that Part, and came to *Adem Arrive at* on the 30*th*, but the Wind growing fcant got not in, till the next *Adem.* Day, after a ftrong Guft had carry'd away our Maft. It was known in the City, who we were by Letters, fent in, the Day before by an *Almadie*, or Boat, and *Xarif Abdela* the Governour of the City expected fome mighty Wedges of *Ethiopian* Gold from us.

Being landed they carry'd us before the Governour, who fent *Detain'd and* us to the *Xabander*, and order'd all we had fhould be carry'd to *cruelly us'd* the Cuftom Houfe. The *Amir*, or Lord of the City, being then *there.* at *Rara* five or fix Leagues from *Adem*, and expecting to get some mighty Treasure, order'd us, and all we had to be carry'd to him, which was accordingly done, and finding nothing but our Bedding, Bisket, and some inconfiderable, necessaries, kept us there several Days Prisoners, with great Threats in case we did not turn *Mahometans*, and tho' he could not prevail on us, he succeeded better with the poor *Abyssines*, who overcome with ill Usage, comply'd, and embrac'd his Sect. At length being inform'd, that the *Baneans* would lend us much Money, because we were very rich in *India*, he sent us back to *Adem*, when the Ships were ready to sail for *Diu*, but would not suffer us to depart that Season, that he might have more Time to treat of our Ransome.

Adem described.

Since we are come to *Adem*, a Place famous in the Histories of *India*, it will be proper to give a short Account of the Condition we found it in. This City is in *Arabia Felix*, and in twelve Degrees of North Latitude, about 20 Leagues without the Mouth of the *Red Sea*, seated at the Foot of high Mountains, which are the Land Marks of Necessity to be observ'd by all the *India* Ships bound for the *Red Sea*, which Generally first make Cape *Guardafuy* in *Africk*, and thence stand over for the Mountains of *Adem*, and as soon as discover'd, being sure of their Course, they steer directly for the Streight of *Babelmandel*, which they generally Pass the same, or the next Day. Formerly most Ships resorted to *Adem*, without entring the *Red Sea*, because all the *Arabian* Merchants met there, with the Wealth of their several Provinces, and carry'd thence the Commodities of *India* to several Fairs, frequented by Merchants of *Damascus*, and all Parts of the lesser *Asia*, who convey'd them along the *Mediterranean* into *Europe*. This Trade enrich'd *Adem*, and made it once so famous, as to vie with the three principal Eastern Marts of *Goa Ormuz*, and *Malaca*.

How it dealt'd.

After the *Turks* made themselves Masters of the Ports in the *Red Sea*, and of the Kingdom of *Yemen*, which is the best Part of *Arabia Felix*, taking the City *Adem*, that Part declin'd, by Reason of the Wrongs the Governours offer'd to Merchants trading thither; who being better treated at *Moca*, *Odida*, *Camarane*, *Gida*, *Suaquem*, and *Mazua*, within the Red Sea, went on thither, leaving *Adem*, which of a rich, and very propulous City, came to be so poor, and thinly inhabited, that we saw most, and those the best Structures in it gone to Ruin, so that scarce one in 15 was standing.

The

The *Arabs* had retaken this City from the *Turks*, five or six *Taken by the* Years before we came to it, having it betray'd to them by the *Arabs.* Guards, who open'd the Gates on the Land Side to them, in the Night, and they entring eafily put to the Sword all the Garifon, being as is faid, about five, or 600 Men, only fuch efcaping as got out of the Sea Gate, into fome Veffels they found there, and fo to *Moca.* At the fame Time the King of *Yemen* obtain'd great Victories over the *Turks*, driving them almoft out of all his Kingdom, and taking all the Inland Cities ; fo that the prime Men being kill'd in feveral Actions, the Towns on the Sea Coaft, believing they could not be long defended, offer'd many Wrongs to the Merchants of *India* trading to them, whereas on the contrary, the *Amir* of *Adem*, being defirous to draw many Ships to his Port, began to fhow them much Favour. Thus *Adem* began again to improve, and we found 18 Ships in the Habour, come that Year from feveral Parts of *India*, richly laden. But it was not long fo fortunate, for the King of *Yemen* ftill preffing upon the *Turks*, two Years after made himfelf Mafter of the Ports in the Red *Sea*, as *Moca*, *Odida*, and *Camarane* and he being ftill more kind to the *India* Merchants, than thofe of *Adem*, he drew almoft all the Trade to himfelf, very few reforting to *Adem*, which foon funk again.

Its Situation is thus, Certain high Clifts, and Headlands run *Its Situation* out from the Land, and Jutting into the Sea, ftretch forth one Arm to the Eaftward, and another to the Weftward for about a League. Thefe Arms confift of very lofty, Craggy Rocks, and Mountains. The Sea runs in on both Sides Eaft, and Weft, forming two large Bays between thofe Promontories, and the Main Land. That to the Weftward is longeft, but fhallow. The other oppofite to the Eaftward, has Water enough for many Ships to Anchor clofe by the Shore, and is fhelter'd from almoft all Winds ; becaufe near the Arm form'd by the Mountains on that Side, there is a high Clift, divided from it by a fmall Channel, and lying to the Eaftward ; breaks off the Sea from the Ships in the Harbour. At the Foot of thefe Mountains is a Spot of Ground, almoft round, about a Falconet Shot Diameter, the bury'd under thofe Hills, like a Kettle. There ftands the City, fo enclos'd, that it needs no Wall, except only one fmall Part, next the Bay, where the Ships Anchor. The Houfes are of Stone, and Clay, as far as the fecond Story ; fuch as are higher being of Brick from thence upwards, all flat roof'd, with many fmall Windows, and wooden Lattices. They are not ill built, and tho' not fo ftrong, for want of Lime, yet they are out of Danger, becaufe it never rains there, all the Year Round, and tho' the Sky is often clouded, never any thing fals above a fmall Dew.

This

Gates &c.   This Furnace, for so we may call it, by reason of the Vehement Scorching of the reflected Sun Beams, is as close as can be imagin'd having but two Gates, or Avenues. The one leads to the Shore, which contains a very small Compass, being terminated by the Rocks of the Mountains enclosing the City, which is in the Shape of a Bow full Bent, the Shore being the String, holding at the Ends of the said Bow, next the swelling Billows, that continually beat upon those Rocks. On the other Side, the Way leads to the Continent, between Rocks, and seems to be hew'd out by Hand, being of prodigious Height, and for above 100 Fathom in Length, in which Space there are three Gates, one behind another, open'd, and shut, at Night and Morning, all of very thick Planks cover'd with Iron Plates, and 12, or 14 Yards High, with *Guerites* over them, on Arches lying a cross the Road, from one Rock to the other. These Gates are continually guarded by above 100 Soldiers, and no Man can go out, without carrying the *Ducam's* Ticket on his Arm.

Strength.   The Mountains, and Precipices on them are a Fortification to the greatest Part of the City they surround. Next the Shore it has a weak Piece of Wall, as being built with Stone, and Clay, and plaister'd without; but the Headland, I said, lies to the Eastward of the Bay, serves instead of a Fort, being very high, and commanding all about, and the Chanel lies very close to the Rocks, of the said Head-land. On the Point of it is a Battery, level with the Water with some Canon on it, which can sink any Enemies Ship that shall come to Anchor there, but a few Men may easily make themselves Masters of it.

Fertility.   The Land about *Adem* is fruitful, where we saw many Fields of Millet, the Reed whereof was as tall, and thick as a Pike-staff, and the Ear so large and full that 10, or 12 would fill a Peck, and what is still more wonderful is, that one and the same Seed Yields three Crops, for it runs up, and is ripe in three Months, when they cut the Reed about a Span, or a Span and a Half from the Ground, and the Stalk left sprouts up again and comes to Maturity in three Months, which being cut again grows up again a third Time, with only this Difference, that tho' the Reeds are still alike, the Ear is fuller the first Time, than the other two following; but the Reed is almost as good as the Grain, being excellent Food for Horses, Camels, and all Sorts of Cattel.

A Camban friend to the Jesuits.   In this Place we continu'd six Months, and suffer'd enough, which had been worse, but that some of the *Bancans* reliev'd us with Alms, and Mony Lent; but we chiefly owe our Lives to a Native of *Cambaya*, whose Name was *Emsarg esar*, and he had

been

been several Years *Xabander*, well belov'd by all Men for his good Temper, and Generosity, besides that he was familiar with the prime *Xarifs*. This Man gave them so good an Account of us, that they began to favour our Pretensions, disliking the *Amirs* scurvy Behaviour towards us, and so far supporting our Intrest, that all Men show'd us Respect, and good Will. An Accident hapen'd at this Time, which indanger'd our Liberty, and even our Lives, and was thus. The *Amir* returning to *Adem*, with his whole Court, several of the *Abyssines* they had taken from us, return'd with their Masters. These now finding an Opportunity, some of them came to confess to us, and be reconcil'd to God, repenting the Sin they had committed, in professing *Mahometanism* with their Mouths, tho' they had never receiv'd it in their Hearts, or sincerely renounc'd *Chrif*, whose Faith they promis'd for the future openly to profess, tho' it cost them their Lives. One of these, to secure his Religion, and get rid of his Master, who was the *Amir*'s Son, and never ceas'd to importune him to repair to the *Mosques*, fled to a Sanctuary, the Slaves in *Adem* us'd to have Recourse to when oppress'd by their Masters ; and it is the Custom there, that the Master can not force them thence, but is oblig'd to sell them to another. The *Amir*'s Son, being much concern'd at it, complain'd to his Father, who be- *They are ba-* lieving that had been done by our Advice, grew inrag'd at us, *nish'd.* and order'd we should depart *Adem*, and be carry'd in Banishment to *Canfar*, a very unhealthy Place, where it would be a wonder if we escap'd with our Lives. Our *Banean* Friend took the Business in Hand, and spoke to the *Xarif Abdela*, Goverour of *Adem*, who obtain'd of the *Amir*, that we should be banish'd to a better Territory, call'd *Lage* ; where we suffer'd much, during our 20 Days Stay, till the *Amir* was somewhat mollify'd.

At length he came to this Resolution, to demand 1200 Pieces *Embark for* of Eight for our Ransom, which some *Baneans* lent us, to be re- *Diu.* paid at *Diu*, with another Sum borrow'd for our Expence in that Country, and the Ransom of four or five *Abyssines*, of those they had taken from us. The little *Monson* coming on, which is about the Beginning of *March*, three Fathers of us embark'd on a Ship belonging to *Diu*, and the 4th, with two of the Patriarch's Chaplains on a small Coasting Vessel of *Mascate*, hoping to get to *Diu* by the End of *April*, and thence to *Goa*, before the Winter. We had a troublesom Voyage, because that *Monson* is very weak, and the Winds scant. Our Ship sail'd out of the Harbour the next Day, with a fair Wind. The other Vessel, not being then quite ready, continu'd there 40 Days, for Want of Wind

Wind to carry her out, all which Time the Paſſengers continu'd
abroad, for Fear of being ſtopp'd again, if they went aſhore.
The 40 Days being expir'd, they ſet Sail, and arriv'd at *Maſcate*,
where they were forc'd to Winter, and got to *Goa* with the
September Monſon.

Our Voyage prov'd no better, tho' we left *Adem* ſooner, the
Winds proving ſo contrary, that we were two Months, and a
half ſailing to *Caixem*, where we winter'd, and came to *Dia* a-
bout the Middle of *September*, F. *Joſeph Giroco* dying by the Way.
Thus far F. *Emannel d' Almeyda.*

C H A P. XII.

*The Patriarch, and Fathers diſpers'd. Moſt of them de-
liver'd to the* Turks, *who put them to Ranſom.
Some paſs over to* Goa. *One ſent to* Lisbon. *Plague,
Famine, and War in* Ethiopia.

Six Jeſuits *go towards the Sea.*

THE new *Abuna*, and his Followers could never be ſatisfy'd,
as long as the Patriarch, and Fathers were in *Ethiopia*, and
accordingly ceas'd not preſſing the Emperor, till at the Beginning
of the Summer, he ſent an *Azage*, with Orders to deliver them to
the *Turks* at *Maxua*. This Officer being well affected towards
them, was very favourable, ſo that they were allow'd to write to the
Emperor, tho' without Hopes of altering his Reſolution, but
only to gain Time. News being brought, that the Emperor was
ſending a ſecond Meſſenger to remove them, the firſt fearing he
ſhould be blam'd for his Remiſſneſs, preſs'd to carry them away
immediately; but the Patriarch poſitively declaring he would
not ſtir, unleſs dragg'd away by Force, and he having no ſuch
Orders, nothing was done at that Time However, for Fear
of exaſperating the Emperor too much, the Biſhop went away,
with ſix of the Fathers to the Province of *Siraoe*, which is nearer
the Sea, where they ſuffer'd very much.

The

The Patriarch, foon after, underftanding, that another Mef- *Others with* fenger was coming to drag them away by Force, privately ne- *draw to a* gotiated with *Joannes Akay*, the *Babar-Nagays*, or Governour of *Mountain.* the Sea Coaft, that he fhould take them all into his Protection, which he confenting to, and fending a Number of arm'd Men to conduct them, they made their Efcape by Night, and came fafe to him. He receiv'd them in friendly Manner, as he did a Prefent they gave him, of the fmall remains of their Shipwrack, and fent them to an *Amba*, or *Ethiopian* Fortrefs, being an high upright Mountain on all Sides, with only two fteep, and difficult Avenues to it, on the Top whereof was a Plain, containing a fmall Village of Thatch'd Houfes, and Cottages, more like Dens of wild Beafts, than Habitations of Men. Here was little Water, and lefs Provifion, the Land being barren, and affording little but fome Millet, and a few Lentiles.

The Bifhop, and his Companions had Notice fent them, to get away the fame Night the Patriarch had fled, but they were fo clofely obferv'd, that it was impracticable ; for one of them *The reft con-* happening only to look abroad a little, it was interpreted that he *fin'd.* intended to fly, and had like to be kill'd, being much hurt. The Lord of thofe Parts being acquainted, that they had attempted to efcape, fent for, and confin'd them to a Shed there was in the midft of his Village, for Cattel ; but thinking that too good a Lodging, at his Departure the next Day, order'd them to be remov'd to a worfe. Being on the Way, F. *Jerome Lobo* went before to beg of the faid Lord, that they might continue in their firft Apartment, but was fain to wait half a Day, before he could fpeak to him, he being then very bufie about difcovering a mighty Treafure his Monks told him lay under a vaft Stone, which when turn'd up, they affur'd him a great Stream of Gold would run out, till it met with another of *Fabulous No-* Water, that ran about half a League from it. The Fable of this *tion of hidden* Treafure was very ancient, and imported, that the faid Treafure *Treafure.* had been always guarded by a very dreadful Devil, who as foon as any dug down to a certain Hole, flew out from under the Stone, in fuch a terrible Storm of Wind, that the Searchers ran away with all Speed, curfing the Devil, and his Treafure. But now an old, blind, praying Monk affur'd them, that the faid ill condition'd Devil was newly dead, and had left only one Son, who was then very far off, and being lame could not come in hafte, and that there was none at that Time but a blind Daughter of his, who fince fhe could not fee, minded nothing, and therefore that was the Day to make their Fortune. This was the Bufinefs that employ'd the *Xumo*, when F. *Lobo* came

K k   to

to him, who tells us in his Commentaries, that 300 Men were at Work, digging, and labouring to remove the Stone ; besides abundance of Monks, and among them the blind one praying heartily, and they had sacrific'd a Black Cow, that the dead Devil might not come to life again. But after all their Toil, and praying, when the Stone was remov'd they had nothing but Weariness for their Pains.

The *Xumo* was much out of Humour, but being told that the Father brought him a present of Value, he admitted him, and granted his Request that they should return to their first Lodging, where the next Day, he search'd their Baggage, and accepted of what they gave him, wondering at their Poverty. Here they receiv'd Advice from the Patriarch, that the Viceroy was coming to *Tygre*, with Orders to carry them down to the Sea, and F. *Lobo*'s Head to Court, fearing, that if he went to *India*,

They escape. he would cause a great Fleet to be sent against *Ethiopia*. This Advice being brought on *Low* Sunday, which the *Abyssines* celebrate with much eating and drinking, the Fathers took the Opportunity of their Guards being dead asleep to give them the Slip, travelling all Night, and lying hid all Day, with much Danger of wild Beasts, but could not escape the Hands of the Lord of a Village, who would have stripp'd them of their very Cloaths, as having nothing else at that time, but that they gave him Security, he should have three Ounces of Gold, as soon as they came to the Place, where the Patriarch was.

The Emperor understanding that the Patriarch, and Fathers were under the Protection of *Joannes Akay*, sent the Viceroy of *Tygre*, to offer him the Command of *Bahar-Nagays*, or Governour of the Coast, and other great Advantages, if he would deliver them up to him, or at least to the *Turks* at *Mazua*. He could not withstand this Temptation, and therefore chose to put them into the Hands of the *Turks*. They being inform'd of this Design contriv'd to divide themselves ; and one *Cafla Mariam*, a powerful Man in the Territory of *Bur*, offering to se-

4 Jesuits pro- cure two on his Lands, the Bishop, and F. *Hyacinth Francis*
tected by E- went to him ; as did the Fathers *Lewis Cardeyra*, and *Bruno*
thiopians. *Bruni*, to one *Cantibazara Joannes* an old Friend of theirs in the same Province. There was no time to dispose of any more, for their Protector *Joannes* soon sent them word, that he would obey the Emperor's Orders, yet not in delivering them up to him ; but would conduct them to *Mazua*, and desire the *Turks* to grant them free Passage ; and accordingly came with the *Azage Ziero*, who deliver'd the Patriarch a Letter from the Emperor, complaining that he had not obey'd him, in departing

his

his Dominions, and threatning him, if he perfifted in his Re- *Two deli-* solution of staying. In fine they were conducted within a Days *ver'd to the* Journey, and a half of *Mazua*, and there deliver'd to a *Turkish* Turks. Officer, who was waiting for them with about 80 Musketiers, and receiv'd them with much Civility, which he continu'd to *Arquico*, where they arriv'd on the 20*th* of *May* 1634. Only the Fathers *Francis Rodrigues*, and *John Pereyra* were permitted by *Joannes Akay*, before the Delivery to stay behind in Disguize, to affift the many *Portuguefes* there were within his Diftrict in *Tygre*.

Mazua as has been said, is a small, flat, and open Ifland, *Mazua, and* without any Fortification, divided from the Continent of *Ethi-* Arquico *def-* *opia* by a Channel about a Musket Shot over. There is never a *crib'd.* fresh Water Spring in it, nor any but what is gather'd in Cifterns, when it rains, which not being fufficient to ferve the Inhabitants, they have it daily brought from certain Wells, on the Continent, near the Sea, and a League and a half from the Ifland, towards the Mouth of the Red Sea. Near thefe Wells is the Town we call *Arquico*. The People of *Mazua* not being able to fubfift without Water, it is requifite for them to be Mafters of *Arquica*, on Account of the Wells, and therefore the *Turks* have there erected a Fort, with four Baftions, and Curtains, but weak, and low, and all the Work feems to be of Stone and Clay, yet fuppofing it were of Lime and Stone, two Hours Battery would lay it level with the Ground, by reafon of its Thinnefs. On the Baftions, there are fome Falconets, and Drakes, fufficient to fright the Natives; but not any that underftand the Art of War. The Governour, whom the *Turks* call *Quequea*, has his Houfe adjoyning to the Fort ; and about it is a Wall of dry Stone, within which the Garrifon Soldiers live, being a-bout 60, or 80 white *Turks*, and as many *Arabs*, and Mungrels.

As foon as the Fathers enter'd this Enclofure, they were re-ceiv'd with Shouts of the Boys, and the reft of the People flock'd to fee them, both on Account of their being Strangers, and be-caufe they thought every one of them was loaded with Gold, and a mighty Treafure came with them to *Arquico*. Thofe who *Ufage of the* were not afoot alighted at the *Quequea's* Door, and went up Jefuits *at* immediately to falute him. He receiv'd them in a Room cover'd Arquico, with Carpets, fitting on a Step rais'd above the reft, and lean-ing on a Cufhion of half Brocade of *Mecca*, being himfelf a Man of a middle Stature, pretty grofs, with a long Beard, a grave Countenance, a Fierce Afpect, and worfe in Conditions, as the Fathers found by Experience. His Veft was of fine Cloath, and on his Head a large Turbant of very fine Muflin.

They

They all came in barefoot, as is the Cuſtom, and touching the Points of his Fingers kiſs'd their own Hands. He bid them ſit down on the Carpet, enquir'd about their Journey, and gave fair Words, promiſing free Paſſage for *India*. All theſe Ceremonies tended to draw from them thoſe mighty Heaps of Gold, Fame had ſpread abroad, they brought out of *Ethiopia*, and accordingly he had order'd his Guards to ſearch their Goods, whilſt he held them in Diſcourſe. They did ſo, and after all their Labour, found nothing but two Silver Chalices. The Governour being told, what had appear'd, gave Directions, they ſhould be ſtrictly ſearch'd, in the next Room, and after all nothing appear'd, but two little gilt Croſſes, ſuch as Prelates uſe to wear, and a few Royals in a Purſe, which would keep them but a very few Days with good Husbandry. This being too little to ſatisfy the Avarice of the *Turk*, he ſent them away to the *Xabandar*'s Houſe, taking for himſelf four *Abyſſine* Boys, which he ſaid fell to his Share. One of them had been Servant to a Monk, who having been poſſeſs'd of many Lands, forſook all to follow the Patriarch. This Monk, being concern'd for the Loſs of the Child, which would be bred a *Mahometan*, and not acquainted with the Barbarity of thoſe People, went indiſcreetly to the *Quequea*, and told him, That Boy was born free, and could not be made a Slave. The *Turk* who was enrag'd to be diſappointed of his conceited Treaſure, drew his Scymeter and would have cut him in Pieces, had not the Standers by mollify'd him, excuſing the Monk's Ignorance. However he caus'd him to be ſo cruelly baſtinado'd, that it had like to coſt him his Life.

Barbarity of a Turk.

That afternoon the Patriarch, and Fathers were hurry'd over to *Mazua*, where the *Amim*, or Chief of the Cuſtom-Houſe, being a better natur'd Man, receiv'd them courteouſly, and ſent them to the Lodgings the *Baneans* had provided. Here they borrow'd 600 Pieces of Eight of the ſaid *Baneans*, which they preſented to the *Quequea*, who obliged them to give him 60 more, to ranſome a *Portugueſe* Boy he would have taken away. They continu'd here above a Month, till the *Baſſa* of *Suaquem* ſent for them, and accordingly they imbark'd on the 24th of *June*, on two ſmall Veſſels, with a Guard of *Turks*, and ſpent 45 Days in their Paſſage, which is generally made in Eight. The firſt welcome they receiv'd at *Suaquem*, was being told, that the *Baſſa* would take no Ranſom for them, being reſolv'd to rid the World of them. However being inform'd, he would quite loſe the Trade of *Diu*, if he murder'd them, he demanded 30000 Pieces of Eight for their Ranſome, which they not being able to pay,

He ſends the Jeſuits to Suaquem.

pay, he after several Abatements came to 4000, which were bor-*They are* row'd, and they provided for their Voyage. When they were *ransom'd for* ready to imbark, he sent Word that only seven should go to *Diu,* 4000 *Pieces* and the Patriarch, with the rest remain there till the next Year, *of Eight.* which was accordingly done.

The Ship set sail on the 26*th* of *August* 1634, and after 52 Days, arriv'd at *Diu,* whence some of them made the best of *Arrive at* their Way to *Goa,* to treat about the Patriarch's Ransome, and *Goa.* making some Provision for *Ethiopia.* They propos'd to the Viceroy *Don Michael de Noronha,* Count *de Linhares,* to send 400 *Portu-guefes,* who would easily make themselves Masters of *Suaquem, Mazua,* and *Arquico,* which last they should Garrison, and it would be a Curb upon both *Turks,* and *Abyssines,* whence the Catholicks in those Parts might be protected, and as to Tempo-rals the Custom-House of *Mazua* was worth 1000 Pieces of Eight a Month, besides that from *Ethiopia* might be had much Wax, *F. Lobo im-* Brimstone abundance, of Hides, and Gold ; but all these Pro-*barks for* jects came to nothing, and therefore *F. Jerom Lobo* was sent into *Lisbon.* *Europe* to negotiate at *Madrid,* and *Rome.* The Ship which car-ry'd him being one of the finest that was ever built in *Portugal,* made so much Water, that they were forc'd to run her aground at *Terra-do-Natal,* on the South Coast of *Africk,* beyond the Cape of *Good Hope,* where whilst they were endeavouring to save what they could ashore, she took Fire, and was consum'd.

The Father, and his Companions remain'd on that desert *Left seven* Shore, seven Months, during all which time, none of them *Months on* dy'd, or was sick, so healthy is that Air. They all labour'd *the Coast of* hard to build two small Vessels, with what Timber the Sea *Africk.* threw up, and what they found ashore, each of them 45 foot Long, about twelve in Breadth, and six in Depth, to attempt in them to weather the Cape of Good Hope. 263 Men embark'd on those two inconsiderable Vessels, which met with such Storms, that one of them was soon forc'd ashore again in the some Place, whence it set out. The other, which they call'd *Nossa Senhora da Natividade,* or Our Lady of the Nativity, in which the Father was, after immense Dangers and Sufferings, arriv'd safe at *Angola,* on the 5th of *March* 1636. Thence the *Gets to An-* Father, embarking on another Ship, sail'd over to *Cartagena* in *gola, thence to* *America,* and came thence in a Galeon to *Cadiz,* whence he went *Lisbon and* by Land to *Lisbon,* then to *Madrid,* and *Rome,* in all which *back to Goa.* Places he obtain'd nothing, but fair Words and Promises, with which he return'd to *Goa* in 1640.

In

Ethiopia de-　In the mean while *Ethiopia* groan'd under all the Calamities
stroy'd by the　it had pretended to dread, on account of Entertaining the Fa-
Rebels and　thers, for notwithstanding their Banishment, the Peasants of
Gallas.　*Lasta*, who before pleaded Religion to countenance their Rebellion, grew more formidable, infomuch that they ravag'd
the greatest Part of the Kingdoms of *Bagameder*, and *Tygre*, as
far as the high Mountains of *Cemen*. The *Gallas* pierc'd into the
Heart of the Kingdom of *Gojam*, plundering, and driving away the
Cattel, under the Conduct of *Chyrilos*, Son to *Ras Cella Christos*,
to revenge the wrongs offer'd to his Father, and defended himself
from being compell'd to renounce his Religion. *Emana Christos*,
Son-in-Law to the same *Ras*, who then Govern'd in *Narea*,
revolted, and refus'd to pay the usual Tribute to the Emperor.
At the same Time, the Plague rag'd in the Kingdom of *Dambea*,
so that the Emperor was forc'd to remove his Court from *Dan-
Plagues Lo-　caz*, to *Lybo*, whither it pursu'd him, destroying several of his
custs, and　Servants, and obliging him to fly thence. Nor did it stop there,
Famine.　but spred into the Province of *Ogara*, the High Mountains of
Cemen, that of *Lamalmon*, and over the Plains of *Tygre*. To
compleat the Miseries of those wretch'd People, such immense
Multitudes of Locusts spread over the Provinces, as devour'd
all the Product of the Earth, which was follow'd by so de-
structive a Famine, as swept away the greatest Part of the Natives the Pestilence had spar'd.

CHAP

C H A P. XIII.

Perfecution and Slaughter in Ethiopia *for Religion.
Capucins fent thither murder'd. The* Gallas *ravage the Kingdom of* Tygre. *A fhort Account
of* Moca, *and the Conclufion of this Work.*

THE Bifhop, and Fathers that remain'd in *Etibiopia*, could
not be fo clofe conceal'd, but that the Emperor had Notice
of it, and fent ftrict Orders to the Viceroy of *Tygre* to deliver
them to the *Turks*, or put them to Death. *Cafla Mariam*, who
protected the Bifhop, and his Companions ftood by them at firft,
till being overcome by threats, he carry'd them towards the Sea,
near *Dafalo*, to a dreadful deep Vale, where he left them, in the
Cuftody of fome *Moors*, defiring they would relieve them with a
little Barley. Here they continu'd till a *Portuguefe* found them
almoft famifh'd, and acquainting *Cafla Mariam* with it, he carry'd them to his own Houfe, till fearing the Emperor's difpleafure, they were forc'd to fly again. *F. Almeyda* to a thatch'd
Houfe, where he lay clofe a Year, and the Bifhop to *F. Rodrigues*'s Retreat, which was fomewhat eafier.

Three others were protected by *Tecla Emanuel*, Governour of
Affa, near *Maegoga*. He being remov'd, and his Brother fucceeding in the Place, and being a mortal Enemy to the Fathers, they
were oblig'd to remove, and he never ceas'd till he had found the
Place where they lay hid, ftripp'd them almoft naked, kill'd *F.
Gafpor Pays*, and three *Portuguefe* Youths, and left the others
dangeroufly wounded, of which Number *F. John Pereyra* dy'd
eight Days after, on a Mountain, whither they had been remov'd by fome *Portuguefes*. This account is given at large by
F. Bruno Bruni, the Surviver of them, in a Letter to the General of his Order, and we have a Confirmation of it in an Au-
thenick Inftrument, fent over by the Bifhop of *Nice*, with the
Affidavit of feveral Witneffes, proving that all thefe Perfons
were thus butcher'd in Hatred to the Catholick Faith.

The Patriarch, and two Fathers were ftill at *Suaquem*, whence
they had writ to the *French* Conful, at *Grand Cairo*, acquainting him with their barbarous Ufage, whereupon an Officer of
the *Baffa* of *Cairo*, to whom he of *Suaquem* was fubordinate,
writ

Jefuits dif-
trefs'd in E-
thiopia.

Two mur-
der'd and o-
thers wounded.

The Patriarch ransom'd for 4000 Pieces of Eight.

writ to acquaint him, that it might coft his Head, if he did not difmifs them. Upon this Advice he demanded 15000 Pieces Eight for their Ranfome, and they offering but 1000, he put them into Irons, where they continu'd till the *Banaans* contracted with the *Baffa* for 4000 Pieces of Eight, which being pay'd, they were difmifs'd, and put aboard on the 24th of *April* 1635, and in a Month arriv'd fate at *Dix*, whence the Patriarch went immediatly to *Goa*, to folicite for *Ethiopia*, tho' without any Succefs.

Others put to Death for Religion.

To return to *Ethiopia*, the Perfecution ran as high as ever there, and fix noted *Ethiopians* were cruelly put to death, for profeffing the *Roman* Faith. In the Year 1628, the Bifhop of *Nice*, and the two Fathers his Companions were deliver'd up by their Protector *Joannes Akay*, to the Emperor's Officers, who conducted them to Court, where they were condemn'd to Death, but their Sentence chang'd into Banifhment, which their Enemies not bearing, after many Suffering, they were all hang'd.

Capucins fent to Ethiopia.

The News of what had happen'd in *Ethiopia* being brought to *Rome*, and fome Perfons reprefenting that what thofe People had done, only proceeded from their Hatred to the *Portuguefes*, they fent fix *French Capucines*, with Paffes from the Great *Turk*, to make their Paffage into *Ethiopia* feveral Ways. Two of them attemped it by the Coaft of *Magadoxo*, and *Pate*, on the Faft-fide of *Afrik*, where they had not travell'd up the Country many Leagues, before they were murder'd by the *Cafres*. The other four went through *Egypt* to *Suaquem*, two of whom pafs'd no farther than *Mazua*, being there inform'd of what had befallen the other two, who ventur'd before into *Ethiopia*.

Ston'd to Death.

Thofe two being F. *Agathangelus* or *Vendofme*, and F. *Caffianus* of *Nants*, enter'd the Kingdom of *Tygre* in the Habit of *Arabian* Merchants, where they were foon feiz'd, and fent Prifoners to Court, and there being examin'd, and owning what they were, immediately fton'd to Death.

Two Jefuits that had lain conceal'd hang'd.

The two Fathers *Lewis Cardeyra*, and *Bruno Bruni* were ftill in *Ethiopia*, under the Protection of *Abeto Xa Mariam*, *Xumo*, and Lord of *Temben*, one of the beft Territories in the Kingdom of *Tygre*. This great Man, withftood all the Emperor's Promifes, and flighted his Threats, difappointing all the cunning Machinations of his Enemies to deftroy him, for defending thofe Religious Men; till after many brave, and honourable Exploits perform'd againft the Viceroy, who befieg'd him, with all his Forces, and was kill'd by him, he was bafely flain by fome of the Enemies, that furpriz'd him alone, and fpent with

Fa-

Fatigue. The News of his Death was soon brought to *Amba Salama*, which signifies the Holy Mountain, where he secur'd the Fathers, yet was not believ'd in three Months, till a Priest came from *Lasta*, with the Confirmation of it. The Inhabitants of this Mountain were all so Zealous, that they resolved to perish, rather than forsake their Spiritual Directors, and accordingly endur'd the utmost Extremities of Want, both of Provisions, and Water, till they all look'd more like Shadows than Men. Thus they all continu'd on the Mountain till the following *March* 1640, being above a Year and a half after the Death of their Protector, who was kill'd, as has been said above. During this Time, the Emperor never ceas'd trying all means to destroy them, and offering fair Conditions for them to quit the Mountain, which they never would regard, well knowing, he valu'd not what he promis'd, being resolv'd not to perform it, till finding it impossible to subsist any longer in that Place, they were forc'd to condescend, the Emperor swearing, he would not oblige them to depart *Ethiopia*, but would assign them a Place, where they might live in Safety, with all the Catholicks that were on the Mountain. Notwithstanding this Solemn Ingagement, as soon as the two Fathers came down from the Mountain, they were carry'd to a Neighbouring Town, where a Fair was kept that Day, and there hang'd in the Sight of a Multitude of People.

The Death of these Fathers was immediately follow'd by an Irruption of the *Gallas*, into the Kingdom of *Tygre*, a great Part whereof they laid waste. The Emperor sent one of his Sons, with the greatest Part of his Army against them, who being joyn'd by the Chief *Saentes*, so they call the Lords of Lands in *Tygre*, gave those Infidels Battel, near the Place, where the aforesaid Fair had been kept, and was himself kill'd, with the *Bahar Nagais*, *Tecla Salus*, the *Xumo Robel*, and the whole Army defeated. The *Gallas*, encourag'd by this Success, return'd the next Year, 1641, with a greater Power, destroying most of the Provinces of this Kingdom, *viz.* Those of *Terta, Sera, Temben, Sorte, Agamea, Auxen, Amba, Canete, Fixo, Maegoga, Debaroa, Angana*, and others, and piercing as far as *Decano*, which we call *Arquico*, the *Turkish* Fort, and had thought of possessing themselves of it, but drew off when the Balls began to fly among them. These Judgments were so heavy, that even the Emperor's Mother, who had been the most violent Enemy to Catholick Religion, and his Brother *Gladios*, look'd upon them as such, and advis'd him to return to it, to prevent the utter Ruin of the Empire; but his Heart was hardned.

Miseries of Ethiopia.

These Accounts we receiv'd in several Relations sent us from *Ethiopia*, and *Mazua*, and by Information the two *Capucins* above mention'd took at the said Town of *Mazua*, from several *Abyssines* both Catholicks and Schismaticks.

The Patriarch in *India* never ceas'd trying all Expedients to send some *Jesuits* into *Ethiopia*, knowing that all those he had left there were dead. The *Bassa* of *Suaquem* was tamper'd with, by means of a rich Present, and offer'd mighty Matters, but was found to do it, only in Order to extort Money from those Fathers, if they had come, being corrupted by the Emperor of *Ethiopia* with a Bribe of 100 Oquees, which amount to 1000 Pieces of Eight. *Antony Almeyda*, upon a Pass sent by the *Aga* of *Moca*, giving Leave for *Jesuits* to go thither, went, to attempt a Passage that Way, in *March* 1643, and return'd in *September* following. He declar'd that Country is still worse than *Mazua*, being so hot that it resembles an Oven, so that there is not a Tree to be seen, nor any sort of Green, nor so much as a River, or Spring, or any Water but of one Well, which is half a League from the Town, and that rather Salt than Brackish. The Houses are very inconvenient, little, and low, and all moulder away into Salt Dust, because the Clay they are made of is moulded with Sea Water. As bad as this Place is, it was formerly much frequented, as being a Port to which the Commodities of *India* were brought, and therefore resorted to by Caravans of Merchants from all Parts of the Lesser *Asia*, or *Natolia*. However since the *Arabs* recover'd that Country from the *Turks*, the aforesaid Caravans failing, the *India* Commodities were not brought, because there was no Vent for them, and consequently Trade ceasing, the Town is gone to Decay, as is that of *Din*, and others that formerly engross'd the Commerce of the *Red Sea*.

Wretched Country about Moca.

In *March* 1648, two *Italian*, and one *French Capucins* were beheaded at *Suaquem*, by Order of the *Bassa*, at the Instigation of the Emperor of *Ethiopia*, who sollicited him to commit that Murder. Their Heads were flead, and the Skins, stuffed with Straw, sent to the Emperor, as a Testimony, that his Will had been perform'd, and to procure the promis'd reward. This Account we receiv'd in a Letter of *F. Torquatus Parisiano*, an *Italian*, sent by our Patriarch, in the Habit of an *English* Man, aboard a Ship of that Nation, from *India* to *Suaquem*, to consult there, about the Affairs of *Ethiopia*, with those Fathers. After touching at *Moca*, they made over to *Dalet*, the largest of all the Islands in the *Red Sea*, being twelve Leagues in Length, and proceeding on their Voyage very slowly, because of of the many Shoals, anchor'd at a place called *Xaba*, whence they fent to acquaint the *Baffa* with their arrival, at which he rejoyc'd, becaufe of the Profit he expe&ted, and return'd a Boat with frefh Provifions. On the *7th* of *May* 1648, the Ship came to an Anchor at *Suaquem*, where the Father Landing a-mong the *Englifh* could hear no News of the *Capucins*, the *Baffa* having forbid all Perfons, on Pain of Death, to difcover that he had murder'd them. At laft the Chief of the *Englifh* told him, how inhumanly they had been butcher'd by the *Baffa*, defiring he would go aboard the Ship, for Fear of the like Fate, fince he could not poffibly fuceeed in what he came about, and might do him much Harm, if difcover'd. The *Baffa* be-ginning to enquire particularly into the Strength of the Ship, the *Englifh*, who fufpe&ted that Infidel might have fome De-fign to feize, went all aboard, and making merry, fir'd their Guns at every Health, to fhow the *Turks* they were ready to receive them. This done, they went afhore, to fhow themfelves, without fuf-fering the Father to land, for Fear of any Difafter, and fo re-turn'd again to their Ship, and in her to *India* in the Year 1649.

All other Means failing, the Patriarch fent one of the *Aby-ffines* he had brought with him, and a *Banean*, both of them Catholicks, hoping the one, as a Native, might be permitted to pafs into *Ethiopia*, and the other find more Favour among his Country Men the *Baneans*. They fail'd from *Diu* in *March* 1651, and touching at *Moca*, in *Arabia*, ftay'd there till *Auguft*; the reafon whereof was this. The *Baffa* of *Suaquem*, who is Com-mander in chief of all that Coaft of *Ethiopia*, kept a Galley cruizing in that Sea, in which there were 60 Chriftians, all *Polanders*, at the Oar, who breaking loofe one Night, flew all the *Turks*, and to be reveng'd on thofe People, play'd the Py-rates, without fparing any thing they met on either Coaft. But they prov'd too bold, for the King of *Arabia* hearing of them, fitted out fome Veffels, which boarded, and took them, after a brave Defeuce. The Men were all put to Death, and the Galley reftor'd to the *Baffa*. He flying into a Paffion, fent the King Word, that he ought to have reftor'd him his Slaves, and not have kill'd them; for he knew how to punifh them himfelf; and fince he had been fo hafty, as to put them to Death, he fhould give him 250 Crowns a Man for them, or he would make Reprifals on his Ships, and ravage all the Coaft of *Arabia*. The King laugh'd at his Meffage, fending him for an Anfwer, That he might begin when he pleas'd, for he had his Revenge in his Hands, and he would cut him off all the Trade of *India*.

The *Turk* hearing his Meſſage, went away to *Mazua*, and vented his Spleen on the Inhabitants of that Place, Robbing and Killing thoſe that were no way concern'd. This Breach with *Arabia* was the Occaſion that none paſs'd from *Arabia* to *Mazua*, or *Suaquem*, and detain'd the *Abyſſine* and *Banean* there ſix Months. Here they receiv'd News from *Ethiopia*, that the new *Abuna Mark* had been publickly depos'd for his moſt infamous Life, and another, whoſe Name was *Michael*, ſent from *Egypt*.

The *Turks* and *Arabs* being reconcil'd, the *Banean* and *Ethiopian*, in *October* paſs'd over to *Mazua*, and thence proceeded to *Engana*, which is two Days Journey farther, ſending Letters to *F. Bernard Nogueyra*, the Patriarch's Vicar General, to meet them there with all Speed. This Father had been appointed Vicar General, by the Patriarch, after the Death of all the others, and was put to Death for the Profeſſion of his Faith. Here *F. Tellez* concludes his Hiſtorical Account of the Travels of the *Jeſuits*, and the Affairs of *Ethiopia*, reaching to the Year 1654, what hapened afterwards we ſhall have from the *Capucins*, who ſucceeded in that Miſſion, and have publiſh'd their Relation in *Spaniſh*.

F I N I S.

THE
CONTENTS.

BOOK I.

The CONTENTS.

The CONTENTS.

The CONTENTS.

The CONTENTS.

M m   The

THE
INDEX.

A

Afsamo

Cam.

Printed in the USA
CPSIA information can be obtained
at www.ICGtesting.com
LVHW011224270124
769852LV00008BA/216